CARLISLE AND CUMBRIA

Roman and Medieval
Architecture, Art and
Archaeology

General Editor   Sarah Brown

CARLISLE AND CUMBRIA
Roman and Medieval Architecture, Art and Archaeology

Edited by
Mike McCarthy and David Weston

The British Archaeological Association

Conference Transactions XXVII

The publication of this volume has been assisted by
generous grants from The Chapter, Carlisle Cathedral,
the Cumberland and Westmorland Antiquarian and
Archaeological Society, Hodge Fund, English Heritage,
the Corpus Vitrearum Medii Aevi, Great Britain,
the Francis Coales Charitable Foundation and
the Nini Isabel Stewart Trust

Cover illustration: Carlisle Cathedral, East Window, D1, Hell.
Photo by D. O'Connor. See page 167 for description.
Cover design: Laurence Keen

ISBN Hardback 1 902653 90 4
Paperback 1 902653 69 6

MANEY
publishing

1004829697

PUBLISHED BY THE BRITISH ARCHAEOLOGICAL ASSOCIATION AND MANEY PUBLISHING
HUDSON ROAD, LEEDS LS9 7DL, UK

Contents

vi

Preface

THE Association's annual conference in 2001 was based in Carlisle and took place between Saturday, 21 and Wednesday, 25 July. It was attended by ninety-five members and guests, from the United Kingdom, Canada, Ireland, Swaziland and the United States of America. Of these five had been awarded conference scholarships. Accommodation was provided in The Old Brewery, Bridge Lane, a university hall of residence, and lectures were given in Tullie House, Castle Street. Twenty-two papers were delivered over the five days, of which versions of seventeen are printed in this volume.

The choice of Carlisle was influenced by the fact, as the editors observe below, that it is among England's least known cities, as, indeed, is the cathedral. Furthermore, the city has been visited only once by the Association, in 1908, over ninety years ago. A return visit, therefore, was long overdue, especially since recent archaeological work has done much to elucidate its development and there have been major publications on the city's medieval history, by Dr Henry Summerson (1993), on the castle, by McCarthy, Summerson and Annis (1990), and on the cathedral, by Canon David Weston (2000). Within the context of this burgeoning interest and new research, the cathedral was the main object of study and ten of the conference papers were devoted to various aspects of its architecture and furnishings.

On Sunday, 22 July, having spent the greater part of the afternoon in the cathedral, the Association was honoured with a reception at Carlisle Castle, and was received by the mayor of Carlisle, Cllr Doreen Parsons, and Malcolm Cooper, English Heritage's Regional Director.

During the afternoon of Monday, 23 July, visits were made to Holm Cultram Abbey, Rose Castle and St Andrew's church Greystoke, where we were welcomed, respectively, by the Revd David Tembey, the Rt Revd Graham Dow, bishop of Carlisle, and the Revd Michael Houston. Returning to Carlisle members were offered a reception in the deanery, by courtesy of the Dean and Chapter, and were welcomed by the dean, the Very Revd Graeme Knowles, now bishop of Sodor and Man.

After morning lectures on Tuesday, 24 July, coaches left for visits to Naworth Castle, where the Hon. Philip Howard welcomed members, then to Bewcastle. Here, the Revd Alan Bartlamb was delighted to receive us as the first visitors since Foot and Mouth: tea and home-made cakes were provided by the ladies of the church. The day's excursion finished at Lanercost Priory, which was examined in detail, followed by a drinks reception and dinner in the Dacre Hall. English Heritage kindly allowed members to stay long into the evening, taking advantage of the perfect weather.

The Association is grateful to all those who gave papers, or acted as guides during visits, and to the Dean and Chapter in particular. A special debt of gratitude is owed to Mike McCarthy and Canon David Weston, Conference Convenors, to Anna Eavis, Conference Organiser, and to Robert Gwynne, Conference Secretary, for arranging such an interesting programme and all the practical details. But for the production of this volume grateful thanks are offered to Mike McCarthy and Canon David Weston for editing it, to the several bodies listed at the beginning of this volume for providing grant aid, and to Linda Fisher, of Maney Publishing, for her expertise in its production.

As the editors remark, the papers published here 'represent a watershed in the understanding and interpretation of important aspects of the cathedral'. As a contribution to research on the cathedral and other monuments in Cumbria this volume will serve as a springboard for new research and investigation. May we hope that the Association's next visit will be in less than ninety years and that, then, there will be new ideas and interpretations to explore.

Laurence Keen, *President*
Easter 2004

Editors' Introduction

FROM most people's perspective, Carlisle, in the far north-west, is among England's least known cities. Its cathedral church has in consequence tended to be overlooked in many recent studies of cathedrals. However, the decision of the BAA to select Carlisle as the venue for its annual conference in 2001 reflects a change that is now taking place. Carlisle and Cumbria are attracting more attention, with a particular emphasis on Hadrian's Wall which runs through the northern suburbs. Recent excavations have, by the richness and unique quality of some finds, served to emphasise the importance of the Roman city, and from that time onwards the almost unbroken sequence of significant finds have served to document this two-thousand-year-old city.

In the planning of the Conference the decision was made at an early stage to concentrate upon Carlisle Cathedral, but also to reassess the Roman background, to include Carlisle Castle, Rose Castle, monastic sites at Holm Cultram and Lanercost, and to consider aspects of Romanesque and Augustinian architecture. In a region rich in historic sites, much had to be omitted. Amongst this, for example, no mention is made in this volume of Anglian and Anglo-Scandinavian sculpture, but an afternoon excursion allowed the addition of the Bewcastle Cross, and we do have the benefit of the magnificent published corpus by Professors Richard Bailey and Rosemary Cramp. Other afternoon excursions, to Greystoke Church and Naworth Castle, helped fill other gaps.

Because Carlisle Cathedral was not well known and not greatly studied, the BAA Conference provided an excellent opportunity to examine the cathedral with fresh eyes. Many of those who came found themselves confronted with an unfamiliar building that presented a range of challenges. The Conference itself, and the papers published here, represent a watershed in the understanding and interpretation of important aspects of the cathedral.

Our special thanks are due to Anna Eavis whose energy and commitment contributed so much to the smooth running of the conference, and to the Dean and Chapter for supporting it so enthusiastically.

Mike McCarthy
David Weston

Abbreviations

Antiq. J.	*Antiquaries Journal*
Archaeol. J.	*Archaeological Journal*
BAA Trans.	*British Archaeological Association Conference Transactions*
Bede, *H.E.*	Bede, *A History of the English Church and People*
BL	British Library
CRO	Cumbria Record Office
CSIR	*Corpus Signorum Imperii Romani* (various volumes, British Academy)
D. & C.	Dean and Chapter
HMSO	Her Majesty's Stationery Office
JBAA	*Journal of the British Archaeological Association*
Med. Archaeol.	*Medieval Archaeology*
OED	*Oxford English Dictionary*
Pevsner, B/E	N. Pevsner et al., *The Buildings of England* (Harmondsworth, various dates)
PRO	Public Record Office
RCHME	Royal Commission on the Historic Monuments of England
RIB	*Roman Inscriptions in Britain, I, Inscriptions on Stone*, ed. R. G. Collingwood and R. P. Wright (Oxford University Press 1965, reprinted Stroud 1995)
VCH	Victoria History of the Counties of England (various volumes)

List of Contributors

DR JENNIFER S. ALEXANDER
School of Continuing Education, University of Nottingham

SHARON CATHER
Courtauld Institute of Art, University of London

JILL A. FRANKLIN
Freelance Art Historian, London

DR JOHN A. A. GOODALL
Freelance Researcher in Architectural History, London

DR CHRISTA GRÖSSINGER
School of Art History and Archaeology, University of Manchester

STUART HARRISON
Ryedale Archaeological Services Ltd, Pickering, North Yorkshire

DR MARTIN HENIG
Institute of Archaeology, University of Oxford

THE RIGHT REVEREND GRAEME PAUL KNOWLES
Formerly Dean of Carlisle Cathedral, Carlisle

DR MIKE MCCARTHY
Department of Archaeological Sciences, University of Bradford

DAVID O'CONNOR
School of Art History and Archaeology, University of Manchester

DAVID A. PARK
Courtauld Institute of Art, University of London

DR RICHARD PLANT
Queen Mary College, University of London

GAVIN SIMPSON
Historic Buildings Research Unit, University of Nottingham

DR HENRY SUMMERSON
Oxford Dictionary of National Biography, Oxford

TIM TATTON-BROWN
Freelance Architectural Historian, Salisbury, Wiltshire

PROFESSOR MALCOLM THURLBY
York University, Ontario, Canada

LIST OF CONTRIBUTORS

DR CHARLES TRACY
Freelance Art Historian, Ipswich, Suffolk

THE REVEREND CANON DR DAVID WESTON
Carlisle Cathedral, Carlisle

DR ABIGAIL WHEATLEY
Usborne Publishing Ltd, London

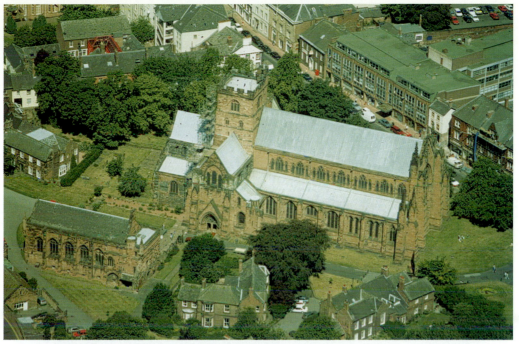

A.   Aerial photograph of Carlisle Cathedral
Photograph: Mike McCarthy

B.   View of Carlisle Castle, Cumberland, from the south-west. The main entrance to the castle,
De Ireby's Tower, stands to the left and the great tower to the right
Photograph: John Goodall

Carlisle Cathedral: crossing, looking north
Photograph: Richard Plant

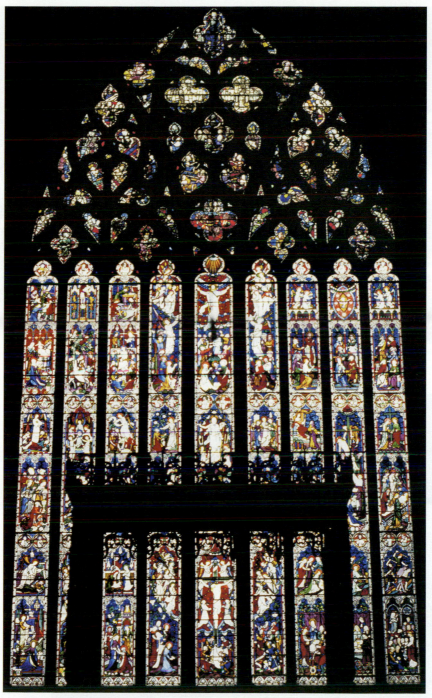

Carlisle Cathedral east window
© D. O'Connor

B.   X1: Christ in judgement
© D. O'Connor

A.   I K1: resurrection of man
© D. O'Connor

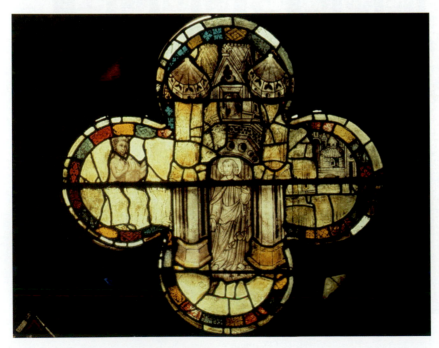

C.   I R2: Heaven
© D. O'Connor

A. I D1: man tortured on spit

© D. O'Connor

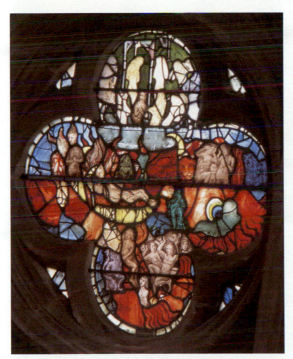

B. Carlisle Cathedral, I D1 Hell

© D. O'Connor

C. I D1: woman hanging from gallows

© D. O'Connor

Choir-stalls: St Augustine cycle
© English Heritage NMR

COLOUR PLATE VII

Choir-stalls: St Anthony cycle
© *English Heritage NMR*

Choir-stalls: St Augustine and the devil
© English Heritage NMR

Choir-stalls: Consecration of St Augustine
© English Heritage NMR

Choir-stalls: Baptism of St Anthony
© English Heritage NMR

Choir-stalls: St Anthony and the beasts bury the Blessed Paul; St Anthony
walks over the flood water

© English Heritage NMR

A. Choir-stalls: St Anthony resists the Spirit of Fornication
© *English Heritage NMR*

B. Prior's Tower ceiling: general view of ceiling
© *English Heritage NMR*

A. Prior's Tower: general view of ceiling
After watercolour of 1890

B. Prior's Tower ceiling: detail of painted design
© English Heritage NMR

A. Prior's Tower
ceiling: angel boss
with *Arma Christi*

© *English Heritage
NMR*

B. Prior's Tower
ceiling: snail-warrior
boss

© *English Heritage
NMR*

C. Prior's Tower
ceiling: boss with
female bust

© *English Heritage
NMR*

The Roman Town of *Luguvalium* and the Post-Roman Settlement

MIKE McCARTHY

Excavations in Carlisle, especially from the 1970s on, have confirmed the importance of Carlisle as a focus of Roman military activity and the civilian settlement. In the angle between the Rivers Eden and Caldew lay a fort, and on its southern side was the town and probable civitas Carvetiorum of Luguvalium, *one of the largest in northern England. On the north bank of the Eden was the great Hadrian's Wall fort at Stanwix, the home of the* ala Petriana. *Occupation continued at a number of places in Carlisle after the end of the Roman period, and there are suggestions that part of the former fort continued to function as a centre of authority. To the south a key focus of ecclesiastical power was established from the 7th century, and this was consolidated in the 12th century with the foundation of a house of Augustinian canons and the creation of a new diocese.*

CARLISLE has excited antiquaries for a long time. Hutchinson recorded much of the sculpture in the late 18th century, and R. S. Ferguson, local mill owner, philanthropist, politician, Chancellor and antiquary added to this through his assiduous researches a century later. It was Peter Salway, whose book *The Frontier People of Roman Britain* that drew serious attention of scholars to the town of Carlisle, comparing it with Corbridge, as well as reviewing evidence for *vici* and the way of life of the population. Dorothy Charlesworth followed this in 1978 with an important paper in the *Archaeological Journal*.[1]

ROMAN *LUGUVALIUM*

IN A.D. 72 the Romans led by Q. Petillius Cerialis left York and headed north-west for the Solway Firth building forts as they went. This was the territory of the Brigantes, a tribe encompassing a vast swathe of land from West Yorkshire to the Scottish border led only a short time before by the formidable Venutius and his equally formidable queen, Cartimandua. After crossing Stainmore the Romans entered the Eden valley and northern Cumbria where they were probably faced with a dispersed population living in isolated farms, and subsisting on generally low-grade soils interspersed with mosses and occasional patches of naturally well-drained land. The post-glacial wildwood had probably all but disappeared under the onslaught of millennia of small-scale farming and stock raising. Unfashionable though the idea of the Celtic cowboy may be nowadays, the local economy in Cumbria was almost certainly geared towards cattle raising with cereals forming a lesser component.[2]

The Romans arrived at Carlisle and may have pressed further north into south-west Scotland, but that point has yet to be confirmed. At all events, the Cumbrian landscape

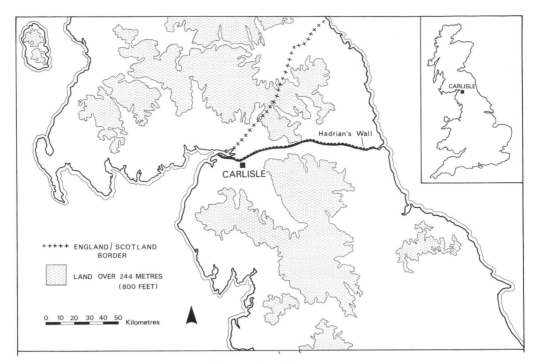

FIG. 1.   Location map
Drawing: Mike McCarthy

was not geared towards supporting thousands of troops with all their associated horses and other beasts of burden, and despite the point that many of their supplies will have been imported, their arrival will have had a substantial impact. The cutting down of both oaks and other wood such as alder for building, or the need for extensive areas of grazing and winter feed for the cavalry horses, will have contributed to altering the general appearance of the landscape.[3]

The fort was probably of standard playing card shape erected on the bluff overlooking the confluence of the rivers Eden and Caldew (Fig. 1). Encircled by an earth and timber rampart, the southern and western defences have been investigated along with the *porta praetoria*, barracks in the *praetentura*, parts of the central range and the *via principalis*. Between its foundation in about A.D. 72 and 103–05, dates firmly attested by dendrochronology, the internal buildings were modified on a number of occasions. One of the important discoveries was the identification of the unit in residence for part of that time, the *ala Sebosiana Gallorum*. Ink writing tablets shed fascinating detail on the unit, including the barley rations required for each troop, or *turma*, for three-day periods and recorded by the decurions. Other documents record the point that some weaponry, namely lances, had gone missing.[4] In another instance a soldier from the Twentieth Legion is recorded as owing a colleague the sum of 100 denarii.[5]

Beyond the southern defences lay a defended annexe, doubtless used amongst other things for the repair and maintenance of equipment, the slaughter of animals for

2

consumption and other uses as suggested by the discovery of scrap armour and well-preserved wooden buildings.[6] Within a generation, up to around A.D. 100, not only had Carlisle acquired a name, but it had become the focus of a region. A writing tablet from Vindolanda tells us of Annius Equester, centurion of the region who was based at *Luguvalium*, Carlisle.[7] The very name is first recorded in a writing tablet found at Castle Street, Carlisle, dating to the mid-80s.[8] What the region comprised, how far it extended, whether it took in an existing tribe, or was a wholly new creation by the Romans is not clear, but the name Carvetii — the deer people — seems to have been attributed to the local population.

By the beginning of the 2nd century *Luguvalium* had expanded. Outside the annexe to the south lay the road to Old Penrith, Brougham and the south. Parts of this road, the modern Blackfriars Street, was occupied by strip-like buildings which in one Flavian phase resemble domestic houses tightly positioned with their gable-end on the street, and occupied, perhaps, by retired soldiers. This arrangement implies pressure on space, a situation similar to that of medieval burgage tenements[9] where space was at a premium in the most populous areas. On the other side of the settlement, perhaps in the later 1st century A.D., a round-house marks the beginnings of activity on the periphery, and this was followed in the reign of Trajan, by a series of properties enclosed by fences with rectangular wooden buildings, yards and associated features. Here the development reflects a combination of agricultural activities and domestic functions. Its use of space certainly contrasts with the area occupied by retired soldiers at Blackfriars Street as well as with adjacent land given over at this time to 'official' buildings. Amongst these was a very large and elaborately constructed timber building with white-painted walls thought to be the *praetorium* of Annius Equester. Next to it, but not necessarily exactly contemporary, was a *mansio* providing accommodation for imperial couriers.[10] Both these buildings seem to have had a short life, the former being dismantled and the remains burnt. Immediately subsequent phases seem to continue the 'official' usage of the area into the mid-2nd century with ranges of buildings the plans of which have a military rather than domestic architectural appearance.

For the first fifty years of its life Carlisle displays fascinating insights into the development of a frontier settlement with fort, annexe, different types of domestic and agricultural areas, and an 'official' zone. During this same period fluctuating frontier policies resulted in many thousands of troops passing through Carlisle on the way north into, or south from, Scotland. Carlisle was a stopping-off place in these troop movements and there are a number of hints of other forts or marching camps in and around the growing core settlement.

Within that same period a series of decisions had been taken about *Luguvalium* that were to lay the foundations for nearly two millennia of development in Carlisle. The Romans could have developed the Brougham, Penrith, area where there is a natural nodal communications point and where a fort and extensive *vicus* are attested, or they could have gone to Cargo and Grinsdale about two miles to the west where a major complex of prehistoric sites has been found. Instead they chose Carlisle, the importance of which was significantly enhanced from the time Hadrian's Wall was built in A.D. 122. The fort at Carlisle was rebuilt after A.D. 105 and continued in use with modifications through to the 4th century, yet Hadrian chose to build another at Stanwix some five minutes' walk away on the opposite bank of the River Eden. It was one of his successors, perhaps Antoninus Pius or Marcus Aurelius, who enlarged the Stanwix fort to accommodate the 1,000-strong *ala Petriana*, the most senior regiment in Britain. The combination of *Luguvalium*, which at its height was nearly twice the size of Corbridge,

FIG. 2.   Stone-built house dating to the 3rd and 4th centuries
Photograph: Carlisle Archaeological Unit

and Stanwix (the two sites must surely be regarded as one for economic and social purposes), the Carlisle area contained all the right ingredients for a single military command centre for the northern frontier in Britain.

Between about A.D. 150 and 250 a whole series of schemes attest to the wealth and civic pride of its inhabitants. Amongst these there are public buildings such as baths, a grid of streets resembling the insulae of towns elsewhere in the empire, rubbish collection, large-scale land reclamation, and a large public building, perhaps a forum, near the Tullie House Museum and Art Gallery. Domestic houses acquired hypocausts and glazed windows, and the history of some can be charted in some detail. One in The Lanes, for example, developed from a simple rectangular timber building in the later 2nd century to a multi-roomed structure with hypocaust and a probable first-floor room, together with a well, metalled yards and an ancillary building by the late 4th century (Fig. 2). Whoever lived here clearly had some means and it is tempting to see the property being occupied throughout by a single family gradually acquiring the means to enlarge their house. Other properties were 'strip-houses' and remained as such for the duration of Roman rule, although they too display many re-floorings and signs of other structural modifications. In some cases evidence of small-scale craft activities is present in the form of ovens, kilns or hearths, although there are few signs of the specific nature of the work being carried out.[11]

To the south of the core settlement lies the modern road of Botchergate, and alongside this in the 2nd century was a series of buildings separated by metalled lanes and with yards and open ground to the rear (Fig. 3). There is evidence here of ovens

FIG. 3.   Roman 'planned' buildings in Botchergate
Photograph: Carlisle Archaeological Unit

and other industrial activities, but there is some doubt as to whether this zone continued to exist for long after the early 3rd century. On the opposite side of this road is a substantial linear feature tentatively identified as an aquaduct running along the eastern bank of the River Caldew and, if correctly identified, probably serving public buildings in the city centre. The banks of the aquaduct were used both as a rubbish tip and as a place for burials from the late 2nd or 3rd centuries.[12]

Pottery kilns are attested immediately outside the centre at one stage, and there is evidence, albeit in a very early context, of a goldsmith.[13] Another trade, also known from early on, is wood-turning, indicated by off-cuts of holly and ash and other species not normally associated with construction work.[14] Glass vessels and metalwork are known from Flavian times onwards, although there is so far no evidence for manufacture in Carlisle. Henig has also drawn attention to the likelihood of a school of gem cutters being based at Carlisle,[15] whilst a number of scholars note the distinct likelihood of a local school of sculptors responsible for some of the fine tombstones and other architectural details.[16] Some of the dedications and sculptures, such as the various *genii*, will have come from niches in the fort or in private houses, but others will have been in temples. A mithraeum, for example, is indicated by the figure of Cautes, one of the god's supporters.[17] Within the fort, probably in the *principia*, architectural elements including the pediment of a shrine and an unusually fine altar found in the castle, demonstrate very high quality work indeed.

Luguvalium may lack mosaic pavements, and the entire region lacks villas, but by the standards of the north Carlisle was undoubtedly prosperous. Evidence of

FIG. 4.   Roof collapse in the barracks
Photograph: Carlisle Archaeological Unit

romanisation is abundant and includes a wider range of crafts and other activities than might be expected in a normal *vicus* outside a fort. This is one of the critical factors, together with its size, that makes Carlisle the most likely candidate for having been a major regional centre, the *civitas Carvetiorum*, a title probably bestowed in the 3rd century. It is fair to say, however, that although the name *Luguvalium* is not equated on any known inscription with the civital capital, a milestone found at Brougham, Penrith, and another at Middleton in Lonsdale, refer respectively to the *civitas Carvetiorum* and the distance 53 miles, being the correct distance from Carlisle.[18]

THE POST-ROMAN SETTLEMENT

FROM the 4th century on some properties fell from use and were abandoned, whilst others were maintained well into the 5th century. One house contained a gold solidus of Valentinian II (375–92) sealed in a hypocaust below a series of later re-floorings.[19] In the late 4th century another 'strip-house' in Blackfriars Street was built with a series of earth-fast posts, unlike the earlier tradition of clay and cobble footings supporting a framed construction, but it was subsequently modified, presumably in the 5th century. The barracks in the *praetentura* of the fort were also abandoned in the mid-4th century and the roofs fell in (Fig. 4), but the buildings[20] of the central range remained, and excavations here demonstrate a sequence of activities, including the erection of timber buildings from the late 4th century on, not unlike those at Wroxeter.

The *principia* was modified several times and shows clear traces of traffic and wear taking place at a very late date.[21] Are these the places where the élite remained, perhaps much like the aisled hall excavated by Wilmott at the Hadrian's Wall fort of Birdoswald?[22] Work at the fort in Stanwix suggests that late- or post-Roman activities may also be occurring there, and we might suppose the same to be true of other forts.[23] Most excavations, however, lack contemporary finds and the post-Roman dating is based upon a sequence of stratigraphic 'events'. This is the case in the *principia* where the events lie firmly rooted in the 4th century through the association with coins and pottery. The duration of these sequences is uncertain but given the 'events' of the 530s and 540s identified by Baillie in the dendrochronological sequences at both Carlisle and at Whithorn,[24] as well as elsewhere in the British Isles, it is possible that some of the tattered remnants of Roman traditions petered out then.

The Northumbrian kings began extending their interests in Cumbria in the 7th century and it is St Cuthbert who, in the company of Ecgfrith's queen, is usually credited with building a monastery in Carlisle in 685. Bede's description of this is instructive. He tells us that St Cuthbert

came to the town of Lugubalia, which the English people corruptly call Luel, to speak to the queen who had arranged to await the issue of the war there in her sister's monastery. On the next day, while the citizens were conducting him to see the walls of the city and the marvellously constructed fountain of Roman workmanship, he was suddenly troubled in spirit . . .[25]

From this several points emerge. First, as the monastery was clearly in existence when St Cuthbert arrived, so the question arises when was it built and why Carlisle was chosen for a monastic house? A possible date is during the period of Northumbrian expansion westwards, perhaps as early as Oswald's reign in 630s, when an alliance was allegedly formed through the marriage of Rhienmelth, great granddaughter of Urien Rheged, with Oswiu.[26]

Second, the famous references to the city walls and the fountain have long been taken to indicate that Roman Carlisle was a walled town with a water supply. However, despite extensive investigations there is no evidence for a defensive wall around the town, although there was an attempt, possibly in the 3rd century, to construct walls. It is much more likely that St Cuthbert saw the remains of the stone wall of the fort which has been found, as well as stone buildings such as those referred to as still standing by Geoffrey of Malmesbury in the 12th century.[27]

Neither is there any evidence for a fountain, although an aquaduct has been tentatively identified near Botchergate and there was a large bath-house in the centre of the town on the site of the present Market. There will almost certainly have been other bath-houses including at the commanding officer's house in the fort. It is the fort, however, that has yielded a multiplicity of drains and wooden and ceramic pipes in the *via principalis* showing that the Romans had addressed problems of flooding as well as water supply to some point in the central range. The presence of a fountain, associated perhaps with the courtyard of the *praetorium* in the fort, or as a water shrine in the town, is entirely plausible.

The location of the Cuthbertian monastery is not known, but is thought to lie within the general vicinity of the present parish church and Cathedral. This is the area that has yielded the greatest concentration of 7th- to 9th-century finds, including coins (mostly stycas), metalwork, glass, sculpture and other finds. St Cuthbert's church is itself incorrectly aligned and the present writer has suggested elsewhere that the position of its eastern end and its orientation may have been determined by the Roman layout.[28]

FIG. 5.   Aerial photograph of Carlisle Castle
Photograph: Carlisle Archaeological Unit

Indeed, it is possible to speculate and suggest that the church originated as a Roman building and was converted, perhaps into a gate-house providing access to a monastic enceinte formed today by the Cathedral precinct.[29]

What is clear is that the area of St Cuthbert's church and the Cathedral precinct lie in the heart of the Roman town, but outside the fort, and that they became the centre of ecclesiastical power for both the town and ultimately the diocese. This has remained the case ever since. It is unfortunate that we know too little of the nature of the Roman buildings in this area, and one wonders whether there was an important public building on the Cathedral site. The excavations of 1988 were inconclusive on that point. Finally we note that Symeon of Durham drew attention to the *paruchia* of the church and that it extended for 15 miles outside the town.

Within Carlisle itself the focus of secular power at this time is not known. Work within the fort has failed to locate features of Anglian date and, unusually for Carlisle, there were no stycas with the central range. Dark-earth deposits are present overlying the Roman and sub-Roman buildings but at the time of writing insufficient work has been undertaken to understand the mechanisms of deposition. Indeed, it is possible that if there was an Anglian period royal residence in addition to the monastic site, it lies in the north-eastern corner of the fort. This is where the castle keep of Henry I and David I is located, and it is also where William Rufus erected an earth and timber castle, probably a ringwork. Economy of hypothesis would suggest that the same site is the preferred location for Dolfin's *villa regia* of the late 11th century[30] (Fig. 5).

When the Normans arrived in 1092 they encountered a site partly covered in the ruins of Roman buildings, as William of Malmesbury tells us, but also a site where there had been a major centre of power and administration from Roman times onwards. Whether or not Dolfin occupied part of the former Roman fort is uncertain, but this was the place that William II and later Henry I chose to defend with one of the largest castles in northern England.[31] Ecclesiastical power was located a little to the south from at least as early as the 7th century and this will certainly have incorporated at least one stone church the location of which can be postulated as lying to the south of the existing Cathedral, probably in the claustral area.[32] There may have been a point in the 12th century when, as happened at other Cathedrals, the site was occupied by two stone churches, the old one continuing to function prior to demolition whilst the Augustinian Priory (founded 1122), the nave of which later doubled up as the diocesan church (1133), was being built. A stone in the south transept of the Cathedral bears a runic inscription reading 'Dolfinn engraved these runes on this stone'. Was this the same Dolfin, son of the very distinguished Gospatric, formerly Earl of Northumberland, who was ejected by William Rufus?

NOTES

1. See, for example, N. Chadwick, *The British Heroic Age* (University of Wales Press, Cardiff 1976), 81, 112; D. Charlesworth, 'Roman Carlisle', *Archaeol. J.*, 135 (1978), 115–37; R. S. Ferguson, *A History of Cumberland* (London 1890); W. Hutchinson, *History of the County of Cumberland and some places adjacent* (Carlisle 1794); P. Salway, *The Frontier People of Roman Britain* (Cambridge University Press 1965), 41–45.

2. For further discussion see M. R. McCarthy, *Roman Carlisle and the Solway Region* (Stroud 2002).

3. M. R. McCarthy, 'Archaeological and environmental evidence for the Roman impact on vegetation near Carlisle, Cumbria', *The Holocene*, 5 (1995), 491–95.

4. R. S. O. Tomlin, 'Roman manuscripts from Carlisle: the ink writing-tablets', *Britannia*, XXIX (1998), 31–84.

5. R. S. O. Tomlin, 'The Twentieth Legion at Wroxeter and Carlisle in the first century: the epigraphic evidence', *Britannia*, XXIII (1992), 141–58.

6. M. R. McCarthy, *Roman Waterlogged Remains and Later Features at Castle Street, Carlisle: excavations 1981–2*, Cumberland Westmorland Antiquarian Archaeological Society Research Series, 5 (Kendal 1991).

7. A. K. Bowman and J. D. Thomas, *The Vindolanda Writing Tablets (Tabulae Vindolandenses II)* (The British Museum Press, London 1994), 221–22.

8. R. S. O. Tomlin, 'The writing tablets', in T. G. Padley and S. Winterbottom, *The Wooden, Leather and Bone Objects from Castle Street, Carlisle: excavations 1981–2*, Fasc. 3, Cumberland Westmorland Antiquarian Archaeological Society Research Series, 5 (Kendal 1991), 209–18.

9. M. R. McCarthy, *A Roman, Anglian and Medieval Site at Blackfriars Street, Carlisle: excavations 1977–9*, Cumberland Westmorland Antiquarian Archaeological Society Research Series, 4 (Kendal 1990).

10. M. R. McCarthy, T. G. Padley and M. Henig, 'Excavations and Finds from The Lanes, Carlisle', *Britannia*, XIII (1982), 79–89.

11. See note 2. M. R. McCarthy, *Roman and Medieval Carlisle: The Southern Lanes. Excavations 1981–2*, Carlisle Archaeology Limited Department Archaeological Sciences, Univ. Bradford Research Report, 1 (Carlisle 2000). See also J. M. Zant, *Roman and Medieval Carlisle, The Northern Lanes. Excavations 1978–82* (forthcoming).

12. J. Zant, and F. Giecco, 'Recent work in Carlisle', *Current Archaeol.*, 164 (August 1999), 306–09.

13. Tomlin, in note 8.

14. See McCarthy, *The Southern Lanes*, note 11.

15. Henig, this volume.

16. E. J. Phillips, 'A Workshop of Roman Sculptors at Carlisle', *Britannia*, VII, 101–10. See also Henig, this volume.

17. J. C. Coulston and E. J. Phillips, *Corpus of Sculpture of the Roman World, Great Britain Volume 1 Fascicule 6: Hadrian's Wall West of the North Tyne and Carlisle* (British Academy, Oxford 1988), 161, and pl. 109.

18. The Brougham milestone was discovered in the *vicus* and reads RPC CAR — *Res Publica Civitas Carvetiorum*, and is housed in the small display area operated by English Heritage at Brougham Castle. The Middleton milestone is in R. G. Collingwood and R. P. Wright, *The Roman Inscriptions of Britain*, 1 (1965), no. 2283. It reads mpLIII (53 miles, which is the distance to Carlisle).

19. G. D. Keevill, D. C. A. Shotter and M. R. McCarthy, 'A Solidus of Valentinian II from Scotch Street, Carlisle', *Britannia*, XX (1989), 254–55.

20. I. D. Caruana, *Excavations on the Roman Fort at Carlisle* (in preparation).

21. Excavations carried out between 1998 and 2001 by Carlisle Archaeology Limited.

22. T. Wilmott, *Birdoswald: Excavations of a Roman fort on Hadrian's Wall and its successor settlements: 1987–92*, English Heritage Archaeological Reports, 14 (1997), especially Periods 5 and 6.

23. B. C. Burnham, 'Roman Britain in 1999', *Britannia*, XXXI (2000), 392. See also Wilmott in note 22.

24. M. G. L. Baillie, *A Slice Through Time: dendrochronology and precision dating* (London 1995), 85, 94; see also M. Baillie, *Exodus to Arthur: catastrophic encounters with comets* (Batsford 2000), 65–68, 78, 125–26.

25. B. Colgrave, *Two Lives of Saint Cuthbert* (Cambridge University Press 1940).

26. M. R. McCarthy, 'Carlisle and St. Cuthbert', *Durham Archaeol. J.*, 14–15 (1999), 59–67. See also Henig, this volume. For Rheged see M. R. McCarthy, 'Rheged: an Early Historic Kingdom in South-West Scotland', *Proceedings Society Antiquaries of Scotland*, 132 (2002), 357–81.

27. William of Malmesbury quoted in Salway, note 1, 42.

28. McCarthy, 1999, in note 26.

29. ibid.

30. M. R. McCarthy, H. R. T. Summerson and R. G. Annis, *Carlisle Castle: A survey and documentary history*, English Heritage Archaeological Reports, 18 (1990), 11, 28 and fig. 32.

31. See also Goodall, this volume.

32. McCarthy, 1999, in note 26, especially pages 63–66.

Murum civitatis, et fontem in ea a Romanis mire olim constructum: The Arts of Rome in Carlisle and the Civitas of the Carvetii and their Influence

MARTIN HENIG

The paper discusses the survival of Roman culture and Roman buildings in Carlisle and its region in the light of the remarkable near-contemporary account of St Cuthbert's visit to Luguvalium *in* A.D. 685 *with its intriguing mention of a wonderful fountain, and of William of Malmesbury's 12th-century description of a 'triclinium' with its dedication. The implication of such survivals for the early Medieval art of the region are immense and have been insufficiently considered in the past.*

It will be suggested that early Northumbrian churches and certain works of art such as the High Crosses had Romano-British prototypes rather than having been derived from Roman art from further afield, and that the Bewcastle Cross, in particular, was deliberately sited within a Roman pagan sanctuary in order to re-sanctify the place to Christ.

CARLISLE was the most northerly city of the Roman Empire. Although situated in a part of Britain dominated by the army, it became the administrative centre for the Carvetii, a native people whose name evidently means 'deer-men'. The degree to which the leaders of Carlisle society were local in origin is uncertain because, in the 'military-zone' of Roman Britain, there was a larger-than-usual proportion of foreigners associated with the army. However, the standard of culture amongst the upper ranks of the civilian population of Carlisle appears to have been high and its sophistication was manifested visually, as early as Hadrianic times, in some remarkably accomplished relief-carvings, mainly on tombstones of women, found here and through the western Hadrian's Wall area (Figs 8 and 9).[1] In addition, numerous attractive small finds have been excavated at Carlisle, attesting civilised life, including an amber finger ring and other fine jewellery, a *balsamarium* as used in the baths in the form of a youthful Bacchus bust, and figurines.[2]

The aims of this paper are first to consider the possible impact of Roman culture on the art and architecture of succeeding periods, and to assess how far any such influence was the result of the survival of Romano-British traditions, and how far they represented rediscovery and revival. Was there, in other words, a continuing tradition, however tenuous, of Romanitas in Cumbria (and neighbouring Northumbria)? Roman influences are very evident in the art of northern Britain in the Northumbrian Renaissance of the 7th and 8th centuries, but, with the exception of George Henderson and John Mitchell, scholars have generally tended to look to Rome and the Mediterranean for sources, although there were others closer to hand, and frequently closer in appearance.[3]

A SURVIVING CIVITAS

THE name *Luguvalium* or *Lugubalium* was still remembered in the 7th century, and indeed it survives in highly corrupted form to this day via the Brythonic *Caer Lliwelydd*. Excavation here as well as at nearby Birdoswald suggests that the collapse of Roman administration in the years around A.D. 400 had no very brutal aftermath. Evidence, indeed, points to buildings and occupation at least as late as the early 6th century just as it did further to the south at Wroxeter. The Roman accounts of the terrors of the northern barbarians, Picts, Scots and Saxons (frequently cited together) essentially provided a *topos*, serving the needs of propaganda. The northern frontier was necessary to Rome in order to mark the *limes* separating the civilised world from what lay beyond it. As a military province Britain served as a source of victory against the barbarians which could be manufactured at will, whether by the Emperor, Septimius Severus who wished to train his sons in war at the beginning of the 3rd century, or at the very end of the 4th century by Honorius' general Stilicho (who surely did not actually campaign in the north).[4]

The civitas seems to have maintained its territorial integrity even after the political structure of the western Empire fell apart, a crisis which, in Britain, may have been occasioned by a widespread revolt towards the end of the first decade of the 5th century. Carlisle's importance may even have enhanced for the territory of the Carvetii who came to call themselves Cumbri or Combogi and their kingdom, Rheged, perhaps extended to Catterick in Yorkshire, probably the *Catraeth* of the Gododdin, and almost certainly included Whithorn in Galloway in the north. This early Christian site known in latin as Candida Casa, was perhaps founded by Nynia (Ninian) in the 5th century. Continuity here is demonstrated by the presence of 6th-century amphorae (B ware), fine table wares (A ware) and glass from the eastern Mediterranean. The name of the site suggests it was a structure of well-coursed masonry with whitewashed walls. This technique of whitewashing is certainly attested in our area earlier as Hadrian's Wall itself was certainly so treated at least in the Severan period. In both cases the structure was meant to gleam out from afar.[5]

EARLY LITERARY SOURCES

IT has been suggested that St Patrick came from our region and the first element of the name of the saint's home town, *Bannavem Taburniae*, would suit Birdoswald, called *Banna* in the sources. If his father's estate was, indeed, located here and his schooling, which manifested itself in writing of remarkable quality, really took place at Carlisle, late in the first decade of the 5th century, this would be highly significant; however, it is at least equally possible on present evidence that Patrick's early life was lived in south-west Britain.[6]

The first certain reference to Carlisle in a literary source is considerably later in date, and concerns the remarkable survival of its Roman buildings. Although little now remains of these architectural splendours, there was clearly plenty to be seen in the early Middle Ages. When St Cuthbert visited the city on 20 May 685, according to the anonymous author of his life written a few years later, he was given a guided tour by a *praepositus* (reeve) called Waga who explained to him 'the city wall, and the fountain formerly built in a wonderful manner by the Romans'. St Cuthbert's mind only wandered from the matter in hand when he had a premonition of the death of King Egcfrith at the hands of the Picts at Nechtansmere.[7] The Roman historian can register a wry smile for, although the Picts are mentioned on several occasions by Roman writers such as Ammianus Marcellinus and Claudian, as one of the main enemies of Rome, it is only now that a well organised Pictish kingdom (with a well ordered, partly Romanised art), had become an active threat to the peoples of the south, now represented by Rheged and the Northumbrian kingdom, which came in part to control it.

In 1125, William of Malmesbury (*c.* 1095–1142) was still able to write of the wall and also of a *triclinium* which was associated with an inscription reading, according to William, 'Marii victoriae'. Amusingly, William thought the Cumbri of Cumberland were the barbarian tribe of the Cimbri, defeated by Marius in 101 B.C. He reckoned that their uncouth dialect, which as we have seen, distorted the name of their city showed them to be barbarians.[8] However, we can easily emend William's reading 'Marii' to Marti, and the inscription could then either record a shrine to Mars Victor, as Dr R. P. Wright believed (Marti Victori Ae[dem]) or alternatively, it could be a dedication to a number of appropriate deities including Mars and Victoria ([. . .]Marti, Victoriae[. . .]) as suggested by Dr Roger Tomlin who posits a building with three recesses (suggesting to William a *triclinium*), which might indicate three deities. If so, the third deity, whether an Olympian such as Minerva, or the Genius or Numen of the Emperor, must remain conjectural.[9]

Both the Anglo-Saxon and Norman sources mention the wall of Carlisle. Roman walls were obviously serviceable, and the circuits remained in whole or in part in most towns still occupied from ancient times in however desultory a fashion, or at least reoccupied. If the temple and fountain suggest the quality of life in antiquity, the wall was a continuing symbol of power, giving *dignitas* to the city and still providing it with security, likely to have been cherished by its inhabitants even more now that there was no standing army in the vicinity.

The wonderful fountain of the anonymous monk and of Bede is rather more interesting. Unfortunately, we are not informed what was remarkable about it. Notionally, it might have been no more than a broken aquaduct of well shaped Roman stone gushing pure water. I have seen how, in the centre of Ithome (Messene) in the Northern Peloponnese, just such an aquaduct has allowed a little village to flourish in an otherwise parched landscape (Fig. 1). In the virtually contemporary Anglo-Saxon poem 'The Ruin', almost certainly about Bath, the gushing hot springs are mentioned but far more prominent are the walls and pavements of a Roman site, still marvellous in its decay.[10] It would have been more likely that just a clean spring would have been mentioned in the account of Carlisle if that had been all that was to be seen.

Equally, no mention is made of the fountain having been carved out of marble or other exotic material, or of it having been embellished with figural carving which is a feature of so many water features from around the Empire, although it may have been. A small quantity of fountain sculpture remains in Britain, a few examples taking the form of figures of Venus or a nymph such as the examples which evidently stood in the pre-Hadrianic fortress at Wroxeter (perhaps in the headquarters), and in the fort bath-house at Duntocher, Dunbartonshire. A dolphin from the fountain-house a simple *exedra* which stood at one end of the rectangular pool in the open *palaestra* of the fortress baths at Caerleon, presumably accompanied Venus. It is not known whether

13

FIG. 1.   Spring gushing from broken aquaduct at Mavrommati, Messene, Greece
Photograph: Martin Henig

the fish-sculpture from the villa or rural shrine at Tockingham in Wiltshire was simply the decorative spout of a pipe or something more elaborate.[11] A relief from Housesteads, depicting Neptune with the nymphs was almost certainly the backdrop through which water debouched into a basin. It is possible that St Cuthbert's fountain was such a structure, also represented in Britain by a plainer example in the *mansio* at Catterick which is embellished simply with hippocamps. A number of such fountains, often simply ornamented, are still to be seen perfectly preserved in the streets of Pompeii (Fig. 2).[12]

An octagonal basin constantly replenished by a spring can be seen at the well known Cotswold villa or sanctuary site of Chedworth (Fig. 3) and a much smaller octagonal fountain, evidently fed from below, has been revealed at the enigmatic and still ill-known complex beside the River Wye in New Weir garden outside Kenchester where it still trickles water (Fig. 4); when the hydraulics were functioning better it would, no doubt, have seemed a marvel.[13] In the Wall region these religious or quasi-religious nymphaea bring to mind two water features at Carrawburgh. Coventina's Well is a rectangular tank which, when excavated in the 19th century, was full of coins, small metal items as well as statuary and altars set up by prefects of the First Cohort of Batavians in garrison at the fort. These dedications had evidently once stood around the tank. On a more intimate scale there was the nearby shrine of the Nymphs and the Genius Loci identified by the altar of Marcus Hispanius Modestus, another *praefectus* of the regiment. The spring is represented by a modest stone-lined tank but with its

FIG. 2.   Street fountain at Pompeii
Photograph: Martin Henig

exedra, a curved bench on which he could sit and contemplate, or perhaps place his offerings, Modestus' *fons* evokes the simplicity of Roman rustic religion.[14]

Both of these water shrines may provide analogues of sorts for the Carlisle *fons* although they were in a relatively remote location, outside a fort. The legionary fortress at Chester may have had a more elaborate version to sanctify the probable source of its water supply to judge from the size and quality of the surviving altar to the Nymphs and Fountains. In an urban setting, the fountain could have been a building embellished with columns. Indeed, modest examples of columnar water shrines occur in the fortress baths of the legionary fortress at Caerleon and at the villa (or sanctuary site) at Chedworth. It is not out of the question that it could even have taken the form of the much more elaborate fountain houses prevalent in the East. Although this might appear to be rather unlikely, the elliptical building in the Chester Fortress was planned to have a fountain at its very centre and, although very different in some ways, the building covering the sacred spring at Bath was probably highly ornamented with architectural sculpture and statuary.[15]

In northern Britain, a still serviceable tank might have been regarded as remarkable enough, even if largely or totally devoid of embellishment. Just possibly it may have been no more than a stone bowl or *labrum* as used in Roman bath-houses, such as remaining examples from the Legionary Baths at Exeter and, again, at Caerleon. In southern Europe and in the East, bowls of life-giving water, often fluted *canthari* were set up in gardens from early Roman times. They were associated at first with the saving power of Bacchus but they later figured in Christian art where doves or hinds are

FIG. 3.   Hexagonal *fons* at Chedworth, Gloucestershire
Photograph: Grahame Soffe

FIG. 4.   Hexagonal *fons* at New Weir Garden outside Kenchester, Herefordshire
Photograph: Grahame Soffe

FIG. 5.   Christian font at Richborough, Kent
Photograph: Society of Antiquaries of London

portrayed refreshing themselves from them. It has been suggested that such a vessel may have been the ultimate inspiration for the design of certain Romanesque fonts, notably in the St Albans region, though it is likely in this case that the inspiration was a medieval import from Italy.[16] It does, however, emphasise that a fountain could never, for a Christian, be merely a dead antiquity. It linked him to the very structure of his faith which itself was, self-evidently, of Roman origin. The octagonal *fons* at Kenchester is paralleled by the use of similar water-features for Christian baptisteries, like the simple example which has been identified at what must be a late-Roman church site at Richborough, Kent (Fig. 5). It is interesting to note that the Chedworth nymphaeum seems to have been Christianised in the late 4th or early 5th century as some slabs from the site cut with the chi-rho symbol very probably derive from the edging of this pool. For Cuthbert and his contemporaries the wonder of the fountain lay largely in that it was a source of living waters, a symbol of faith in itself.[17]

William of Malmesbury's temple, if that is what it was, is, likewise, not described in any detail. As a building this was certainly not a unique case of survival in north Britain. Indeed, Arthur's O'on, a circular domed structure remained virtually complete in the Carron Valley in Scotland until recorded by Dr Stukeley and others in the 18th century. It was only then destroyed by a philistine local landowner in order to build a dam. Interestingly, it may have held a statue of Victory and have served to mark a Roman triumph against the northern barbarians.[18] The mithraea at Carrawburgh

(Fig. 6) and Housesteads, for instance, were *triclinea*, each with two dining benches along their main axes, though, to judge from its inscription, the Carlisle building was not a mithraeum. With regard to what could be regarded as a dining-bench, we have seen that the shrine of the Nymphs and the Genius Loci had a simple *exedra* with curved *stibadium*-like bench, but it seems from the context that William was thinking more of a building than a dining area. A small temple with a single apse at one end, not unlike the Carrawburgh mithraeum in plan, has been excavated at Benwell (Fig. 7), and Roger Tomlin has suggested to me that William was describing a rather more elaborate version of such a structure. Much further south in Britain the mid-4th-century triconch building at Littlecote, Wiltshire seems to have served both as a dining room, a *triclinium*, and, as its mosaic suggests, a shrine to Bacchus and his associated prophet, Orpheus.[19] The dedicatory inscription, if *in situ*, is likely to have been on the architrave or in the pediment of the building. It would seem to show that the cult here was military and official, to Mars or to Mars combined with Victory. One thinks of the *scholae* from Corbridge, one of which was associated with another warrior deity of the Romans, Hercules, here shown battling against the Hydra. However, no sculpture is mentioned, if it ever existed, at the Carlisle 'triclinium'.[20]

SURVIVAL AND REVIVAL

THE strands making up the culture of the successor states to Rome are sometimes hard to disentangle. In Britain the problem is exacerbated because, for some reason, little in the way of sculpture and inscriptions was produced after the 3rd century. The rather attractive Carlisle-school sculptures cannot, then, have had a direct influence on the sculptors of the succeeding ages. We can be certain, however, that a great deal was still visible in Cumbria and Northumbria because of the testimony of travellers from the 16th to the 18th century, and collections actually made during the 'early modern' period. Thirty years ago George Henderson made a telling comparison between the figure of St John, as depicted in the Lindisfarne Gospels, and the seated woman on a tombstone from Murrell Hill, Carlisle (Fig. 8). The comparison between the clinging garments with their tubular folds is striking. An equally sound comparison might be made with the two seated women, presumably goddesses, on an unfortunately destroyed relief from Housesteads, or a seated statue of Fortuna from Birdoswald.[21] A miniature from a copy of Cassiodorus' commentary on the Psalms in Durham Cathedral Library showing King David standing holding a palm and a wreath, is equally closely attuned to the earlier tradition of the Carlisle School sculpture.[22] Especially notable in this respect are the standing men on two tombstones from Housesteads. The stylised head is, however, more reminiscent of that of a woman shown two dimensionally on a stele from Vindolanda whose competence falls very far short of the skill displayed by other Carvetian sculptures we have been considering.[23]

The most important stone monuments of the region are much later in date; the High Crosses, notably those at Ruthwell and Bewcastle, culturally belong to the 'Northumbrian Renaissance'. Henderson wrote of the former, and the same could be said of the latter, that it 'was carved in deep relief in evident formal and technical emulation of Romano-British tomb sculpture', a theme recently taken up by John Mitchell who cites such exempla as a relief of Victory (from Housesteads), another of Dea Brigantia (on a dedication slab from Birrens) and, perhaps rather incongruously in this case, the centurion M. Favonius Facilis (portrayed standing within a niche on his 1st-century tombstone from Colchester, Essex).[24] The full-length figures wearing rich, linearly

FIG. 6. Mithraeum at Carrawburgh, Northumberland
Photograph: Martin Henig

FIG. 7. Temple of Antenociticus at Benwell, Northumberland
Photograph: Martin Henig

FIG. 8. Tombstone of woman with bird found at Murrell Hill, Carlisle

Photograph: Tullie House Museum and Art Gallery

folded drapery set in round-headed niches on the Bewcastle cross have ready analogues in the Carlisle School tombstones. In particular, the famous tombstone from Murrell Hill, Carlisle (Fig. 8) which Henderson, as we have seen, contrasted with the St John the Evangelist illumination from the Lindisfarne Gospels, and another from Bowness on Solway (Fig. 9) with their stylised clothing, are good examples. Incidentally, both are associated with birds and it is easy to see how the sculptor of the 'falconer' relief at Bewcastle (Fig. 10) may have modelled his work on something like the Bowness carving.[25] This is not to deny that there are elements from southern Europe as well, especially in aspects that could easily be adapted from small objects such as ivories and as Mitchell suggests, small reliquaries: the vine scrolls, for example, would seem to have had a Mediterranean origin as most surviving Romano-British examples are simpler.[26]

There is, however, another possible source for the Northumbrian High Crosses and Mitchell rightly notes the Jupiter columns of north-western Europe. These are primarily associated with Celtic (rather than Germanic) religion and have a distribution centered on the Rhine and Moselle region although there are quite a number even in Britain, albeit most surviving British examples are rather fragmentary. They often had registers

FIG. 9. Tombstone of woman with bird found at Bowness-on-Solway, Cumbria

Photograph: Tullie House Museum and Art Gallery

FIG. 10. The falconer relief, Bewcastle cross

Photograph: Martin Henig

of sculptural embellishment, but in their essentials they were stylised trees, generally with 'imbricated' shafts to represent leaves or bark. They were surmounted by Corinthian capitals, sometimes inhabited, as in the case of a large capital at Cirencester which contains half-length Bacchic figures. At Cirencester this or, more probably, another column of this type, set up in the 2nd or 3rd century, seems to have been a victim of Christian iconoclasm under Constantine or his sons before being re-erected to the 'prisca religio' by Lucius Septimius, the *praeses* of the province of Britannia Prima, probably in the reign of Julian 'the Apostate'.[27]

Another Jupiter column may be recognised in the most easterly of the central columns in the crypt Chapel of the Holy Innocents on the north side of the choir ambulatory of Canterbury Cathedral. It may have been a survivor from a temple on the site reused first in St Augustine's Christ Church. Perhaps we should see in it a reflection of the policy to be found in the letter of Pope Gregory to Abbot Mellitus in A.D. 601, asking that the temples of the heathen should not be destroyed but re-dedicated to the service of God for 'in this way, we trust that men, may abandon the worship of idols but still come to these places as before'. Its prominent place before the altar in the Norman chapel shows it was still regarded as especially significant even in the 12th century. This, of course, introduces a possible element of continuity in the re-employment of such monuments.[28]

Bewcastle has long been celebrated as the site of an outpost fort 'beyond the Wall', although it does not appear to have been garrisoned as such after about A.D. 360, when, if it were regarded merely in military terms, its importance should have come to an end.[29] However, its hexagonal shape is very odd for a fortification of the Roman army as is its curious positioning of which, in their published report, Richmond, Hodgson and St Joseph wrote:

Although the site dominates the little valley in which it lies, it nevertheless does not command, as do most Roman forts, an extensive outlook. It is hemmed in by hills, which restrict the view in all directions except the west. Since, however, alternative sites with a wide view lie near at hand, the choice must be regarded as deliberate and explicable by other than immediate circumstances.[30]

In fact, the site was clearly a religious sanctuary throughout its history, whatever its other uses. Examples of polygonal sanctuaries are not unusual; we might note examples at Farley Heath, Surrey and at Coblenz. The 'sacellum' of the strong room seems to have been (or doubled up as) a temple *favissa*; it contained two silver votive plaques of a type frequently found at sanctuaries, depicting, in this case, the god Cocidius, as well as parts of two bronze letters of a type best known in Britain from Lydney Park, Gloucestershire and Woodeaton, Oxfordshire. There was also what the excavators described as 'the stone base for a life-sized Imperial statue'.[31] This, however, looks far more like the seating for a votive column as its top consists of a circular depression with a moulding around it. Four altars dedicated to Cocidius have been found at or near Bewcastle and it appears more than likely that this is the *Fanum Cocidi* ('Temple or Sanctuary of Cocidius') of the Ravenna Cosmography. Cocidius, who was sometimes equated with the Roman Mars and sometimes with Silvanus, is, incidentally, figured on a red jasper intaglio found at South Shields, Co. Durham, but attributable to the North British (probably Carlisle) gem workshop which flourished around the end of the 2nd century A.D. This, it may be noted, exhibits a rather similar aesthetic in the patterning of the garments of the god as does the near contemporary Carlisle sculpture studio with regard to the dress of the women portrayed on its tombstones.[32]

It is highly probable that the sanctity of Bewcastle not only anticipated but also long outlasted the fort, and the still potent god may be assumed to have attracted local worship at least as late as the 5th century. The place almost certainly long retained many of the features of a Romano-Celtic sacred landscape such as a grove and a spring, and perhaps even buildings, whilst amongst its appointments there could still have been a sacred column, even if the one attested by the base in the 'strong room', which seems to have been associated with some thirteen coins of A.D. 268–75, was no longer extant. A slight problem is that we do not know whether Cocidius would ever have been allotted a column just like those which are attested for Jupiter, or whether he might actually have shared his sanctuary with Jupiter (who was presumably regarded as his father in any case). An altar to Jupiter and a dedication from a temple to Jupiter Dolichenus are, incidentally, attested here from the military phase of the site. However, it may be noted that the device on the central *emblema* of a silver votive dish from the rural sanctuary at Berthouville in northern France shows Mercury standing between two columns, with a sacred tree for good measure on one side.[33]

It is highly plausible that the Bewcastle cross (Fig. 11) was a deliberate replacement for this column, marking the Christianisation of a long-hallowed sacred site. Mitchell comments that 'of the principal uses of these stone crosses seems to have been to mark places of prayer and foci of Christian assembly in locations where there were no churches to serve as places of worship', further, that the imagery on the principal face

Fig. 11. The Bewcastle cross. West face with Christ in Majesty and falconer relief

Photograph: Martin Henig

of the Ruthwell cross and the west face of Bewcastle 'may have been designed to serve as back-drops (retables) to altars'.[34] If he is right that the eucharist would have been celebrated there, we are surely back to Mellitus' conversion of the heathen temples mentioned above. At Ruthwell, as well as the carving, there are, of course, portions of the text of a poem 'similar to, but distinct from, lines 39–65 of the "Dream of the Rood" in the Vercelli Book', thus emphasising the tree imagery so clearly to be seen in the pagan columns as here in the Christian High Crosses.[35]

As well as being charged with a sacramental significance, the High Crosses can also be regarded as potent 'monuments of imperial power' as would seem to have been partly the case with King Oswald's wooden votive cross at Heavenfield. One source could have been transmitted knowledge of Trajan's Column at Rome, but there may well have been smaller Imperial monuments still extant in northern Britain, such as that represented by two pieces from a commemorative Victory inscription found reused in Jarrow church.[36]

The key factor in appreciating such monuments has to be continued literacy and the survival of the Roman tradition of letters. At first this may seem rather hard to substantiate because, as with sculpture, 'the epigraphic habit' largely died out in the 3rd or at best the early 4th century, not to be revived, as it was in western Britain, at the earliest until the 5th century. One of the latest examples of the earlier Roman series is the tombstone of Flavius Antigonus Papias, a Greek who was buried at Carlisle, and who was most probably a Christian judging from the language of his epitaph.[37]

Inscriptions, like sculpture, were still to be seen in the intervening period as they were much later: we have William of Malmesbury's testimony to that. One could have seen such inscriptions not only in Roman sites but in isolated places along the roads. One example found in 1894 in the bed of the river Petteril, a couple of kilometres south of Carlisle, bears an inscription to Constantine as Caesar (A.D. 307–08) replacing one to the British usurper Carausius (A.D. 286–93) on the other end.[38] Such inscriptions played their part in the epigraphic 'renaissance' when it came in the 5th century. An arresting feature of this revival is the continued, or else revived, use of the same Romano-Celtic names, most probably the former because there is no evidence for massive population change.

It is self-evident that the practice of epigraphy could only have been revived in a literate population, but in the case of northern and western Britain there is no evidence that the art of writing had ever been lost. Christianity had only arrived here in late Roman times when it is attested, for example, by inscriptions on two silver vessels from Corbridge as well as on the Papias tombstone. It is possible, as noted above, that St Patrick himself came from the Carlisle region. Certainly, from the *episcopus* Nynia's Whithorn there is an important stone set up by a certain Latinus and his daughter, and evidently dedicating the church, in the same manner that for example pagan temples had been dedicated in the past. The language is oblique and employs a tradition of numerology which had already begun in Britain before the 4th century. This allowed comparison to be made with Solomon's Temple.[39] At Kirkmadrine the gravestone of two priests, Viventius and Mavorius, and at Low Curghie, some 12 km to the south, that of the *subdiaconus* Ventidius, equally point to a flourishing church at this time. The use of English on the Ruthwell Cross is a deliberate move to create yet another 'Imperial' language, that of the Northumbrian dynasty.[40]

Even the Picts could join in this game of imitating Rome; although well beyond our area, the earliest Pictish carvings, often of animal images like bulls and eagles, seem to be related to naturalistic Roman art. The symbols that appear, such as mirrors and combs, perhaps also hint at Romanising prototypes. Words are not used but pictures are, perhaps, substitutes for them. The interest of this art in the present context is that it shows the continued influence of Rome far beyond what can still be regarded as part of the civilised world, not only in subject matter but in the erection of commemorative stones.[41]

A major aspect of this tradition must have consisted of a large number of (mainly lost) insular manuscripts. Most of these were probably quite plain but some may have been illuminated. Dr Ken Dark and I have suggested that a surviving Vergil manuscript might be of insular origin, though even if it is, a south-western provenance is far more likely here than the northern frontier. There could have been figural decoration analogous to that in the Lindisfarne tradition and itself copied from Rhegedian manuscripts. This would have provided a link between the Carlisle sculpture and Lindisfarne but it is essentially not provable. One clue, however, is to be seen in a charred leaf from a manuscript from the Lindisfarne *scriptorium* showing the Lion of St Mark. The patterned pelt, consisting of a number of tiny waves, is paralleled by the pelt of rather a similar feline on the bowl of a silver-gilt spoon in the late-4th-century treasure from Thetford, Norfolk, itself possibly derived from a contemporary insular manuscript tradition.[42]

THE ARCHITECTURAL LEGACY OF ROMAN BRITAIN

ROMAN buildings were a ready source of building materials and sometimes survived sufficiently complete to influence the ecclesiastical architecture of the Middle Ages. Amongst the best-known and most obvious examples of that in our region are the chancel arch of St John's church, Escomb, County Durham and the tower-arch at St Andrew's, Corbridge. They were both reconstructed from arches taken from Roman sites, the former from Binchester and the latter surely from the Roman supply base of *Coria*. The monolithic columns from the nave of the mid-12th-century church of St Giles, Chollerton were presumably robbed from Chesters.[43] Architectural history, dealing as it does with influences passing across Europe from exemplar to model, requires the former to survive. The importance of the Romano-British legacy, reduced so drastically by later builders, has thus been consistently underestimated. Models for the comparatively simple but solid buildings of Monkwearmouth, Jarrow and Escomb lay much nearer to hand than Italy or even Merovingian Gaul. In such simple basilican structures as are now represented by the foundations of temples of Mithras at Carrawburgh and Rudchester, the temple of Antenociticus at Benwell and Scola 1 at Corbridge. Unfortunately, we have little more than the ground plan and lower portions of the walls of these. The Carlisle 'triclinium' must have been yet another. That is not to deny the skill of the builders of the late-7th-century churches of Northumbria which survive, or perhaps those which once existed in Cumbria which do not, and it would be absurd to ignore influences from the Continent, which are certainly present as well, but in re-cutting and re-shaping masonry the architects of simple single-cell churches like Escomb would have been most directly influenced by the plans and structures of the buildings they were dismantling. In some measure then, they were the legatees of the Roman Britons, from whom some of them may actually have been descended.[44]

The settlement at Carlisle that survived into the days of Cuthbert was not a classical Roman city, but we should not expect it to have been like that. In many ways there was a very pronounced break between the flourishing provincial Roman town of the 2nd and early 3rd century and the Carlisle that the saint visited, but the cultural *caesura* had in fact occurred during the period when the official writ of Rome was still strong, in the 4th century. Carlisle may have continued through the 5th and 6th centuries during which time there was no mass influx of barbarians from across the frontier to threaten the cultural cohesion of the region. Northumbrian conquest from the east certainly cannot be seen in this light. 'The things we thought would happen did not happen; unexpected things God makes possible . . .', to take the traditional words which end a Greek drama. But, in 685 St Cuthbert looked north from Carlisle with well founded trepidation, for the Picts who had so frequently been used as a 'topos' in Imperial Roman sources had slain the King, Ecgfrith of Northumbria, who, in so many respects would have been seen as the contemporary version of Roman authority. His death on the field of Nechtansmere thus marked a real moment of crisis in the history of northern Britain. Ironically, it seems possible, that a Pictish sculptor took the Roman way and actually commemorated the battle in a relief, which was erected at Aberlemno, Angus.[45]

NOTES

1. For the name, 'Carvetii', cf. A. L. F. Rivet and C. Smith, *The Place-Names of Roman Britain* (London 1979), 301–02. The sculpture workshop was first published by E. J. Phillips, 'A workshop of Roman sculptors at Carlisle', *Britannia*, VII (1976), 101–08.

2. M. R. McCarthy, T. G. Padley and M. Henig, 'Excavations and Finds from The Lanes, Carlisle', *Britannia*, XIII (1982), 84–85, for jewellery including a carved gemstone depicting a satyr (probably from Carlisle studio; see n. 32 below), and a lead figurine, 88–89 for the amber ring. J. Webster, 'A bronze incense-container in the form of Bacchus from Carlisle'; *Transactions Cumberland Westmorland Antiquarian Archaeological Society*, ns, LXXIII (1973), 90–93.

3. Typical of the 'Mediterranean approach' is J. Lang, 'Survival and Revival in Insular Art. Northumbrian Sculpture of the 8th to 10th centuries', in *The Age of Migrating Ideas. Early Medieval Art in Northern Britain and Ireland*, ed. R. M. Spearman and J. Higgitt (National Museums of Scotland, Edinburgh 1993), 261–67; J. Hawkes, 'Anglo-Saxon Sculpture: Questions of Context', in *Northumbria's Golden Age*, ed. J. Hawkes and S. Mills (Stroud 1999), 204–15. Contra, see G. Henderson, *Early Medieval*, Style and Civilization series (Harmondsworth 1972), 119–21; and see especially J. Mitchell, 'The High Cross and Monastic Strategies in Eighth-century Northumbria', in *New Offerings, Ancient Treasures. Studies in Medieval Art for George Henderson*, ed. P. Binski and W. Noel (Stroud 2001), 88–114, especially 94.

4. Rivet and Smith, *Place-Names*, 402. T. Wilmott, *Birdoswald. Excavations of a Roman fort on Hadrian's Wall and its successor settlements 1987–92*, English Heritage Archaeol. Rep., 14 (1997), esp. 408–09. On Wroxeter cf. P. A. Barker, R. H. White, K. B. Pretty, H. Bird and M. H. Corbishley, *Wroxeter, Shropshire: Excavations on the site of the baths basilica, 1966–90*, English Heritage Archaeol. Rep., 8 (1997). For recent work at Carlisle cf. McCarthy, this volume; see also M. McCarthy, *Roman Carlisle and the Lands of the Solway* (Stroud 2002). Texts on the Picts are assembled by S. Ireland, *Roman Britain, a sourcebook*, 2nd edn (London 1996), esp. ch. xiii.

5. P. Hill, *Whithorn and St Ninian. The Excavation of a Monastic Town, 1984–91* (Stroud 1997), ch. 3; R. Woodside and J. Crow, *Hadrian's Wall. An Historic Landscape* (The National Trust, London 1999), 39, fig. 17 and 112 for evidence of whitewashing.

6. C. Thomas, *Christianity in Roman Britain to AD 500* (London 1981), ch. 13; Rivet and Smith, *Place-Names*, 261–62.

7. B. Colgrave, *Two Lives of St Cuthbert* (Cambridge 1940), especially the Anonymous Life by a monk of Lindisfarne, cap. VIII (pp. 122–23) written around A.D. 699 x 705, and Bede's Life, cap. XXVII, 242–43.

8. *Willelmi Malmesbiriensis Monachi Gesta Pontificum Anglorum, Libri quinque*, ed. N. E. S. A. Hamilton (Rolls Series, LII, London 1870), Prologus Lib.iii.208–09, written *c.* 1125. I am grateful to Giles Gasper for first drawing my attention to this source.

9. R. G. Collingwood and R. P. Wright, *The Roman Inscriptions of Britain* (henceforth *RIB*), I (Oxford 1965, new edn with corrigenda by R. S. O. Tomlin, Stroud 1995) no. 950.

10. Barry Cunliffe, 'Earth's Grip Holds Them', in *Rome and the Northern Provinces. Papers presented to Sheppard Frere*, ed. B. Hartley and J. Wacher (Trowbridge 1983), 67–83.

11. For Wroxeter see M. Henig, *The Art of Roman Britain* (London 1995), 86 ill. 54; for Duntocher see L. J. F. Keppie and B. J. Arnold, *CSIR Great Britain, I fasc. 4. Scotland* (British Academy, Oxford 1984), 55 no. 151; for Caerleon see J. D. Zienkiewicz, *The Legionary Fortress Baths at Caerleon. I. The Buildings* (Cardiff 1986), 277–80; for Tockenham see Henig in P. A. Harding and C. Lewis, 'Archaeological investigations at Tockenham, 1994', *Wiltshire Archaeological Natural History Magazine*, 90 (1997), 35–36.

12. For Housesteads see J. C. Coulston and E. J. Phillips, *CSIR Great Britain, I, fasc. 6. Hadrian's Wall West of the North Tyne, and Carlisle* (British Academy, Oxford 1988), 32–33, no. 88; for Catterick see S. R. Tufi, *CSIR Great Britain, I, fasc. 3. Yorkshire* (British Academy, Oxford 1983), 73–74 no. 127; cf. P. Zanker, *Pompeii. Public and Private Life* (Cambridge Mass. and London 1998), 120–21 fig. 63 and see also 100 fig. 50 (Pompeii).

13. R. Goodburn, *The Roman Villa at Chedworth* (National Trust Guidebook 1972), 23–24; R. Shoesmith, 'The Roman buildings at New Weir, Herefordshire', *Transactions Woolhope Naturalists' Field Club*, 43 (1980), 134–54, especially 137, pl. 1 and fig. 3.

14. L. Allason-Jones and B. McKay, *Coventina's Well; a shrine on Hadrian's Wall* (trustees of the Clayton Collection, Chesters Museum 1985); D. J. Smith, 'The shrine of the nymphs and the *genius loci* at Carrawburgh', *Archaeologia Aeliana*, 4th ser., 40 (1962), 59–81.

15. For Chester see Henig, 'Chester and the Art of the Twentieth Legion', *BAA Trans.*, XXII Chester, 8 fig. 11; for Caerleon see Zienkiewicz, *Fortress Baths I*, 146–47; for Chedworth see Goodburn, *Chedworth*, 23–24; D. J. P. Mason, *Excavations at Chester. The Elliptical Building: An image of the Roman World? Excavations in 1939 and 1963–9* (Chester 2000), 29 and see reconstructions pl. III 36a-m (Elliptical building, Chester);

B. Cunliffe and P. Davenport, *The Temple of Sulis Minerva at Bath. I: The site*, Oxford University Committee for Archaeology Monograph No. 7 (1985), 39–43 (Bath).

16. See M. Thurlby, 'The Place of St Albans in Regional Sculpture and Architecture in the second half of the Twelfth Century', in *Alban and St Albans Roman and Medieval Architecture, Art and Archaeology*, ed. M. Henig and P. Lindley, *BAA Trans.*, XXIV (Leeds 2001), 162–75, figs 3 and 5.

17. P. D. C. Brown, 'The church at Richborough', *Britannia*, II (1971), 225–31, pls xxx-xxxii; Goodburn, *Chedworth*, 24, pl. 11; Thomas 1981, ch. 8 for baptisteries in Roman Britain.

18. K. A. Steer, 'Arthur's O'on: A lost shrine of Roman Britain', *Archaeol. J.*, 115 (1958), 99–110; idem, 'More light on Arthur's O'on', *Glasgow Archaeological J.*, 4 (1976), 90–92; M. Henig, *Religion in Roman Britain* (London 1984), 208–09.

19. I. A. Richmond and J. P. Gillam, 'The Temple of Mithras at Carrawburgh', *Archaeologia Aeliana*, 4th ser., 29 (1951), 1–92; C. Daniels, 'Mithras Saecularis, the Housesteads Mithraeum and a Fragment from Carrawburgh', *Archaeologia Aeliana*, 4th ser., 40 (1962), 105–15; Smith, 'The shrine of the nymphs' (Carrawburgh); F. G. Simpson and I. A. Richmond, 'The Roman fort on Hadrian's wall at Benwell', *Archaeologia Aeliana*, 4th ser., 19 (1941), 37–39, pl. 1; B. Walters, 'The "Orpheus" Mosaic in Littlecote Park, England', in R. Farioli Campanati, *III colloquio internazionale sul mosaico antico* (Ravenna 1984), 433–42. For scaled plans see M. J. T. Lewis, *Temples in Roman Britain* (Cambridge 1965), 185, fig. 71 (Benwell, Antenociticus temple); 193, fig. 102 (Carrawburgh Mithraeum), fig. 103 (Housesteads Mithraeum).

20. I. A. Richmond, 'Roman legionaries at Corbridge, their supply-base, temples and religious cults', *Archaeologia Aeliana*, 4th ser., 21 (1943), 127–224 at p. 132 for scholae and 171–72 for Hercules relief.

21. Henderson, *Early Medieval*, 120–21, ill. 75 = Coulston and Phillips, *CSIR Hadrian's Wall*, 167–68 no. 497 (Murrell Hill, tombstone of Regina); 128 no. 349 (two women, Housesteads); 7–8 no. 15 (Fortuna, Birdoswald).

22. L. Webster and J. Backhouse ed., *The Making of England. Anglo-Saxon Art and Culture AD 600–900* (British Museum, London 1991), 125–27 no. 89.

23. Coulston and Phillips, *CSIR Hadrian's Wall*, 84–85, nos 202–03 (Housesteads); 87 no. 211 (*Vindolanda*).

24. Mitchell, 'The High Cross', 94 (see n. 3 above). Better references include for Housesteads, Coulston and Phillips, *CSIR Hadrian's Wall*, 36–38 no. 99, also no. 100; for Birrens, Keppie and Arnold, *CSIR Scotland*, 7–8 no. 12; for Colchester, J. Huskinson, *CSIR Great Britain, I, fasc. 8. Eastern England* (British Academy, Oxford 1994), 23 no. 47.

25. See n. 21 and for Murrell Hill, Phillips in 'A workshop of Roman sculptors', 101, pl. xii; Bowness on Solway, 103 and pl. xivA; see also E. Kitzinger, 'Interlace and Icons: Form and Function in Early Insular Art', in *The Age of Migrating Ideas. Early Medieval Art in Northern Britain and Ireland*, ed. R. M. Spearman and J. Higgitt (National Museums of Scotland, Edinburgh 1993), 3–15 at p. 11, fig. 1.10 (Falconer Relief, Bewcastle).

26. Mitchell, 'The High Cross', 95. See J. Lang, *The Anglian Sculpture of Deira: The Classical Tradition* (Jarrow Lecture 1990).

27. G. Bauchhenss and P. Noelke, *Die Iupitersäulen in den Germanischen Provinzen*, Beihefte Bonn.Jb., 41 (Bonn 1981); see also M. Henig, *CSIR Great Britain, I, Fasc. 7. The Cotswold Region* (British Academy, Oxford 1993), 8–9 no. 18; cf. *RIB*, 30–31 no. 103; cf. p. 758 in 1995 reprint, although I reject Tomlin's earlier date. The use of the *praenomen* in Roman Britain is attested upon two mid-4th-century mosaics from Britannia Prima and the reign of Julian seems by far the likeliest restoration to a *prisca religio*. For a Jupiter column from Wroxeter see R. White and P. Barker, *Wroxeter. Life and Death of a Roman City* (Stroud 1998), 93–94, fig. 47.

28. Bede, *H.E.*, I, 30; cf. Mitchell, 'The High Cross', 107; the recognition of the Canterbury capital is my personal observation but the use of a special column in a key position representing Christ, is found in other buildings of the early Middle Ages, cf. J. Onians, *Bearers of Meaning. The Classical orders in Antiquity, the Middle Ages and the Renaissance* (Princeton 1988), 79, fig. 49 (Fulda, c. 820); 81–82, fig. 51 (Quedlinburg, c. 930).

29. J. P. Gillam, I. M. Jobey and D. A. Welsby, *The Roman Bath-House at Bewcastle, Cumbria*, Cumberland Westmorland Antiquarian Archaeological Society Research Series, 7 (1993), 39–40.

30. I. A. Richmond, K. S. Hodgson and K. J. St Joseph, 'The Roman fort at Bewcastle', *Transactions Cumberland Westmorland Antiquarian Archaeological Society*, XXXVIII (1938), 196.

31. M. Lewis, *Temples in Roman Britain*, 198, fig. 117 (Farley Heath temenos); 199, fig. 118 (Coblenz temenos); Richmond et al., 208; cf. Coulston and Phillips, *CSIR Hadrian's Wall*, 151 no. 464 for the pedestal.

32. Evidence for Cocidius, *RIB*, 328–31, nos 986, 987 (two silver plaques); 985, 988–89, 993 (altars). For the name *Fanum Cocidi* see Rivet and Smith, *Place-Names*, 363. For the intaglio see M. Henig, 'The huntsman intaglio from South Shields', *Archaeologia Aeliana*, 4th ser., 49 (1971), 215–30 and, for two gems from same studio, see idem, 'Intaglios from Castlesteads and the Roman fort at Kirkbride', *Transactions Cumberland Westmorland Antiquarian Archaeological Society*, ns, LXXII (1972), 57–65 especially 60–62, for the gem

showing Bonus Eventus from Castlesteads and see McCarthy, Padley and Henig, 'Excavations and Finds' in note 2 above for satyr gem actually from Carlisle.

33. Altar to Jupiter, *RIB*, 330–31 no. 991; dedication to Jupiter Dolichenus, no. 992. For the Berthouville *phiale*, see M. Henig, *A Handbook of Roman Art* (Oxford 1983), 145, ill. 112.

34. Mitchell, 'The High Cross', 103.

35. D. Howlett, 'Inscriptions and design of the Ruthwell Cross', in *The Ruthwell Cross. Papers from the colloquium sponsored by the index of Christian art, Princeton University*, ed. B. Cassidy (Princeton 1992), 71–93, esp. 85–93.

36. F. Orton, 'Northumbrian Sculpture (The Ruthwell and Bewcastle Monuments): questions of difference', in *Northumbria's Golden Age*, ed. J. Hawkes and S. Mills (Stroud 1999), 222. For King Oswald's wooden cross at Heavenfield, Bede, *H.E.*, III, 2. For the Jarrow inscription, *RIB*, 349–51 no. 1051, presumably derived from a *tropaeum* on the eastern side of Hadrian's Wall.

37. *RIB*, 317–18, no. 955.

38. ibid., 718, nos 2290–92.

39. C. Thomas, *Christian Celts. Messages and Images* (Stroud 1998), 102–14.

40. ibid., 114–21.

41. On the art itself see C. Hicks, 'The Pictish Class I animals', in Spearman and Higgitt, *The Age of Migrating Ideas*, 196–202; also L. Alcock, 'Image and icon in Pictish Sculpture', in ibid., 230–36. The most convincing attempt to 'read' the symbol-stones is that of R. Samson, 'The reinterpretation of the Pictish symbols', *JBAA*, 145 (1992), 29–65.

42. M. Henig, *The Art of Roman Britain*, 157–58; K. R. Dark, *Civitas to Kingdom: British Political Continuity 300–800* (Leicester 1994), 184–91. The lion from the Otho-Corpus Gospels, Webster and Backhouse ed., *The Making of England*, 117 no. 83a should be compared with the late Romano-British silver pantheress from Hoxne, R. Bland and C. Johns, *The Hoxne Treasure: an illustrated introduction* (British Museum, London 1993), 24, cat. no. 30.

43. For Escomb see E. Fernie, *The Architecture of the Anglo-Saxons* (London 1983), 54 ill. 29; for Corbridge see Pevsner, *Northumberland* B/E (1957), 130, pl. 15b; T. Eaton, *Plundering the Past. Roman stonework in Medieval Britain* (Stroud 2000), 25 and 27, fig. 11 (Chollerton).

44. Fernie, *Architecture of the Anglo-Saxons*, 48–50, ill. 22 (Monkwearmouth); 50–52, ills 23–24 (Jarrow); 54–57 (Escomb).

45. Alcock, 'Image and icon', 233–24 for the Aberlemno stone possibly showing the Battle of Nechtansmere.

Medieval Carlisle: Cathedral and City from Foundation to Dissolution

HENRY SUMMERSON

The fortunes of Carlisle Cathedral in the Middle Ages were inseparable from those of the city in which it stood. The documentary record for each is imperfect, but it is often possible to deduce the fortunes of one from those of the other. Together they interacted with external forces: potentially benevolent ones like the English crown which brought both into existence, or the bishops who usually resided close at hand in Rose Castle, from where they often promoted works or appeals for funds; dangerous ones like hostile Scots or other disruptive agencies on England's northern border. In recurrent times of crisis city and cathedral supported one another. The cathedral, especially through its focal cult of the Virgin, gave spiritual and emotional sustenance to the city, which also benefited economically from the recourse of pilgrims and others who for any reason came to the mother church of the diocese. The townsfolk for their part were constantly involved in the affairs of the cathedral (whose fabric comprised both a monastic and a parish church), to the point of taking part in disputes among its clergy (who must often have been their relations), and many remembered it in their wills. In the early 16th century city and cathedral prospered together: the refoundation of the latter in 1541, following the dissolution of the Augustinian cathedral priory a year earlier, was certainly an important and beneficial factor in the continued development of the former.

THE purpose of this paper is to present a coherent account of Carlisle Cathedral from the early 12th century to the reign of Henry VIII, and of the context in which it developed. It is unfortunately necessary to admit that there is a great deal about it that we do not, indeed cannot, know. A series of disasters, the product of war, crime and misadventure, has almost entirely deprived us of the medieval cathedral's archive. The cartulary of the cathedral priory, which might have been expected to form the basis of any study of its fortunes, has disappeared so completely that it is purely a matter of presumption that one ever existed. Where written records of a building are wanting, it is usual for scholars to console themselves with an intensified study of its standing remains. At Carlisle even that recourse is limited, by the demolition of five of the seven bays of the cathedral nave in the mid-17th century. The manuscript evidence is usually fragmented, and decidedly uneven in its chronological distribution — of all the medieval centuries, the 14th is by far the best documented. The narrative that follows is probably best likened to a mosaic, many of whose pieces are missing and in which nuances of light and shade are rarely detectable.

The continuous history of Carlisle Cathedral begins less in shade than in pitch darkness. The oldest sections of the surviving fabric are of the 12th century. Archaeology has recently established that there may have been an earlier church on its site, probably of the 10th century, but that is all. Who built it, for whose use, its size and shape — all are utterly unknown.[1] The recovery of this church, and of the community implicitly associated with it, is important not least in contradicting the statement by the chronicler John of Worcester that Carlisle lay unoccupied for some two centuries after its destruction by Vikings in the late 9th century.[2] Objectively considered, it would have been surprising had that been so. Carlisle is an ancient site. In the Roman period, under the name of *Luguvalium*, it was an important settlement, a garrison town and centre for civilian government. Afterwards it seems to have retained something of the latter character into at least the late 7th century, and to have become an estate centre, and perhaps more, afterwards. Its significance, one which makes it unlikely to have been deserted for long, lay in its position. This is now masked by buildings. The Roman and medieval town lay on a rising spur of land protected on three sides by rivers — the Petteril to the east, the Eden to the north, the Caldew to the west. The ground slopes up from south to north, and the spur ends with a sharp drop to the flood-plain of the Eden below.[3] Until it was embanked in the 19th century, the Eden *did* flood, so that the town was protected by marshes as well as watercourses. The valleys of the rivers which thus made the site defensible also provided the means of communication to and from it, in particular to its southern hinterland down the Eden valley. Moreover, Carlisle dominated the crossings of the Solway, less than ten miles to the north, and had easy access both to southern Scotland and to north-east England through the Tyne valley to its east. In both the Roman and medieval periods a road ran behind Hadrian's Wall from Carlisle to Newcastle.

The position of Carlisle inevitably made it a site of military occupation, while the needs of its garrisons brought settlers and traders. This was as true in 1092, when William Rufus occupied Carlisle and built a castle where the Roman fort had once been, and brought in a population of peasants to support it, as it had been 900 years earlier. The political status of Carlisle and its region in 1092 is uncertain, but they were probably attached to the kingdom of the Scots.[4] Rufus's annexation was certainly resented by successive Scottish kings, and his importation of settlers was a device employed elsewhere in the Anglo-Norman *regnum* to hold disputed territory — it was practised on a massive scale in Pembrokeshire. In other respects, too, there were similarities between Carlisle and the Welsh marches. In the latter a combination of castle, burgh and religious house was a common formula for places of strategic importance. At Carlisle the castle came first, but it is no surprise that a monastery should have soon followed, or that its foundation should have been an act of royal policy. The beginnings of what became Carlisle Cathedral emerged from decidedly secular considerations.

No charter survives for the foundation of the Augustinian priory of Carlisle, but it is highly likely that this event took place in 1122, when Henry I is known to have visited Carlisle.[5] The monastery stood on royal demesne.[6] It occupied the site of the earlier church but clearly covered much additional ground. Indeed, its position as part of a large complex in the very centre of the future city, next to the market-place, in itself argues for a royal association. An Augustinian house was relatively cheap to establish by comparison with a Benedictine one, and at Carlisle the builders had the additional advantage of access to Roman masonry, recorded by William of Malmesbury as still standing above ground in the early 1120s.[7] But considerations of economy did not prevent Henry I from planning on a fairly grand scale, as the surviving remains of the 12th-century church, both above and below ground, make clear. As well as land for the site, he gave money for building — in 1130 the canons had £10 of the king's gift for works on the church[8] — and in 1133 he organised the detachment of what became Cumberland and Westmorland from the diocese of York, to form a new diocese with its cathedral at Carlisle. The first bishop was, or had been, Henry's confessor.

Carlisle as a burgh also originated in 1092, but took longer to attain a separate existence. The city's first charter dates probably from 1158, effective self-government only from 1231. Like the cathedral priory, the urban community grew to maturity under the supervision of the crown, but never constituted an ecclesiastical burgh. This was an important factor in Carlisle's development, in that although town and cathedral were always of great importance to one another, the former was never dominated by the latter. At first the townsfolk were probably mainly important to the priory as suppliers of goods and labour. Apart from the king, the lay people most involved in its development were local magnates who acted as benefactors. Several gave lands, and one also gave relics. Alan son of Waldeve, lord of Allerby in the second half of the 12th century, is said to have given bones of SS Paul and John the Baptist, two fragments of the Holy Sepulchre and a portion of the True Cross.[9] In doing so he probably laid the foundations for the cathedral's important role as a place of pilgrimage. It was one which doubtless contributed to the priory's apparent early prosperity, achieved in spite of the lack of a bishop between 1157 and 1204. Henry I died before he could endow the see properly, which was consequently so poor that nobody could be found willing to occupy it for nearly half a century. Entries on the 1188 pipe roll, after Henry II had tried in vain to install a bishop, record work in progress on the cathedral, involving the high altar and a pavement, and also the building of the canons' dormitory.[10]

The scale on which it was conceived was such as to make it inevitable that the completion of the cathedral would be long-delayed, and its history during the 13th century is largely one of attempts to achieve this, involving the efforts of the king, the canons and (once the sequence resumes) the bishops. The latter had to be endowed from the property of the canons, whose resistance to the division delayed a final arrangement.[11] Even so, the present choir, with its rectangular east end, is usually associated with Bishop Hugh of Beaulieu, a Cistercian perceived as having overseen its construction in the style with which he was familiar.[12] It was a very substantial undertaking, which may well have increased by half the cathedral's length in comparison with the Norman building, and it is hardly surprising that finishing it took a long time and much expense. Henry III gave money in 1246 and 1253, Edward I gave timber in 1280.[13] The involvement of the canons is attested by a reference to one of them in 1285 as 'former warden of the works on St Mary's Carlisle'.[14] But in the end it was Bishop Ralph Irton who brought the work to completion, by a tax levied on his diocese — Lanercost Priory had to find £24.[15]

Irton could have justified his levy by reference to the cathedral's centrality in the religious life of his diocese — and not only the religious life. A papal mandate issued in 1217, when Carlisle was briefly in Scottish hands, referred to the way that 'the church of Carlisle being on the border exercises much influence either for or against the king and his realm'.[16] In 1282 Irton confirmed the appropriation of Addingham church to Carlisle Priory on the grounds of the burden which the cathedral church had to bear as a result of its geographical position and the frequency with which clergy and people gathered there.[17] It seems reasonable to assume that those people included the townsfolk, though it is impossible to say how they saw the cathedral in this period. They may not have perceived it as the architectural unity apparent to the art historian, since most of the nave formed the parish church of St Mary, while the choir and crossing constituted the priory church where the canons worshipped. Presumably screens separated the two parts. In an age when devotion often focused on shrines, images and lights, the people of Carlisle may have had a somewhat dispersed view of the cathedral in their midst.

Nevertheless, canons and townsfolk could have lamented for one another as well as for themselves when the cathedral (only just finished) and the city went up in flames together on 19 May 1292, the result of an act of arson. Only the Dominican friary at the south end of the city escaped the fire which swept across the city from west to east. The *Lanercost Chronicle* records gleefully that it destroyed Irton's tomb, though not that of his predecessor Robert de Chaury (probably the bishop whose fine if battered effigy survives in the choir's north aisle).[18] To make matters worse, Edward I's ambitions to dominate, then rule, the Scots led in 1296 to the outbreak of centuries of intermittent war. Almost the first blow in the hostilities was aimed at Carlisle, and resulted in another fire.[19] Cross-border trade had flourished in the 13th century, as had other links with Scotland — Holyrood, Jedburgh and Melrose Abbeys all had property in the city.[20] Such connections now largely withered away. At first the effects of the hostilities were limited, while English armies held the military initiative and often camped in and round Carlisle, spending money there. Edward I stayed several times, and made an extended visit of some three months in 1307, residing in the priory. Among his offerings was one to 'the sword of St Thomas the Martyr', first recorded ten years earlier, when Robert Bruce swore allegiance on it, but probably there long before — it seems likely that it was the weapon used by Hugh de Morville, a member of a great northern family, when Becket was slain.[21] Such relics were doubtless exploited to raise funds for rebuilding the cathedral, a process which started almost as soon as the ashes were cold. Indulgences were promised to donors in 1293, the king gave oaks for timber in 1294 and 1296, and at the end of his life gave Castle Sowerby church for the benefit of the fabric; as late as 1318 the archbishop of York licensed the collection of funds in his diocese.[22]

By that time the process of rebuilding was grinding to a halt, as the Scots, now masters of the battlefield, reduced the north of England to dust and ashes. The annual revenues of bishop and priory fell to £20 each.[23] The canons had to be dispersed to other houses of their order, and the bishop was apt to take refuge in his Lincolnshire manor of Horncastle.[24] Occasional passing references, like one in a lawsuit of 1331 in which Robert of Grinsdale alleged that some ten or fifteen years earlier he had been forcibly taken to St Mary's in Carlisle and there compelled to subscribe a deed,[25] suggest that parts of the cathedral, at least, had remained in or returned to use at this time, but the processes whereby this came about were not ones which have left their mark on the records. It has been suggested that the stylistic idiosyncrasies of the chancel's east window are due to its having been designed during the reign of Edward II but not installed, for lack of funds, for some forty years.[26] That Edward III, in 1335 making the last visit to Carlisle by any English king for nearly 300 years, was able to make an offering at the high altar, and the endowment in 1342 of the cathedral's first chantry, dedicated to St Katherine and located somewhere in the nave,[27] both suggest a continuance of religious life, but these events have to be seen in the context of a militarisation of life which affected the whole of Cumbrian society. In 1345 a brawl at a miracle play in the market place developed into a riot by the castle garrison against the citizenry. Urged on by the warden of the castle, the militant Bishop John Kirkby, the soldiers rampaged through the streets, killed a townsman in the cathedral cemetery and pelted the door of St Mary's with arrows.[28] In 1349 the Black Death reduced the population of the city by at least a third and probably more.[29]

The middle of the 14th century saw the fortunes of Carlisle city and cathedral at their lowest ebb. It is possible that signs of improvement for both after 1350 are primarily owing to better sources. It is only after 1352, for instance, that the bishops' registers, which survive in a continuous sequence for the period 1292–1395, contain transcripts of wills, in which the cathedral features regularly. But even if we accept that we are in a position to know more, there are still grounds for believing that the impression conveyed by the improved documentation, of a real if uneven recovery, is correct. With the English victory at Neville's Cross in 1346, the pressure from the Scots eased. They would return many times to endanger Carlisle, but never again was the threat as *sustained* as it had been in the first half of the 14th century. No less important, the death of the violent Kirkby in 1352 led to the appointment of a series of resident bishops, often local men, who were prepared to give practical assistance to the maintenance and enhancement of their cathedral. The king was usually concerned with other things. But he may have had an indirectly beneficial effect on the cathedral when he provided money for works on the castle. There were links between these two major structures. In 1381/2 and 1384 lead for the castle was recorded as having been smelted at 'the abbey',[30] and it does not seem unlikely that they sometimes shared masons and a workforce as well as facilities. Ideas may have circulated as well — the motif of the mermaid and mirror, found on a cathedral misericord, also occurs among the so-called 'prisoners' carvings' in the castle keep.

At the cathedral the lead was taken by the bishop, starting with Gilbert Welton, who in 1354 issued an indulgence for those who contributed to works in the choir, and so launched a major programme of restoration, attested by a string of further indulgences granted by Welton and his successor Thomas Appleby.[31] It lasted until at least 1367 and clearly continued thereafter in a lower key, presumably directed by the canon listed in 1374 as 'master of the fabric of Carlisle church'.[32] The early indulgences were given specifically for the choir, later ones for the cathedral. The distinction may have been genuine, but it seems more likely that the works usually involved the whole fabric. Perhaps John of Salkeld, who in 1359 left 100s. to the fabric of the church of Carlisle Abbey, and 40s. to make a new window in the chancel there (so helping to date the east window),[33] was indeed thinking of the choir alone, but it seems improbable that testators who bequeathed money or goods (the latter including an ox, a cow and a cart) either to the fabric of St Mary's or to the works there, were only thinking of the parish church, especially as they often left money to the priory as well. The bequests were quite numerous. Some 160 wills survive, but many are bare notes, without details.[34] Of the rest, 39 contain bequests to the priory, 22 specifically to the cathedral fabric. Revealing in many different ways, they show above all the centrality of the cult of the Virgin to Carlisle's religious life. She was always an important figure there. The cathedral was dedicated to her, and the city's annual fair opened on the feast of the Assumption (15 August). Although there were no relics, by 1370 there was an image whose lights had an endowment with its own keeper.[35] Where the image stood is unknown — a will of 1356 shows that that there were lights dedicated to the Virgin in both choir and nave[36] — but the will of 1380 which contains the bequest of a silver belt 'to the image of the Blessed Mary in Carlisle church' provides additional evidence for the prominence of the cult.[37]

It was a cult which intensified as the city resumed its position at the centre of regional defence. After years of rising tension open war with Scotland broke out again in 1384. A year later, according to the chronicler Henry Knighton (an Augustinian canon, and well informed about Carlisle), the Scots invaded the western march and attacked Carlisle, where it was said and believed, they were put to flight by a miracle. For a woman appeared and declared that the king of England was coming with his army, and when they looked, they seemed to see the king's standard advancing, and thus dismayed they abandoned their ladders on the wall, and their machines, and fled. And the woman was believed to have been the glorious Virgin Mary, Carlisle's patron, who ever watches over her townsmen'.[38]

In the years which followed the cult of the Virgin at Carlisle seems to have attracted devotees outside the city, and even outside the diocese. Thomas Irland, king of arms for Ireland, making his will in 1414, instructed that a man should go as a pilgrim from London to Whithorn in south-west Scotland, via a number of major shrines, Walsingham, Beverley, Bridlington, York, and last in the list, St Mary of Carlisle.[39] In 1472 a Yorkshire testator left money for pilgrims to visit shrines which included that of the Blessed Mary of Carlisle.[40] In 1451 an indulgence was drawn up for those who contributed towards ornamenting with gold and gems a silver-plated image of St Mary, thereby glorifying God and the Virgin and intensifying the ardour of pilgrims flocking to Carlisle. The work was so excellent, so notable, so sumptuous.[41] The indulgence was never issued, and perhaps an existing image was refurbished. But there clearly was a famous statue of the Virgin in Carlisle Cathedral. In 1469 the rector of Lamplugh, in a bequest which also sheds a little light on the cathedral's liturgical practice, bequeathed property to the priory on condition that 'every night on which after compline the antiphon Salve Regina is sung by the convent, they provide five candles in honour of the five joys of the Blessed Virgin Mary before her image in the said conventual church'.[42]

The property thus granted was in Carlisle itself. Occasional bequests by outsiders notwithstanding, the cathedral and priory remained primarily the recourse for Cumbrian devotion. The canons bore mostly northern names, and were closely involved in the affairs of the city. Following a disputed election to the priorate in 1381, both parties found supporters among the townsfolk and even in the castle garrison. When Bishop Appleby tried to intervene there were unseemly brawls even in the cathedral, involving 'several of the more important people both from the clergy and the citizens of Carlisle city'.[43] The city had an interest in the cathedral that extended beyond its religious function. Pilgrims could be a source of profit to both. The townspeople could also profit from the cathedral's role as the physical and administrative centre of the diocese, to which parish clergy came for twice-yearly synods, and where, as Appleby ordered in 1372, the clergy were obliged to come yearly and perform an annual homage in procession, wearing surplices.[44] Such activities raised the status of Carlisle, as well as presumably benefiting the city's shops and hostelries.

As Appleby's injunction shows, the bishop retained a place of prime importance in the fortunes of the cathedral. In 1380 the crossing tower, perhaps a new and insecure structure, blew down and devastated the north transept.[45] It was Bishop William Strickland (1400–19) who restored the transept and rebuilt the tower when the task proved beyond the canons' means.[46] Strickland was buried in the cathedral, as was his successor Roger Whelpdale (1419–23), whose bequest of £200 probably endowed another chantry, dedicated to St Roche, and who also left vestments to the cathedral.[47] Whelpdale's successor William Barrow (1423–29) in his will left the cathedral a silver image of the Resurrection, and bequeathed his body to the chantry of St Katherine in the nave.[48] Marmaduke Lumley (1429–50), a pillar of Henry VI's government, died as bishop of Lincoln after twenty-one years at Carlisle. But in 1438, at a time of fierce Anglo-Scottish hostilities, he was said to be maintaining the impoverished canons, and he also left money to fund a light before the blessed sacrament, one which was still burning in his memory in 1535.[49] Works in the canons' choir, including the bishop's throne and the choir screen, are traditionally associated with Bishop William Percy (1452–62).[50] Richard Scrope (1464–68) provided for his own interment before the high altar.[51] Richard Bell (1478–95), formerly prior of Durham, brought with him across the Pennines a manuscript of the miracles of the St Cuthbert whose illuminations have been convincingly proposed as the source for the paintings of those same miracles on the back of the choir screen.[52] Bell resigned his see in 1495, a very old man, but does not seem to have left Carlisle, since he is commemorated to this day by a superb brass in the middle of the choir. All these prelates, whatever their other commitments, associated themselves with their cathedral, and do not appear to have shirked their responsibilities to it.

The bishops were not the only contributors to the maintenance and embellishment of Carlisle Cathedral, however. Indulgences and licenses to collect alms show that appeals for funds went on being made for much of the 15th century, being recorded in 1410, 1421, 1422, 1443, 1445, 1454, 1462 and 1472.[53] Very few wills, or any other forms of evidence, survive to give any idea as to how successful such appeals were. Perhaps they paid for 'the chapel inside the burial ground of the church of the Blessed Mary of Carlisle' referred to, for the only time, in a will of 1430,[54] and for the handsome exterior implicit in the comment of the Flemish diplomat Ghillebert de Lannoy, when he passed through Carlisle a year later, that the cathedral was 'very fine'.[55] The cathedral establishment remained one to which members of important city families remained willing to belong: in 1441 John Blenerhasset, a scion of just such a family, remembered the day twenty-one years earlier on which his own eldest son had joined the convent.[56] For lesser folk, the cathedral doubtless went on being visited and used as it had always been. The same proof of age that records the fall of the tower in 1380 claims that on the same day different people went to the cathedral to attend a baptism, a wedding and a funeral, and pursued to it a suspected criminal who fled there for sanctuary.

The late 15th century saw what appears to have been a deliberate policy of beautifying the interior of Carlisle Cathedral. At any rate in the choir, this policy is associated particularly with Prior Thomas Gondibour, who enriched it with paintwork and wooden screens and recorded his achievement in a Latin inscription.[57] He may have had the encouragement, rare for the late Middle Ages, of a royal gift, when in October 1483 Richard III (closely associated with Carlisle as warden of the west march before he became king) gave £5 for a glass window in the priory.[58] It seems highly likely that the window was in the cathedral, but the grant does not specify its location. Still more important, however, was the improvement in the priory's economic fortunes which came in the years on either side of 1500, a development associated above all with the reign of Henry VII. As Henry worked towards establishing peace with Scotland, so cross-border links were re-established that had been broken for centuries — in 1493 the canons of Carlisle and Holyrood made arrangements for the mutual commemoration of their deceased brethren.[59] Such links may help explain the Scottish influence that some have seen in the Gondibour screen.[60] Peace brought material prosperity as well. By the time of its dissolution the priory's annual revenues amounted to nearly £600 per annum, just over £100 of which came from properties in and round Carlisle, where the convent must have been easily the largest single landowner; it had 52 burgages in Castle Street, for instance, and 123 in the city overall.[61] Economically and also physically — a point conveyed forcefully by the British Library drawing of about 1560 — the priory, centred upon the cathedral, dominated Carlisle.[62] The city's court rolls attest the priory's continued importance as employer and purchaser, while the house's wealth helped to maintain the canons in a very comfortable if somewhat secularised lifestyle, one nicely encapsulated in the 4*d*. tip which, in around 1533, the earl of Cumberland bestowed upon the prior's fool.[63]

The wealth of Carlisle Priory was not used only to benefit the cathedral. Gondibour built the so-called tithe barn and rebuilt the fratry. The prior's tower, now part of the deanery, with its superb painted ceiling, is associated with his successor Simon Senhouse, and an inscription attributes the gatehouse at the north-west corner of the priory complex to the next prior but one, Christopher Slee.[64] Like Furness and Shap in Cumbria, and like many other monasteries elsewhere, Carlisle Priory was adding to the whole of its fabric in the last decades of its existence. A papal indulgence of 1514 shows that the cathedral was not being neglected.[65] That a list of canons from 1521 includes a keeper of the relics as well as a keeper of the fabric shows that traditional sources of revenue, and also of devotion, persisted.[66] In 1535 the two offices were said to be combined in one, with an annual income of £15;[67] the fusion was appropriate, given the extent to which the well-being of the fabric had formerly depended on the cathedral's role as a centre of pilgrimage. In the following year the relics were said to be a portion of the True Cross, the girdle of St Bride, and the sword with which St Thomas of Canterbury had been martyred.[68] The last was appearing in the written record for the first time for centuries, but it had clearly remained important, in view of the anxiety which arose in the cathedral immediately after the priory's dissolution, over a service book from which the service of St Thomas, now illegal, had not been erased.[69]

All the signs are that when the Henrician axe fell on Carlisle Priory in January 1540 it did so on a prosperous and self-confident house, qualities reflected in the cathedral it served. Able to maintain its numbers — about fifteen canons — right to the end, it displayed its wealth in the 767 ounces of plate (whether sacred or secular is not specified) removed by the king's commissioners,[70] and also in images, fine vestments, lights — dedicated to the Holy Cross, The Trinity and St Sitha as well as to the Virgin[71] — and music; four lay clerks and six boys were employed to reinforce the canons.[72] Carlisle in the 1530s was a heavily clericalised city. On the evidence of a muster roll from 1534, which unusually lists the clergy as well as the able-bodied laymen, approximately one in every seven men was a canon, a priest or a friar.[73] On the evidence of their names, the canons were still commonly members of families important in or near Carlisle. Local recruitment was just one of the ways in which the cathedral anchored itself in the community at its gates, where, it may be surmised, the refoundation of the cathedral in 1541, with all its old endowment and much of its old personnel, was greeted with considerable relief.

NOTES

1. D. W. V. Weston, *Carlisle Cathedral History* (Carlisle 2000), 7; M. McCarthy, *Carlisle: history and guide* (Stroud 1993), 38–40. Mike McCarthy adds: the evidence takes the form of a three-phase cemetery attributed to the 10th century found below the nave of the present church. It is considered probable that the cemetery was accompanied by a church to the south, probably in the vicinity of the cloister and fratry. Further archaeological investigation in the future would probably resolve the issue as to the date at which the cemetery and putative church were established. See also M. McCarthy, *Roman Carlisle and the Lands of the Solway* (Stroud 2002).
2. P. McGurk ed., *The Chronicle of John of Worcester*, III (Oxford 1998), 63.
3. A. Garnett, *The Geographical Interpretation of Topographical Maps*, 3rd edn (London 1953), 152–58.

4. H. Summerson, *Medieval Carlisle: the city and the borders from the late eleventh to the mid-sixteenth century*, Cumberland Westmorland Antiquarian Archaeological Society, Extra Series, XXV (1993) [i], 14–15, 47–49.

5. Symeon of Durham, *Opera Omnia*, ed. T. Arnold (Rolls Series, LXXV, 1885), ii, 267.

6. PRO, JUST/1/131 m 13.

7. William of Malmesbury, *De Gestis Pontificum Anglorum,* ed. N. E. S. A. Hamilton (Rolls Series, LII, 1870), 208–09.

8. J. Hunter ed., *Pipe Roll of 31 Henry I* (London 1833), 141.

9. VCH, *Cumberland*, II, 139.

10. *Pipe Roll 34 Henry II*, Pipe Roll Society, 38 (1925), 7–8.

11. H. Summerson, 'The king's *clericulus*: the life and career of Silvester de Everdon, bishop of Carlisle, 1247–1254', *Northern History*, 28 (1992), 70–91.

12. C. G. Bulman, 'Carlisle Cathedral and its development in the thirteenth and fourteenth centuries', *Transactions Cumberland Westmorland Antiquarian Archaeological Society*, ns, XXXXIX (1949), 87–117.

13. *Calendar of Liberate Rolls 1246–1251*, 70; F. H. M. Parker ed., *The pipe rolls of Cumberland and Westmorland 1222–1260*, Cumberland Westmorland Antiquarian Archaeological Society, Extra Series, XII (1905), 161 (misdated by the editor).

14. PRO, E32/5 m 22.

15. H. Maxwell ed., *The Lanercost Chronicle 1272–1346* (Glasgow 1913), 23.

16. *Calendar of entries in the papal registers: letters, 1198–1304*, 48.

17. J. Raine ed., *Historical papers and letters from the northern registers* (Rolls Series, LXI, 1873), 251.

18. Summerson, *Medieval Carlisle*, I, 177–78.

19. ibid., I, 194.

20. ibid., I, 76–77.

21. PRO, E101/370/16, f. 16; H. Rothwell ed., *The Chronicle of Walter of Guisborough*, Camden 3rd series, 89 (1957), 295–96.

22. C. M. L. Bouch, *Prelates and People of the Lake Counties* (Kendal 1948), 71; *Calendar of the Close Rolls 1288–1296*, 377, 489; J. Raine ed., *The priory of Hexham I: its chroniclers, endowments, and annals*, Surtees Society, 44 (1864), lxii-lxiii.

23. Bouch, *Prelates and People*, 69.

24. *Calendar of the Patent Rolls 1313–1317*, 426; for the bishop's movements see W. N. Thompson ed., *The register of John de Halton, bishop of Carlisle, 1292–1324*, 2 vols, Canterbury and York Society, 12–13 (1913).

25. PRO, JUST/1/1404 m 28d.

26. Bulman, 'Carlisle Cathedral and its development', 108–17.

27. BL, Cotton MSS Nero C VIII, f. 202v; *Calendar of the Patent Rolls 1340–1343*, 468.

28. Summerson, *Medieval Carlisle*, I, 276–78.

29. ibid., 279–81.

30. PRO, E101/554/24; E101/40/6 m 10.

31. R. L. Storey ed., *The register of Gilbert Welton, bishop of Carlisle, 1353–1362*, Canterbury and York Society, 88 (1999), nos 198, 230, 300, 358, 413, 534, 557, 599; Cumbria Record Office, Carlisle, DRC1/2, 206–07; *Calendar of entries in the papal registers: petitions to the pope, 1342–1419*, 437.

32. BL, MS Harleian 669, ff. 175–79.

33. R. L. Ferguson ed., *Testamenta Karleolensia*, Cumberland Westmorland Antiquarian Archaeological Society, Extra Series, IX (1893), 20.

34. As well as *Testamenta Karleolensia*, Borthwick Institute, York, Reg. 14 Arundel, ff. 77, 77v; CP E139 (6); Probate Register III, ff. 282, 282v.

35. Cumbria Record Office, Carlisle, TL 542/6, f. 81.

36. *Testamenta Karleolensia*, 11.

37. ibid., 139.

38. G. H. Martin ed., *Knighton's Chronicle 1377–1396* (Oxford 1995), 337.

39. BL, MS Add. 9010, ff. 10, 10v.

40. J. Raine ed., *Testamenta Eboracensia III*, Surtees Society, 45 (1865), 199–201.

41. *Priory of Hexham I*, xcvii-xcviii.

42. J. Raine ed., *Wills and inventories from the registry of the archdeaconry of Richmond*, Surtees Society, 26 (1853), 6–8.

43. Cumbria Record Office, Carlisle, DRC1/2, 351–52.

44. VCH, *Cumberland*, II, 134–35.

45. *Calendar of Inquisitions post mortem 1399–1405*, no. 856.

46. Bouch, *Prelates and People*, 110–11.

47. *Testamenta Eboracensia III*, 65–68.

48. J. W. Clay ed., *North Country Wills*, Surtees Society, 116 (1908), 39–40.

49. *Calendar of the Patent Rolls 1436–1441*, 185; J. Caley ed., *Valor Ecclesiasticus temp. Henr. VIII*, V (Record Commission 1825), 269.

50. Bouch, *Prelates and People*, 124.

51. ibid., 126.

52. B. Colgrave, 'The St Cuthbert paintings in the Carlisle Cathedral stalls', *Burlington Magazine*, 73, (1938), 17–21.

53. *Priory of Hexham I*, xcvii (note); *Calendar of the entries in the papal registers: papal letters, 1404–1415*, 220; ibid., *1417–1431*, 225; Bouch, *Prelates and People*, 115, 123–24.

54. F. W. Ragg, 'Early Lowther and de Louther', *Transactions Cumberland Westmorland Antiquarian Archaeological Society*, ns, XVI (1916), 158–59.

55. C. Potvin ed., *Oeuvres de Ghillebert de Lannoy* (Louvain 1878), 168–69.

56. PRO, C139/107, no. 42.

57. Bouch, *Prelates and People*, 128–29.

58. R. Horrox and P. W. Hammond ed., *British Library Harleian Manuscript 433*, II (London 1980), 28.

59. F. C. Eeles ed., *The Holyrood Ordinale*, Old Edinburgh Club 7 (1914), 19–20.

60. C. G. Bulman, 'The Gondibour and Salkeld Screens in Carlisle Cathedral', *Transactions Cumberland Westmorland Antiquarian Archaeological Society*, ns, LVI (1957), 104–11.

61. Summerson, *Medieval Carlisle*, II, 598–600.

62. BL, Cotton MSS, Aug I.i.13.

63. Chatsworth, MS Bolton 2, f. 46v.

64. Summerson, *Medieval Carlisle*, II, 602–03; Weston, *Carlisle Cathedral History*, 98–100.

65. *Letters and papers, foreign and domestic, of the reign of Henry VIII*, I/2 no. 3617 (p. 1531).

66. Borthwick Institute, York, Reg. 27 Wolsey, f. 136v.

67. *Valor Ecclesiasticus*, v, 274.

68. *Letters and papers* 10, no. 364 (p. 140).

69. *Letters and papers* 15, nos 619, 633.

70. PRO, SC6/Henry VIII/7373 m 3.

71. *Testamenta Karleolensia*, 150.

72. PRO, SC6/Henry VIII/480 m 12; C1/1223/36.

73. PRO, E101/549/13, ff. 190–94.

The Great Tower of Carlisle Castle

JOHN A. A. GOODALL

This article aims to set the great tower or keep of Carlisle Castle in the wider context of 12th-century castle architecture. After some general observations on the distinctive character of great tower architecture in England, it first reconstructs the original design of the building and then explores its similarities with two other northern great towers: Bamburgh and Richmond. The architecture of both these buildings is briefly described and discussed and the terms of their relationship to Carlisle defined. From a combination of architectural evidence and historical circumstance the three towers are attributed and dated. It is argued that Carlisle and Bamburgh were probably both begun by Henry I, and Richmond by Conan, duke of Brittany. Of the three, Bamburgh is represented as being the earliest, its design probably directly inspired by the Tower of London. This was followed by Carlisle, a simplified version of the Bamburgh design, probably begun after 1133. The last in the sequence is the great tower at Richmond, probably built in the 1160s. In a short final section the influence of these great towers on two later buildings — Newcastle and Conisbrough — is briefly discussed.

SINCE the Middle Ages two great buildings have dominated the skyline of Carlisle. Rising above the clustered roofs of houses in the south of the town is the cathedral, with its curious massing of choir, central tower and truncated nave. And on a rocky bluff to the north, ringed by fortifications, is the stocky form of the castle keep or great tower (Col. Pl. IB). These two landmarks represent architecturally the two principal authorities that have presided over the development of Carlisle since the 12th century: the Church and the king. And it was only the construction of the A595 in 1972 — a spectacularly insensitive piece of urban vandalism — that finally severed, after more than eight hundred years, a sense of their close physical relationship.

The keep at Carlisle has long been recognised as an important surviving example of a Romanesque great tower. But beyond acknowledging this fact and describing its physical form in appropriate detail, no recent attempt has been made to place this building in a wider architectural context or consider its design in the light of new discoveries about English great tower architecture.[1] To do so, I believe, sets Carlisle in an entirely new perspective. Not only can the original form of the tower be reconstructed, but several very unusual features of its design can be used to identify it as one in a group of northern great towers. This group of buildings — it will be argued — owes its architectural inspiration to the great tower of Bamburgh Castle, which in turn drew its design directly from the Tower of London. Using a combination of architectural and historical evidence, the tower of Carlisle can also be convincingly attributed to Henry I in the years after 1122.

As a group great towers, or keeps so-called, constitute the most impressive and ambitious examples of surviving secular architecture from the Anglo-Norman world. A great deal of scholarship has been published on these buildings in recent years, some of which has served to challenge the fundamental premises of their received analysis. It would be absurd in so short an article as this to attempt a summary of the debates to date or attempt a full survey of the literature. But this situation makes it essential briefly to outline a few of the issues under discussion and my own impression of how these buildings can be categorised and understood.

Romanesque great towers are generally characterised by their rectangular plans; their design with three or more storeys; and by their massive construction, which allows for the incorporation of stairs, rooms and passages within the thickness of the walls. The larger great towers are divided internally by partition or spine walls, to facilitate flooring and roofing. Typically the principal apartments of a tower are set above a basement level and entered directly through a raised doorway on one side of the building. To judge from Henry II's Pipe Rolls, which provide evidence for dating several important late-12th-century examples of great towers, they were also spectacularly expensive to construct.[2]

The first great towers to be built in England were erected in the aftermath of the Norman Conquest. There is clear evidence that this first generation of keeps was directly informed by buildings in Normandy.[3] But the English tradition of great towers quickly developed its own distinctive characteristics. Perhaps the most striking of these was the sheer scale on which the largest English examples were built. In complement to their size English great towers also developed more complex internal arrangements than their French counterparts. The spine wall, for example, which is comparatively unusual in French designs, was widely employed in English towers and was sometimes richly ornamented for internal architectural effect. Some keeps — such as Canterbury or Colchester — were so big as to require two such walls, a feature unparalleled on the Continent.[4]

Another of feature of great tower architecture that was particularly developed in the English tradition was the forebuilding, a subsidiary tower that housed the external stair to the main, raised entrance of the keep. Some early French great towers — notably Loches — have elaborate structures of this kind.[5] But it is really in England that the most sophisticated forebuilding arrangements may be found and where, from about 1100, such structures become an essential element of the grandest keep designs. The largest forebuilding towers — as at Rochester, Dover or Newcastle, for example — not only receive grandly proportioned entrance stairs but also incorporate numerous chambers (often including a chapel). Some were possibly designed with external timber galleries as well.[6] Conventionally interpreted as defensive structures, the scale and detailing of many forebuildings also suggest that they were conceived as ceremonial entrances.[7]

Curiously, square great towers also remained popular much longer in England than in France, particularly in royal castles. Although some towers were constructed into the 13th century — for example at Brougham[8] — the tradition is usually represented as culminating with the keep at Dover, built by Henry II from 1182.[9] The persistence of square keep designs has been a matter of confusion to architectural historians. It is the received wisdom that the angles of a square keep were vulnerable to attack by catapults and mining. Consequently — to counter this weakness — polygonal, and later round, great towers came into fashion during the second half of the 12th century.[10] But this military explanation for architectural change entirely fails to square with the evidence of the buildings themselves. For example, Henry II built his first polygonal keep at Orford in 1165–72[11] and possibly his first round great tower at Chinon in the 1180s.[12] Had he believed these designs to be militarily more effective, his construction of a square tower at the vastly ambitious and strategically vital castle of Dover from 1182, for example, makes no sense at all. If we are to accept the military explanation for change, Dover should have at least a polygonal tower.

More will be said about the late-12th-century interest in polygonal great towers towards the end of this article, but the question remains of why the square great tower remained popular for so long in England. One explanation is that it became a classic architectural form and the hallmark of the greatest castles. Indeed, given the widespread construction of great towers in the century after the Norman Conquest and the prestige attached to buildings such as the White Tower at London, it is easy to see how this kind of association might have grown up. And it is an association which, arguably, far outlived the Middle Ages. The periodic remodelling of ancient keeps as the living focus of castles remained common into the 17th century, and such new Jacobean buildings as the Little Castle at Bolsover or Lulworth clearly owe much to this tradition.[13]

In these terms the square plan of the great tower at Dover receives a ready explanation. The castle appears to have been constructed as a royal response to the developing cult of St Thomas Becket at Canterbury and was intended as a statement of Henry II's power.[14] What could be more appropriate in this circumstance than a classic great tower designed on a gargantuan scale? The Angevin association with square towers might also explain why in France Philip Augustus adopted a design of keep — the round *Tour Phillipienne*, so-called — that stands in such striking architectural contrast to that of his rivals. Whatever their military advantages, Philip clearly used these towers to stake a visual claim over the towns and castles he captured and nowhere is this usage more striking than at the great stronghold of Falaise. Here Philip's round tower stands in dramatic juxtaposition to the square keep of his vanquished rivals.

Until recent years it has been believed that most large keeps were grand residences recast in tower form. In the absence of much documentary evidence, therefore, interpreting their internal layout has conventionally been a matter of marrying the plan of a particular building to a list of the rooms believed to be necessary for grand living in the period, such as the great hall, solar and chapel.[15] This kind of formal analysis is often perfectly convincing, but it regularly fails to account for any but a handful of the internal spaces in any individual great tower. Moreover, the whole premise on which it is founded — that the keep is coherent unit of determined function — has recently been called into question.

Although in some cases, such as Norwich, Castle Rising and Middleham, the physical evidence overwhelmingly suggests that keeps might house complete suites of domestic and service chambers, this is by no means universally true, even amongst the largest English great towers.[16] Equally, a keep might constitute one element of a house (most typically a chamber block, as probably occurred at Sherborne, Dorset) or, as in the case of Castle Hedingham, serve primarily as a ceremonial building.[17] Regardless of their original intended function, it was this latter ceremonial purpose that gradually came to claim a large number of royal keeps. This seems apparent from the fact that many castles with great towers are also documented to have had separate royal lodgings within them. The Tower of London, for example, was so provided by at least the mid-12th century.[18]

With these general observations about great towers in mind, let us turn now to Carlisle. William Rufus first established Carlisle Castle in 1092, when he refounded the town on this naturally defensible bluff above the conjunction of the Rivers Caldew, Eden and Petteril.[19] Presumably this fortification occupied the same position as the present castle at the north-western tip of the city defences, but nothing is securely known about its original form. In its present condition the castle comprises a roughly triangular enclosure with the principal castle entrance, De Ireby's Tower, facing the town midway along its south side (Col. Pl. IB). Divided off at the eastern corner of this enclosure by a wall and ditch is the inner bailey, which is entered through a second gatehouse, the Captain's Tower. From the evidence of the fabric it is clear that the essentials of this plan were established by the late 12th century and it is perfectly possible that they reflect those of Rufus' castle too.

The great tower stands at the south-west corner of the inner bailey. Siege damage, neglect, radical renovation and, some time before 1576, the explosion of a gunpowder magazine within the building have rendered its fabric a complex patchwork of repairs, many of them unsatisfactorily dated. In what follows I wish simply to distinguish the primary fabric of the structure with a view to reconstructing the original 12th-century design of the keep. This design may have been modified during the course of construction, but not to the extent that renders such a distinction problematic. For a detailed description of the entire fabric accompanied by numerous plans and drawings and a selection of excerpts from relevant documents, the reader should refer to M. R. McCarthy, H. R. T. Summerson, and R. G. Annis, *Carlisle Castle: A Survey and Documentary History*, English Heritage Archaeological Report no. 18 (London 1990).

Before describing the keep it is worth making a prefatory remark about the dating of the building. Discounting some of the more eccentric assertions on the subject, it is generally accepted that the keep at Carlisle was erected during the 12th century. Nevertheless, scholars have variously attributed it to three different patrons within this period. In order these are Henry I, after 1122 — when he ordered the fortification of Carlisle;[20] King David of Scotland between his seizure of the city in 1135 and his death in 1153;[21] and Henry II between his resumption of Northumbria 1157 and the first documentary reference to the tower in the Pipe Rolls in 1187.[22] There is no architectural detailing surviving in the building that can reasonably be deployed in favour of any one or other of these men and the documentary evidence, which will be discussed later, is only slightly more satisfactory. But the overall design of the great tower and the buildings it can be compared to will be used here to argue for an attribution to Henry I. He may either have begun it in 1122 or in conjunction with the foundation of the bishopric at Carlisle in 1133, a circumstance which may have led to the completion of the keep by King David of Scotland.

In common with most buildings of its kind the great tower at Carlisle is massively conceived on a square plan with a complex system of mural chambers and stairs (Figs 1 and 2). Today the building stands four storeys high, each storey corresponding to a floor, and is topped by a parapet with deep embrasures for cannon. Broad clasping buttresses articulate the corners of the building and the north and east faces also have a centrally placed pilaster buttress rising up the wall. A similar buttress may have existed on the south side — the face of which has been cut back — but the arrangement of windows and the patches of surviving Romanesque masonry on the west side suggest that this has always been plain. The different faces of the building are also divided horizontally by chamfered off-sets. Apart from this external articulation the keep and its architectural features — such as doors and windows — are entirely devoid of ornament.

The principal entrance to the keep is a door, formerly closed by a portcullis, at ground level at the northern end of the east wall. In its present form this doorway is entirely Tudor but, as will be argued, it clearly stands in place of the original entrance to the building. Passing through it the visitor can either go directly into the basement or

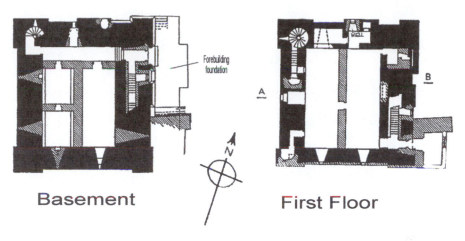

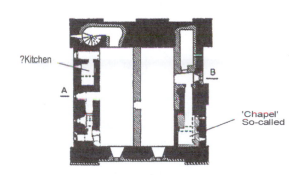

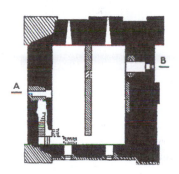

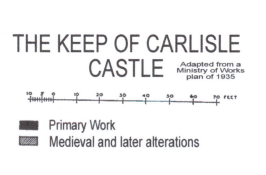

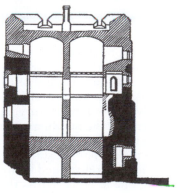

THE KEEP OF CARLISLE CASTLE

Adapted from a
Ministry of Works
plan of 1935

■ Primary Work
▨ Medieval and later alterations

Fig. 1. Plans and section of the keep of Carlisle Castle
© *English Heritage*

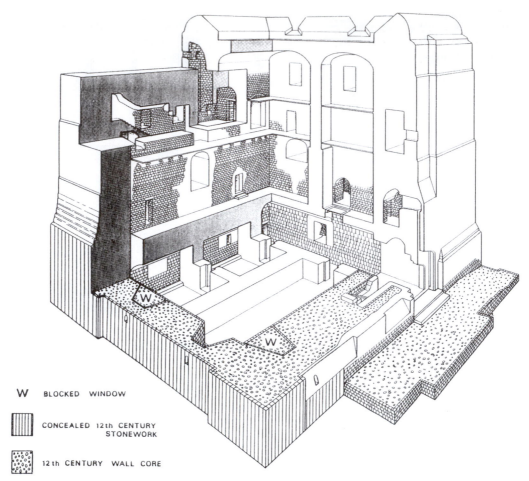

W   BLOCKED WINDOW

CONCEALED 12th CENTURY
STONEWORK

12th CENTURY WALL CORE

FIG. 2.   Cutaway of Carlisle keep from the south-east
Drawing by Richard Annis. © English Heritage

up a straight flight of stairs rising within the thickness of the east wall to the first floor. Straight internal stairs independent of a vice are a rarity in English keep design, occurring only in a handful of 11th-century towers, such as Chepstow and Ludlow, and in several 12th-century northern keeps. The Carlisle staircase has been entirely refaced internally in the 16th century, apparently in an attempt to strengthen the structure of the tower. But the building has nevertheless subsided since and wide gaps have opened between this strengthening skin and the original fabric. Looking along these gaps it is possible to see that the staircase originally had a barrel-vaulted roof. Moreover, there was a wide, barrel-vaulted lobby at the head of the stairs.

Facing one another across the lobby today are two doors. That to the right of the arriving visitor (west) leads onto the first-floor interior of the great tower and appears to be an original feature of the building. Opposite it — to the left (east) — is a doorway into a modern chamber projecting out to the east of the keep. This doorway has a round-headed arch but is so much reworked as to be impossible to date securely. Since — as will be argued — the keep was originally planned without any projecting structures, this door must be an insertion within the fabric. It probably replaced a large window or an internal recess and the 12th-century ashlar facing for the embrasure of this feature is still visible behind later skins of masonry.

Internal access between the floors of the keep was provided by a 12th-century spiral stair in the north-west angle of the building. This spiral stair now only rises from basement to second-floor level, at which point it is roughly capped by a mass of rubble masonry. As surviving areas of 12th-century stonework indicate, it originally gave access to both the first and second floors of the tower, the former through a short, straight mural stair in the west wall. Sufficient 12th-century masonry survives in the wall facings at third-floor level to demonstrate that there was no means of access to the spiral stair at this level. Presumably, therefore, the stair originally rose unbroken from the second floor up to the parapets. There it must have emerged from one of the four corner turrets which are known once to have crowned the building, a typical arrangement in great towers at this date.[23]

That there is no 12th-century means of access to the third floor is one of several pieces of evidence which suggest that the roof of the building originally sat at this level, deeply countersunk within the stone shell of the tower. Though the matter remains controversial, there is, in my opinion, an overwhelming body of evidence to demonstrate that such countersunk roofs were, with a few important exceptions, a universal feature of English keeps from the Tower of London onwards. Certainly, all the keeps to which Carlisle will be compared show clear evidence for roof arrangements of this kind. Given the low-set roof, Carlisle originally comprised only three floors — a basement, first and second floor within its four-storey structure. Access to the third floor is today provided by a modern mural stair, forced awkwardly through a Romanesque passage lit with windows in the west wall. Connecting this top floor with the roof is a modern flight of wooden steps.

The interior of the tower is divided through its full height by a spine wall, which creates two chambers on each floor. In its present form this wall is an essentially Tudor structure and whether it replaces a Romanesque original is an open question. The interior dimensions at Carlisle (13 x 10 m) places it within the category of great towers which, for reasons of scale, usually incorporated a spine wall. Indeed, the only great tower of commensurate breadth demonstrably to lack one is Kenilworth (14 x 10 m).[24] But although it may seem reasonable to propose the existence of a Romanesque spine wall on the basis of scale, therefore, there are two problems in doing so.

First, there is no Romanesque masonry in the spine wall today at all, even at ground level, where a considerable amount 12th-century facing masonry otherwise survives. Second, there is a centrally placed window in the north wall of the basement, directly on the line of the putative spine wall. This window could, of course, still be accommodated with a spine wall in one of two ways. Either the spine wall could be set on a diaphragm arch at first-floor level — in the manner of the spine walls at Hedingham and Scarborough.[25] But the first floor is demonstrably too low in proportion to its width to accommodate an arch of this kind. Alternatively, the basement could have been vaulted and the spine wall sat on top of this vault. There are, however, no traces of vault scars in the exposed 12th-century masonry to the north and south of the basement. It is difficult to see, therefore, how a spine wall could have been incorporated within the original design and the likelihood is that the 12th-century tower lacked such a feature.

At basement level today, the interior of the building is divided up into a series of barrel-vaulted chambers constructed within the shell of the Romanesque structure. These were probably built in the 16th century. The floors above are all laid in timber, the material presumably used for all the original floors. There are several subsidiary mural chambers at both the first- and second-floor level. Those on the first floor comprise a chamber over the main door, later adopted to house a portcullis mechanism; a latrine in the south-west corner; and two connected spaces in the north wall, one of which opens on to a well bored through the depth of the external pilaster buttress.

On the second floor within the west wall is a largely pristine 12th-century chamber with a large fireplace and wall flue, possibly a kitchen. The east wall opposite has been radically remodelled at this level but a small 12th-century chamber in the southern extreme, which was approached down a corridor, can still be identified. A transverse arch spans the chamber and the blocked embrasure of an original window is still visible. Incorrectly orientated and without architectural ornament, the popular labelling of this interior as a chapel seems tendentious.[26] Only a few courses of 12th-century facing masonry survive at third-floor level, which has been largely rebuilt. Nevertheless, it is clear from what does survive that there were no mural chambers at this level in the 12th century, further evidence that this storey enclosed the roof.

In comparison with other great towers, the most unusual feature of Carlisle is the form of its present main entrance. By the 12th-century English keeps on this scale characteristically possess an entrance stair housed in a structurally distinct forebuilding. And for this reason alone the present arrangement at Carlisle — where the forebuilding stair has effectively been swallowed into the east wall of the tower and a ground-level door created — seems unlikely to be original. Moreover, excavation of the area immediately to the east of the keep has revealed the footings for what appears to be an external stair and forebuilding (Figs 2 and 3).[27] This stair presumably gave access to the first-floor lobby through the much-altered external door at that level. But although this evidence makes it clear that a forebuilding has existed at Carlisle it is equally apparent that the structure must have been an addition to the original design.

There are two reasons for making this assertion. First, the basement preserves evidence of a 12th-century window embrasure immediately beneath the first-floor door. Had there been a forebuilding planned initially, this window must have been obscured by it. Presumably, therefore, the window was built before the forebuilding was planned or erected. Much more compelling, however, than this anomaly of design are the existence of two other buildings in the north of England which closely match the peculiar design of Carlisle: the great towers of Bamburgh and Richmond.

The great tower at Bamburgh is often represented as being an essentially modern building, ruined as a medieval structure when it was restored to use by a certain Dr Sharp for the Lord Crewe Trustees between 1757 and 1766.[28] At this time all the windows, previously narrow slits, were widened, and the interior extensively altered to create two new upper floors within the medieval fabric (Figs 4 and 5). Shortly after 1900 it was further adapted by Lord Armstrong as a house, subsequent to which no plans of the building or any analysis of its fabric have, to my knowledge, been printed. But in fact the original form of this building, despite these alterations, is still relatively easy to read. Although the building preserves little in the way of architectural ornament, aside from an astonishingly elaborate 12th-century moulded plinth,[29] it is amongst the most complex in its design of any great tower in England.

Bamburgh keep is square-planned and comprises four storeys, each of which today corresponds to a floor. Its entrance arrangement precisely reproduces that found at

Fig. 3.   North-east face of
Carlisle keep and the remains
of the forebuilding stair
Photograph: John Goodall

Carlisle. To the left of the ground-floor doorway to the building (set in the eastern face
of the tower) a straight mural stair rises up to first-floor level. The entrance door also
gives direct access to the basement, which is groin vaulted in nine bays. Two different
types of vault are used: intersecting barrel vaults in the eastern half of the building and
regular groin vaults in the three western bays. This curious contrast probably reflects
the differences in bay size to either side of the great tower and is also found in the
vaulting on the floor above. The basement is heavily restored and most of its vaults
appear to have been largely rebuilt or repointed. That they are an original feature,
however, is indicated by the articulation of the wall interior with pilasters, which
course into the wall masonry.

There are very few examples of vaulted basements within English great towers and
(with the exception of Norwich) all the most important examples are in the north of
the country, such as Middleham and Newcastle. It is quite common to find such points

FIG. 4.   North-east view of the great tower of Bamburgh Castle, Northumberland

Photograph: John Goodall

of architectural similarity between keeps in a particular locality and this circumstance constitutes evidence for what I conceive to be regional styles in the design of great towers, a phenomenon which is rarely accorded the attention it deserves.[30] In the north-west corner of the keep a spiral stair rises to the battlements. It is entered through a door with a gabled lintel and recessed tympanum, the only piece of extant architectural detailing in the building. Some of the windows at this level may be unaltered. These are curiously set in rectangular embrasures with seating for a shutter chased around their inner face.

Two intersecting spine walls rise the full height of the building, dividing up its interior into rooms. A sufficient number of 12th-century doors can be identified within these spine walls at basement, first- and second-floor level to prove that both are

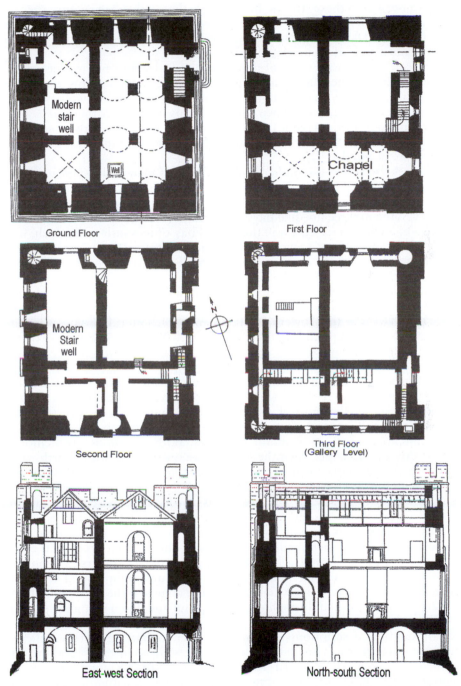

Ground Floor

First Floor

Chapel

Modern stair well

Well

Modern Stair well

Second Floor

Third Floor
(Gallery Level)

East-west Section

North-south Section

FIG. 5.   Plans and cross-sections of the keep of Bamburgh Castle, Northumberland
Adapted from G. T. Clark, 'Bamburgh Castle', *Archaeol. J.*, 46 (1889)

original features within these storeys. It is possible that in the 12th century they created four principal chambers around an unequal cross-shaped division at every level, as still occurs on the second floor. But demolition, rebuilding and other alterations have served to obscure some details of their original arrangement.

In the basement the eastern arm of this cross plan is lacking and it is not clear from the restored fabric whether there was originally a medieval wall at this point. Pre-1900 published plans also show that the north-east spine extended only two bays across the room, the northern bay standing open. Although this may reflect the medieval plan, it seems more likely from the layout of elements within the interior that one section of this wall was demolished in the 18th century. Just to confuse matters, since 1900 this loss has been made good.

On the first floor there is no southern arm to the cross plan of the spine walls. Today, therefore, the floor comprises three principal chambers: two arranged lengthways within the northern half of the building and one along its southern width. This third chamber is vaulted in three unequal bays and terminates to the east in an apse. There is also an apse-like window casement in the central bay of its south wall which, if it is an original feature at all, is now a wholly faced in modern materials. Inconsistencies in the masonry along the line of the north-south spine wall suggest that some internal feature has been lost from the interior at this point.

There is a strong circumstantial case for identifying this last room as a chapel. The only English parallels for large, vaulted first-floor chambers within the body of a great tower are the chapels at the Tower of London and Colchester, buildings with internal arrangements closely comparable to that of Bamburgh.[31] Moreover apses are themselves a great rarity in keeps and always appear to be associated with chapels. Beside the examples found at London and Colchester they may be found in the forebuilding chapels of Rochester[32] and in an angle of the great tower at Norwich.[33] It should be said that the identification of this chamber at Bamburgh as a chapel has previously been rejected on very curious grounds. First, because the chamber is incorrectly aligned to serve as a chapel and, second, that rooms with religious purpose were never placed below secular apartments in medieval buildings. Both assertions are demonstrably untrue.[34] If this was a chapel, then the lost feature on the line of the north-east spine wall could have been an ornamented transverse arch, intended to articulate the division between the chancel and nave.

The second floor — as already described — is divided cross-wise into four principal rooms. It incorporates in its southern side a curious mural chamber approached down a short barrel-vaulted passage built along the line of the north-south spine wall. This is one of several mural chambers, most of them much altered, that open off the first and second floors of the keep. As at Carlisle, however, no mural chambers exist on the third floor. Instead, there is a long mural gallery that runs right round the building, connecting the three spiral stairs which exist in the angles of the building at this level. This gallery is barrel-vaulted throughout and steps up and down along the eastern wall of the building.

Two antiquarian descriptions of the keep demonstrate that this gallery level originally enclosed the roof: one published by Francis Grose in 1775[35] and the other by the learned but eccentric Edward King in 1804. Both accounts provide similar information, but King's deserves quoting at length. Working with drawings of the keep which had been made in exemplary fashion by Dr. Sharp prior to his alterations and which are now, sadly, lost he writes:

There appears to have been a roof set in low, beneath the top of the building as at Portchester and Peveril; — and even to have been placed no higher than the top of the second storey from the ground; — in so much that the middle old small window of what is now the third storey must have been a mere large loop, or used as a sort of *lookout*, between the slopings of the roof, to which the walls, carried up so much higher all round, were a defence. In subsequent ages the tower was covered at the top of the third floor, but the vestiges in the side walls of the stone mouldings in the form of a V, remained until Dr. Sharp's time.

It clearly appeared also that *originally* all the rooms beneath were lighted, only by very narrow loops, or small slits in the wall: and even the chief room on the first story only by a window near its top, three feet square. . . whilst in each of the deep gable ends of the old roof, was a window only one foot broad.[36]

Although this description (as well as Grose's) might be variously interpreted as regards the form of the roof — how many pitches it had and whether these ran from east to west or north to south or both — one thing at least is clear. Given that this gallery level is at the top floor of the building, the roof must originally have been sprung from below it. One further detail of the roof can perhaps be gleaned from Clark, who states that the lost mouldings (evidently already obscured by the time of his visit) were 'concealed in the east and west walls'. Unfortunately Clark does not cite his authority for this statement, which, if reliable, would settle at least the issue of the orientation of the roof.[37]

Whatever the precise reconstruction of the roof system, the enclosure of the roof within a gallery storey has three extant parallels of importance to this paper: the Tower of London, Dover and Newcastle. In each parallel case there is modern scholarly literature which attempts to treat these galleries as internal elements of the building.[38] And in each case, in my opinion, such an interpretation fails to square with the physical evidence for the position of the roof. In the Tower this comes in the form of a roofline and gutters;[39] at Newcastle from the extant sockets for the roof timbers;[40] and at Dover from the remains of the gutter and water system.[41] More of this in a moment.

In its original form, therefore, I would suggest that Bamburgh comprised a basement, first and second floor with a gallery storey corresponding to the roof level. Crowning the whole structure were battlements and four corner towers, now rebuilt but clearly on the footings of originals. Access to the interior was through a straight mural stair rising from a ground-floor entrance and communication between the floors was provided by a spiral stair in the north-west angle, which rose to the parapet. In sum, the form of the building is strikingly similar to that I have proposed for Carlisle. But I would also like to give equal emphasis to the similarities of Bamburgh with the Tower of London, particularly in the form and arrangement of its chapel.

Unfortunately the construction of the keep at Bamburgh is entirely undocumented. The consensus of scholarly opinion is that Henry II built or completed it. Various entries in the Pipe Rolls have been used to corroborate this, including £4 of expenditure on the tower in 1163–64 and the documented failure of two tenants to assist in unspecified work to the castle in 1169–70.[42] In fact, there is a good case for dating this exceptional building rather earlier. Bamburgh was already an ancient centre of government in the 11th century and after its capture by William Rufus in 1095, the castle became the principal royal stronghold north of York. By reason of its strategic and historic importance it was also the administrative centre of the shire of Northumberland during Henry I's reign, a position it maintained after it passed into the control of Henry, earl of Huntingdon, the son of King David of Scotland during the 1140s.[43]

But in the second half of the century Bamburgh lost its pre-eminent place in the administration of Northumbria to Newcastle, where Henry II began a new great tower in 1168. In these circumstances the most likely date for a building of this ambition at Bamburgh is the period of the castle's greatest importance, during the first half of the 12th century. Added to this, the architectural sources for the design, particularly, I suspect, in the Tower of London, suggest that it was intended as a statement of English royal authority. The attribution of this building specifically to an English monarch will be elaborated on subsequently. These facts combined make Henry I its most likely patron and, it is worth pointing out in this connection, that there is reference to a *cimentarius* called Osbert working here in 1131. Might he be the man responsible for the erection of the keep?[44]

An attribution to Henry I can be justified on more than circumstantial evidence. In architectural terms, the articulation of the basement and chapel vaults best compares with late-11th- or early-12th-century architecture, rather than, say, Henry II's work at Newcastle. Of particular importance as a parallel for the single pilaster bay articulation at Bamburgh is the *c.* 1121 basement vault within the nearby keep at Norham.[45] The dating of Bamburgh to Henry I's reign, however, is most forcibly suggested by a consideration of its architecture in relation to Carlisle and that of the third building in this group of related northern great towers.

The great tower of Richmond Castle in Yorkshire dominates the surrounding town in the most spectacular fashion.[46] Like Bamburgh and Carlisle it is designed on a square plan and comprises four storeys with a crowning parapet level (Fig. 6). Despite alteration in the late 13th century, when the basement was vaulted, and restoration in the 19th century, this keep is exceptionally well preserved. The exterior is articulated with plain buttresses and off-sets. Most of the windows are very small, a point of comparison with Bamburgh before its restoration, and at each corner there is a projecting turret.

The entrance to the building is through a raised door at first-floor level, but this arrangement, which might seem to connect Richmond with the mainstream of English keep design, probably has a practical explanation. The keep is built over the 11th-century enclosure wall of the castle and the entrance door has simply been raised over this structure.[47] That the raised door can be explained in terms of practical convenience is apparent for two reasons. First, because Richmond apparently never had a stone forebuilding, the natural counterpart to a first-floor entrance in a great tower of this ambition and scale.[48] But much more important than this, however, because leaving the basement level aside, the design of the tower compares very closely with those of Carlisle and Bamburgh.

From the entrance door the visitor can either pass directly into the first floor of the keep or turn left up a straight stair that rises in the thickness of the wall to second-floor level (Fig. 6). At the top of this stair is a small lobby lit by a large external window — now partially blocked — and furnished with a stone bench. In its present form the bench is a modern feature, but scars in the fabric suggest that it could replace a 12th-century original. In combination these arrangements strongly suggests that the lobby was intended as a holding space for visitors to the great tower. From the lobby a door opens into the body of the building. No spine wall exists at Richmond, which is smaller in plan than either Carlisle or Bamburgh, and the central spaces on both the first and second floors are without internal partition. There are subsidiary chambers, however, contrived within the thickness of the walls on both these two levels.

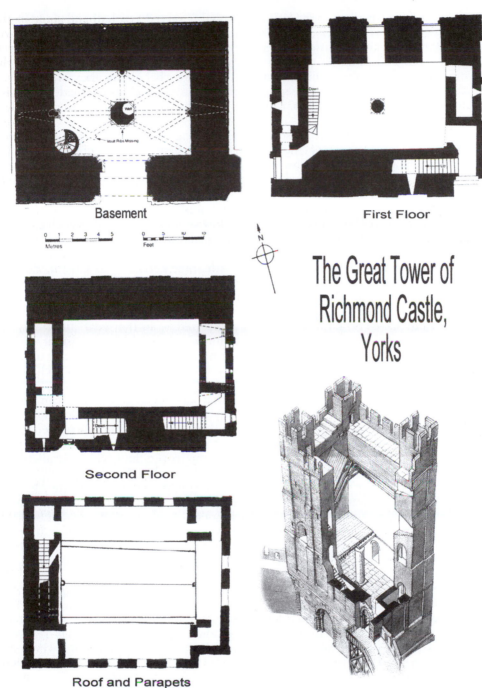

Basement

First Floor

0 1 2 3 4 5
Metres

0 5 10 15
Feet

N

The Great Tower of
Richmond Castle,
Yorks

Second Floor

Roof and Parapets

FIG. 6.   Plans and cut-away of the great tower of Richmond, North Yorkshire

© *English Heritage*

The second-floor chamber of the building probably served as a hall and stands open to the roof, which was countersunk within the top storey of the building. Like the top storeys of Bamburgh and Carlisle this upper level of the building lacks mural chambers. The form, pitch and position of the roof can be precisely reconstructed from the surviving sockets for timbers and a supporting stone corbel at the apex of the gable. Significantly, one window of the keep must always have stood above the level of this low-set roof, a parallel in this comparatively diminutive design for the external gallery at Bamburgh.

One detail of this perfectly preserved roof arrangement at Richmond deserves particular comment in view of the current controversy on the subject generally. Opening onto the leads in the south-west corner of the tower is a small service door, a feature which can be identified in many buildings with countersunk roofs of this kind, including the Tower of London and Dover (where it is largely blocked up). One of the openings in the gallery level at Bamburgh might be similarly interpreted.[49] The existence of these openings proves beyond doubt that the low setting of the roof in each case was a designed feature of these buildings, not a reflection of botched or interrupted construction.

The keep at Richmond can be attributed with some certainty to Conan, duke of Brittany between 1156 and his death in 1171. Not only did late medieval tradition celebrate Conan as the builder,[50] but Henry II's Pipe Roll of 1171 documents work to the tower.[51] The expenditure demonstrates that the great tower stood complete — or as some scholars have chosen to argue, was completed — in that year. Internally the building uses a repertoire of architectural detailing which would be consistent with an 1160s date, including billet mouldings and cushion capitals.[52] This decoration has apparently been used systematically to sign-post the principal doors, inner chambers and thoroughfares within the interior.

It is to be hoped that from the descriptions that have been given there can remain little serious doubt that these three 12th-century great towers at Carlisle, Bamburgh and Richmond are directly related to one another. Their entrance arrangement in particular stands in notable contrast to the mainstream of English great tower design in this period. Other points of comparison between the towers find wider parallels, but nevertheless further substantiate the case for their relationship. Bamburgh and Carlisle both possess a spiral stair rising the full height of the building in the opposite corner of the tower from the main entrance. Similarly both these great towers comprise a basement and two main upper floors. That Richmond is a substantially smaller building may suggest that it was intended to function in connection with the other domestic buildings in the castle, particularly Scolland's Hall and the Chapel of St Nicholas.[53] Perhaps Carlisle and Bamburgh — in contrast — were designed as complete domestic suites.

In all three buildings the roof of the tower was countersunk within the upper storey and the building crowned by corner turrets, both features widely encountered in keep design of the period. That the former detail occurs at Bamburgh, however, seems to me particularly important to our understanding of the original design of the Tower of London, constituting further substantive evidence that the latter was originally designed with a low-set roof. Incidentally, it should be said that with its original parapet and turret arrangement Carlisle must have stood higher than it does today.

It is necessary next to consider the order in which these three buildings were constructed. In purely typological terms Richmond is likely to be the last of the three. Not only is it the one tower in the group that incorporates rich decoration, but the smaller scale of the design and its odd first-floor entrance door — an adaptation of a distinctive entrance system to suit the site — mark it out in architectural terms as being a follower of the Bamburgh and Carlisle designs rather than their inspiration. It should not be forgotten in this respect either that Bamburgh and Carlisle were both major royal strongholds and the probability is, therefore, that their keeps set the architectural pace in the region.

Of these latter two buildings, Bamburgh seems likely to be the earliest. Not only is it the largest of the great towers, but it is far the most complex and ambitious. It also appears to draw architectural inspiration from the Tower of London, a very appropriate model for a great tower built by a king in the ancient seat of Northumbrian royal power. Carlisle is not so closely aware of its architectural roots, and appears for this reason to be a copy of Bamburgh. Placing the three in order — Bamburgh, Carlisle and finally Richmond — on this basis, may seem tendentious, but it is a chronology which makes cumulative sense.

On the basis of historical and architectural evidence, it has already been suggested that Bamburgh was built by Henry I around 1120 and Richmond by Duke Conan between 1156–71. On this basis Carlisle might be loosely dated between the two to *c.* 1120–60. But in fact this dating margin can be narrowed considerably in the light of political events. In 1135 King David of Scotland invaded Cumberland and seized Carlisle, which remained in Scottish hands until 1157.[54] This year, therefore, can be considered a watershed for the commissioning of the keep at Carlisle, though not necessarily for its construction of course.

On the face of it a Scottish attribution post-1135 is attractive because the *Scotichronicon* for the year 1138 specifically attributes the construction of the keep at Carlisle to King David.[55] But there is a problem with this. The close similarity of Bamburgh, Carlisle and (to a lesser extent) Richmond demands explanation through some common circumstance of patronage. If David commissioned Carlisle (rather than simply completing it, which is what the *Scotichronicon* might really record), therefore, it seems reasonable to expect some plausible connection with the work at Bamburgh and Richmond. This is the more particularly true since square great towers are otherwise an exclusively English phenomenon.

The circumstances of David's conquests in Northumberland might provide such a connection, but not comfortably. Bamburgh held out successfully against the 1135 Scottish invasion and was specifically reserved to the English king when the area was ceded to David's son, Henry, earl of Huntingdon in 1139. Confusingly, however, a charter issued here, probably in the 1140s, shows that it did later come into Henry, earl of Huntingdon's possession.[56] To further substantiate this change of ownership, Bamburgh was specifically listed amongst the castles received back by Henry II when he reclaimed Northumberland from the Scottish king in 1157.[57] Richmond never passed out of the control of the dukes of Brittany in this period.

Leaving this last fact aside, however, let us assume for the purposes of argument that David did commission Carlisle and that this group of buildings reflects common Scottish royal patronage. If this was the case, the relative chronology would necessarily be as follows: Carlisle (after 1135), then Bamburgh (copied by David's son in the 1140s), both followed — for some unknown reason — by Richmond (in the 1160s). Bamburgh's place in such a sequence is extremely uncomfortable and the objections to it numerous. Why should David build in his principal Border city a smaller keep than that constructed by his son at Bamburgh? In typological terms, how can the sophistication of Bamburgh be born of the relative simplicity of Carlisle, particularly since Bamburgh appears to have a specific architectural source in the Tower of London or Colchester? And finally, what are we to make of Bamburgh's architectural affinities to early-12th-century architecture, particularly the *c.* 1121 work at Norham?

Added to these difficulties is a circumstantial point: if Carlisle and Bamburgh are by David and Henry, earl of Huntingdon, why did their work stimulate no tradition of comparable great tower architecture in Scotland? This fact is the more mysterious because the Anglo-Scottish border was clearly permeable to architectural ideas, as is well testified, for example, in the influence of Durham Cathedral, and David as well as his son and many of their nobility were Anglo-Norman either in origin or persuasion. Nevertheless, no square towers appear to have been constructed north of the border in the 12th century. The sheer expense of such commissions may well have been an important factor in limiting their construction, but as the 12th century progressed this consideration may have been reinforced by another: the symbolic associations of towers of this kind with the English kings. To understand why this might have been the case, it is necessary to seek an alternative rationalisation of the relationship between Bamburgh, Carlisle and Richmond.

Much more convincing than a Scottish attribution for the former two towers, is that both were commissioned by Henry I as part of his attempt to control the North of England in the early years of the 12th century. I would suggest that the architectural and historical evidence points to Bamburgh being the first of the group to be built, probably in the second or third decade of the 12th century. Modelled specifically, I suspect, on the Tower of London, it was intended as a statement of Henry I's authority in the north of England at a time when Bamburgh remained the pre-eminent castle of Northumbria and the greatest royal castle north of York.

Bamburgh was then followed by Carlisle, which is essentially a simplified and reduced version of it. The great tower at Carlisle might either have been begun around 1122, when Henry I refortified the city, or in symbolic counterpart to the foundation of the Bishopric in 1133. This latter date is in some ways preferable, because it would allow for King David to work on the tower as the *Scotichronicon* records. In these terms Bamburgh and Carlisle could both be directly related to one another through the person of Henry I and his attempts to consolidate and advertise his political control of the north of England. Duke Conan could be understood to have aped these buildings in his own keep at Richmond in the 1160s because of their prestige as the principal local, royal buildings of this type.

As well as answering the historical and architectural evidence that has been discussed, this putative chronology might also help explain why Scotland never developed its own tradition of square, great towers in the 12th century. Allowing that Bamburgh and Carlisle were constructed by Henry I, all the principal 12th-century great towers in the region would be directly connected with attempts by English kings to absorb the area within their own realm. Should we perhaps understand these not merely as the grandest type of secular residence at this date but also specifically symbolic of English royal authority in the region? Was Henry I (and later Henry II at Newcastle) attempting to stake out his territorial claims in this area with buildings iconic of Anglo-Norman power?

Whether or not this is the case, it is worthwhile concluding this article with a few comments on the subsequent northern tradition of great tower architecture. It has already been observed that in general terms the buildings that have been described incorporate two features which, while always unusual in great tower design, are more common in the north than elsewhere: namely vaulted basements and straight mural stairs. It is tempting to trace their influence in more specific ways and two further buildings deserve consideration in this context. The first of these is Henry II's keep at Newcastle, constructed by Maurice the Engineer between 1168–78.

Newcastle follows generically in the tradition of these northern keeps with an elaborate vaulted basement, several straight mural stairs, and a gallery enclosing the roof. These features all arguably show an awareness of the existing great towers in the region. One other curious feature of the building is the existence of a richly decorated room at the head of the forebuilding stairs.[58] Could this be a waiting room based on the Richmond model? Such a chamber also exists at Maurice's other known great tower at Dover, a building which shares many further similarities of design with Newcastle.[59]

The second building worthy of consideration in the context of these designs is the great tower at Conisbrough, Yorkshire (Fig. 7), to judge from its sculptural detail a work of the 1160s or 1170s.[60] This tower is usually discussed exclusively in terms of the new generation of late-12th-century round or polygonal keeps in England, such as Orford, Tickhill or Chilham. It has also been compared to the keep at Mortemer, a building which does indeed bear a striking similarity to the overall form of this Yorkshire tower.[61]

But the formal design of Conisbrough is actually best paralleled in the local rectangular keeps we have discussed in this article and particularly Richmond. Conisbrough great tower is entered through a raised door up a stone stair, which is now largely ruined. In the manner of Richmond, this stair was not housed in a forebuilding. The main door gives direct access both to the first floor of the tower — which is set above a vaulted basement — and to a mural stair that curves gradually upwards in the thickness of the wall. Similar stairs connect the upper floors and there is pattern of arched and square-headed interior doorways, as is to be seen at Richmond. Aside from Barnard Castle, also a northern building, all other English round or polygonal keeps of the late-12th-century use spiral stairs to connect their floors. This distinctive stair arrangement at Conisbrough is, therefore, more than likely to be inspired by the buildings we have been looking at.

The architectural debt of Conisbrough to a local architectural tradition of square keeps is of great importance, particularly if it is acknowledged that polygonal and round forms were not primarily adopted for reasons of military efficiency. Such designs might be explained instead by a fascination with the potential complexities and symbolism of polygonal forms or, more mundanely, as a means of constructing reduced-scale great towers, without making the design seem absurdly pocket-sized.[62] Whichever the case, these polygonal and round keeps also need to be understood in the context of ambitious mural towers, which begin to be constructed in major castles from around 1180, such as the Avranches Tower at Dover, The Bell Tower at London and the Butavant Tower at Corfe.[63]

At the conclusion of this paper it is also worth observing that one important building in the north of the country would certainly merit discussion in relation to Carlisle but remains inaccessible. The keep at Lancaster is still part of a prison and its interior has been extensively altered. From the evidence that is available it is not clear that the keep at Lancaster does show any affinities with this group of northern keeps; but then very little evidence is available.[64] Indeed, even the date of this building effectively remains a matter for speculation. Jason Wood, who has seen the interior, kindly informed me that he recalled seeing no evidence for the original setting of the roof or of any Romanesque detailing within the building. He felt confident that the spine wall was original and as well as some of the window openings. Our ignorance of this important

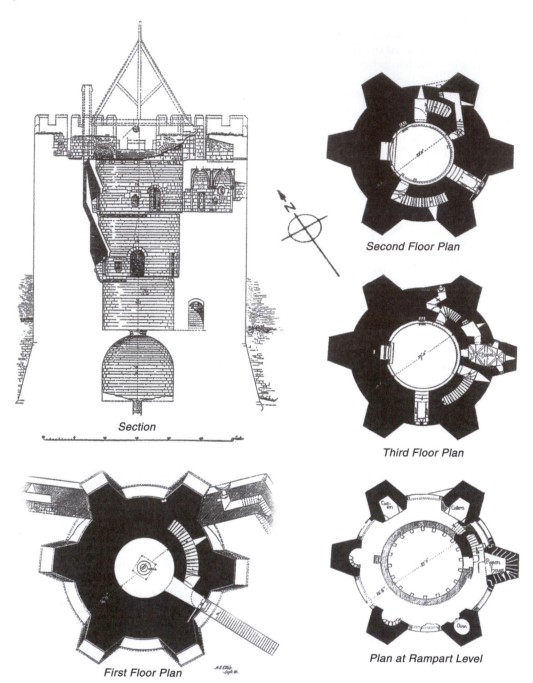

Section

Second Floor Plan

Third Floor Plan

First Floor Plan

Plan at Rampart Level

FIG. 7.   Plans and section of the keep of Conisbrough Castle, West Yorkshire by A. S. Ellis.
Reproduced from G. T. Clark, *Military Architecture*, vol. 1

great tower is a serious handicap to our understanding of castle architecture in this area.

The keep at Carlisle Castle has generally been discussed simply as one example of a legion of rectangular Romanesque great towers erected across England and France in the 11th and 12th centuries. While the geographical spread of these buildings is both remarkable and important, the scholarly emphasis on their points of similarity, significant though they are, has tended to eclipse their differences. As this article has sought to argue, the architecture of Carlisle has both an English and a regional flavour. By appreciating its similarities to other buildings in the area — particularly the keeps at Bamburgh and Richmond — it is not only possible to understand the design of the original building more fully but also to reconstruct some of its lost or obscured details. And combining this architectural evidence with the political circumstances of Carlisle in the 12th century, it is further possible to date the keep and attribute it to Henry I as part of his efforts to stake out his claims to this disputed border area.

ACKNOWLEDGEMENTS

I would like to acknowledge the assistance and kindness of many people in completing this article. In particular I would like to thank Anna Eavis, David Weston, Kate Eavis and Jo Pillman for all their practical kindnesses. Mr Francis Watson-Armstrong generously gave me access to all the corners of Bamburgh keep and Ron Bewley very kindly showed me around the building. Rachel Moss, Karen Lundgren, Kevin Booth, Jonathan Coad and Edward Impey have all wittingly or unwittingly shared their expertise with me on various points. Richard Plant kindly discussed the keep with me on-site. I must also particularly thank Jeremy Ashbee, who is unfailing generous to me with his considerable knowledge of castles and who nobly read the first draft of this article.

NOTES

1. Carlisle Castle has attracted a considerable bibliography. Besides those listed below, the principal works used in the preparation of this article were: G. T. Clark, *Medieval Military Architecture*, I (London 1884), 350–58; E. S. Armitage, *The Early Norman Castles of the British Isles* (London 1912), 123; R. A. Brown, H. M. Colvin, and A. J. Taylor, *The History of the King's Works: The Middle Ages*, ed. H. M. Colvin, II (London 1963), 595–600; D. F. Renn, *Norman Castles in Britain*, 2nd edn (London 1973), 133–34; and G. Neilson, 'The Keep of Carlisle Castle', *Notes and Queries*, 8th series, 8, 321–23.

2. For a tabulation of expenditure on royal castles in the Pipe Rolls see R. A. Brown, 'Royal Castle Building in England, 1154–1216', *English Historical Review*, 276 (1955), 353–98.

3. Particularly important in this respect is Edward Impey's forthcoming work on Ivry-la-Bataille. This building provides a precedent for the project apse form found at the White Tower at London and at Colchester keep.

4. For a recent and well illustrated survey of French great tower architecture see J. Mesqui, *Chateaux et Enceintes de la France Medievale*, I (Paris 1991), 89–220.

5. For a full discussion of this building see J. Mesqui, 'La Tour Maitresse du Donjon de Loches', *Deux Donjons Construits Autour de L'An Mil en Touraine*, Société Française D'Archéologie (1998).

6. The doorways opening into space above the forebuilding entrances at both Dover and Newcastle, the former now transformed into a window, may well have been intended to serve timber galleries. At Castle Rising there is an anomalous, elevated door in the east face of the forebuilding. This has been described either as a postern or a later insertion in R. A. Brown, *Castle Rising*, English Heritage Guidebook (1994 edn), 40, but it might originally have given access to an external gallery.

7. The theatrical qualities of castle keep design have been emphasised by several authors in recent years. See, for example, P. Dixon, 'Design in castle-building: the controlling of access to the Lord', *Château Gaillard*, 18 (1996), 47–57 and also the notes below.

8. Which must have been constructed after *c.* 1214. H. Summerson, S. Harrison and M. Trueman, *Brougham Castle, Cumbria*, Cumberland Westmorland Antiquarian Archaeological Society Research Series, 8 (1998), 8–10 and 89–108.

9. *The King's Works*, II, 630–32. See also J. A. A. Goodall, 'Dover Castle, i', *Country Life*, 193, no. 11 (18 March 1999), 45, for a suggested chronology of construction.

10. For one of many statements of this theory see A. Hamilton-Thompson, *Military Architecture in England during the Middle Ages* (Oxford 1912), 160–87.

11. *The King's Works*, II, 769–71 and R. A. Brown, *Orford Castle*, HMSO Guidebook (London 1966). For further references to Orford see below.

12. La Tour du Moulin, Mesqui, *Châteaux et Enceintes*, I, 167.

13. The keeps of Dover and Corfe, for example, were both still in use as residences in the 17th century. Quite how directly 15th- and 16th-century great towers are related to earlier medieval models remains a matter of debate. To my mind, however, the formal similarities between the two are usually compelling. An instance of the debt of Jacobean architects to the medieval castle tradition is discussed in J. A. A. Goodall, 'Lulworth Castle, Dorset', *Country Life*, 194, no. 2 (13 January 2000), 34–39.

14. J. A. A. Goodall, 'Dover Castle, ii', *Country Life*, 193, no. 11 (25 March 1999), 110–13.

15. Amongst many books which approached the subject formally is M. W. Thompson, *The Rise of the Castle* (Cambridge 1991).

16. See T. A. Heslop, *Norwich Castle Keep* (Norwich, 1994). The ground floor of Middleham is generally described as a kitchen on the basis of its large fireplace — see J. Weaver, *Middleham Castle*, English Heritage Guidebook (1998 edn), 7–9. If this feature is 12th-century it should be noted that the arrangement of the fireplace in the spine wall (as opposed to an external wall) is unique in a Romanesque great tower in England.

17. P. Dixon and P. Marshall, 'The great tower at Hedingham Castle: a reassessment', *Fortress*, 18 (1993), 16–23.

18. In 1166–67 payment was made '*in operatione domorum Turris Londoniarum*' and four years later for '*reparatione domorum Regis in balia turris de Lundon*'. Respectively, *The Great Roll of the Pipe for 13 Henry II 1166–1167*, Pipe Roll Society, 11 (1889), 1 and *The Great Roll of the Pipe for 18 Henry II 1171–1172*, Pipe Roll Society, 18 (1894), 144. I am grateful to Jeremy Ashbee for these references.

19. For the early history of the town see H. R. T. Summerson, *Medieval Carlisle: The City between the Borders from the late 11th century to the mid-16th century*', Cumberland Westmorland Antiquarian Archaeological Society, Extra Series, XXV (Kendal 1993), 1–54.

20. *The King's Works*, II, 595–96 sets out the possibilities and concludes that a date in the 1130s cannot be ruled out.

21. R. A. Brown, *English Castles*, revised edn (London 1977), 70.

22. Thompson, *Military Architecture*, 120; S. Toy, *The Castles of Great Britain*, 2nd edn (London 1954), 92.

23. An account of 1308 (PRO E372/153) strongly suggests the existence of corner turrets in stone. In this year springalds were erected in 'houses' on the corners of the tower. These 'houses' were probably of wood — and were later repaired in that material in 1321 (PRO C145/86) — but they were almost certainly erected within stone turrets. This is clear because in 1308 stone was also provided to repair the stairs to two of the turrets on the keep. The references are quoted from McCarthy et al., *Carlisle Castle*, 94.

24. For a useful table of keep dimensions see Thompson, *The Rise of the Castle*, 64–65. It should be noted that this list reflects the inaccuracies of the literature it draws on, and is structured to suit Thompson's own formal analysis of these buildings. For example he does not note the existence of spine walls set on arches — such as occur at Hedingham and Scarborough, and omits mention of the spine wall at Corfe.

25. See Dixon and Marshall, 'The great tower at Hedingham Castle' and J. A. A. Goodall, *Scarborough Castle*, English Heritage Guidebook (2000) respectively.

26. For drawings of this interior see McCarthy et al., *Carlisle Castle*, 84.

27. McCarthy et al., *Carlisle Castle*, 69 and 75.

28. The most valuable works on this site are G. T. Clark, 'Bamburgh Castle', *Archaeol. J.*, 46 (1889), 93–113; C. J. Bates, 'Bamburgh', *Archaeologia Aeliana*, ns, 14 (1891), 223–82; and revised from this last account, E. Bateson, *A History of Northumberland*, I (Newcastle 1893), 17–79; and 'Bamburg', *Newcastle-upon-Tyne Society of Antiquaries Proceedings*, ns, 8 (1898), 233–38.

29. Clark, 'Bamburgh', 107 illustrates this. He considered it to be a feature of the 18th-century restoration, but although parts of it have certainly been renewed, this does not seem likely. The commonest plinth moulding in castle architecture at this period is the plain chamfer. Though this form is sometimes used to striking architectural effect, as for example, at Conisbrough or Kenilworth keep, more complex forms are very rare. At Hedingham (Essex) and Canterbury, where only a fragment survives, the plinth face is subtly articulated with shallow rolls, an unusual point of comparison between the two buildings. The bold Bamburgh design, however, is perhaps best paralleled by the plinth at Newcastle, which is topped by a heavy roll.

30. The existence of local styles in church architecture has long been recognised but the subject is rarely addressed in studies of castles. One fruitful treatment of the subject is Heslop, *Norwich Castle Keep*, 56–66. This places Norwich — with its rich external articulation and turret-less outline — in both a local and international architectural context.

31. The similarity of Bamburgh to these buildings is sometimes commented upon but never discussed. For a recent discussion of the Tower of London and Colchester see E. Fernie, *The Architecture of the Norman England* (Oxford, 2000), 55–67. As will be apparent later, however, my analysis of these buildings does not agree in all points with Fernie's.

32. There are problems with identifying the upper chamber in the Rochester forebuilding as a chapel, in particular its original difficulty of access (over a portcullis chase). But the existence of an apse seems difficult to discount as evidence for this identification.

33. The chapel apse at Norwich is set in the angle of the keep and should perhaps, therefore, be conceived of as a mural chamber opened up to the interior of the building, rather than a full internal apse. As such it would compare with a wide range of chapel arrangements in castle keeps, which use the wall thickness to create a vault over the altar.

34. Bateson, *A History of Northumberland*, I, 64.

35. F. Grose, *The Antiquities of England and Wales*, III (London 1775), unpaginated.

36. E. King, *Monumenta Antiqua*, III (London 1804), 222.

37. Clark, 'Bamburgh Castle', 112. Note that Clark deemed the chapel apse to be north facing, which means that — if he is correct — the roof ran at right angles to this interior.

38. For example, the Tower of London, see Fernie, *The Architecture of the Norman England*, 60–61. He acknowledges that a countersunk roof did exist but argues that it was not originally intended. Rather, that the upper floor of the Tower was conceived as a two-storey hall under a high-set roof and sums up his case as follows: 'Both the one-storey [ie. with a countersunk roof] and two storey [i.e. with a high roof] solutions have their difficulties, but the choice between them can be encapsulated as one between a design which is contradictory in itself and one which has a consistent structure at the start and becomes contradictory through alteration in the course of the building.' For Dover see R. A. Brown, *Dover Castle*, HMSO Guidebook (1965 edn). The form and position of the Newcastle roof have been variously represented, see R. O. Heslop, 'Notes on a recent examination of certain structural features of the great tower or keep of the castle of Newcastle upon Tyne', *Archaeologia Aeliana*, ns, 25 (1904), 101–03.

39. The most detailed exposition of the countersunk roof at the Tower of London to date is G. Parnell, 'The White Tower, the Tower of London', *Country Life*, 192, no. 28 (9 July 1998), 86–89. It should be added to the case he puts forward that, (1) this countersunk roof arrangement is widely encountered in keeps of this period and was therefore presumably not considered 'contradictory' in the 12th century, as Fernie asserts. Moreover, Jeremy Ashbee has pointed out to me that, (2) while all other examples of the two-storey keep interiors treat the clerestorey level as a half-storey, at the Tower the interior would have been the equivalent of a full two-storey elevation.

40. I am very grateful to John Nolan for providing me with photographs of his work to the upper storey of the keep. For a good description of the building see W. H. Knowles, 'The Castle, Newcastle upon Tyne', *Archaeologia Aeliana*, 4th series, 2 (1926), 1–51.

41. Goodall, 'Dover Castle', ii, 110.

42. Bates, 'Bamburgh', 223–82.

43. C. H. Hunter Blair, 'The Sheriffs of Northumberland, pt. 1, 1076–1602', *Archaeologia Aeliana*, 4th series, 20 (1942), 11–90.

44. J. Harvey, *English Medieval Architects*, rev. edn (Gloucester 1987), 223.

45. P. Dixon and P. Marshall, 'The great tower in the 12th century: the case of Norham Castle', *Archaeol. J.*, 150 (1993), 410–32.

46. For Richmond Castle see Fernie, *The Architecture of the Norman England*, 60–61; *VCH, North Riding*, I (London 1914), 1–16; J. A. A. Goodall, *Richmond Castle and St Agatha's Abbey, Easby*, English Heritage Guidebook (2001); and *Registrum Honoris de Richmond*, ed. R. Gale (London 1722).

47. Fernie, *The Architecture of the Norman England*, correctly points out that the tower does *not* incorporate an earlier gatehouse, as asserted, for example, in C. Peers, *Richmond Castle*, HMSO Guidebook (1981 edn), 16.

48. This is apparent because the masonry around the door shows no sign of having been laid to receive such a structure. Added to this no forebuilding is either described in the 1538 survey of the castle (PRO E36/159, ff. 28–31) or shown in views of the keep from the late 17th century onwards. Of particular importance in this latter respect are the drawings of F. Place, copies of which are to be found in the Witt Library of the Courtauld Institute, London.

49. A detail which would corroborate the north south alignment of the roof, see n. 37 above.

50. For the late medieval attribution see London, British Library, Cotton MSS, Faustina B VII, f. 94, printed in W. Dugdale, *Monasticon Anglicanum*, V (London 1825), 574.

51. *Et in operatione domorum de Richmont et turris — LI libri. The Great Roll of the Pipe for 18 Henry II, 1171–1172*, Pipe Roll Society, 18 (1894), 5.

52. Fernie, *The Architecture of the Norman England*, 71–72 suggests an earlier date in the 1140s. Without feeling strongly on the subject, however, I am inclined to compare its richness of decoration, as we have seen an unusual feature amongst keeps in this area, as well as the generic details of that decoration with those of the great tower at Newcastle, built between 1168–78.

53. BL Cotton MSS, Faustina B VII, f. 85v clearly represents the chapel of St Nicolas as occupying the 11th-century mural tower in the east wall of the castle enclosure, not a later chapel to the south-west of the castle, as shown in N. G. J. Pounds, *The Medieval Castle in England and Wales* (Cambridge 1990), 48–49. Confusion over the arrangement of chapels at Richmond seems to stem from the erroneous suggestion that a chapel formerly existed over the west gate of the castle. The supposed window of this chapel is probably a rebuilt portcullis frame, as Jonathan Clark has suggested to me.

54. Summerson, *Medieval Carlisle*, 39–47.

55. W. F. Skene ed., *Chronicles of the Picts . . . of the Scots and other Early Memorials of Scottish History* (Edinburgh 1867), 212.

56. London, British Library, Lansdowne MSS, no. 863, f. 79 and printed in W. S. Gibson, *The Monastery of Tynemouth*, II (London 1847), p. xvii no. xxiv.

57. Bateson, *A History of Northumberland*, I, 27–28.

58. This room has now been entirely stripped of decoration. Some traces of this remained to be engraved in J. C. Bruce, *A Guide to the Castle of Newcastle-upon-Tyne* (1847). To judge from the 1817 plans of the keep engraved for the Society of Antiquaries of Newcastle, the interior was articulated with a wall arcade.

59. Amongst the luxuries of the Dover stair chamber was a basin with running water. Flues rising through the vault from the chamber below may also suggest that it was heated. The comparison between Dover and Newcastle is worthy of an article in its own right. It is the more curious because the architectural detailing of the two buildings is completely different, a circumstance which implies a great deal about the role of Maurice in the creation of these buildings.

60. A late-12th-century date for the tower is generally accepted in the most useful discussions of the building and accords well with Hamelin Plantagenet's ownership of the castle between 1163 and 1201. See Clark, *Medieval Military Architecture*, I, 431–53; H. Sands, H. Braun and L. C. Loyd, 'Conisbrough and Mortemer', *Yorkshire Archaeological J.*, 32 (1936), 100–15; and S. Johnson, *Conisbrough Castle*, English Heritage Guidebook (1997 edn), 20–21. An 1189 endowment by Hamelin and his wife of a priest to serve the chapel of Ss Philip and James within the castle may demonstrate the completion of the keep by this time. But even if this chapel is one and the same as that in the keep — rather than another in the bailey — the endowment could have been formalised some time after the building was finished.

61. Sands et al., 'Conisbrough and Mortemer', 100–15. It is not clear to me why Conisbrough *necessarily* follows Mortemer, as these authors assume. It should be noted that Mortemer appears to have had a spiral stair — not a passage stair in the manner of Conisbrough — and was without a basement vault.

62. The two are by no means exclusive. Orford, for example, seems to me to be a 'rounded' square, designed in the style of south-eastern keep architecture. Its form may be dictated by its relatively small scale, but an interesting case has also been put together for its possible symbolic importance. See T. A. Heslop, 'Orford Castle, nostalgia and sophisticated living', *Architectural History*, 34 (1991), 36–58.

63. D. F. Renn, 'The Avranches Traverse at Dover Castle', *Archaeologia Cantiana*, 84 (1969), 78–92; G. Parnell, *The Tower of London* (Batsford 1993), 25–26. The Butavant Tower awaits anything more that the description provided in RCHME, *An Inventory of Historical Monuments in the County of Dorset*, II, South-East Part i (London 1970), 70. Other towers of this kind which still await proper analysis are the chamberblock tower and Cockhyll Tower at Scarborough and Lunn's Tower at Kenilworth.

64. The literature on Lancaster Castle is very thin, amongst the more useful articles is E. W. Cox, 'Lancaster Castle', *Historical Society Lancashire Cheshire Proceedings and Papers*, 48 (1896), 95–122.

'King Arthur lives in merry Carleile'

ABIGAIL WHEATLEY

Both the city and castle of Carlisle feature as important locations in medieval Arthurian literature. This paper compares this literary and legendary evidence with the material evidence of medieval Carlisle and its castle to ascertain the particular significance of this choice of setting. The location of Arthurian legends in specific, identifiable cities and castles around Britain is by no means unusual, even though the medieval legends are often set back in a distant period of the past shortly after the Roman occupation of Britain. This is sometimes specified as the 5th century A.D. and is, therefore, long before the introduction of castles to this country at the Norman Conquest.

This paper also addresses the possible rationale behind this backdating of identifiable medieval castles to the Arthurian period. It can be shown by textual analysis that the identification of Carlisle specifically, and of castles in general in the Arthurian legends, was founded on a simple series of medieval mistakes and misreadings. The way in which these mistakes were accepted and consolidated, however, allows wider conclusions to be drawn about medieval perceptions both of ancient history and of castle architecture. It is suggested that the extant Roman remains and traditions of Roman occupation at Carlisle and other sites may have provided the impetus for links with the great rulers and architecture of the past. The transference of this ancient heritage from the Romans to King Arthur may have been dictated in some cases by nationalist politics. However, the identification of medieval castles with the Roman remains which surrounded them was probably due to the lack in the Middle Ages of the precise dating systems which can now be employed to distinguish between different periods in historical architecture.

IT is acknowledged amongst the literary scholars of the Middle Ages that Carlisle has an important role to play in certain of the English Arthurian legends.[2] Both the town and the castle, for example, occur in Malory's *Morte D'Arthur* which was completed in 1469.[3] Close to the final denouement of the narrative, in Book 22 entitled 'Slander and Strife', Carlisle Castle provides the setting for a trap aimed at betraying Launcelot and Gwenyver. This episode plays a pivotal role in the development of the narrative. The importance of the architectural setting is given particular emphasis by the terms of Malory's description:

So on the morne kynge Arthure rode an-huntyng and sente worde to the quene that he wolde be oute all that nyght. Than sir Aggravayne and sir Mordred gate to them twelve knyghtes and hyd hemselff in a chambir in the castell of Carlyle.[4]

Naturally, Gwenyver summons her lover to her chamber, and she and Launcelot are trapped inside the chamber by the conspirator knights. Launcelot is forced to improvise armour from furnishings, and uses the thick door of the chamber as a shield while he takes on the knights one by one. Once the main body of the posse retreat, Launcelot is able to leave the queen and return to his own chambers. The architectural element of this setting is sufficiently non-specific that it cannot be linked directly to Carlisle, or to any particular castle. It is nonetheless presented in a forceful, physical fashion. Malory invokes a substantial building and identifies it by name with a castle which was a very substantial reality for medieval Carlisle. In doing this Malory seems to encourage his readers to locate this Arthurian episode within the real world of medieval Britain.

This episode is certainly not the only one of its kind in the *Morte D'Arthur*. Castles are in fact one of the most prominent features which Malory's Arthurian landscape shares with medieval Britain. Just after the episode described above, for example, once Launcelot has saved Gwenyver from Arthur's retribution, he carries her from Carlisle to his castle, Joyous Garde.[5] Malory is careful to provide real locations for this building too. Later he reports, 'somme men say it was Anwyk, and somme men say it was Bamborow'.[6] This makes good geographical sense: either of these famous medieval castles would provide a fairly convenient but sufficiently distant retreat from Carlisle. This detail emphasises once again the way in which Malory encourages his audience to link the Arthurian legends to the actual landscape of medieval Britain, whether in terms of geographical relationships or architectural features.

Such topographical awareness is shared in different degrees by many other medieval Arthurian romances. Carlisle, for example, is identified as a location in a substantial number of the extant Middle English Arthurian romances, including the texts known as the *Stanzaic Morte Arthur* and the *Alliterative Morte Arthure*, on which Malory is known to have drawn, as well as *Sir Gawain and the Carle of Carlisle*, *The Awntyrs off Arthur*, *The Greene Knight*, *The Marriage of Sir Gawain* and several other related texts.[7] While the castles of the Carlisle region play a relatively minor role in several of these texts, other local landmarks are emphasised. Carlisle Cathedral comes in for an occasional mention, too. *Sir Gawain and the Carle of Carlisle* describes its foundation by an uncouth, giant man, the 'Carle', successfully freed from an enchantment.[8] Inglewood Forest and, within it, the Tarn Wathelene or Wadling, are also both used as settings for significant events in these narratives.[9]

This association of Arthurian legend with specific places and their architecture may not surprise modern readers. We are used to seeing filmic depictions of Arthurian legends replete with props and scenery which evoke a Hollywood version of the Middle Ages. Medieval castle locations may even be used in such depictions to increase the period flavour.[10] This reinforces the strong Arthurian associations which locations like Tintagel and its medieval castle still have in the modern mind. Such conventions often reflect details of description and setting in the medieval Arthurian romances, which tend to reproduce the language, costume and architectural detail of their own periods. For example, Tintagel Castle is identified as an Arthurian site as early as Geoffrey of Monmouth (who finished his *magnum opus*, the *Historia regum Britannie*, in 1138)[11] and as late as Malory.[12] However, the medieval flavour of such tales can seem to come into conflict with the chronologies set out by such texts. Medieval texts often explicitly set Arthur and his court far back into the distant past, into the period after the withdrawal of the Roman occupation of Britain.

For example, in the 12th century Geoffrey of Monmouth calculated that Arthur died in A.D. 542.[13] This location of the legendary Arthur in the distant but real past was still relevant by the time Malory came to tackle the material in the 15th century. He set the start of the Grail Quest 454 years after Christ's death, providing a dated midpoint for Arthur's reign.[14] Within these dating parameters, the use of identifiable locations is not problematic. However, the presence of castles within this context seems somewhat incongruous to our historical sensibilities. It is an accepted fact that the castle did not arrive in Britain until the Normans introduced it shortly before the Conquest.[15] Why, then, might medieval authors such as Malory and his precursors have introduced castles — especially specific, datable medieval castles — into the Arthurian legend? What was the nature of their perception of Britain's landscape in the ancient past, such that it allowed them to imagine castles in it? And what might be the particular significance of Carlisle and its castle within this context? These are the questions to which this paper will be addressed.

In fact both these questions can be answered at a simple level by the discovery of some fairly straightforward mistakes in the medieval interpretation of sources. However, the ways in which these slips were subsequently perpetuated and justified have important implications for the medieval understanding of the past and of castle architecture. As much of my argument rides on the origination and reception of these mistakes, it seems worthwhile examining how they came about in some detail, before exploring their wider consequences.

It has been noted that several of the texts which cite Carlisle as an Arthurian setting form a distinctive group. These texts concentrate on the character of Sir Gawain and have been collected in the useful volume entitled *Sir Gawain: Eleven Romances and Tales*.[16] They are of various dates, regions and qualities, tending towards the popular end of the spectrum, and several represent variant versions of one another or of well-known tales of Sir Gawain's adventures also found elsewhere.[17] It has been suggested, accordingly, that Gawain himself provides the connection with the Carlisle region. Given that his father was widely identified as King Lot of Orkney, a location close to the Scottish border might have seemed appropriate for Sir Gawain.[18]

However, it has also been suggested that the place-name of Carlisle in these texts may result merely from a mistaken reading of Cacrleon,[19] the town on the River Usk in Gwent, which is specified as an Arthurian site from the early development of the legend. Geoffrey of Monmouth, for instance, dwells at some length in his *Historia Regum Britannie* on Arthur's ceremonial crownwearing at Caerleon after his first round of wide-reaching conquests. In this instance Geoffrey calls Caerleon the City of Legions (*Urbs Legionum*), and in other places, Caerusc.[20] However the similarity of the more familiar names of Carlisle and Caerleon in their variable medieval spellings, which could both be written using the same prefix of 'K/Caer', certainly seems a likely source of confusion. One instance of such a switch can be found, interestingly, in a Welsh version of Geoffrey's *Historia*, dated around 1500.[21] Here 'kaer Lleon' is substituted in Geoffrey's account of the foundation of 'Kaerleil' (Carlisle) by Leir, king of Loegria.[22] It is easy to see how a similar mistake might be made in reverse, substituting Carlisle for Caerleon, in other circumstances. There are many parallel examples of such toponymic confusions in Arthurian legend, and this does indeed seem to be a convincing explanation for the genesis of Carlisle's Arthurian associations.

Circumstantial details in the Arthurian tradition provide confirmation of this switch. For example, Geoffrey associates the festivities after Arthur's first major round of victories with a Whitsuntide crownwearing at Caerleon, as I have already mentioned. In the *Alliterative Morte Arthure* this gathering occurs at Christmas and at Carlisle.[23] In *Sir Gawain and the Carle of Carlisle* there seems to be additional evidence of elision between Carlisle and Welsh locations. In this text some of Arthur's knights set out one morning on a hunt from Cardiff and become lost; when they seek shelter the same night in a nearby castle, it is said to be that of the Carle of Carlisle.[24] This seems an unlikely association in geographical terms, and might be explained through some confusion between Carlisle and the name of a Welsh location closer to Cardiff, such as Caerleon.

ABIGAIL WHEATLEY

These examples provide an account of the origins of Carlisle's association with the Arthurian canon. However, it is by no means clear at what stage such confusions might have occurred in the transmission of any of these narratives. The Gawain texts especially are often the result of a confusing textual history, with only a few late manuscript versions surviving.[25] Even with the example from the Welsh version of the *Historia Regum Britannie* (mentioned above), there is nothing to show that the switch between Carlisle and Caerleon was originated in the extant manuscript. It is therefore not possible to pin-point a particular source or date-range in seeking the origin of this confusion. On the contrary, a more general and diffused series of mistakes may even have been responsible for various switches in a variety of contexts.

However, the association between the location and the legend in many of the Arthurian texts I have mentioned seems to express more than a simple mistake. It has been remarked that, in the Gawain-texts especially, 'Carlisle operates as the indispensable end place of the plots, the centralised narrative site where everything is brought home and made secure'.[26] That is, the place itself is made a feature of considerable narrative significance. The frequent mentioning of local landmarks, which I have mentioned as a feature of several of these texts, suggests more than a mere substitution of names. It demonstrates an active appreciation of the whole Carlisle area as a suitable *locus* for Arthurian events. Indeed, Carlisle's replacement of some of the functions originally applied to Caerleon place it in a position of considerable royal and ceremonial significance. Once an initial mistake had been made, then, it seems that Carlisle was fitted readily into the Arthurian framework. There are several indicators in the medieval historiography of Carlisle which help to explain this development.

For example, Carlisle is included in its own right in Geoffrey's *Historia Regum Britannie*, as has already been mentioned. It is not given the extended description or Arthurian associations of Geoffrey's Caerleon on Usk, but Geoffrey does provide Carlisle with its own eponymous founder: one Leil, who was supposedly one of the early kings of Britain.[27] At least from the late 1130s, then, Carlisle was being portrayed as an ancient city with its own legendary history, once the favourite northern town of a British king. A subsequent connection with King Arthur may well have seemed more likely within this context.

Physical evidence of the town's ancient origins seems also to have been available to its visitors and inhabitants from an early stage. Other papers in this volume detail the evidence of Carlisle's Roman origins and extant archaeological remains, which were even more noticeable in the Middle Ages. There is evidence that the city's Roman remains were identified and admired from the early Middle Ages. Bede, for example, in his *Life of St Cuthbert*, describes how the saint was shown the Roman city walls and a Roman well or fountain, displayed proudly by the city reeve as evidence of the city's ancient status.[28] Here is another reason why it might have been easy for medieval writers and their audiences to accept that Carlisle had had an important part to play in ancient British history.

It seems to me more than a coincidence that precisely this same kind of physical evidence formed the foundation of Caerleon's claim to an ancient past. Geoffrey of Monmouth and subsequent medieval writers are thought to have been inspired directly by the sight of Caerleon's impressive Roman remains. Indeed, Tatlock has shown that Geoffrey's description of Arthurian Caerleon is based closely on the archaeological reality of the site.[29] It may well be that a similar knowledge of Carlisle's Roman origins lay behind the various tales of its role in Britain's legendary past. As Michael Greenhalgh points out, Roman remains are a recurrent theme in medieval British literature, provoking ongoing speculations about the ancient culture which created them.[30]

Geoffrey's use of Caerleon, however, also shows that ancient architectural remains could be equated in the medieval perception with periods of history, and with rulers of Britain's past, other than the Romans. It is possible that, in Geoffrey's case especially, this was a matter of national pride. Several scholars have argued convincingly that the whole creation of the literary figure of Arthur follows patterns created for British challenges to the historical dominance of the Romans.[31] In Geoffrey's history Arthur was the king who refused to pay the tribute demanded since Caesar's conquest of Britain. He took martial vengeance on the Romans for daring to demand such tribute. In the end he was prevented from conquering Rome only by Mordred's final treachery.[32]

Geoffrey's choice of Caerleon, as well as other sites with Roman remains, for setting Arthur's story may, then, have an element of architectural usurpation built into it. He reclaims the impressive remains of the Roman culture for the British, attributing them instead to British founders and associating them with the British repudiation of Roman dominance. There does seem to be a deliberate juxtaposition in Geoffrey's *Historia* of the material remains of the Roman past with British anti-Roman feelings. For example, Geoffrey specifically notes that the gold-painted roof gables of Arthur's Caerleon were 'a match for Rome'.[33] It is at Caerleon that Arthur receives the Roman ambassadors who come to ask for tribute, and also at Caerleon that he rejects their demands, rehearsing Britain's historical resistance to the Romans with great rhetorical flourish. It is there that he plans his terrible vengeance on Rome.[34] In later versions of the Arthurian legend, however, as in the *Alliterative Morte Arthure*, these significant events are transferred to Carlisle.[35] Through Carlisle's comparable associations with the Roman past, it too could become a part of the legendary history of Britain's resistance to the Romans. Its ancient architecture, like Caerleon's, was appropriated for the native British past and associated not with the invading Roman Empire, but with the greatest of the nationalist British kings.

The medieval mistake of introducing Carlisle into the Arthurian legend does, then, carry with it a definite logic, according to the patterns of British legendary history. However, this explanation does not immediately account for the introduction of the medieval castle into the town's ancient past, the second of the medieval slips I mentioned at the start of this paper. Nevertheless, it seems to me that this, too, may be justified with reference to Roman remains: those of medieval Carlisle specifically, and, more generally, of other sites in medieval Britain. This is the subject I will tackle in the remaining section of this paper.

It is widely accepted that the castle was an architectural innovation of the Normans, introduced to Britain shortly before the Conquest.[36] However, it is not clear that the castle was always understood in medieval thought as a new architectural form.[37] Actual castles are mentioned by name throughout medieval legendary histories of Britain.[38] Many are even connected with specific ancient founders, some of them from Classical antiquity. For example, a large number of castles, including the Tower of London and Dover Castle, are attributed to Julius Caesar in various different sources.[39] One might assume that this is due to simple anachronism, or that the word *castle* is used loosely in these contexts to refer to ancient fortresses which preceded medieval castles. However, when the evidence is examined in detail, it becomes clear that this is not the case.[40] There is, in fact, much textual evidence to show that the actual medieval buildings were understood as relics of the ancient past by contemporary observers. I will provide just one example which, I think, will shed some light on the case of Carlisle and its

Arthurian castle. It should also help to explain how the remains of Roman architecture, such as those at Carlisle, are implicated in this issue. It is interesting to note that, in this case, too, a mistaken identification of a place-name is involved.

Geoffrey of Monmouth, describing the first Roman invasion of Britain led by Julius Caesar, mentions that the Roman fleet landed near a town called 'Dorobellum'.[41] He derived this information from a 9th-century Welsh text known as the *Historia Brittonum*, where 'Dolobella' was probably meant as a personal name rather than a place-name.[42] Nevertheless, the Roman landing would have required a coastal location on the south coast. Wace's *Roman de Brut* of 1155, and the Anglo-Norman version of Geoffrey's History, therefore transpose one of the later invasions by Caesar to Dover ('Dovre').[43] The superficial linguistic similarity between Dorobellum and Dover may have been a contributing factor in this choice. However, as with the case of Carlisle, it seems likely that the extant Roman remains at Dover may have convinced Wace of the likelihood of his identification. The most prominent example is the Roman *pharos* or lighthouse which still stands today within the enclosure of Dover Castle.[44] Wace is believed to have known Britain from his own travels,[45] so it is possible that he was influenced personally by such remains at Dover.

However, the later history of this episode also underlines the significance of the Roman remains at Dover for the area's legendary history. As I have already mentioned, Dover Castle is amongst the monuments supposed by some medieval authors to have been built by Julius Caesar. This idea is attested, for example, in Nicolas Trevet's Anglo-Norman *Cronicles*, written probably between 1328 and 1335.[46] Trevet is very casual in his attribution of several castles to Caesar, including them in a long list:

Julius Cesar... en moustrance de la Conqueste faite sur la terre du Brutaine, q'ore est dit Engleterre, edifa le chastel de Dovre et de Canterburi et de Roncestre et de Loundres[47]

(Julius Caesar... in demonstration of the Conquest made of the realm of Britain, as England was called, built the castle of Dover and of Canterbury and of Rochester and of London).[48]

A similar reference also appears in the alliterative poem of around 1370, *The Parlement of the Thre Ages*:

> Thane Sir Sezere hymselven, that Julyus was hatten,
> Alle Inglande he aughte at his awnn will
> When the Bruyte in his booke Bretayne it callede.
> The trewe toure of London in his tyme he makede,
> And craftely the condithe he compaste thereaftire,
> And then he droghe hym to Dovire and duellyde there a while,
> And closede ther a castelle with cornells full heghe[49]

This represents quite a leap from the reference in Wace to Caesar's landing at Dover. However, a monastic chronicle apparently shows how this came about. This text is known as *Cronicon Sancti Martini de Dover*, in British Library manuscript Cotton Vespasian B XI. It links the Roman *pharos* at Dover with Julius Caesar, stating that he built the tower as his treasury. The *pharos* is identified with great clarity in this passage, which specifies that 'this very same tower now stands in Dover Castle next to the church' (*quidem Turris nunc stat ibidem in Castro Doverr' iuxta ecclesiam*).[50] Although this chronicle now exists only in a manuscript of the 15th century,[51] it seems to preserve an intermediate stage in the development of the legendary history of Dover Castle. It bridges the gap between Wace's identification of Dover as Caesar's landing place, and Trevet's suggestion that the whole of Dover Castle was built by Caesar. It shows that the *pharos* was correctly identified as Roman architecture, and was associated with

Caesar, the most famous Roman visitor to Britain. Only a relatively small step would have been needed to extend this identification to the surrounding architecture of the castle, some of which was, by the 14th century, nearly 300 years old in any case.[52]

It should also be noted that early medieval castles in Britain were frequently associated with Roman remains. N. J. G. Pounds reckons that, of the 37 royal castles established before 1100, 20 were built within town defences, and twelve of these were in towns of Roman origins.[53] This does not include London, arguably the most important of the new Norman castles, and also situated in the corner of the Roman town walls.[54] Yet more castles were associated with Roman remains of other kinds. At Pevensey the corner of the Roman fort was used for a castle during the Conquest of 1066, and was followed by Portchester (around 1120), Brough-on-Stainmore (around 1100) and Bowes (1170s onwards), where Norman keeps were all built inside the substantial remains of Roman forts.[55] Other castles such as Dover (1066 onwards) and Scarborough (from 1127) were sited on or close to Roman remains of different kinds.[56] Carlisle Castle (from 1092) should also be added to this list, as it too is situated on the site of a Roman fort, adjacent to the Roman town of Luguvalium.[57]

The sight of castles in this kind of close association with ancient architecture was common in medieval Britain. Especially in the late medieval period, once the novelty of the Norman castles had worn off, it is not difficult to imagine how parts of medieval castles, or whole fortresses, might gradually become assimilated in the minds of observers with the more ancient buildings surrounding them. This might be expected in those places where local pride in, or knowledge of, ancient remains had been perpetuated.

It should, perhaps, also be noted that even the more learned of medieval observers did not have the accurate architectural dating skills, or the archaeological knowledge, to which modern historians have access. Such benefits are of a surprisingly recent date. Well into the 19th century, for example, certain parties believed the Tower of London to be a Roman building. In 1840 Henry Hart Milman, the Dean of St Paul's and a noted London antiquary, could describe the Tower as 'the work of the great Caesar'.[58] Such misconceptions were presumably assisted by the similar forms of Roman and Romanesque architecture. For those medieval scholars, such as the authors of the legendary histories, who did have access to pre-medieval texts, there would be no certain way of ascertaining the form or dating of historical buildings. Caesar and Vegetius, for example, describe the defensive forts of the Romans as *castella* (singular: *castellum*).[59] This is exactly the same Latin word used throughout the Middle Ages for the medieval castle.[60] There is no reason to suppose that medieval readers would have made substantial differentiation between the two concepts.[61] Such similarities can only have assisted in the idea that the castle was a form of architecture which could be associated with the ancient past, with figures such as Julius Caesar and with the architecture of the Roman occupation of Britain.

The Arthurian question can once again be fitted into this architectural and ideological legacy. As I have mentioned, it is accepted that authors of the legendary history of Britain used Arthur quite deliberately as a reply to the Roman occupation and cultural dominance of Britain. Arthur is a native Caesar, subduing the world, including Rome, to the might of the British Empire. Scenes such as the reception of the Roman consuls at Caerleon (or Carlisle) are deliberately drafted as replies to portrayals of the Roman Conquest of Britain.[62] Other episodes, such as Caesar's Dover invasion, also find their echoes in the Arthurian legend. In the Stanzaic *Morte Arthur*, Arthur is called home from his conquest of Rome to confront the treachery of Mordred in the dramatic final battle. Echoing Caesar's invasion of Britain, he too lands at Dover and in the subsequent battle Mordred kills Gawain, the most faithful of Arthur's knights.[63] In Malory's version of this final denouement, he further increases the local significance of the Dover battle and the symmetry of the Arthurian cycle's imperial narrative.[64] He specifies that Gawain is buried in a chapel within Dover castle, adding that 'there yet all men may se the skulle of hym'.[65] Dover castle, believed to be founded by Julius Caesar, is thus appropriated for the commemoration of a truly British hero.

Carlisle and its castle provide a close parallel, as I hope I have shown. Its own Roman associations led, paradoxically, to its integration into the legends of Gawain and Arthur. As I have already noted, even the cathedral and abbey are drawn into this mythography: they become part of the Arthurian architectural heritage of the city through their supposed foundation by the Carle of Carlisle, on the occasion of his admission to the Round Table. Through identifications such as these, the illustrious history of the city is linked to its medieval present. The landmark buildings of medieval Carlisle are endowed with long histories, and are transformed into points of contact with the many layers of Britain's past, as well as indicators of its medieval prestige. To the popular imagination, then, the architectural monuments of medieval Britain could communicate the cultural reality and proximity of British history and legend as well as the physical reality of medieval style and craftsmanship. Arthur, and Caesar for that matter, was commemorated in castles as much as in romances.

The advanced analytical systems of current archaeological and architectural methods produce ever more accurate descriptions of the planning, construction and patronage of medieval buildings. Such techniques are perfected to get inside the brains of medieval architectural craftsmen and patrons. They reveal in astonishing detail the processes and products of medieval building. However, it is worth remembering occasionally that such specialist knowledge was quite alien to more popular medieval modes of thought about architecture. Castle and cathedral architects may have been constantly on the cusp of each new development in stone technology. At the same time, however, their buildings were claimed as part of a thriving medieval heritage industry, which did not respect the niceties of stylistic dating as much as the cultural and imaginative ideas which medieval architecture was capable of communicating.

NOTES

1. From *The Marriage of Sir Gawain*, in T. Hahn ed., *Sir Gawain: Eleven Romances and Tales* (Michigan 1995), 359–71, 363, l.1. All subsequent references to Hahn refer to items within this collection.

2. R. Barber, *King Arthur: Hero and Legend*, 2nd edn (Woodbridge 1973), 105; Hahn, 'Introduction', 1–46, 29–31.

3. Thomas Malory, *The Works of Sir Thomas Malory*, ed. E. Vinaver, 2nd edn, I (Oxford 1967), 'Introduction', xiv.

4. Malory, III, 1164.

5. Malory, III, 1178: 'And so he rode hys way wyth the quene, as the Freynshe book seyth, unto Joyous Garde, and there he kepte her as a noble knyght shulde'.

6. Malory, III, 1257.

7. For a full list see Hahn, 'Introduction', 4. For Malory's use of the Stanzaic and Alliterative Arthurian cycles, see F. Riddy, 'Contextualizing Le Morte Darthur: Empire and Civil War', in *A Companion to Malory*, Arthurian Studies, 37 (1996), 55–73, 63.

8. Hahn, *Sir Gawain and the Carle of Carlisle*, 103, ll. 649–54: 'A ryche abbey the Carle gan make / To synge and rede for Goddis sake / In wurschip of Oure Lady. / In the towne of mery Carelyle / He lete hit bylde stronge and wele; / Hit is a byschoppis see.'

9. Barber, 105; Hahn, 'Introduction', 29–30.

10. Richard Fawcett tells me that Castle Stalker and Doune Castle, both in Argyll, were used in filming *Monty Python and the Holy Grail*, for example.

11. Geoffrey of Monmouth, *The Historia Regum Britannie of Geoffrey of Monmouth*, ed. N. Wright, I (Cambridge 1985, reprinted 1996), 'Introduction', xv-xvi. In all subsequent references to the works of Geoffrey of Monmouth, unless otherwise specified, references to the Latin text will cite the above edition, while references for translations will cite L. Thorpe ed. and trans., *Geoffrey of Monmouth: The History of the Kings of Britain* (London 1966).

12. Geoffrey, I, 97: 'At Gorlois . . . cum magis pro uxore sua quam pro semetipso anxiaretur, posuit eam in oppido Tintagol' ('Gorlois . . . as he was more worried about his wife than he was about himself . . . left her in the castle of Tintagel'; Thorpe, 205). Malory, I, 8: 'And so his wyf dame Igrayne he putte in the castell of Tyntagil'.

13. Geoffrey, I, 132: 'Set et inclitus ille rex Arturus letaliter uulneratus est; qui illinc ad sananda uulnera sua in insulam Auallonis euectus . . . anno ab incarnatione Domini .dxlii.' ('Arthur himself, our renowned king, was mortally wounded and was carried off to the Isle of Avalon, so that his wounds might be attended to . . . this in the year 542 after our Lord's Incarnation'; Thorpe, 261).

14. Malory, II, 855: 'Four hondrid wyntir and four and fyffty acomplyvysshed aftir the Passion of oure Lord Jesu Cryst'.

15. See, for example, C. Platt, *The Castle in Medieval England and Wales* (London 1982), 1; N. J. G. Pounds, *The Medieval Castle in England and Wales: A Social and Political History* (Cambridge 1990), 6; J. R. Kenyon, *Medieval Fortifications* (London 1990), 3.

16. Texts from this collection which use Carlisle as a location are *The Wedding of Sir Gawain and Dame Ragnelle*, *The Marriage of Sir Gawain*, *Sir Gawain and the Carle of Carlisle*, *The Carle of Carlisle*, *The Avowyng of Arthur*, *The Awntyrs off Arthur* and *The Green Knight*.

17. Dates for these texts range from about A.D. 1400, with some also recorded in the Percy Folio in about 1650: Hahn, 'Introduction', 24–35; A. E. Hartung ed., *A Manual of the Writings in Middle English 1050–1500*, I (New Haven 1967–98), 57–66. Dates for these texts range from about 1400, with some also recorded in the Percy Folio in about 1650.

18. Hahn, 'Introduction', 4; N. J. Lacy, *The New Arthurian Encyclopedia*, 4th edn (New York 1996), 178.

19. Hahn, 'Introduction', p. 4, n. 6.

20. Geoffrey, I, 30, 109–11.

21. See A. Griscom ed., *The Historia Regum Britanniae of Geoffrey of Monmouth* (London 1929), 149.

22. Griscom, 260, includes the variant reading from the Welsh text in Oxford, Jesus College Library MS LXI; compare Geoffrey, I, 18: 'Leil . . . qui et prosperitate regni usus est, urbem in aquilonari parte Britannie aedificauit: de nomine suo Kaer Leil uocata.' ('Leil took advantage of the prosperity of his reign to build a town in the northern part of Britain which he called Kaerleil after himself'; Thorpe, 80).

23. This, despite the fact that 'Caerlion' itself is mentioned only three lines beforehand: *Alliterative Morte Arthure* in L. D. Benson ed., *King Arthur's Death: The Middle English Stanzaic Morte Arthur and Alliterative Morte Arthure* (Exeter 1986, reprinted 1986), 115–238, 117–30, ll. 61, 64–480.

24. Hahn, *Sir Gawain and the Carle of Carlisle*, 85–89.

25. See note 17.

26. Hahn, 'Introduction', 31.

27. Geoffrey, I, 18; see note 22.

28. B. Colgrave ed. and trans., *Two Lives of St Cuthbert: A Life by an Anonymous Monk of Lindisfarne and Bede's Prose Life* (Cambridge 1940), 244–45, ch. xxvii. See also the Anonymous Life in the same volume, 122–23, for a very similar account. See also Henig and McCarthy, this volume.

29. J. S. P. Tatlock, *The Legendary History of Britain: Geoffrey of Monmouth's Historia regum Britannie and its Early Vernacular Versions* (Berkeley 1950), 69–70.

30. M. Greenhalgh, *The Survival of Roman Antiquities in the Middle Ages* (London 1989), 21 and passim.

31. J. Gillingham, 'The Context and Purposes of Geoffrey of Monmouth's History of the Kings of Britain', *Anglo-Norman Studies*, 13 (1990), 99–118, 100–01; Geoffrey, I, 'Introduction', xix and passim; M. B. Shichtman and L. A. Finke, 'Profiting from the Part: History as Symbolic Capital in the Historia regum Britannie', *Arthurian Literature*, 12 (1993), 1–35, 4 and passim; A. Gransden, *Historical Writing in England c. 550 to c. 1307* (London 1974), 204–05.

32. Geoffrey, I, 116–29.

33. Thorpe, 226; Geoffrey, I, 110: 'aureis tectorum fastigiis Romam imitaretur'.

34. Geoffrey, I, 112–16.

35. Benson, *Alliterative Morte Arthure*, 117–30, ll. 64–480.

36. See note 15.

THE AUGUSTINIAN REGULAR CANONS

REGULAR canons — 12th-century pedants enjoyed ridiculing the tautology — were communities of clergy, distinguishable from their secular counterparts by virtue of their adherence to a conventual rule.[7] In England, regular canons were a post-Conquest phenomenon. One of the earliest English houses was that established at Huntingdon before 1091, but the nature of the rule adopted then is not recorded.[8] The Augustinian regular canons followed the so-called Rule of St Augustine, unknown in England until the beginning of the 12th century.[9] Augustinian observances were introduced from Northern France early in the reign of Henry I, probably at St Botolph's, Colchester (Essex), before 1107.[10]

The popularity of the Augustinians within court circles during Henry I's reign is well documented. Henry's pious queen, Mathilda, was one of the Order's earliest English lay patrons.[11] Archbishop Anselm was instrumental in introducing the Augustinians into the country and Mathilda's enthusiasm for them may have grown with her wish to gratify her implacable mentor.[12] For Anselm, champion of the papal reforms in England, the Augustinians were allies in the effort to steer lay patronage within the Church towards acceptable ends. The Augustinians were popular among the episcopate in general during Henry's reign. Unlike the other orders which developed in response to the reforms, the Augustinians were immediately answerable to their diocesan bishop, as the secular clergy had always been.[13] There was no General Chapter before 1215.[14] Augustinian priories constituted an arm of the pastoral system which bishops had always had a responsibility to maintain. In sponsoring Augustinian houses, bishops were effectively discharging an aspect of their parochial duties. As canons, the inmates of an Augustinian house were destined, at least notionally, for ordination. Bishops would, therefore, have been more intimately involved with the Augustinian communities in their diocese than with those of the Cistercians or Cluniacs. Anselm would have been aware of the potential here for reinforcing episcopal authority. Before his death in 1109, early in the Augustinian's history in England, Anselm himself had supported the foundation of at least five Augustinian houses.[15]

The Augustinian canons were especially popular with Henry's nobility. Over three-quarters of the Augustinian foundations of Henry's reign were the work of the royal entourage.[16] Henry's curia favoured them partly because they were relatively inexpensive.[17] Augustinians could colonise communities of clergy, appropriating any existing buildings and income. The initial endowment of an Augustinian house might thus be comparatively small.[18] Also, as private patronage of churches became increasingly unacceptable in the wake of the papal reforms, Augustinian foundations provided legitimate outlets for baronial piety. At Thurgarton (Notts.) in the 1130s, the founder endowed his new Augustinian priory with all the churches of his barony.[19]

Augustinian canons are normally discussed together with the so-called Reformed Orders, such as the Cistercians, Premonstratensians and reformed Benedictines. These emerged in response to the desire for a return to the ethos of the early Church, given substance in the papal reforms of the later 11th century.[20] The Augustinians are somewhat overshadowed in this context by the more rigorous Cistercian Order. Both Augustinians and Cistercians undoubtedly sought a return to the spirit of the Primitive Church and were equally committed to the *Vita Apostolica* but, whereas for the Augustinians adherence to the Apostolic Life implied an element of mission, the pastoral obligations of the Cistercians were strictly of an agricultural nature. There were fundamental differences between them, not least that the Cistercians were primarily monks. The Augustinians were, by definition, clerks or priests. As Anselm of Laon said, 'Clerks are chosen for preaching and teaching, monks for prayer'.[21] Augustinians in Holy Orders might serve the laity as priests. How diligently Augustinian communities served the parish altars for which they were responsible is hard to determine, but clearly some did.[22] They relied upon their dependent churches for income, a practice eschewed by the Cistercians. While the Cistercians insisted on an undeviating reading of the Rule of St Benedict, the rule followed by the Augustinians, based partly on the still earlier writings of the priest-bishop St Augustine, was famously open to interpretation. In short, despite their common inspiration, the Augustinians and the Cistercians occupied different spaces in the religious landscape.

The Augustinians are considered remarkable for the flexibility of their ordinances and their rapid proliferation has been attributed largely to this quality. Their overarching concern was the pursuit of the *Vita Apostolica*; beyond insisting that brethren led a full common life, there were few other strictures. Thus, although most of their foundations were new, such as Dunstable Priory (Beds.), they could equally embrace existing communities: groups of hermits, as at Nostell (West Yorks.) and of priests, whether formerly serving an oratory, as at Llanthony (Gwent), parish church, as at Bridlington (East Yorks.), secular college, as at Cirencester (Gloucs.), or hospital, as at St Gregory's, Canterbury (Kent).[23] Was this adaptability matched by an appropriately multifarious architecture?

CARLISLE CATHEDRAL IN THE CONTEXT OF CONTEMPORARY AUGUSTINIAN ARCHITECTURE IN THE REGION: THE ELEVEN HOUSES OF THE NORTH

THE Augustinian priory at Carlisle was founded *c.* 1122. The Romanesque cathedral church was a cruciform building, datable to the second quarter of the 12th century, aisled in presbytery and nave, with a three-storey elevation, including a dark nave triforium and a clerestorey wall-passage.[24] It had relatively narrow transepts with commensurately low crossing arches to north and south and a single transeptal chapel apiece. The plan of the eastern termination of the presbytery is a matter for speculation. The nave piers are cylindrical and uniform, the capitals are mostly variations on the scallop and some of the bases have spurs. The arch profiles are particularly varied and include plain, square-sectioned mouldings, hollow-chamfers, soffit-rolls, nook-rolls and the double-roll-and-arris. To what extent are these the characteristics of contemporary Augustinian churches in the locality, in the dioceses of Carlisle, Durham and York?

Of the eleven Augustinian priories founded in Henry I's reign in this northern region, five are lost: Bridlington, Drax (North Yorks.), Embsay (West Yorks., relocated to Bolton *c.* 1155), Nostell and Thurgarton. One of the surviving six, Kirkham (North Yorks.), had an aisleless, cruciform plan.[25] A further three may have had a similar plan but with the addition of an aisle on the north side of the nave, namely Hexham and Brinkburn, both in Northumberland, and Gisborough (Cleveland). At Hexham in 1113, Augustinian canons from Huntingdon were given the ancient church by Archbishop Thomas II of York, and later supported by his successor, Thurstan. The material evidence for a 12th-century church at Hexham is slight, but the predecessor of the 13th-century building was apparently cruciform in plan and either aisleless, or with a single north nave aisle.[26] At Brinkburn, Augustinian canons were installed between 1130–35 in the church built by one Osbertus. The earliest surviving part of the restored building at Brinkburn is the late-12th-century north portal. The church is cruciform with a single aisle on the north side of the nave. The standing structure at Brinkburn is clearly not that built by Osbertus, although the plan could be his, perhaps minus the north aisle.[27] Gisborough was founded, again with support from Thurstan of York, perhaps in the 1120s and excavation has revealed part of the plan of the 12th-century nave. It may have had a north aisle but the evidence for a south aisle is unclear.[28]

Apart from Carlisle, therefore, the only contemporary Augustinian church in the region with a fully-aisled nave is Worksop (Notts.), founded after 1119. There, the surviving nave bays are of two periods, in the earlier of which cylindrical piers occur with a scallop capital comparable, but not identical, to some at Carlisle. Worksop appears to share with Carlisle the dark triforium, but otherwise the nave elevation is more articulated and somewhat idiosyncratic.

CARLISLE CATHEDRAL IN THE CONTEXT OF COMPARABLE PATRONAGE: HENRY'S FIVE AUGUSTINIAN FOUNDATIONS

HENRY I supported the foundation of a number of Augustinian houses but there are just five for which he is considered directly responsible.[29] In addition to Carlisle, these were Cirencester (Glos.), Dunstable (Beds.), St Denys at Portswood-by-Southampton (Hants.) and Wellow-by-Grimsby (Lincs.). Two of the five, Cirencester and Wellow, were abbeys, a rare distinction among English Augustinian houses.[30] Carlisle was the only English house of the Order to be elevated to cathedral status. Both St Denys, Southampton and Wellow-by-Grimsby had sensitive coastal locations, but have left almost no trace. All three of Henry's other Augustinian churches were sited close to major secular buildings: Carlisle and Cirencester, near castles, perhaps Henry's own in both cases, and Dunstable close to the palace Henry had built for himself.[31] The king placed Dunstable priory at the heart of his own 'planted' new town. Carlisle priory was, equally, built in a town only recently established, by means of immigration.[32] All three were on the arterial roads of medieval Britain.[33] At all three, the early 1130s were significant; at Cirencester the first abbot was consecrated *c.* 1130; Dunstable priory was founded *c.* 1132; the first bishop of Carlisle was appointed in 1133.[34]

Did the king's Augustinian churches have common architectural features? Romanesque Carlisle and Dunstable are now fragments and Cirencester virtually erased but all three were aisled in the 12th century. At both Carlisle and Dunstable, similar grooved, scallop capitals and spur bases occur. The nave elevations of Carlisle and Dunstable possess the same elements, but at Dunstable there is greater articulation and the piers, albeit with columnar properties, are all compound. Moreover, Dunstable's elevation, unified by a variant of the giant order, is more harmonious than Carlisle's.

AUGUSTINIAN ARCHITECTURE IN THE REIGN OF HENRY I: THE HOUSES OF THE FIRST AUGUSTINIAN GENERATION THROUGHOUT THE KINGDOM

BY the end of Henry's reign, the Augustinians had founded some 56 houses in England, Wales and Scotland in under 30 years, about 20 more than the Cistercians during their first three decades in England. Of these 56 houses, in what could be called the Order's first generation in Britain, 22 of the churches are lost and their 12th-century plan unknown. Of the 27 with a Romanesque plan whose details are known, only nine certainly had an aisled nave at some stage in the 12th century: Colchester (Essex), Aldgate and Smithfield in London, Worksop, Oxford, Dover (Kent), Carlisle, Dunstable and Cirencester. A larger number, eleven, had a cruciform plan with an aisleless nave:

a   b   c   d   e

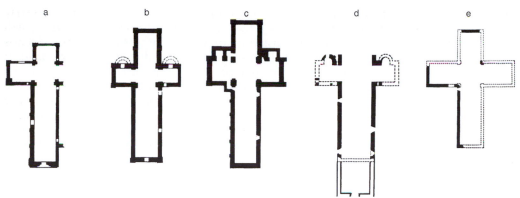

Some aisleless cruciform churches of Augustinian houses founded in the reign of Henry I:
a   Portchester
b   St Leonard Stanley
c   Norton
d   Gt Bricett
e   Kirkham

FIG. 1. Some aisleless cruciform churches of Augustinian houses founded in the reign of Henry I

a–c: after D. Baker in B. Cunliffe, Excavations at Portchester Castle, *Society Antiquaries of London (1977), fig. 70. d: after F. H. Fairweather,* Proceedings Suffolk Institute Archaeology *(1926), 102. e; after G. Coppack, S. Harrison and C. Hayfield,* JBAA, *CXLVIII (1995), Fig. 2A*

Merton (Surrey), Bricett (Suffolk), Leonard Stanley (Glos.), Norton (Cheshire), Portchester (Hants.), Kirkham, Kenilworth (Warks.), Haughmond (Salop), Breedon and Ulverscroft (Leics.), and Holyrood (Lothian) (Fig. 1).[35] In addition, there are three churches, all but lost, which may also have had an aisleless cruciform plan: Little Dunmow (Essex), St Gregory's, Canterbury (Kent) and Llanthony (Gwent).[36] Lastly, there are the three discussed above which were cruciform with a single north aisle possibly added later: Hexham, Brinkburn and Gisborough. Adding those possible candidates to the known examples gives a total of 17; almost twice as many aisleless churches as aisled ones in the period. Moreover, not included in this total are the aisleless cruciform 'ghosts' which may lie beneath later, fully aisled, churches. For example, at Augustinian St Frideswide's in Oxford, founded by 1122 and coeval with Carlisle, the present Romanesque church is datable no earlier than the 1160s. There is, however, evidence of an earlier cloister and indications of an earlier church on the same site.[37] The architectural spectre at St Frideswide's is, perhaps, not the secular minster which the Augustinians inherited, but an unrecorded aisleless, cruciform church, built in the 1120s and replaced some 40 years later by the present one. Something comparable is discernible at Bridlington, founded *c.* 1113, where again the cloister contains the clue.[38] The cloister quadrangle that can be reconstructed at Bridlington is extremely small in relation to the existing 13th-century nave. If the diagonal of the quadrangle approximated to the length of the nave of the lost 12th-century church, the latter terminated short of the Gothic façade, at a point coinciding with an abrupt change of style in the present south nave arcade. The Gothic south nave aisle at Bridlington is over a metre narrower than the north aisle, due, perhaps, to its having been adapted from the Romanesque north cloister walk.[39]

The figures given above for aisleless, cruciform Augustinian churches founded in Henry I's reign, do not include the hypothetical candidates at Oxford and Bridlington.

Nonetheless, the numbers suggest a preference among Augustinian patrons of the time for the unaisled cruciform plan, with nearly twice as many aisleless, as aisled churches. It should also be noted that the nine aisled churches of this first generation do not certainly represent the primary plan in each case, as opposed to a later 12th-century rebuild. At Worksop, for example, an earlier plan has been discovered beneath the present 12th-century nave, not itself a homogeneous structure.[40] At Cirencester, archaeologists have established that the presbytery walls (as opposed to the presbytery aisle walls) were originally 'load-bearing and external', indicating that the Abbey had at least an aisleless choir originally.[41] The nine aisled Augustinian buildings, all in foundations established during Henry's reign, but with standing structures of the 1120s-60s, are a diverse collection. Most commonly occurring features are the columnar pier, found at Colchester, Smithfield, Carlisle, and, in an alternating system, Oxford and Worksop, and the dark nave triforium at Carlisle and, perhaps, Dunstable and Worksop. There is one surviving ambulatory, at Smithfield, and one true giant order, at Oxford. There are, then, some features common to several of the nine, but these also occur in non-Augustinian contexts and do not represent a specifically Augustinian vocabulary. In fact, there is considerable diversity here, which is perhaps what underlies Clapham's judgement on Augustinian architecture as the *tabula rasa* of Romanesque. It has never been argued that these nine aisled churches constitute a group. By comparison, the aisleless cruciform churches do form a group, or the remains of one.

THE POPULARITY OF THE AISLELESS CRUCIFORM PLAN AND ITS SOURCES

THE patronage of the Augustinian houses founded between Henry's death in 1135 and the end of the 12th century was less socially exalted than that of those founded during the king's lifetime (Fig. 2). Proportionately, the losses have been far greater: of some 94 houses in England, Wales and Scotland of this later generation, the churches of 61 are lost. Of those 34 whose plan is known, 16 (47%) were aisled in the 12th-13th centuries. A smaller proportion, seven (20%), were certainly aisleless.[42] A further five (18%) had just a north aisle, or were possibly aisleless originally.[43] Taking the 12th century as a whole, the evidence suggests that the Augustinians built marginally more aisleless cruciform churches than aisled ones, with possibly 29 (48%) aisleless and 25 (42%) aisled out of a total of 60 known plans. But taking Henry's death in 1135 as a *terminus*, it seems that the popularity of the aisleless cruciform plan declined among the Augustinians afterwards. Combining certain examples with possible ones, of a total of 27 known plans, some 63% of Augustinian churches of houses founded before Henry's death were aisleless, as opposed to only 38% after it. If the majority of Augustinian canons and their patrons in the first four decades of the 12th century favoured a distinctive building type, some explanation should be sought.

AUGUSTINIAN PREFERENCE FOR THE AISLELESS CRUCIFORM PLAN IN THE REIGN OF HENRY I

IT seems unlikely, in an order noted for its capacity to absorb and adapt, that this was a type of plan proper to the Augustinians, one which they might impose wherever they were established. In any event, the aisleless cruciform plan is far from uncommon, in a non-monastic context. Several authorities on the early Church in Britain have associated its occurrence in the landscape with the presence of a community of priests.[44] Among the reformed monastic orders, Cistercian, Premonstratensian and Benedictine examples

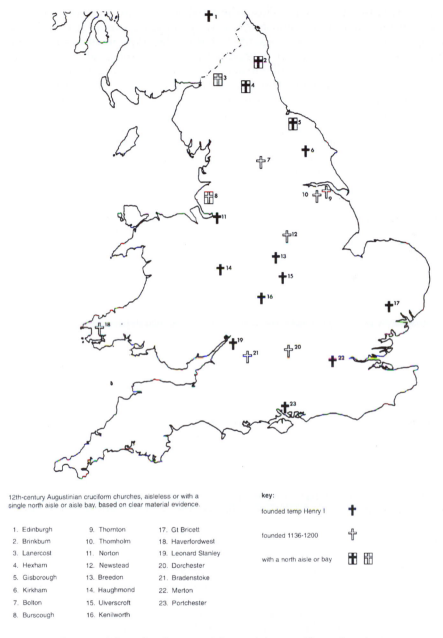

12th-century Augustinian cruciform churches, aisleless or with a
single north aisle or aisle bay, based on clear material evidence.

1. Edinburgh	9. Thornton	17. Gt Bricett
2. Brinkburn	10. Thornholm	18. Haverfordwest
3. Lanercost	11. Norton	19. Leonard Stanley
4. Hexham	12. Newstead	20. Dorchester
5. Gisborough	13. Breedon	21. Bradenstoke
6. Kirkham	14. Haughmond	22. Merton
7. Bolton	15. Ulverscroft	23. Portchester
8. Burscough	16. Kenilworth	

key:

founded temp Henry I

founded 1136-1200

with a north aisle or bay

FIG. 2. Map of 12th-century Augustinian cruciform churches
Drawing: Jill A. Franklin and Jan Kuzminsksi

of the plan have also been cited.[45] The earliest aisleless cruciform Cistercian church was that of the Order's first English house at Waverley (Surrey), founded in 1128.[46] Waverley was thought to have been the progenitor of this plan-type in monastic Britain until attention was drawn to an earlier Augustinian example, the church begun in 1125 at Merton, also in Surrey, sufficiently close to Waverley for any direct influence to have travelled from the Augustinian to the later Cistercian house.[47] It is worth recalling that Cistercian Rievaulx and Fountains were largely founded by Walter Espec and Archbishop Thurstan respectively, both patrons of the Augustinians for a decade. Indeed the founder of Waverley, Bishop William Giffard of Winchester, had already established an Augustinian priory at Taunton, c. 1120.[48] Of the 86 Cistercian abbeys in the British Isles, only six appear to have possessed an aisleless cruciform church at some stage, all in foundations of the second quarter of the 12th century.[49] One Benedictine example of the cruciform unaisled plan has been cited, at Ewenny (Mid Glamorgan).[50] This apparently monastic church was once thought to have been built for the Benedictine priory established in 1141, but has since been identified as the building recorded on the site before 1126.[51] Formerly a rogue Benedictine example of the aisleless cruciform plan, Ewenny can now be reinterpreted as the church built originally, perhaps, for a community of priests and subsequently appropriated by Benedictines. As for the Premonstratensian canons, they, too, used the aisleless plan but were latecomers to monastic Britain; their first house in England was founded in 1143, 15 years after the arrival of the Cistercians and over 35 years after the Augustinians.[52]

Liturgy

IT is difficult to gauge, given the paucity of information on 12th-century Augustinian customs, whether this plan-type was particularly appropriate to Augustinian liturgical requirements.[53] The various architectural strategies deployed by the Augustinians to circumvent the limitations of the aisleless nave, however, certainly suggest that the plan, far from evolving in response to Augustinian liturgy, had shortcomings in this respect.[54]

Patronage

THERE is nothing in the distribution of the aisleless Augustinian churches to suggest that the preference was localised; examples occur as far North in the British Isles as Edinburgh, and as far south as Hampshire; from Gloucestershire in the west, to Suffolk in the east (Fig. 2). The earliest Augustinian example at Merton of 1125, has been discussed in conjunction with Holyrood Priory in Edinburgh, founded some three years later and with a similar plan.[55] The connection between these two far-flung sites was one of patronage. The first canons at Holyrood came from Merton. The first canons at Merton had come, in their turn, from Augustinian Huntingdon, for Merton's founder was Gilbert, Sheriff of Surrey but also of Huntingdon. It is Huntingdon which provides the link, for the founder of Holyrood was David of Scotland, holder since c.1114 of the vast estates in the East Midlands and Yorkshire comprising the Honour of Huntingdon.[56] Gilbert was sheriff in David's territory. David, brother of Queen Mathilda, was an avid sponsor of religious foundations. Of the Augustinian houses which he and his son supported, Holyrood had an aisleless plan, Llanthony was certainly cruciform, and Brinkburn and Hexham were cruciform with perhaps a single north aisle. David gained the Earldom of Huntingdon upon marrying the widow of the previous holder, Simon

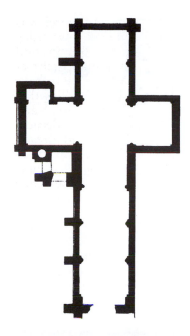

Fig. 3.   Senlis, St Vincent: plan
Drawing: Jill A. Franklin after R. J. Johnson

of Senlis. One of the first English Augustinian houses was that established by 1108 at Huntingdon, in the heartland of Simon's territory, but nothing survives of its church. One of the earliest houses of regular canons in northern France was that at Senlis, at the Abbey of St Vincent, founded probably in the 1060s.[57] The church at Senlis is heavily restored but retains, intriguingly, a cruciform aisleless plan (Fig. 3).[58]

Iconography

THE suggestion that canons favoured a distinctive church plan in the first half of the 12th century revives the issue of the perceived difference between monks and canons at that time.[59] Possibly to the laity, little distinguished Augustinian canons from Benedictine monks. But canons in Holy Orders were set apart from the rest of humanity, including most monks, by the act of ordination. Certainly, in the 12th century, to those within the Church, the difference was real enough; when the Augustinian canon William of Corbeil became Archbishop of Canterbury in 1123, the Benedictine Orderic Vitalis was outraged, accusing the canons of one-upmanship.[60] The rancour between canons and monks is epitomized in the struggle between the metropolitan sees of Canterbury and York. Lanfranc's success in achieving York's submission died with him. The grievance persisted, driving Eadmer of Canterbury to collude in forgery and Archbishop Thurstan of York into exile. Thurstan, however, enjoyed papal support and King Henry was obliged to acknowledge York's independence. While in exile, Thurstan elicited papal protection for Nostell, and possibly Bridlington and Gisborough.[61] After his reinstatement in 1121, he continued to promote Augustinian foundations within the diocese at Embsay, Worksop, Kirkham and Thurgarton.[62] In *c.* 1122, King Henry made his only journey to Carlisle, establishing the Augustinian priory there.[63] Also at this time, the king intervened in the foundation of Nostell, located reassuringly close to Pontefract castle.[64] Nostell's position in the

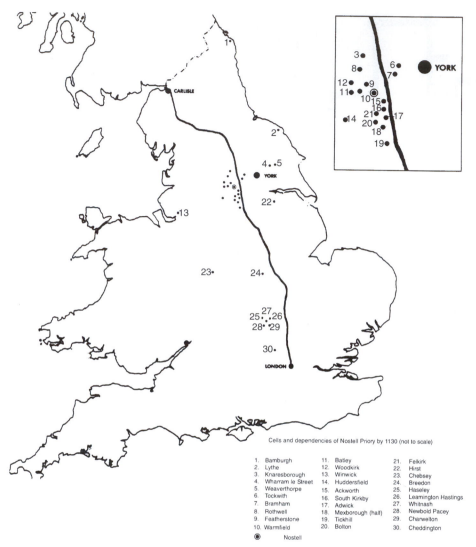

Cells and dependencies of Nostell Priory by 1130 (not to scale)

1. Bamburgh	11. Batley	21. Felkirk
2. Lythe	12. Woodkirk	22. Hirst
3. Knaresborough	13. Winwick	23. Chebsey
4. Wharram le Street	14. Huddersfield	24. Breedon
5. Weaverthorpe		25. Haseley
6. Tockwith	15. Ackworth	26. Leamington Hastings
7. Bramham	16. South Kirkby	27. Whitnash
8. Rothwell	17. Adwick	28. Newbold Pacey
9. Featherstone	18. Mexborough (half)	29. Charwelton
10. Warmfield	19. Tickhill	30. Cheddington
	20. Bolton	
⊚ Nostell		

FIG. 4. Map of cells and dependencies of Nostell Priory by 1130
Drawing: Jill A. Franklin and Jan Kuzminsksi

region came to be pivotal, both as an outpost of royal authority and as a centre of Augustinian control. It was crucial to the development of the diocese of York in the 12th century. Its first prior, Athelwold, who was also Carlisle's first Augustinian prior and first bishop, occupied a prebendal stall at York.[65] Nostell supplied the canons for Scone, the first Scottish Augustinian house, whence came Robert, bishop of the major diocese of St Andrews.[66] Within ten years of its foundation *c.* 1122, Nostell possessed twenty-nine dependencies, not all nearby (Fig. 4).[67] An Augustinian mother church, such as Nostell, presiding over a network of lesser, 'ministry' churches, seems to have assumed the role of the Saxon Head Minster. Most of Nostell's possessions have vanished, but two, Kirkham and Breedon, were cruciform and aisleless and another, Knaresborough (North Yorks.), possibly was.[68] Knaresborough, transferred to York Cathedral in the 13th century and much altered, retains sufficient of its original form to warrant discussion in connection with the majestic aisleless church of *c.* 1140 at North Newbald (East Yorks.). Like Nostell, North Newbald was a prebend of York and had possibly been created 'in the image of its cathedral mother'.[69] What if Nostell had a similar form? Nostell and Carlisle were both held by Athelwold, in plurality. Perhaps Nostell and its army of cruciform dependencies stationed along the Old North Road, should be seen as markers on the route linking London with Athelwold's other Augustinian house at Carlisle!

The role of the York episcopate in the expansion of the Augustinian Order during the reign of Henry I was significant. The Province of York, together with the Honour of Huntingdon, may also have played a part in the proliferation of the aisleless cruciform plan among the Augustinians. Between them, they could probably account for the geographical spread of the plan-type, given the size of their respective territories, including York's ancient claim to jurisdiction in Gloucestershire.[70] Thomas of Bayeux's cathedral at York with its vast aisleless nave, seems almost assertively distinctive in the context of contemporary Anglo-Norman cathedral architecture, notwithstanding the latter's diversity. Its very form proclaims its separate identity, perhaps as a house of canons, in contradistinction to its rival metropolitain, monastic Canterbury. Were Thomas and his successor, Thurstan, responsible for promoting a similar church plan, on a reduced scale, among the Augustinians, placing the stamp of York firmly on the map, within the diocese and beyond? The Cathedral of York, dedicated to the Prince of the Apostles, was perhaps built in the image of an Early Christian predecessor, as other churches were in the West in the late 11th century. S. Nazaro, Milan, for example, rebuilt after 1075 and likewise served by canons, incorporated within its cruciform structure the 4th-century Ambrosian Church of the Apostles, itself built in the form of an aisleless latin cross in conscious emulation of Constantine's Apostoleion and, like the Constantinian building, a reliquary church for the apostles (Fig. 5).[71]

THE PLAN OF THE AUGUSTINIAN CHURCH AT CARLISLE

WHAT of Romanesque Carlisle in the context of these unaisled Augustinian churches? Its unique cathedral status apparently conferred the distinction of a fully-aisled church plan, grander, by design, than its humbler aisleless contemporaries in the region. There are, however, points to note in this connection. Despite the view that the scheme for the new diocese was coeval with the priory's foundation *c.* 1122, the proposal was not ratified until 1133.[72] Moreover, the only dated reference to building work at the church seems to belong to 1129–30.[73] The Romanesque church lacks homogeneity. For its size, its arch mouldings are unusually varied. The nave elevation has the layered horizontality of Worksop, but displays a faltering attempt at vertical articulation that was ultimately abandoned; the openings in each bay are centred one above the other but the mysterious half-shaft rising from the nave capitals would be wildly off-centre if continued upwards through the middle storey, for the triforium piers are not aligned with those of the arcade below. This perhaps results from an error in setting-out, for the first bay of the nave is narrower by some 500 mm than those to the west, a discrepancy which throws the elevation out of true. And, finally, the nave arcade rests upon an impressive piece of masonry over 2 m wide and at least 2 m deep, a portion of which is exposed at the western end. This is interpreted as the sleeper wall of the Romanesque nave arcade, but

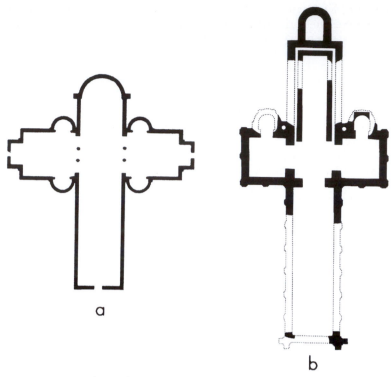

FIG. 5.   Plans of (a) Milan, Holy Apostles, (b) York Minster

a; after R. Krautheimer, Early Christian and Byzantine Architecture *(New Haven 1986), fig. 38. b; after*
E. Fernie, Architecture of Norman England *(2000), © English Heritage*

given the character of Carlisle's Augustinian contemporaries, it is worth speculating that it may represent, instead, the remains of an earlier nave wall, that of Carlisle's unrecorded aisleless Augustinian priory church.[74]

CONCLUSION

TAILOR-MADE for the medieval reformation, the Augustinians were ideally suited to missionary work in frontier and pioneer towns, and Henry I may have used them strategically in the 1120s-30s for his new projects at Carlisle and Dunstable, and perhaps Nostell. Although the aisleless cruciform plan was by no means exclusive to the Augustinians, it was, it seems, used first by them in a 12th-century conventual context in England. It was the preferred plan-type among them during the 1120s-40s, a time when they were particularly favoured by Henry I, Archbishop Thurstan and protégés such as Athelwold. The plan is effectively that of the late-11th-century cathedral at York, writ small. The support of the York episcopate for the Augustinians reinforces that connection. The role of Nostell, vis-à-vis Carlisle, York and the Crown, was crucial during this period, prompting speculation that its plan, too, may have taken this form. An iconographic source is suggested for the plan in Early Christian architecture, perhaps selected by canons to emphasise their identity. The plan was not adopted for Carlisle Cathedral, although it is tentatively suggested that it was used there for a short-lived priory church, discernible in aspects of the Romanesque fabric.

NOTES

1. J. T. Micklethwaite expressed the view that the aisleless nave was characteristic of 12th-century Augustinian churches; *Archaeol. J.*, XXXIX (1882), 458. J. F. Hodgson argued the opposing case, in favour of variety, without restricting his discussion to primary plans, in a series of papers; *Archaeol. J.*, XLI (1884), 374ff.; ibid., XLII (1885), 96ff., 215ff., 440ff.; ibid., XLII (1886), 53ff., 290ff., 403ff.

2. W. H. St John Hope and H. Brakspear, 'Haughmond Abbey, Shropshire', *Archaeol J.*, LXVI (1909), 281–310, 285 where again the authors did not confine their discussion to primary plans and also included buildings of independent Augustinian congregations, such as the Arrouasians.

3. A. W. Clapham, *English Romanesque Architecture After the Conquest* (Oxford 1934), 83–84.

4. S. Heywood, 'The Priory of St Mary in the Meadow of the Order of Peterstone, Beeston next the Sea, Norfolk', *Norfolk Archaeology*, XL (1989), 226–59, 235.

5. J. P. Greene, *Norton Priory* (Cambridge 1989), 85. N. Coldstream in *The Cistercian Abbeys of Britain*, ed. D. Robinson (London 1998), 40. R. Halsey in *Cistercian Art and Architecture in the British Isles*, ed. C. Norton and D. Park (Cambridge 1986), 65–85, 68 n. 22 suggests the reformed canons may have been following their own tradition.

6. D. Baker in B. Cunliffe, *Excavations at Portchester Castle, Reports of the Research Committee of the Society of Antiquaries of London*, xxxiv, III (London 1977), 117.

7. J. C. Dickinson, *The Origins of the Austin Canons and their Introduction into England* (London 1950), 61.

8. Regular canons had been installed at St Mary's Huntingdon before 1091; W. Dugdale, *Monasticon Anglicanum*, ed. J. Caley, H. Ellis and B. Bandinel, VI, part 1, 79 no. 1; W. A. Morris, 'The Office of Sheriff in the Early Norman Period', *English Historical Review*, 33 (1918), 145–75, 152n. Augustinian observances had been introduced there by 1108; D. Knowles and R. N Hadcock, *Medieval Religious Houses in England and Wales* (Cambridge 1971), 160.

9. The authoritative account of the early history of the order in England is that by J. C. Dickinson, *The Origins of the Austin Canons and their Introduction into England* (London 1950) which cites the documentation for all the Augustinian foundations mentioned in the present paper. The expansion and later history of the order is analysed and discussed in D. M. Robinson, *The Geography of Augustinian Settlement in Medieval England and Wales*, British Archaeological Reports, Brit. Series 80 (Oxford 1980).

10. The evidence for the foundation date of Colchester is discussed in Dickinson, 98–103.

11. Mathilda founded Holy Trinity Priory, Aldgate, in 1107. The first canons came from Colchester; Corpus Christi College Cambridge MS 59, f. 154v; Dickinson, 109–11.

12. For Mathilda's relationship with Archbishop Anselm, see R. W. Southern, *St Anselm and his Biographer. A Study of Monastic Life and Thought* (Cambridge 1963), 191–93.

13. A. Hamilton Thompson, 'Bolton Priory', *Transactions Thoresby Society*, XXX (1924), 9.

14. Dickinson, 82.

15. Anselm was involved in establishing Colchester, Aldgate and possibly Dunmow, Llanthony and St Giles, Cambridge; Dickinson, 126–27, 103 n. 4.

16. J. C. Dickinson's figure for the number of Augustinian foundations of Henry's reign is 43, some 33 of which involved curial patronage; Dickinson, 128.

17. One estimate puts the cost of maintaining a Benedictine monk in the early 12th century at three times that of an Augustinian canon; R. W. Southern, *Western Society and the Church* (Harmondsworth 1970), 246.

18. For example, in 1121 Bishop Richard of London was able to hand over to Augustinian canons the ancient church of St Osyth in Essex, previously served by the four priests installed by his predecessor, Maurice; F. Neininger ed., *English Episcopal Acta XV: London, 1076–1187* (Oxford 1999), xlvii–xlviii, n. 43; Dickinson, 112–13, 113 n. 2. Over 60 Austin houses were established in pre-existing sites in this way, the property of the latter being used to endow the new community in many cases; Robinson, *Augustinian Settlement*, 276.

19. T. Foulds ed., *The Thurgarton Cartulary* (Stamford 1994) f. 143r.

20. B. Bolton, *The Medieval Reformation* (London 1983), 17–54.

21. Dickinson, 214 n. 1.

22. The Augustinian priories of Leeds, Gisborough, Bridlington and Nostell, for example, all sent canons to serve dependent churches in the 12th century; Dickinson, 237. See ibid., 214–41 for a detailed discussion of this issue.

23. For Dunstable, see VCH, *Bedfordshire*, I (1904). For Nostell, J. Burton, *The Monastic Order in Yorkshire, 1069–1215* (Cambridge 1999), 71–77. For Bridlington, ibid., 69–71. For Llanthony, I. N. Soulsby in D. H. Evans, 'Further Excavation and Fieldwork at Llanthony Priory, Gwent', *The Monmouthshire Antiquary*, V (1983), 1–61, 50–52. For Cirencester, A. K. B. Evans in D. J. Wilkinson and A. D. McWhirr, *Cirencester Anglo-Saxon Church and Medieval Abbey* (Cirencester 1998), 14–18, 15. For Canterbury, T. Tatton-Brown, 'The Beginnings of St Gregory's Priory and St John's Hospital in Canterbury', in *Canterbury and the Norman Conquest. Churches, Saints and Scholars*, ed. R. Eales and R. Sharpe (London 1995), 53–86.

24. For the Romanesque structure see Plant this volume.

25. G. Coppack, S. Harrison and C. Hayfield, 'Kirkham Priory: the Architecture and Archaeology of an Augustinian House', *JBAA*, CXLVIII (1995), 55–136, 63–65.

26. E. Cambridge, 'C.C. Hodges and the nave of Hexham Abbey', *Archaeol. Aeliana*, 5th series, VII (1979), 158–68.

27. F. R. Wilson, *An Architectural Survey of the Churches of the Archdeaconry of Lindisfarne* (Newcastle-upon-Tyne 1870), 142. The most recent study of Brinkburn is that by J. Cunningham in 'Buildings and Patrons: Early Gothic Architecture in the Diocese of Durham, *c.* 1150–*c.* 1300' (unpublished Ph.D. thesis, University of London, 1995), ii, 71–84. In Dr Cunningham's view the north aisle is integral to the present nave and not an addition to it. I am most grateful to Jane Cunningham for discussing this with me.

28. D. H. Heslop, 'Excavation within the Church at the Augustinian Priory of Gisborough, Cleveland 1985–6', *Yorkshire Archaeological J.*, LXVII (1995), 51–126; ibid., LXXI (1999), 89–128. If it is argued that the Romanesque nave at Gisborough had a south aisle, it must also be assumed that the latter was subsequently engulfed by the cloister. It seems most unlikely, however, that a south-lying cloister would have been extended northwards.

29. Dickinson, 125–26.

30. Apart from Holyrood in Scotland, Cirencester and Wellow were the only Augustinian houses founded during Henry I's reign which were abbeys from their inception.

31. The first castle at Carlisle was built by William Rufus in 1092; H. Summerson, *Medieval Carlisle: The City and the Borders from the late 11th to the mid-16th century* (Kendal 1993), I, 16. Henry I visited Carlisle *c.* 1122 and ordered it to be fortified by a castle and towers; *Symeonis Monachi Opera Omnia*, ed. T. Arnold, ii, (Rolls Series, LXX, 1885), 267. The Augustinian priory was situated near the castle. Henry paid for work to the city walls in 1129–30; *Pipe Roll 31 Henry I*, ed. J. Hunter (London 1833), 141. For a discussion of Carlisle Castle, see Goodall this volume. The castle at Cirencester, which adjoined the abbey, was destroyed in 1142; *Gesta Stephani*, ed. K. R. Potter (Oxford 1976), 138–40. The castle may have been Henry I's recorded 'new work' of 1117 at Cirencester, rather than the abbey, for which the earliest evidence is the reference to the abbot *c.* 1130, contained in *Pipe Roll 31 Henry I*, 80, 126; A. K. B. Evans, 'Cirencester's Early Church', *Transactions Bristol Gloucestershire Archaeological Society*, CVII (1989), 107–22, 117 n. 3; ibid., CIX (1991), 99–116, 99–100. At Dunstable, Henry built a royal residence, known later as Kingsbury, celebrating Christmas there in 1122. He established the Augustinian priory to the south of it in 1131–32; R. A. Brown, H. M. Colvin and A. J. Taylor, *The History of the King's Works: The Middle Ages*, ed. H. M. Colvin, II (London 1963), 924.

32. Henry created the borough of Dunstable *c.* 1119, clearing the site for building and encouraging settlers. He placed his palace, and later the priory, at its centre; M. W. Beresford, *New Towns of the Middle Ages: town plantation in England, Wales and Gascony* (London 1967), 349. Having established a castle at Carlisle, William Rufus brought in settlers to populate the town; Summerson, 16.

33. Dunstable was established at the intersection of Watling Street with the Icknield Way; *VCH*, Bedfordshire, III (1912), 350. Cirencester stood on the Fosse Way and Ermin Street; T. Darvill and C. Gerrard, *Cirencester: Town and Landscape* (Cirencester 1994), 51–52. Carlisle was at the junction of several Roman roads and was linked with London via the Old North Road; Summerson, 13. J. M. Steane, *The Archaeology of Medieval England and Wales* (London 1985), 106.

34. The dating of Abbot Serlo of Cirencester's consecration is discussed in A. K. B. Evans, 'Cirencester Abbey: the first hundred years', *Transactions Bristol Gloucestershire Archaeological Society*, CIX (1991), 99–116, 99. For Dunstable's foundation date, see Dickinson, 115. For the creation of the see at Carlisle and Bishop Athelwold's consecration, ibid., 245–51, 247.

35. For Merton, D. G. Bird, G. Crocker and J. S. McCracken, 'Archaeology in Surrey 1988–9', *Surrey Archaeological Collections*, LXXX (1990), 201–27, 219. For Bricett, F. H. Fairweather, 'Excavations on the site of the Augustinian Alien Priory of Great Bricett, Suffolk', *Proceedings of Suffolk Institute of Archaeology and Natural History*, XIX (1926), 99–109. For Leonard Stanley, C. Swynnerton, 'The Priory of St Leonard Stanley', *Archaeologia*, LXXI (1921), 199–226. For Norton, Greene, XI, fig. 4. For Portchester, A. Borg in Cunliffe, 107, fig. 67. For Kirkham, Coppack, Harrison and Hayfield, fig. 2A. For Kenilworth, N. Pevsner and A. Wedgwood, *Warwickshire* B/E (1966), 319. For Haughmond, J. Cherry in 'Medieval Britain in 1979,' *Med. Archaeol.*, XXIV (1980), 218–64, 240–41, fig. 6. For Breedon, C. A. R. Radford, 'Breedon on the Hill Church of St Mary and St

Hardulf', *Archaeol. J.*, CXII (1955), 170–72. For Ulverscroft, N. Pevsner, E. Williamson and G. K. Brandwood, *Leicestershire and Rutland* B/E, 2nd edn (1984), 415–17. For Holyrood, C. Wilson in J. Gifford, C. McWilliam, D. Walker, C. Wilson, *Edinburgh* B/Scot (1984), 130–31.

36. For Little Dunmow, RCHME *Essex, North-West* (1916), 175–80, 176. For Canterbury, T. Tatton-Brown, 'St Gregory's Priory, Canterbury', *Current Archaeology*, XI (1991), 100–06. The site is complex. According to Tatton-Brown's interpretation, the aisled church at St Gregory's, which replaced an aisleless cruciform structure, dates from the introduction of Augustinian canons, 1123–36. It is possible, however, that the aisled church post-dated the fire of 1145. For Llanthony, Evans, 'Llanthony Priory', 2 and fig. 1. The first conventual church, of perhaps *c.* 1118, was certainly cruciform.

37. R. Halsey, 'The Twelfth-Century Church of St Frideswide's Priory', in *St Frideswide's Monastery at Oxford*, ed. J. Blair (Gloucester 1990), 115–67, 117–22.

38. J. A. Franklin, 'Bridlington Priory: an Augustinian Church and Cloister in the Twelfth Century', *Medieval Art and Architecture in the East Riding of Yorkshire, BAA Trans.*, IX (1989), 44–61, 49.

39. ibid., 54.

40. N. Pevsner, revised by E. Williamson, Pevsner, *Nottingham* B/E, 2nd edn (1979), 386.

41. Thus, what was to become the sleeper wall of the south choir arcade was originally an external wall; Wilkinson and McWhirr, 43 with plan, fig. 33, and section, fig. 35.

42. Churches of Augustinian houses founded 1135–1200: aisleless: Bradenstocke (Wilts.), Bolton (West Yorks.), Dorchester (Oxford), Haverfordwest (Dyfed), Newstead (Notts.), Thornholm and Thornton (Lincs).

43. Churches of Augustinian houses founded 1135–1200: possibly aisleless originally: Canons Ashby (Northants.), Ixworth (Suffolk), Lanercost (Cumberland), Letheringham (Suffolk). With a single north aisle, or north aisle bay: Burscough (Lancs.), Lanercost (Cumbria).

44. J. Blair, 'Secular Minster Churches in Domesday Book' in *Domesday Book; a Reassessment*, ed. P. Sawyer (London 1985), 104–42, 137. E. Cambridge, 'Early Romanesque Architecture in North-East England: A Style and its Patrons', in *Anglo-Norman Durham 1093–1193*, ed. D. Rollason, M. Harvey and M. Prestwich (Woodbridge 1994), 141–60, 145.

45. Greene, 85.

46. H. Brakspear, *Waverley Abbey* (London 1905).

47. Wilson, 32. See also Eric Fernie, *The Architecture of Norman England* (Oxford 2000), 41.

48. Dickinson, 118, notes 7 and 8.

49. Waverley (founded 1128), Neath (1130), Tintern (1131), Rievaulx and Fountains (1132) and Sawley (1147); D. M. Robinson ed., *The Cistercian Abbeys of Britain. Far from the Concourse of Men* (London 1998); P. Fergusson and S. Harrison, *Rievaulx Abbey: Community, Architecture, Memory* (New Haven and London 1999).

50. D. Baker in Cunliffe, 118–19; Greene, 85.

51. M. Thurlby, 'The Romanesque Priory Church of St Michael at Ewenny', *J. Society Architectural Historians*, XLVII (1988), 281–94. In Thurlby's view, the north aisle at Ewenny is integral to the nave, not an addition.

52. Knowles and Hadcock, 183.

53. The only surviving Augustinian customary of English origin is that of the late 13th century of Barnwell Priory; J. W. Clark ed., *The Observances of Barnwell Priory* (Cambridge 1897).

54. For example, the inclusion of the single aisle bay at otherwise aisleless Lanercost; H. Summerson and S. Harrison, *Lanercost Priory, Cumbria. A Survey and Documentary History. Cumberland Westmorland Antiquarian Archaeological Society Research Series* No. 10 (Kendal 2000), 181.

55. Wilson, 32.

56. W. Farrer, *Honors and Knights Fees*, II (London 1924), 296.

57. M. Prou, *Receuil des actes de Philippe Ier* (Paris 1907), xliii.

58. R. J. Johnson, *Specimens of Early French Architecture* (Newcastle-upon-Tyne 1864), pl. 9.

59. C. N. L. Brooke, 'Monk and Canon. Some Patterns in the Religious Life of the Twelfth Century', *Studies in Church History*, XXII (1985), 109–29. C. W. Bynum, 'The Spirituality of Regular Canons in the Twelfth Century: A New Approach', *Medievalia et Humanistica*, ns, 4 (1973), 3–24.

60. *Orderic Vitalis*, XII, 31.

61. Hugh the Chanter, *The History of the Church of York 1066–1127*, ed. C. Johnson, rev. edn, M. Brett, C. N. L. Brooke and M. Winterbottom, Oxford Medieval Texts (Oxford 1990), 124 n. 3.

62. D. Nicholl, *Thurstan Archbishop of York* (York 1964), 128. The prior of Thurgarton held a stall in the chapter of the Archbishop of York's minster at Southwell; Foulds, xvii.

63. Dickinson, 246.

64. J. Herbert, 'The Transformation of Hermitages into Augustinian Priories in Twelfth-Century England', in *Monks, Hermits and the Ascetic Tradition*, ed. W. J. Sheils (Oxford 1985), 131–45, 140.

65. J. Le Neve, *Fasti Ecclesiae Anglicanae 1066–1300*, VI, York, ed. D. E. Greenaway (London 1999), 60.

66. G. W. S. Barrow, *The Kingdom of the Scots* (London 1973), 170–71.

67. Nostell's possessions are listed in Hamilton Thompson, 'Bolton Priory', 27–28.

68. For Knaresborough, see R. Morris, *Churches in the Landscape* (London 1989), 283.

69. Morris, 283. Knaresborough was transferred from Nostell to York in 1230; J. Burton, *Monasticon Eboracense* (York 1758), 306.

70. A. Hamilton Thompson, 'The Jurisdiction of the Archbishops of York in Gloucestershire', *Transactions Bristol Gloucestershire Archaeological Society*, XLIII (1921), 85–180.

71. R. Krautheimer, *Early Christian and Byzantine Architecture* (Harmondsworth 1975), 86 n. 36, pl. 38. See, also, the comparable example of S. Simpliciano, Milan, whose aisleless plan and tall blank arcading are found again at late-11th-century York Minster; ibid., 87, pls 39 and 40. For York, see E. Fernie, *The Architecture of Norman England* (Oxford 2000), 122–24.

72. The evidence cited to support the view that the scheme to establish the new diocese was contemporary with the priory's foundation *c.* 1122 is the dispensation of Pope Calixtus II (1119–24), allowing Athelwold to hold his priorate in conjunction with another office. The inference that this second office was the bishopric is drawn from a Nostell chronicle which, in recording the papal dispensation, refers to Athelwold as bishop; J. Wilson, 'The Foundation of the Austin Priories of Nostell and Scone', *Scottish Historical Review*, VII (1910), 141–59, 159. The Nostell chronicle, however, was written in the late 14th century. It cannot be discounted, therefore, that the second office for which the dispensation was granted was the priorate, rather than the bishopric, of Carlisle.

73. *Pipe Roll 31 Henry I*, ed. J. Hunter (London 1833), 141.

74. This suggestion offers an alternative interpretation to that based on the excavation involving part of the north nave arcade in 1988, summarized by M. R. McCarthy in 'The Origins and Development of the Twelfth-Century Cathedral Church at Carlisle', in *The Archaeology of Cathedrals*, ed. T. Tatton-Brown and J. Munby, Oxford University Committee for Archaeology, XLII (Oxford 1996), 31–45, 36, 43. See also n. 41 above.

The Romanesque Fabric of Carlisle Cathedral

RICHARD PLANT

*The Romanesque fabric of Carlisle Cathedral survives in a very fragmentary state, and
has been comparatively little studied. While certain aspects of its original form can only
be recovered through further excavation, careful examination of the remaining masonry
can reveal something of its architectural affiliations and a number of hitherto unnoticed
aspects of its design. The church, largely built during the first half of the 12th century,
appears to draw on building practice of the western part of England and of the north-
east. It had a crossing in which the arches were lower than the vessels to which they led,
and hence falls into a small group of larger 12th-century churches which shared this
feature.*

INTRODUCTION

THE Romanesque fabric of Carlisle Cathedral has attracted less attention than that of
most others in England, probably because of the poor state of its preservation. Nothing
remains of the choir, but part of the crossing although not the tower, one transept, and
two bays of the truncated nave, the easternmost of which is marked by subsidence,
survive.[1] It would be hard to argue that what remains represents the most immediately
enticing example of 12th-century Romanesque, giving, as it does, an impression of
extreme plainness. However, the building presents a number of intriguing problems of
interpretation, and in the absence of a well-developed local tradition of Romanesque
stone building, its architectural affiliations have to be sought beyond the immediate
vicinity. This paper will start with a description of the fabric, along with a discussion
of what archaeology has revealed, before putting the building into the wider context of
English 12th-century architecture.

THE EAST END

THE eastern arm has completely disappeared, though this has not, of course, stopped
speculation as to its original form. The most assured statement is by Ferguson in 1898,
who claimed that during the time of the restorations of the 1850s the foundations of the
east end had been uncovered, and it was 'apsidal, or circular at the east end and eighty
feet in length'.[2] Bulmer, writing in the 1930s, claimed that he had found the springing
of the apse in the footings under the choir stalls, giving a choir length of two bays,
rather shorter than Ferguson's east end which, at that length, would probably have had
three bays.[3] My own attempt to locate this springing proved fruitless, as did that of
McCarthy. Rather damningly, Bulmer himself altered, without comment, the plan of
the Romanesque church in his 1949 publication of the Gothic church, extending the
choir by one bay, though in his text it remained at two.[4]

The building itself offers only ambiguous information. The Early English choir, discussed elsewhere in this volume by Jennifer Alexander, was begun at its north-west corner outside the line of the Romanesque choir, allowing the old choir to remain in use. The south aisle, which was built on the same line as the Romanesque aisle, shows a number of changes of window pattern, possibly indicating a pause at a point where the new work encountered the old. However, this raises too many possibilities to be useful; the last bay to continue the window pattern of the north aisle is the fifth bay from the west, the four bays following to the west of this having a variety of arrangements of lancets. Unfortunately, even this *terminus* proves unreliable, as the Early English appearance of the fifth window is the product of restoration; up to 150 years ago there was a perpendicular window in this position.[5] Even assuming that by chance the restorers had provided an accurate reproduction of the 1220 state of affairs, we would still not know whether the new work altered one bay to the east of the old, at the point where the new work joined the old, or indeed whether the aisles terminated at the same point as the central vessel.

More information about the choir can be gained from remains within the building. The choir south aisle entrance survives from the Romanesque period, as, concealed behind the choir stalls and organ loft, do parts of the former entrance to the north choir aisle, where a base is preserved under the dean's stall, and a capital can be seen on the stairs rising to the organ loft. The entrance to the south choir aisle from the south transept is of an outer square order, on both faces, with an inner order of a soffit roll on a deep dosseret, which has hollow chamfers on each side. Each order is supported by scalloped capitals, five heavy bulbous double scallops with thick spur-like fillets between them, but more ornate multi-scallops on the choir aisle wall side. Above this there is a fairly narrow blocked opening, the top of which is cut by the Gothic vault of the choir aisle, which once presumably led to the middle storey of the choir. Since the choir was enlarged to the north during the Gothic rebuilding, traces of the aisle opening and of the opening to the intermediate storey can be seen on the west wall of the main vessel. The top of this upper opening has a lintel and a tympanum, composed of several stones, below an arch (Fig. 1). This is an unusual position for a tympanum (a rare parallel is at St Andrew's in Scotland), and this level of elaboration suggests that the exit from the nave gallery was of some importance, despite its narrowness and the unpromising passage on to which it leads.[6] Above this is the scar of a roof, presumably that of the Romanesque period. There is no sign of a vault for the intermediate storey, suggesting that, like the nave, the choir had an unvaulted gallery.

TRANSEPT AND CROSSING

OF the two arms of the transept, that on the south is much better preserved, the north transept having been partly destroyed by the collapse of the tower in 1380. The impression the south transept gives is of massiveness and austerity, though the thickness of the wall is, at 81 inches (2.06 m), not completely disproportionate to the thickness of the plinth of the nave arcade which is 76 inches (1.93 m) (Fig. 2). The elevation is, however, very plain: although a passage runs through the thickness of the walls at roughly the same height as the nave gallery and the openings over the choir aisle, it is only visible through three openings, one in the east wall at the south end, and two in the west, at the south and north ends. The former is in front of a window, the latter in front of the (reconstructed) entrance to the nave gallery. In all earlier English transept passages at triforium level, from the earliest surviving at St Alban's onwards, these

FIG. 1.   Carlisle Cathedral: west wall of choir, detail
Photograph: Richard Plant

passages open through an arcade to the interior of the church, though the scheme was somewhat reduced at Chester St Werburgh's.[7]

The transept had no aisles; the east wall of the south transept has two openings at ground-storey level, one to the choir aisle and one to a chapel. The choir aisle opening, whose counterpart on the north side survives though blocked, has the only chevron on the interior of the building, a hollow and a roll of centrifugal chevron not projecting from the blocks into which it is carved. The lack of chevron is one aspect that marks the interior of the cathedral as being unusually plain for a major 12th-century building.

The chapel opening is of two plain orders; the chapel is now Gothic, but evidence excavated in the 19th century on the north side suggests that it opened to an unusually small apse. Foundations for an apse with a diameter of only 7 feet 9 inches (2.35 m) were excavated under the north choir aisle, giving a depth of the apse of only about 4 feet (1.2 m).[8] This implies that some part of the transept must have been taken up when any altar placed in this apse was in use. Transeptal apses are not uncommon in English Romanesque great churches, usually providing enough liturgical space not to infringe on the transept. Occasionally, however, one finds, as at Hereford Cathedral,

FIG. 2.   Carlisle Cathedral: south
transept, looking south-east
Photograph: Richard Plant

provision for altars against the east wall of the transept. Above the openings to aisle
and chapel is a string-course, which has sagged markedly towards the crossing, in
indication of the subsidence that plagued the building. The wall above is quite plain
apart from an unadorned opening to the passage already mentioned. Above this is the
clerestorey string-course, and above this string the stone used changes from a pinkish
colour to grey on all sides of the transept. The clerestorey, which has a wall passage,
has two windows on both east and west walls, with a large opening in front of the
window flanked by smaller arches on the internal face of the passage, in the standard
Anglo-Norman fashion. The arch of the window opening has an angle roll, the small
arch-heads are monoliths. These arcades, which are separated by stretches of plain
wall, are supported by monolithic columns, with capitals of a variety of scallop and
other forms, markedly more elaborate than those found below. The north capital of
the south triplet on the west side is a cat head, swallowing the column (Fig. 3). All the
monolithic heads of the minor arches are incised with lines, as if to give the impression
that they are composed of several stones, but on one of them enough fragments of paint
survive to show that they were in fact painted white, with red lines marking the (false)

Fig. 3.   Carlisle Cathedral: south transept, clerestory capital, west side, second from south

Photograph: Richard Plant

masonry joints. Other areas of paint in the clerestorey show that the barrel vault was also painted white and marked out with false masonry lines, and one of the nave capitals retains some traces of paint. There is a change in construction technique between the passage at the lower level and the clerestorey. On the lower level the voussoirs of the arches into the passages are of rubble, while in the clerestorey they are of cut stone.

In the south wall the Romanesque clerestorey has been replaced by a Gothic three-light window, but Romanesque shafts survive at the east and west corners, suggesting the arrangement of the south wall was not radically different to that of the east and west walls. Below this the south wall is partly rebuilt, with a Victorian portal filling the lower section, though antiquarian images give no indication of there having been one there previously. The west wall has two windows, at lower and intermediate levels, at its southern end. They are, however, not aligned with the clerestorey window above, being pushed slightly to the north, perhaps to light the chapel opposite. The opening in the intermediate storey is stepped, perhaps, like a splay, to give more light to the chapel opposite.

The crossing forms an irregular square. The openings of the crossing are wider north-south than east-west, with a width of about 21 feet (6.4 m) north-south and about 14 feet 6 inches (4.42 m) east-west, that is the openings to the transept, although the main vessel of the nave is the same as the width of the transept. The difference is only partly caused by the absence of any shafts on the north and south faces of the crossing piers, which were almost certainly omitted to accommodate the choir stalls running into through the crossing and into the nave. The crossing piers are much longer east-west than north-south.

The capital type of the shafts of the crossing arches is slightly different to those of the lower section of the transept, with multi-scallop capitals, usually with the shields marked out with an incision, a fairly common type. The bases of the shafts have spurs. More remarkable is that the Romanesque capitals of the crossing are set very low, while the Gothic crossing arches spring from a much higher level (Col. Pl. II). No capitals survive for the north-south arches, but the abaci of those opening to the transept are at the same height as the string-course of the intermediate storey. The abaci are continued around on to the inner faces of the crossing piers as a short string-course, which is approximately at the same height as the nave gallery string. Pevsner claimed that the crossing capitals had been reset, but the continuation of this string course argues against this interpretation.[9] The current crossing post-dates the collapse of the tower; the masonry above the abaci and string courses on both sides of each crossing pier appears to be from this period, or at least of a different character to that of the Romanesque masonry below. On the east and west faces the shafts are continued, but the masonry is more finely jointed and the shafts have a slightly different profile; on the north and south faces the stretch of wall is composed of longer, and deeper, blocks of stone. The obvious interpretation of the transept capitals is that an arch sprang from the capitals, at the height of the gallery sill. This would almost certainly have been for a low diaphragm crossing arch. The alternative explanation, of a transept platform, like those once at the abbey church of Jumièges among others,[10] must be discounted. There is no evidence for platforms elsewhere in the transepts, and the capitals are too high for a platform at gallery height, the usual arrangement.

The case for reconstructing the east and west crossing arches is less clear. The western crossing arch is the easier to examine (Fig. 4), where the masonry immediately above the Romanesque string-course is somewhat irregularly coursed, and the point of a half-cone shaped corbel sits immediately above the string. This in turn supports the shaft which, in turn, supports the crossing arch. To judge from the coursing, the shaft and walling around it were built together, and form a straight joint with the neighbouring (Romanesque) nave masonry. The alternatives for the east and west arches are that the crossing rose to the height of the main vessel, and the inner faces of the crossing were rebuilt when the tower was rebuilt, or that the crossing arch sprang from somewhere close to the height of the string course. There is no parallel for a crossing with low transeptal arches and full-height east-west arches — unless the transepts themselves were low — that I know of. It would, however, be unusual to spring the crossing arches directly from the string-course; on the other hand the lowest courses above the string and of the corbel are somewhat thinner than those of the masonry above. It is possible that they represent a survival of Romanesque masonry and the crossing arches sprang from capitals supported on conical corbels, an arrangement that can be paralleled at the roughly contemporary church of St Bartholomew in Smithfield, also an Augustinian house. This reconstruction, which seems the most likely, is not unproblematic, the springing of the arches to nave and

FIG. 4.   Carlisle Cathedral: north-
west crossing pier, south face, detail
Photograph: Richard Plant

choir would have been higher than that of those to the transepts, and, coupled with the greater width of the openings to nave and choir would have resulted in higher crossing arches to these vessels.[11]

THE NAVE

ONLY a stump of the nave survives; two bays, with the remains of two columns preserved in the exterior buttressing of the west wall (Fig. 5). The nave was destroyed in the middle of the 17th century, and there has been persistent debate as to how many bays once existed, the most recent view being that there were seven.[12] The only detailed view of the church before the destruction of the nave, that by Daniel King, is of little help, since, as Browne Willis said, 'might pass as well for any other church as this'.[13]

    The length of the two remaining bays is markedly dissimilar, 9 feet 8 inches (2.94 m) for the east bay, 11 feet 3 inches (3.42 m) for the second bay, measured base to base. This, along with the sagging of the masonry at this point, has resulted in a distortion in the construction of the first arcade arch, which appears slightly stilted. However, the

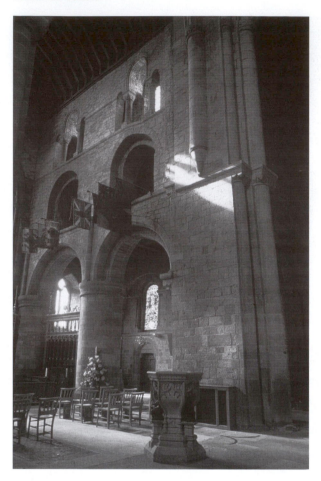

FIG. 5. Carlisle Cathedral: nave, north side

Photograph: Richard Plant

disparity is probably because of the length of the western crossing piers, which project into the nave. The interior elevation is of three storeys, the intermediate storey is a gallery with a wooden roof and a wooden floor; the clerestorey is much as it is in the transepts. Once more a change from pinkish to grey stone can be noted, though in the nave it is lower down the elevation than in the transepts, between arcade and gallery.

Excavation of the footings of nave arcade and aisle walls led to the observation that they were of one build.[14] They are very different in thickness, the nave plinths are 76 inches (1.93 m), the aisle walls are a meagre 30 (0.76 m), and there is a difference in the way in which the aisle walls on each side are treated. Both have been heavily reworked, but on both aisles there are triple responds, as if in anticipation of an aisle vault. There are no vaults; on the south side the responds are topped by rather messy replacement masonry; on the north side the responds were joined by super arches, indicating that by this point no vault was intended.

The nave has cylindrical piers, with triple responds on the west side of the crossing piers. Above the piers half-shafts rise to the height of the gallery string, which runs over them, but no further, and there is no evidence that they ever continued any higher.

Above the nave-side responds on the west side of the crossing piers there are quadrant shafts, which almost fill the angle between the arcade wall, and the crossing pier, which projects inside the line of the arcade wall. This too ceases, with a capital, at gallery string-course level, but above there is a pilaster. This masonry is very cracked, and since the quadrant shafts course badly with the surrounding masonry they may have been inserted to mask cracks between the nave arcade, which sags at this point, and the crossing pier. Both nave and gallery arcades are of two orders, the nave with hollow chamfers on the corners, the gallery plain, except for an offset at the springing point. This may have been used for centring for construction of the arches, a technique also found for the barrel vaults in the gallery at St John's in the Tower of London. The gallery openings, which are unsubdivided, are smaller than those of the arcade. Billings's illustrations of the cathedral show the east side of the north clerestorey window sagging and distorted; this is not apparent now, the masonry appears to be Romanesque, and nor are there signs of a repair, though it is difficult to examine close to. However, the eastern shaft of the clerestorey arcade is set lower than that to its west, and since they are the same length, the arch framing the window is asymmetrical, a solution also employed where subsidence affects the transepts. This disjunction is very apparent on the exterior, and, since it affects the string-course east and west of the window it cannot be the result of a localised repair.[15]

The windows of both aisles are modern replacements; on the north are Victorian Romanesque, on the south side Gothic.[16] Aisle responds and entrances have multi-scallop capitals, but the entrances differ from those in the choir aisles in having paired rolls with an arris on the soffit and no chevron. The spurs on the bases disappear after the first bay west of the crossing. Unusually the north and south arcade capitals do not match, and there are no decisive chronological features to determine which came first. On the south side, the side of the cloister, which may suggest chronological primacy if any existed, there are multi-scallop capitals, on the north simple moulded capitals.

EXTERIOR (Fig. 6)

ON the exterior (Fig. 6) of the transepts the distinction between grey and pink masonry that was apparent on the interior can also be observed, but on the exterior it is four or five courses below the clerestorey sill. The transept clerestorey has broad pilaster buttresses, as does the north nave aisle, though not the south one, nor the nave clerestorey. Although much of the corner buttressing of the transepts is Gothic, the inner parts especially higher up, are clearly of the Romanesque style. The south aisle has a blocked door in the east bay. At the base of the west side of the transept, partly obscured by gravel, there is a plinth of large blocks, with a raised chamfered course.

All the clerestorey windows are decorated, though the lower windows of the transept are not. These are of two plain orders, and are set toward the middle of the transept with respect to the clerestorey window above, perhaps to light the chapel opposite. The clerestorey windows have an inner splayed order, and an outer order on monolithic shafts (many of them renewed), of a roll and hollow, fringed with geometric ornament. The decoration is a varied, but systematic, billet on the east side of the transept, and triangular pieces, somewhat like chevrons with stepped edges giving a fret motif, on the west (Fig. 7). The nave clerestorey has two similar forms of chevron, on the east windows there is a billet hood-mould, and point-to-point chevron on the order, on the west windows a row of lateral chevron has replaced the billet, while there is a row of frontal chevron in a hollow on the face of the order, the two rows of chevron forming a

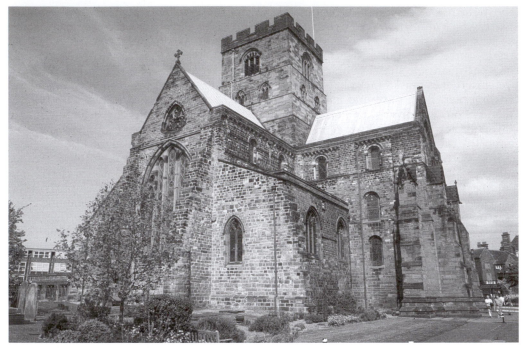

FIG. 6.   Carlisle Cathedral: exterior from west
Photograph: Richard Plant

poor approximation of a point to point arrangement. The two decorative types match on opposite sides of the nave. The corbel table is unusual, consisting of triangular wedges with paired rolls on the diagonals, almost like a section through a set of mouldings, with a head at the base (Fig. 7). The corbels encroach on the outer order of the clerestorey windows, a miscalculation it is hard to explain.

Finally, at the west end of the nave two columns are preserved in the buttressing of the west wall. The southern one has inverted sections of a capital on it. This is a multi-scallop capital: the scallops have sheaths, which have stepped edges, somewhat like the fret motif on the transept clerestorey windows. While there is no reason to assume that this capital comes from this column, it is on the southern side where multi-scallops are found on the interior.

DISCUSSION: SOURCES, DATE, AND SIGNIFICANCE

THERE appears to have been no well-established tradition of masonry architecture in the region before the cathedral. The two most local Romanesque buildings, the castle, discussed elsewhere by John Goodall, and the parish church of Warwick, discussed by Malcolm Thurlby, share constructional traits found at the cathedral, notably the monolithic arch heads found in the clerestorey. At Warwick these are found on the exterior decoration of narrow blind arcades on the apse. This has led to the suggestion that a similar decoration might have been found on the apse of the cathedral, although it is hard to imagine it scaled up, or indeed on the apses of the transepts.[17] The church

FIG. 7.   Carlisle Cathedral: south transept, exterior, south-west window
Photograph: Richard Plant

at Warwick appears to have been built by masons who had been active at the cathedral, the arch at the west of the church has a roll on the soffit flanked by hollow chamfers, like the entrance to the choir aisle at the cathedral, and spur bases, both motifs found around the crossing of the cathedral. The church at Warwick is not firmly dated, but a charter of Henry I confirmed the possession of the parish, and its *capella*, to St Mary in York in 1131–32.[18] The only documentary evidence we have for construction at the cathedral is from a grant of £10 by Henry I to the priory for works on the church in 1029.[19] As will be seen, nothing in the surviving fabric, of which the east end, usually the earliest part, is destroyed, precludes a starting date in the 1120s. This would indicate that the present cathedral was begun to house the Augustinian canons, who were settled there in 1122, although it has been argued that the idea to found a diocese centred on Carlisle dates from when the house was founded. While an earlier church for the canons cannot be ruled out, the only parallel example of a pre-existing foundation being raised to episcopal status, at the monastery in Ely, entailed no major change in scheme.[20]

Internal evidence for the chronology of the building suggests a progression from east to west as would be expected. The capitals of the crossing are more complex than those of the choir aisles, and those of the nave more complex still, at least those that are decorated. The change in materials from pink to grey stone offers only rather ambiguous evidence. The masonry change is at slightly different levels on the interior and exterior of the transept, at the clerestorey sill on the interior, below it on the exterior, suggesting that it perhaps does not represent a break at a convenient point, and may simply represent a change in resources. Likewise, although the change in material comes at an apparently more logical point in the nave, at the gallery sill, this is too low to mark the point at which enough of the nave was built to buttress the tower, a relatively common point for a pause in construction.[21] Should this change in masonry amount to a break in construction, we are presented with contradictory evidence about the work that followed. In the transept clerestorey we find the most elaborate capitals, along with those in the nave clerestorey, while on the nave gallery wall, the half-shafts of the arcade spandrels were seemingly abandoned, and the gallery arcade itself is unusually plain. The clerestorey, however, must have been built after the subsidence had affected the masonry below. Subsidence mainly affects the areas around the crossing piers, and the shafts for the clerestorey nearest the piers are set lower than their neighbours, though they are of the same length, resulting in asymmetrical arches framing the clerestorey windows. The clerestorey capitals, while more elaborate than those below, do not display any features, such as water-leaf, which point to a date well into the second half of the 12th century.

The absence of earlier local buildings leads us to look for buildings outside the region for the sources of its various features. Uncertainty about the form of the east end is unhelpful, and the plan of the church in general is not exceptional, except in the rather negative aspect of the smallness of the transept chapels. Columnar naves are more common in the west of England, and either the west, or the north-east of England are the most obvious places geographically to look for parallels to the features of the cathedral; it seems that both provide either sources or parallels to the decorative repertoire.

While columnar elevations were widespread in English Romanesque, they were probably more common in the west than the east, and appeared there at Shrewsbury, Gloucester and Tewkesbury. These churches also had plain moulded capitals rather than decorated ones, like those on the north side of the nave. The alternative form, rings of scallops, is also common, although to find the two together is more uncommon, though can be paralleled at Hereford Cathedral, begun probably between 1109 and 1115.[22]

The fret motif, found both on the transept west clerestorey and the inverted capital outside the south arcade, can also be found in Herefordshire. At Hereford Cathedral once more, a number of fragments with this motif are built into the aisle wall above the vault, a result of the rebuilding of the nave after the collapse of the western tower in 1786. These fragments may have once formed the gallery string-course of the nave, if evidence from antiquarian drawings can be believed, and a similar motif is found on a capital in the nave.[23] The motif was also found in a few other places in the vicinity of Hereford, in Monmouth, for example.[24] There are more western parallels; scallop capitals with thick fillets between the cones occur at Hereford, Gloucester and Swindon (Glos.). The motif of the column swallower found in the transept clerestorey is also more widely found in western England, forming part of the repertoire of motifs found there with some link to the west of France. There are cat-heads swallowing columns at Elkstone in Gloucestershire and Leominster in Herefordshire.[25]

Outside the west country, a number of parallels can be found in the north-east. The unusual corbels, with paired rolls in section, are closely comparable to those at Adel church, near Leeds, probably from the mid-12th century, and thus possibly later than Carlisle.[26] Hollow chamfers, or chamfers of any sort on arches or ribs, are surprisingly rare, though standard on string-courses. A comparison from an early date comes from the arcade arches at Durham Cathedral, easily missed in the multiplicity of mouldings

FIG. 8.   Carlisle Cathedral: nave, south-west pier, capital
Photograph: Richard Plant

there. Another Durham feature is the form of the external plinth, with a raised course of masonry, which is also found on the pier plinths there. It did not originate at Durham, being found at Jumièges Abbey (Seine-Maritime) and Verdun Cathedral (Meuse) earlier in the 11th century, and later at Selby Abbey and, on the western side of the Pennines, at Kirby Lonsdale as noted by Thurlby in this volume. Finally there is one relatively unusual form of scallop capital, that at the east end of the south nave arcade has leaves between the cones of the scallops (Fig. 8); something similar occurs in the bell-ringer's chamber in the central tower of Winchester Cathedral, rebuilt in the first half of the 12th century after the collapse of the tower in 1107, and on more elaborate capitals, at Bridlington, where the fragmentary remains date from the second half of the 12th century.[27]

This range of buildings, found in the west or north-east, all date from the late 11th or first half of the 12th century, the exceptions being at Adel and Bridlington. Beyond these smaller details, three major aspects of the design stand out which are not so easily localised. The first is perhaps a rather negative one, the great plainness of the building, not only the nave but also the transept, which is most unusual in having three storeys, but only showing two of them. There may have been a self-conscious programme of austerity at work here, though its impact was rather patchy, as the chevron on the choir aisles and the clerestorey exterior shows.[28] The reason may be the very practical one of limited funds for the new diocese.

Shafts rising from the abacus of the columns, such as those in the nave, were a relatively common form of bay articulation in 12th-century buildings. These appear at

Colchester St Botolph's, as pilasters, not shafts, Melbourne in Derbyshire, in the Peterborough transepts, but not the choir, in the nave of Rochester, where they have been cut back to the same height as those at Carlisle, Malmesbury Abbey, Oxford St Frideswide's and Tutbury in Staffordshire, and this list is probably not exhaustive. These buildings span the first half of the 12th century, and continue into the second, when the form also appeared in Gothic buildings. As well as providing bay articulation for churches with columnar supports, some of them, Oxford for example, support roof joists. The shafts at Carlisle do not rise high enough for this to happen, and one can only imagine that the shafts were abandoned part of the way through construction; once more, one can only speculate as to the reason; they can hardly have been a costly element of the building process.

The phenomenon of a crossing with low arches is one which, when noted in 12th-century architecture in Britain, is treated as somewhat anomalous. In general the crossings of major Romanesque churches, where they survive, rise to the full height of the clerestorey, though occasionally, as, for example, at Chichester Cathedral, they spring from somewhat lower than the clerestorey sill. The result, even when the arch itself rises to the height of the clerestorey arches, is still something that would appear to be a diaphragm arch, separating the crossing from the arms of the building, but much less apparent, obstructive indeed, than those at Carlisle. However, a number of other examples of low crossings in Britain have been discussed recently, at Worksop Priory, at St John's in Chester, and at Dunfermline. In addition to these, Melbourne in Derbyshire has a low crossing, though there, as shall be seen, it has a functional purpose. While low crossings occur in pre-Romanesque architecture, sometimes with very restricted openings,[29] the immediate background is in Normandy. At La Trinité in Caen (Calvados), begun around 1060, the arches to the transepts are much lower than the main vessel, and springers for the arches on the east and west sides, which were subsequently heightened, are still visible.[30] The arrangement was repeated at Graville Ste-Honorine (Seine-Maritime), of around 1100.[31] At La Trinité the longitudinal arches were raised when a vault was inserted in the 12th century.[32] Perhaps partly for this reason the low crossing form is seen as somewhat old-fashioned, and its alteration at La Trinité cannot have been separated by many years from the construction of the crossing at Carlisle.

Low crossings of 12th-century date in Britain have, therefore, appeared to require an attempt at special explanation. For Dunfermline, Eric Fernie tentatively postulated that it was a response to the unusually narrow nave.[33] Richard Gem, noting that the crossing arches spring from half-way up the gallery level at Chester St John's, considered it possible that this was an alteration from the original scheme, and 'a reduction in the intended ambition of the primary scheme'.[34] Finally, at Worksop Malcolm Thurlby suggested influence from Flanders, where a similar low set of crossing arches is to be found at Soignies, though this is not the standard form of crossing even there.[35] The final example, Melbourne in Derbyshire, is an exceptional case. The low crossing contains a passage, which connected, via the broad clerestorey (the building is of only two storeys) a western gallery with an upper chapel over the chancel. This unusual arrangement falls into the tradition of two-storeyed episcopal and royal chapels that goes back to Charlemagne's church at Aachen, and it can be argued that the arches of the crossing were kept low so that the passage would run at a continuous level from west to east. The church was given by the king to Bishop Athelwold of Carlisle in 1133, but it has been persuasively argued that the church pre-dates this, at least in its important parts.[36] The evidence presented above suggests that in part the cathedral does too, and this, along with the absence of a function for the low crossing at Carlisle, suggest the Melbourne crossing has no direct bearing on that at Carlisle.

Chester, begun perhaps around 1100, is the earliest of the other buildings in this group, Dunfermline being consecrated in 1150, and Worksop is also work of the 12th century. Of the four buildings the crossing at Carlisle is the lowest, the others have or had their springing in the gallery storey, rather than at its sill. All had columnar naves, but they are not otherwise easy to connect, although Worksop was also an Augustinian house, and they do not all obviously look to a common source. It cannot be argued that buildings are in other ways old-fashioned. Dunfermline, for example, with Scottish royal patronage, is clearly affiliated to Durham Cathedral. The employment of a low crossing appears, therefore to have been an acceptable alternative to a full-height one to 12th-century patrons and builders, even if it has hardly been recognised. It is possible, if not likely, that a number of others have been lost, and it may be that a Romanesque church of an earlier generation, perhaps more directly influenced by La Trinité in Caen made this an acceptable arrangement. There is little likelihood that architecture of the Anglo-Saxon period was being evoked, as the transeptal arrangements are otherwise close to those in other Anglo-Norman great churches.[37] The employment of an architectural form that appears anachronistic to us is a reminder both of the patchy state of our knowledge of the buildings of the period, and a warning against a straightforward model of the development of medieval architecture.

Carlisle Cathedral cuts against the grain of our expectations of 12th-century great church architecture in England. It does not partake in the elaborate decorative repertoire which became prevalent after the construction of Durham Cathedral from 1093, a choice perhaps influenced by financial considerations. It also employs an unusual form of crossing, one often thought old-fashioned in a 12th-century context, but which closer inspection reveals was present at a number of 12th-century sites. In the absence of a local building tradition the builders seem to have used motifs from the west side of the country, to the south of Carlisle, and from the north-east, the area from whose episcopal jurisdiction the diocese was carved.

ACKNOWLEDGEMENTS

In writing this short paper I have incurred a large number of debts: to John Goodall, Hazel Gardner, Ron Baxter and the Corpus of Romanesque Sculpture, Anna Eavis and family, Rita Wood, John McNeil, Jenny Alexander, Stuart Harrison and particularly to Canon David Weston who facilitated access to various parts of the building and, more importantly facilitated egress.

NOTES

1. The most recent general discussions have been, D. W. V. Weston, *Carlisle Cathedral History* (Carlisle 2000), esp. 10–12; M. R. McCarthy, 'The Origins and Development of the Twelfth-Century Cathedral of Carlisle', in *The Archaeology of Cathedrals*, ed. T. Tatton-Brown and J. Munby (Oxford 1996), 31–45, with a thorough description of the fabric. In more general studies it is usually noted, if at all, for its unusual status as an Augustinian Cathedral. Perhaps the fullest treatment of the building is that by R. W. Billings, *Architectural Illustrations, History and Descriptions of Carlisle Cathedral* (London 1840).

2. R. S. Ferguson, *Carlisle Cathedral* (London 1898), 26.

3. C. J. Bulmer, 'The Norman Priory Church at Carlisle', *Transactions Cumberland Westmorland Antiquarian Archaeological Society*, ns, XXXVII (1939), 56–66, at 58–59. Translating Ferguson's dimensions

into a number of bays is made difficult by the paucity of information; is 80 feet an internal or external dimension, and does he mean an apse-ambulatory or apses in echelon, and so on?

4. C. J. Bulmer, 'Carlisle Cathedral and its development in the Thirteenth and Fourteenth Centuries', *Transactions Cumberland Westmorland Antiquarian Archaeological Society*, ns, XXXXIX (1949), 87–117; McCarthy, 'Origins', 41–42.

5. Visible in Billings, *Architectural Illustrations*, pl. 22.

6. For English Romanesque tympana see D. B. C. Givans, 'English Romanesque Tympana: A Study of Architectural Sculpture in Church Portals *c*.1050–*c*.1200' (unpublished Ph.D. thesis, University of Warwick, 2001). For portals leading to service areas, usually stair-vices, Vol. 1, 106–07 and tables iiib and iiid.

7. For Chester see Richard Gem, 'Romanesque Architecture in Chester *c*. 1075 to 1117', *Medieval Archaeology, Art and Architecture at Chester*, ed. A. Thacker, BAA Trans., XXII (Leeds 2000), 31–44, esp. 35–36.

8. C. J. Ferguson, 'Carlisle Cathedral, Apse in the East Wall of the Transept', *Transaction Cumberland Westmorland Antiquarian Archaeological Society*, XIV (1897), 208–10. The broadest part was 6 inches to the east of the west side of the apse.

9. N. Pevsner, *Cumbria and Westmorland*, B/E (1967), 90.

10. Transept platforms were uncommon in the 12th century. E. C. Fernie, *The Architecture of Norman England* (Oxford 2000), 256. For a late example see J. S. Alexander and J. F. King, 'The Architecture and Romanesque Sculpture of Tutbury Priory', in *Staffordshire Histories: Essays in Honour of Michael Greenslade*, ed. P. Morgan and A. D. M. Phillips (Keele 1999), 13–46.

11. The problem of the disparity in height of (full height) crossing arches over unequal openings was resolved at St Bartholomew's by the use of pointed arches to the transepts, which raise the transept arches to the height of those to nave and choir. The earliest English pointed arches are generally taken to be the transverse vault arches in the nave at Durham Cathedral of before 1133.

12. On the circumstances of the destruction of the nave, D. R. Perriam, 'The Demolition of the Priory of St Mary, Carlisle', *Transactions Cumberland Westmorland Antiquarian Archaeological Society*, ns, LXXXVI (1987), 127–58; for the length of the nave see D. R. Perriam, 'The search for the west end of Carlisle Cathedral', *British Archaeology* (1989), 11, 19.

13. Browne Willis, *A Survey of the Cathedrals of York, Durham, Carlisle etc.* (London 1727), 285.

14. M. McCarthy, 'Excavations at Carlisle Cathedral', *Transactions Cumberland Westmorland Antiquarian Archaeological Society*, ns, LXXXVI (1987), 270–71; 'Origins', 43.

15. Billings, *Architectural Illustrations*, pls 3, 4, 5.

16. McCarthy, 'Origins', 35.

17. Pevsner, *Cumbria and Westmorland*, B/E, 198. The suggestion was made to him by Neil Stratford.

18. T. H. R. Graham, 'The Parish of Warwick', *Transactions Cumberland Westmorland Antiquarian Archaeological Society*, ns, XIII (1913), 87–112.

19. *Magnum Rotulum Scaccarii*, ed. J. Hunter (London 1833) 141.

20. See Franklin, this volume. For the foundation of the diocese, and the possibility it was intended from 1122, see H. Summerson, *Medieval Carlisle: The City and the Borders from the Late-Eleventh Century to the Mid-Sixteenth Century* (Kendal 1993), 30–33; for Ely and the integrity of its original ground plan, E. C. Fernie, 'Observations on the Norman plan of Ely Cathedral', in *Medieval Art and Architecture at Ely Cathedral*, ed. N. Coldstream and P. Draper, BAA Trans., II (Leeds 1979), 1–7.

21. Fernie, *Architecture of Norman England*, 294–95.

22. M. Thurlby, 'Hereford Cathedral: the Romanesque Fabric', *Medieval Art and Architecture at Hereford Cathedral*, ed. D. Whitehead, BAA Trans., XV (Leeds 1995), 15–28. The form of the Hereford east end and its close relative St John's, Chester, which both had a square east wall with parallel apses, should warn us of too-easy assumptions about the range of possibilities for the choir at Carlisle.

23. The string-course *in situ* is shown in a print of the ruined nave of Hereford Cathedral by James Wathen, published by Middiman and Jukes in 1789, reproduced in Thurlby, 'Hereford Cathedral', fig. iib, though rather indistinct.

24. M. Thurlby, *The Herefordshire School of Romanesque Sculpture* (Little Logaston 1999), 131–32, where Pauntly (Glos.) is also cited.

25. Amongst other examples are, Siddingham (Glos.) Avington and Great Shefford (Berks.). At Kilpeck (Herefs.) and Elkstone (Glos.) cat heads on the vault bosses perform a similar action with the ribs. A rarer example in the east of England is to be found in the nave dado arcade at Peterborough. In western France there is an example at Cunault, among other places, and the motif spread as far as northern Spain, where there is a Moorish column-swallower at Puente la Reina.

26. For Adel see N. Pevsner and E. Radcliffe, *Yorkshire: The West Riding*, B/E (1986) 338–39; P. Ryder, *Medieval Churches of West Yorkshire* (Hunstanton 1993), 28–30.

27. For a discussion of the Bridlington sculpture, in which it is dated to the third quarter of the 12th century, M. Thurlby, 'Observations on the Twelfth-Century Sculpture in Bridlington Priory', in *Medieval Art and Architecture in the East Riding of Yorkshire*, ed. C. Wilson, *BAA Trans.*, XII (1989), 33–43.

28. A taste for architectural austerity at non-Cistercian houses has been proposed by J. P. McAleer, 'Southwell Worksop, and Stylistic Tendencies in English Twelfth-Century Façade Design', in *Medieval Architecture and its Intellectual Context: Studies in Honour of Peter Kidson* ed. E. C. Fernie and P. Crossley (London and Ronceverte 1990), 61–72.

29. For the wider European context in the early Romanesque period see H. E. Kubach, *Romanesque Architecture* (London 1988), 22–24, and 48–50.

30. For La Trinité see M. Baylé, *La Trinité de Caen: sa place dans l'histoire de l'architecture et du décor romans* (Geneva 1979).

31. For Graville see M. Baylé, 'Graville Ste-Honorine', in *L'architecture normande au Moyen Age*, Vol 2, ed. M. Baylé (Caen 1997), 114–17.

32. The exact date is controversial; L. Grant, 'Architectural relationships between England and Normandy, 1100–1204', in *England and Normandy in the Middle Ages*, ed. D. Bates and I. Curry (London 1994), 117–29 at 127.

33. Although he observes that there is 'no obvious explanation for this oddity'; E. C. Fernie, 'The Romanesque Churches of Dunfermline Abbey', in *Medieval Art and Architecture in the Diocese of St Andrews*, ed. J. Higgitt, *BAA Trans.*, XIV (Leeds 1994), 30.

34. Gem, 'Romanesque Architecture in Chester', 40.

35. M. Thurlby, in *Southwell and Nottinghamshire Medieval Art, Architecture and Industry*, ed. J. S. Alexander, *BAA Trans.*, XXIII (Leeds 1998), 101–10, esp. 103. The other British example he cites, Lindisfarne, had an elevation which was also exceptional in other ways. Soignies is a building the dating of which is highly controversial; it has been argued that some of its elements, including pier alternation and a gallery, derive from Norman architecture; J. C. Ghislaine, *La Collégiale romane de Soignies et ses trésors* (Gembloux 1975); X. Barral i Altet, *Belgique Romane* (La Pierre-qui-Vire 1989), 67–70.

36. R. Gem, 'Melbourne Church of St Michael and St Mary', *Archaeol. J.*, 146 (1989); Supplement: The Nottingham Area, 24–29; see also Fernie, *Architecture of Norman England*, 239–42, where a number of other examples of low crossings in smaller churches are also noted.

37. E. C. Fernie, *The Architecture of the Anglo Saxons* (London 1983), 112–36. Stow is perhaps the best parallel Fernie, *Architecture of Norman England*, 241, n. 16 adds Newton, in Norfolk.

The Construction of the Gothic Choir of Carlisle Cathedral, and the Evidence of the Masons' Marks

JENNIFER S. ALEXANDER

The Gothic choir was rebuilt during the 13th century on a new axis, set further north than its 12th-century predecessor. The north transept was also enlarged at this date and given an eastern aisle, whereas the south transept merely had its apsed chapel replaced by a square one. Fire in 1292 destroyed the choir, although its aisles were saved, and rebuilding took place over the next sixty years. The eastern aisle of the transept survived the fire but was damaged in the partial collapse of the tower in 1380 and not rebuilt. The 13th-century choir arcade arches were re-erected on new piers, the aisle vaults rebuilt using the original ribs, and the arcades and aisles extended one bay to meet the presbytery east wall. Here a radically different method of vaulting was started, but abandoned, and instead the new work was carefully integrated into the old. The progress of reconstruction was smooth with no obvious breaks and analysis of the masons' marks enables its sequence to be demonstrated.

THE choir of Carlisle Cathedral is an imposing eight-bay building with its east wall filled by an elaborate window that was constructed in the 13th century and rebuilt in the 14th (Fig. 1). It dominates the cathedral by its sheer size and overshadows the reduced 12th-century nave. There have been few studies of the choir, apart from comments on the east window, and the architectural literature makes little reference to it. The most complete account remains that of Robert William Billings published with his superb drawings and plans in 1840.[1] Geographically the building is isolated, the county is large and remote, and there were few other monastic sites or major churches that had building operations at a similar time to Carlisle's. Calder Abbey was built during the first half of the 13th century, and there may have been an exchange of architectural ideas between the two sites, but contact would have been difficult as it is situated about 90 km (60 miles) away on the other side of the Cumbrian mountains.[2]

The Romanesque choir was demolished by the builder of its 13th-century replacement and no trace of it remains above ground east of the crossing, but it is reasonable to assume that it was shorter than its successor. Following standard practice, the 12th-century canons' stalls extended westwards through the crossing to create a ritual choir that ended in the eastern bays of the nave. The shafts on the east and west crossing arches are corbelled off at the base of the nave gallery to allow for the stalls. This arrangement became impossible when the decision was made to move the axis of the choir to the north as part of the 13th-century rebuilding. The canons' 46 stalls now occupy the first three bays of the choir, and although the stalls are not from the

FIG. 1.   Choir interior from the north-west
Photograph: Jennifer Alexander

13th century it is likely that the earlier stalls will have occupied the same site. By moving the stalls out of the nave and crossing the canons will not have sacrificed a great deal of space since their new choir extended for a further four or five bays. The canons would, however, have created a distinction between their more up-to-date and richly ornamented new choir and the rather austere architecture of the Romanesque nave, and would have increased the separation from the parish church situated there.

The change in axis has had such a profound effect on the layout of the building that the reasons behind it need investigation. It was not done, as most writers hold, to avoid the conventual buildings on the south side.[3] Were the new choir to have retained the nave axis then the new outside walls would have projected a mere 1.8 m (6 ft) beyond the limits of the Romanesque walls, hardly enough to justify a realignment. It is also not apparent which of the claustral buildings would have been affected by an encroachment since the cloister lay to the west of the transept and the buildings of its east range did not extend into the area affected. The reasons for the change in alignment lie elsewhere.

The main difference in the size of the new choir, apart from its length, is the width of the centre vessel; the side aisles are actually 300 mm (c. 1 ft) narrower than the nave aisles, and the piers are also 300 mm thinner, giving a rectangular aisle bay of c. 5.5 m by 5 m (18 ft by 16.5 ft). The nave aisle bays are 5.3 m squares (17.5 ft). The choir's central space is now 12.2 m (40 ft) wide against the nave's 8.5 m (28 ft). The decision to build the new south aisle wall on the site of its predecessor resulted in all the extra width being accommodated on the north side. Although the 13th-century masons were able to exploit the existing foundations on the south side, there was little room to work with on the north since the new piers reached to within 600 mm (c. 2 ft) of the inner face of the 12th-century wall and their foundations will have cut though the earlier footings.

The north transept was also affected and this provides an alternative explanation for the change in alignment. The north jamb of the arch from the transept into the old choir aisle was taken down, its arch filled in, and the small transept apse removed (Fig. 2).[4] However, instead of opening a new arch through the transept wall the master mason demolished the whole remaining east and north walls of the transept and built a two-bay arcade to provide the entrance to the choir aisle and to a new east chapel that rose to the same height as the aisle. He had to demolish most of the 12th-century transept since the new arcade pier was to be sited very close to the corner of the earlier transept, assuming that was the same size as the south transept, and its respond would lie outside the north-east corner.

The new chapel has since been demolished but its early Gothic arcade pier remains, partly encased in later masonry, together with one arch and the springing of the second (Fig. 3). The former existence of the chapel is shown by the vault respond at the west end of the north aisle arcade since this respond is really a pier. It is a slender clustered pier of six shafts attached to a section of wall turning northwards to form the east wall of the chapel (Fig. 4). The plinth beneath the wall arcade also turns north at this point. The pier supports the diagonal and transverse ribs of the chapel's vault, matched by ribs springing from the arcade pier (Fig. 5). The chapel must have been damaged by the collapse of the tower in 1380 and removed, and a blanking wall built at an angle across its entrance from the choir aisle. This wall, with its Perpendicular window, has been modified more than once; it now has a doorway to a vestry built on the site of the chapel in the 19th century, but before that date the main door into the cathedral was

FIG. 2.   Remains of 12th-century north
transept wall from nave aisle
Photograph: Jennifer Alexander

FIG. 3.   North transept arcade pier from choir
aisle
Photograph: Jennifer Alexander

sited beneath the window.[5] The irregular angle of the blanking wall allows the arcade
pier to remain entire and it may have been intended as a temporary repair.

Further evidence for the chapel can be seen on the exterior where the choir aisle
window arches continue on to a wall running north at a right angle. The first window
jamb has been cut back to form a buttress and the 19th-century vestry wall has been
built on top of the lower courses of the chapel east wall. The spur of its demolished
south-east corner can still be seen in the irregular coursing at the corner (Fig. 6). The
continuation of the choir aisle window arrangement also establishes that the transept
chapel was built as part of the same campaign as the aisle.

The transept arcade pier is made up of a coursed series of filleted shafts with smaller
keeled shafts inset into the angles and has a moulded capital with a substantial row of
nailhead in the abacus. The corbelled respond on the south repeats the nailhead in its
abacus but has a foliage capital with the same type of tightly bunched foliage as the
chapel pier. The respond's abacus originally continued to join that of the choir arcade
respond but it has been cut off and the stonework beneath it dressed back (Fig. 7). The
corbelled respond with its tightly bunched foliage also occurs in the nave of Lanercost
Priory from the middle of the 13th century, in a building described as being dependent
upon Carlisle.[6]

FIG. 4.   Choir north aisle from west with east
chapel pier
Photograph: Jennifer Alexander

FIG. 5.   Detail of east chapel pier
Photograph: Jennifer Alexander

The transept archmoulding is richly decorated with a row of large-scale dog-tooth and closely resembles the archmouldings of the main choir arcade, with the exception of its east bay. The rear face of the arch is simpler and has two orders of chamfer with two further chamfered orders added when the transept wall was thickened (Fig. 2). This was most probably part of the post-1380 repairs following the collapse of the upper parts of the tower. The repair work has also destroyed the evidence for the appearance of the 13th-century east wall above the arcade. The wall has been rebuilt very simply, and massively, and finishes just above the choir aisle roof. It clearly had a clerestory at some stage, certainly by the 14th century, since the blocked entrance to its passage can be seen in the choir clerestory passage at the west end.[7]

The south transept also has an early Gothic east chapel, but this was a much simpler reworking in which only the Romanesque apse was replaced and the 12th-century arches into the choir aisle and the chapel were retained.[8] The chapel was not intended to be integrated with the aisle, the new vault is not aligned with the aisle vault and is set lower (Fig. 8). The aisle's south-west vault respond is only that and supports no further ribs. Clearly the south transept was to be less imposing than the new north transept.

To allow for the extra length of the south wall of the new chapel both its outside walls have been offset by a few degrees to avoid the east wall meeting the aisle bay across a window. There is little correspondence between the exterior walls at this point;

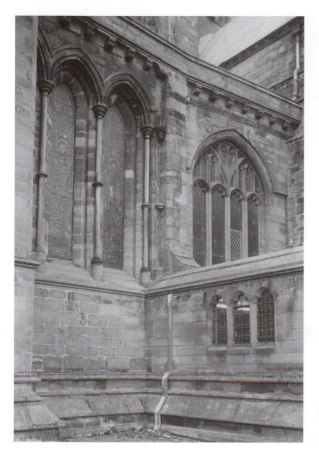

Fig. 6.   North aisle west end, junction with east chapel

Photograph: Jennifer Alexander

although the chapel window shares the design of the western aisle windows it sits lower, the corbel table is lower and their roofs never met. The roof scar on the transept below the Romanesque window is from the 13th-century aisle roof and would not have been needed if the two roofs were on the same level (Fig. 9). The evidence strongly suggests that the south transept chapel was not planned with the south aisle but was built after it.

The choir aisles have seven bays of wall arcades with cinquefoil-headed moulded arches on shafts under a string course below the windows. The window arrangements differ with the north side consistent except for its east bay, while the window designs on the south side are more varied. On the north side the windows are paired lancets flanked by blind arches at the ends of the bays, ornamented by *en délit* shafts with rings on both the interior and exterior. The flanking arches on the interior are dropped on one side to bring their capitals level with those of the vault responds and all the shaft rings are set at abacus level (Fig. 10). These arches are further integrated with the vault responds; the capital repeats the form of the respond capitals as part of a subtle alternation scheme in which moulded and foliage capitals are alternated for the vault shafts, with the result that each bay is a mirror image of its neighbour. The pattern stops after the sixth respond with the seventh respond, that is the east chapel pier,

FIG. 7.   North aisle west end arch into transept
Photograph: Jennifer Alexander

FIG. 8.   South aisle from west with arch into
transept chapel
Photograph: Jennifer Alexander

repeating the foliage capital. The north wall arcade has a row of dog-tooth in the arch heads and a narrow row is also included in the window arches.

The third bay from the east had a Perpendicular-style window with a raised parapet that was replaced in Ewan Christian's restoration by a replica of the arrangement in the adjacent bay. It was matched by a similar five-light window on the south side and both served to provide extra light for the high altar that was situated in the third bay.[9] The next bay to the east has only three arches to its wall arcade with a section of blank wall beyond, the most eastern of these arches is a blocked piscina that has been converted to a cupboard.

The south wall arcade is similar, although the dog-tooth row is omitted from the arches and all the vault respond capitals are moulded after the second bay. A filled-in piscina is evident in the second bay, as on the north side. The windows of the south aisle after bay two are not the same as those on the north side. Bay three is Ewan Christian's replica of bay two and bays four to seven have grouped lancets under a single head. Progress of construction was east to west with a change now visible in bay four where the grouped lancets have part of the rear arch from the bay two design that has been modified to extend over the arched head; bays five to seven retain the same jamb moulding but it is extended upwards to form the window rear arch.

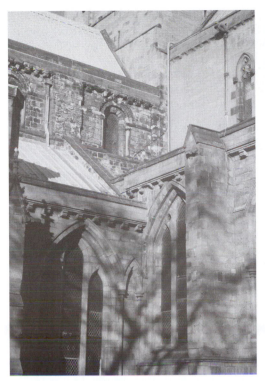

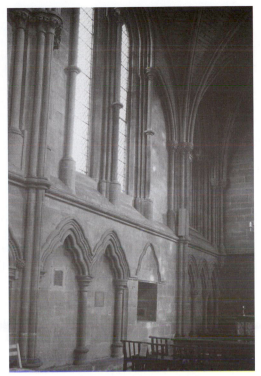

FIG. 9.   South aisle and transept east chapel
exterior

Photograph: Jennifer Alexander

FIG. 10.   North aisle east two bays

Photograph: Jennifer Alexander

Billings's engraving of the south side exterior before restoration shows a pair of shafts flanking the Perpendicular window in bay three on the south side. This presumably provided Christian with the evidence he needed to restore a two-light lancet window resembling that of bay two. However, similar shafts occur on the exteriors of bays four and six where the windows are grouped lancets and there must therefore be some doubt over the point at which the window design changed.[10]

The north transept east arcade and the choir aisles can be dated to the second quarter of the 13th century, with construction of the west end of the south aisle, and transept chapel, extended into the later 13th century. The aisles are related to buildings in Yorkshire and further south. The asymmetric arches flanking the windows are similar to those of the choir aisles at Beverley, in turn derived from Fountains, both from the early 13th century.[11] Carlisle differs, however, in bringing the vault shafts down to the ground and interrupting the wall arcade and there are also two aisle windows instead of the single window at Beverley and Fountains. Carlisle is closer to Beverley in its use of pointed rather than round flanking arches and in the greater amount of decoration, both in the pierced quatrefoils in the spandrels, and in the dog-tooth moulding on the wall arcade. The Cistercian abbey of Calder also has paired lancets and blind quatrefoils in the south transept, used with appropriately simpler chamfered arcade arches, from before 1240, and provides an exemplar within the region.[12] The transept pier is a northern type, its use of keeled diagonal and filleted main shafts is comparable to one of the pier types of the choir of Whitby from the early 13th century, and its capital with the heavy nailhead abacus and fillet continued up into the neck is very similar to capitals in the choir of Southwell, finished by 1240.[13]

The cinquefoil arches of the wall arcade are more commonly found in buildings in the south of England, they are present in the blind arcading on the Galilee porch at Ely from the early 13th century, the chapter house at Salisbury from the middle of the century, and used for the micro-architecture of the Purbeck arcade from the 13th-century shrine of St Swithun at Winchester. Further north cinquefoil arches can be seen on the west front of Newstead Priory, Nottinghamshire, from the end of the 13th century.

Documentary evidence for the building campaign is limited and circumstantial. Bulman has suggested that Hugh, the ex-abbot of Beaulieu who was bishop of Carlisle from 1218–23 after an interregnum, was a major force behind the building project which is probably correct, although responsibility for the works would have lain with the priory.[14] There was a gift of 20 marks from Henry III out of the issue of the bishopric to the priory for the works of the church in 1246 and the resolution of the dispute between bishop and priory in 1249 will have facilitated further work on the building operations. The choir campaign was clearly protracted and was probably brought to an end by Bishop Ireton, between 1280–92. At his first synod in 1280 he levied a diocesan-wide payment for work on the building and the following year petitioned for the gift of an advowson for funds. The presentation of a Becket relic before 1290 will have encouraged pilgrims, and an Indulgence of 1291 will also have generated revenue.[15]

The east bay of both choir aisles clearly differs from the other bays, most obviously in the windows, which have tracery of the first half of the 14th century (Fig. 11). The wall arcades are also of this period but match the 13th-century work closely, reproducing the moulded cinquefoil arches, but the shafts are now coursed in, not monoliths, heads appear as label stops and the arches are less pointed (Fig. 12). Slight changes are made to the sub-bases which are polygonal not round, and foliage capitals replace the moulded ones of the other bays. The vault responds differ only in having hollows between the shafts. It is clear that the east bay has been designed to integrate very closely with the work further west.

By contrast, the vault intended for the east bays shows a radically different, and uncompromising, attitude to the existing work. The main aisle vault is a simple quadripartite rib vault without bosses, except for three bays at the west end of the south side that have small bosses of single roses, sprung from responds. In the east bay, however, the vault springers emerge from the soffit of the archmoulding to create a completely new design for the east end (Fig. 13). The north bay has the rib crossed over part of the arch soffit, resembling the intersected moulding of the north chapel of Beverley St Mary from c. 1330–40 (Fig. 14), whereas the south does not (Fig. 15), but in both cases the ribs are then developed as flying, or skeletal ribs, without vault webs.[16] These occur on a small scale in the Easter Sepulchre at Lincoln from c. 1290, can also be found in the Southwell pulpitum from c. 1320–40 (Fig. 16), where in both cases the span is less than 2 m (c. 6.5 ft), and at Bristol in the ante-chapel to the Berkeley chapel where the vault measures about 2.5 m (8 ft). In each of these examples the vaults spring simply from corbels, or capitals. Flying ribs to span an aisle, that are integrated with archmouldings, would have been a new departure that would have been unprecedented in England in the first half of the 14th century.[17]

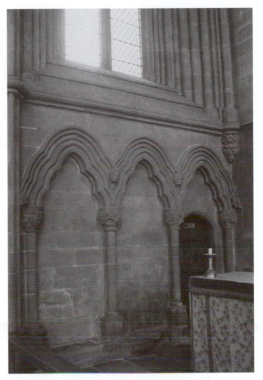

FIG. 11.   North aisle east end
Photograph: Jennifer Alexander

FIG. 12.   North aisle east bay wall arcade
Photograph: Jennifer Alexander

The new vault may represent the start of a remodelling of the aisle that would have involved replacing all the arcade arches and the aisle vault ribs but the scheme was abandoned before a single bay of vaulting had been raised. Instead a conventional rib vault was built over the east bay, but with the diagonal rib corbelled off awkwardly above the archmoulding (Fig. 11). On the south side a cranked section of rib had to be cut to align the diagonal rib above the pier. The new arch moulding itself was intended to spring from a corbelled shaft, still visible as a scar on the wall and easier to see in Billings's engraving, but this was changed to a corbel at capital height.[18] The north side has the same foliage as that used for the arcade capitals, the south side has a figure.

It is now possible to offer a reconstruction of the 13th-century aisles. The evidence in the second bay establishes that the aisle ended there. The extra width on the east side was taken up by the thickness of the end wall and its buttress on the exterior and there were altars in these two bays. In the 14th century it was decided to extend the aisles by one short bay on each side; Bulman suggested that this was to create a square ended building instead of one with a short projecting presbytery, by extending the aisles to meet the east wall.[19] Unfortunately the presence of 13th-century masonry cannot be identified in the centre of the east wall to test this theory due to 19th-century scraping of the surfaces. Bulman's theory is attractive, if only to explain why it was worth lengthening the aisles by less than a full bay. Two different designs were started, an

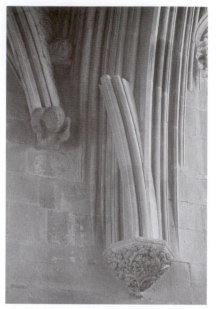

FIG. 13.   Detail of arcade arch, north
aisle east bay
Photograph: Jennifer Alexander

FIG. 14.   Beverley St Mary chancel
north chapel vault springer
Photograph: Jennifer Alexander

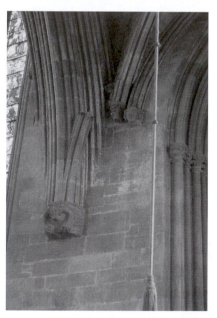

FIG. 15.   South aisle east end arcade
arch
Photograph: Jennifer Alexander

FIG. 16.   Southwell pulpitum vault
Photograph: Jennifer Alexander

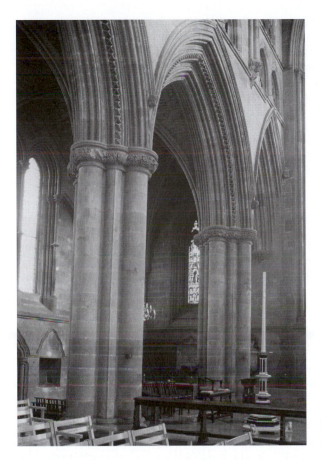

FIG. 17.   Choir north arcade east bays
Photograph: Jennifer Alexander

integration scheme to match the existing work in the aisle wall, and a radical new design for the arcade and vault, with the first design preferred.

The other structural element of the 13th-century choir to survive is the arches of the choir arcades (Fig. 17). The heavily moulded arches with a row of dog-tooth clearly belong to the same period as the choir aisles and have already been compared to the new arches in the north transept. Parallels for the use of dog-tooth in this way can be found in a number of buildings from the period *c.* 1220–60, such as the choir of Ely from 1234–52, Southwell choir from before 1240, or the Angel Choir at Lincoln after 1255.

Close examination of the arches reveals that they are crudely assembled with wide mortar joints that do not fit together well. The arch in bay two on the north side is particularly badly fitted. The moulding of the arcade east bay has a different profile, since it was made new at the time that the aisles were extended. There are also anomalies in the construction of the aisle vault, most noticeable at the west end of the north aisle, where the fit of the stones is badly managed. There we have the unusual situation of a pier and its respond well aligned but the transverse rib of the vault is twisted between the two. It is also apparent that the crown of the aisle vault sits some

400 mm (*c.* 16 in.) lower than the wall ribs and the arch mouldings. It would seem that the arcade arches and the aisle vaults have been taken down and rebuilt.

The rebuilding was necessitated by the devastating fire that swept through Carlisle, destroying much of the city in 1292. It was started outside the castle and spread eastwards, reducing the cathedral to ruins and destroying Ireton's own tomb.[20] If, as seems likely, the choir was wood roofed without a stone vault then the damage may well have been as catastrophic as that suffered by Canterbury in 1174. There Gervase's account tells of a fire starting in the roof under the leads and of the burning timbers falling on top of the choir stalls to create a conflagration that rose *c.* 7 m (*c.* 25 ft) and severely damaged the choir piers. The choir arcade was compromised by the damage to its piers and had to be taken down, but the outside walls of the aisles were saved and the new choir piers were raised on the sites of their predecessors.[21]

The extent of Carlisle's restoration shows that the damage may well have been as severe as Canterbury's. The arcade piers have all been replaced, and, as with the east bay of the aisles, care has been taken to integrate the new work by repeating elements from the earlier period. The new piers are clustered eight-lobe piers with fillets to the minor shafts with inhabited foliage capitals. The pier bases still retain a water-holding element but immediately beneath this moulding the lobed bases become polygonal and are clearly of a 14th-century date (Fig. 18). The capitals are carved with labours of the months and have the bubbly, post-naturalistic, foliage of the second quarter of the 14th century, seen in the Lady Chapel at Ely from the late 1320s and the Percy Tomb at Beverley from *c.* 1340–47.

Everything above the arcade also belongs to this date, the second quarter of the 14th century, and so it cannot be the case, as suggested by Bulman and repeated by most writers since, that the 13th-century arches were supported and the piers either replaced or faced back.[22] The whole elevation was taken down, and the arch mouldings were re-erected on new piers built on the sites of the old ones to maintain the bay size dictated by the aisle bays. One section of a 13th-century base, to the north-west respond, still survives behind the choir stalls, showing that it is in precisely the same place as the 14th-century one, and it is of the same profile as the base of the north transept pier. The aisles, being stone vaulted, would have been better protected against the fire but, with the piers down, the aisle vaults would have had to be dismantled as well, and the rebuilding caused the anomalies to occur. Either because the damage was most severe at the east end, or possibly just taking advantage of the opportunity, the repair work included extending the aisle and creating another arcade bay on each side.

It may be assumed that reconstruction work started quickly after the fire in 1292, gifts of timber were made immediately and continued at regular intervals until 1300, with a petition for further grants in 1316. In 1307 Edward I was in Carlisle for over three months, housed with an entourage in the priory, and he is known to have had a private chapel in the cathedral in which his own relic collection was kept. His recorded donation to the Becket relic may well have stimulated other gifts to the building operations in progress.[23] The period of 1314–15 was marked by Border raids, Carlisle was besieged and priory revenues must have been affected. There is evidence that fund-raising continued beyond the middle of the century with licences given by Bishop Welton from the start of his episcopate in 1353 that resulted in donations to the fabric fund in the ensuing years.[24] The construction of the aisle and high roofs in the 1350s will have completed the structure of the choir, but indulgences to pay for its completion and furnishing continued to be issued until 1367.[25]

FIG. 18.   Choir from east end
of north aisle
Photograph: Jennifer Alexander

No trace remains of the upper levels of the 13th-century choir but the roof-scar visible on the exterior of the south transept east wall shows that its proportions were different with a taller triforium. The new choir elevation has a narrow triforium under a tall clerestory with the upper levels divided into bays by ceiling shafts that descend to the triforium string (Fig. 19). Each triforium bay has three arches, except the narrower east and west bays that have two, with two-light quatrefoil headed tracery set back under arches with continuous mouldings that spring from polygonal bases. The clerestory also has triple moulded arches, with the moulding on the taller, centre one dying into the jambs. The arches frame the windows in the outer face of the wall behind a deep wall-passage. A quatrefoil parapet is set at the base of these arches. The windows themselves show a surprising variety of flowing tracery forms and are arranged in pairs that, in most instances, match across the building. The exterior of the clerestory echoes the plainness of the interior. There is no vertical division between the

FIG. 19.   Choir upper levels from north-west
Photograph: Jennifer Alexander

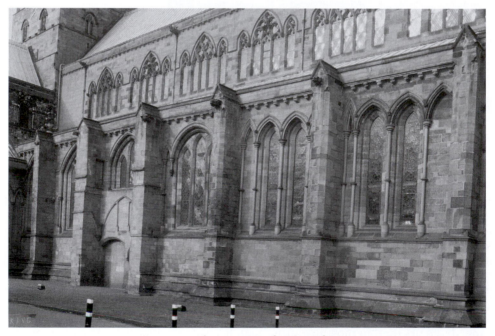

FIG. 20.   Choir exterior from south-east
Photograph: Jennifer Alexander

groups of windows and the only articulation is a narrow hood-moulding linking all the window heads in a continuous line that further emphasises the lack of a stone high vault to the choir (Fig. 20). The north side is more elaborate than the south with the addition of panels with a blind wavy-line tracery design at the base of the windows and the use of blind traceried windows in the west bay next to the tower.

There is considerable uniformity throughout the 14th-century work with no indication of building breaks, or changes in design, despite the probable length of the building operation, post-1292 to *c.* 1350. There are minor changes in detail but these are randomly distributed throughout the upper levels. Analysis of the large numbers of masons' marks found on the 14th-century sections of the choir at all levels and their distribution, however, does provide evidence for its construction.[26]

THE EVIDENCE OF THE MASONS' MARKS

A total of nearly 1,200 marks has been recorded in the choir and transepts (Fig. 21). These occur in small numbers on the south transept chapel east and south walls and on the east side of the north transept. There is a considerable number of marks on the piers and on the walls of the triforium and clerestory of the choir, and fewer on the aisle outside walls where there is a great deal of restored stonework.[27] The walling around the head of the east window produced a few marks, but none was recorded on the lower sections of the wall.

Statistical analysis of the marks is most reliable when there is a large number of occurrences of each mark and single appearances of marks are usually excluded from the data. Single, or very low-use marks can, however, sometimes provide insights when considering the significance of variations in marks. If the two marks are identical except in handedness then in most cases one form is dominant and the second occurs on neighbouring stones, supporting the observation that these are the same mark. For example, 6x14 occurs 33 times, whereas 6x13, the same mark in mirror-image, is found only twice and on adjacent stones to 6x14. It must be the same mark (Fig 21).[28]

The piers, which are all similar eight-lobed coursed piers, show no signs of prefabrication, instead the courses, each made up of four segments, have irregular heights, doubtless due to the availability of the beds. Each pier must therefore have been constructed individually. There is a large number of masons' marks visible both on the blocks, and on the pier-bases, and with a high proportion of marked stones it is possible to estimate the size of the team that worked on each pier. The average is twelve, with 16 in the largest team, drawn from a possible workforce of 36 masons, that included a specialised group of 17 individuals who worked exclusively on the piers. It is clear that there is a difference between the north and south piers that suggests that two foremen with different preferences were in charge. On the south side it is more usual to find only the cardinal stones marked whereas the north side has marks more randomly distributed across all the lobes of the piers. This ties in with the grouping of the marks that shows that thirteen of the 17 specialist pier-masons worked predominantly on one side or the other, mostly on the south side, although two masons worked equally on both. One of these, whose mark was found 40 times, may have been a particularly significant mason; his mark is one of the script type marks.[29] Work replacing damaged stone in the aisle outside walls was undertaken by seven masons who worked on the piers, and nine masons were kept on to cut stone for the upper levels of the choir.

FIG. 21.   Carlisle Choir masons' marks codes, not to scale, single occurrence marks omitted

Drawing: Jennifer Alexander

The disappearance of the 17 pier masons shows that the stone-cutting team had been reduced since the next phase involved mostly mason-setters. These men re-erected the 13th-century arcade arches on the new piers and then raised the aisle vault, again reusing stone, in this case ribs from the earlier vault. This joined the arcades to the outside walls to provide their support before the upper levels of the building were constructed. Canterbury's rebuilding after 1174 was carried out in this way, with the arcade piers and their arches linked to the undamaged aisle walls by vaults before the upper levels were raised.[30]

The masons' marks found on the two west responds demonstrate that these were prepared after the arcade piers since they share few marks with the other piers.[31] Significantly certain of these marks, 4c2, 4v8 and 4w2, also occur in the triforium, suggesting that the upper levels were constructed from west to east once the piers were completed. The walling of the triforium is continuous between the bays and there is a great deal of consistency in the distribution of the marks along each side, indicating that the work was carried out in a single campaign. Where there is a large number of a single mark, such as 6x11, or 6x14, it is mostly restricted to one side. 6x11's work for example is only found in the three west bays on the south triforium, occurring on 28 ashlars, and 6x14's some 27 blocks are all on bays two to five on the north side, with one stray found in bay three on the south. 4c2 cut four blocks for the north side but 41 that were used on the south. Other masons' work was used on both sides, such as 4h3 who cut 23 blocks for the north and 26 for the south, and 2t8 who prepared 15 ashlars for the north and 31 for the south. Some 29 different marks were identified in the walling of the triforium and in the staircases leading up to that level, with a further 12 that only were found once in these areas and have therefore been removed from the analysis. Nine of the group of 29 had been kept on after the piers had been completed, including the three who had worked on the responds, but the remainder was newly recruited. It is possible that these nine masons, 2t3, 2t8, 2v1, 3a4, 3h7, 3z14, 4c2, 4v8, 4w2, had remained as a core-team to maintain expertise as has been recorded at Lichfield. There the master mason made an appeal to keep on his stone-cutters in 1385 because they were trained in methods of cutting and shaping stone which, he claimed, it would take other masons a year to learn.[32]

The arches of the clerestory screen are built to a single design and there are 23 different masons' marks found on the soffits of the arches and on the walling stone. The masons' marks establish that the most easterly bay on the south side of the triforium and clerestory, and the walling above the east window, were under construction at the same time. Marks 3h7, 2v1 and 3h1 are all found in the east bay of both the triforium and the clerestory on the south side and 3h7 is also found with 3v3 and 4w2 above the east window. The one clerestory occurrence of mark 4c2, that is found otherwise mainly in the south triforium, is in the first south bay. This vertical linkage in the first bay is logical in the building sequence since the east wall had to be raised to its full height before the roof could be built and the east end of the clerestory provided its support.[33]

Fewer stones in the clerestory are marked than at the other levels in the building and more single occurrences of marks are found so it is less easy to distinguish the teams at work. It is evident, however, that 14 masons worked on both the triforium and clerestory, and that in most cases their work appears in the same bay in each zone, further supporting the theory that both the upper parts of the choir were built in one continuous campaign. Of the remaining nine masons, only one, 6x12, marked sufficient stone for it to be clear that he was a new member of the team.

In conclusion, it can therefore be shown that the choir of Carlisle Cathedral Priory is a building of more than one period in which care had been taken to integrate the new work with the old. A radical plan was formed in the 13th century to demolish the 12th-century choir and replace it with a magnificent new structure that was on a new axis. The new work increased the importance of the north transept that was also rebuilt more splendidly with an eastern arcade and chapel. Shortly after its completion at the end of the century a disastrous fire destroyed the new building and work had to restart. A debate ensued and two designs were explored, with the more conservative option adopted in which the arcade arches were reused from the damaged building and a simple two-level upper elevation raised. The fragments of the abandoned flying ribs in the east bay of the aisles provide a single clue to the alternative rebuilding plan that would have resulted in a dramatically different building rising from the ruins. The reconstruction work proceeded swiftly, with the evidence of the masons' marks showing that a large number of men were taken on to create the new piers and a core-team was established who remained on the building until its walling was complete. The expense of employing the masons for a 50-year period must have been considerable and fund-raising had to continue long after the masons had handed over the building.

ACKNOWLEDGEMENTS

I should like to thank Canon David Weston, for his help and encouragement in my research, and the team of vergers in the cathedral whose unfailing assistance made access to all parts of the building simple. Gavin Simpson was also invaluable as a recorder of masons' marks.

NOTES

1. Robert William Billings, *Architectural Illustrations, History and Description of Carlisle Cathedral* (London 1840). The choir has been considered by A. Hamilton Thompson, 'Carlisle Cathedral', in the Report on the Royal Archaeological Institute's Summer Meeting at Dumfries, *Archaeol. J.*, 96 (1939), 320–21; C. G. Bulman, 'Carlisle Cathedral and its development in the thirteenth and fourteenth centuries', *Transactions Cumberland and Westmorland Antiquarian Archaeological Society*, ns, XXXXIX (1949), 87–117; see also Kusuma Barnett, 'The East End of Carlisle Cathedral: chronology of its design during the 13th and 14th centuries' (unpublished M.A. dissertation, University of London, 1998). The most recent study of the whole building and its history is Dr David W. V. Weston's *Carlisle Cathedral History* (Carlisle 2000). The documentary and historical background is covered by Henry Summerson, *Medieval Carlisle: The City and the Borders from the late Eleventh to the mid-Sixteenth Century*, Cumberland and Westmorland Antiquarian and Archaeological Society, Extra Series, XXV (1993), 2 vols, Kendal.
2. Calder was founded first in 1134 but the monks returned to Furness and a second foundation was established in 1142. It was under the patronage of the owners of Egremont Castle: Thomas de Multon had rebuilt the stone church and convent by his death in 1240 after damage sustained in a Scottish attack of 1216. D. Robinson ed., *The Cistercian Abbeys of Britain* (London 1998), 84–85.
3. For example, Hamilton Thompson, 320; also Bulman, 95.
4. The apse was rediscovered in 1892 when the floor was trenched. It was found to have a maximum diameter of 2.79 m (9.75 ft). C. J. Ferguson, 'Carlisle Cathedral. Apse in East Wall of Transept', *Transactions Cumberland Westmorland Antiquarian Archaeological Society*, XIV (1897), 208–10.
5. For the tower collapse of 1380 see below, n. 7. The entrance is visible in Billings's drawing, pl. xxiii. Billings noted the extra shafts on the vault respond of the wall arcade and suggested that the transept east chapel may have been intended for a chantry chapel, Billings, 32.
6. For Lanercost Priory see S. Harrison, 'Description of the Standing Fabric', in H. Summerson and S. Harrison ed., *Lanercost Priory, Cumbria*, Cumberland Westmorland Antiquarian Archaeological Society

Research Series, no. 10 (2000), 95–140. Large nail-head also occurs at Lanercost in the south nave clerestory abaci.

7. The crossing tower was brought down by high winds in 1380 and the damage seems to have been sustained in the area of the north transept. Bishop Strickland (1400–19) is credited with completing the repairs to the transept and raising the crossing tower (Summerson, 355). The thickening of the east wall and reduction of the height of the transept can presumably be attributed to this restoration, together with the distortion of the transept arch. However, there is evidence of earlier work in the transept. The north wall may contain 13th-century masonry, although it is hard to identify, but it is sited in the position that the early Gothic wall will have occupied. The present north window was installed by Ewan Christian in the 1850s to replace the uncusped Perpendicular-style window from 1732 that Billings published in 1840. An earlier window is shown in an engraving of 1715 that bears some resemblance to the east window of the choir, illustrated in Weston, 20.

8. The south transept apse was rediscovered during Ewan Christian's restoration of the 1850s. See Ferguson, 209.

9. Ewan Christian, 'Report on the Cathedral Church of St Mary Carlisle descriptive of its present condition and of the repairs and alterations necessary or desirable to be made therein', Carlisle Cathedral Archives 79.0, 81.0–87.0. The high altar had been moved to its current position in the restoration of 1764, removing the purpose of these windows, Weston, 21.

10. The archaeological evidence suggests that the outside south wall of the 12th-century choir was left standing until the new work approached it and there should, therefore, have been a break in construction while this was demolished. Bulman cited the evidence of a section of wall under the fifth pier from the east on the south side that appeared to be part of the main apse and he accordingly reconstructed the 12th-century east end with three bays ending in apses *en echélon* (Bulman, 89 and fig. 1). This would place the break between bays four and five, where there is a change in the window archmoulding. In a recent re-examination of this evidence McCarthy was unable to support Bulman's reconstruction although he was in broad agreement about the form of the east end. M. McCarthy, 'The Origins and Development of the Cathedral Church at Carlisle', in *The Archaeology of Cathedrals*, ed. T. Tatton-Brown and J. Munby, Oxford University Committee for Archaeology Monograph, 42 (Oxford 1996), 31–46. It is unfortunate that the point at which the change in window design occurred in the Gothic aisle cannot now be established.

11. For a discussion of the relationship between Beverley and Fountains see Christopher Wilson, 'The Early Thirteenth-Century Architecture of Beverley Minster: Cathedral Splendours and Cistercian Austerities', in *Thirteenth Century England III*, ed. P. R. Cross and S. D. Lloyd, Proceedings of the Newcastle upon Tyne Conference 1989 (Woodbridge 1989), 181–95.

12. N. Pevsner, *Cumberland and Westmorland* B/E (Harmondsworth 1967). The greater elaboration of the nave with its alternation sequence has, however, been described as having 'little obviously Cistercian in character about it', Robinson, 84.

13. For Southwell see J. McNeill, 'The Chronology of the Choir of Southwell Minster', in *Southwell and Nottinghamshire Medieval Art, Architecture and Industry*, ed. J. S. Alexander, *BAA Trans.*, XXI (1998), 24–32. Keeled shafts and octofoiled piers can also be found at St Bees and Shap in the region, but not used with filleted main shafts.

14. Bulman, 92.

15. Summerson, 157–58.

16. Intersected mouldings can be found at a number of sites in the 13th century, used for example on the eastern arcade of Salisbury where the choir arcades meet the arches at the entrance to the Trinity chapel at right angles, from the second quarter of the 13th century, but ribs are rarely encountered in this setting. At Beverley the wall-rib is sprung from a position in front of the diagonal ribs resulting in the ribs crossing. There is no suggestion that the Beverley mason intended to use flying ribs.

17. Complex vaults with flying ribs are more familiar in buildings in Eastern Europe and Germany, seen in an early example in the sacristy of Prague Cathedral from *c.* 1350–60. This is now thought to have been based on precedents in southern Germany. P. Frankl, revised by P. Crossley, *Gothic Architecture* (New Haven and London 2000), 200, 347 n. 56D. The chancel of St Mary's Warwick, finished by 1392, has a form of flying rib used in its vault.

18. Billings, title page.

19. Bulman, 93–96.

20. Summerson, 178.

21. *Gervase of Canterbury's History of the Burning and Repair of the Church of Canterbury*, from R. Willis, *The Architectural History of Canterbury Cathedral* (London 1845). Reprinted in E. G. Holt ed., *A Documentary History of Art; Volume 1 The Middle Ages and Renaissance* (New York 1957), 52–62.

22. Bulman, 100.

23. Summerson, 210, 215, 257.

FIG. 3.   The west end of the chancel vault
Photograph: C. R. Salisbury

Tie-beams at regular intervals were generally still used *c.* 1200 to prevent the roof from pushing the walls apart and to provide a firm base for the principal trusses. In the absence of any other structural solution by medieval architects the length of the tie-beams available determined the width of the principal parts of the church. The roof and its tie-beams might be completely hidden above a stone vault, or above a flat ceiling of boards nailed to the soffits of the tie-beams, or could simply be left open to the rafters.

A roof with many tie-beams put a limit on the height of a ceiling or vault beneath, whether it was of wood or stone. As tie-beams were generally the largest timbers they became increasingly difficult to obtain, and so expensive to buy. This provided an incentive for development of various designs of truss without tie-beams which could be used to make complete roofs with few, or even no, tie-beam trusses. Such trusses over the stone vault of the chapter-house vestibule of Lincoln Cathedral (*c.* 1220d), have collar-beams with struts, and straight soulaces and ashlar-pieces (Fig. 5B). The late-12th-century open roof of the choir of the church at Branches, just north of Auxerre, is structurally almost identical to the Lincoln chapter-house roof, and only a little earlier, but here soulaces below the collar-beam have become arched-braces to make a rounded profile, more like a barrel-vault.[9] The Greyfriars' Church at Lincoln has a roof of similar design and is probably a few decades later. Here again there are arched-braces, curved ashlars, no tie-beams, and the soffits were originally boarded over to make a true barrel-vault (Figs 6 and 7).[10]

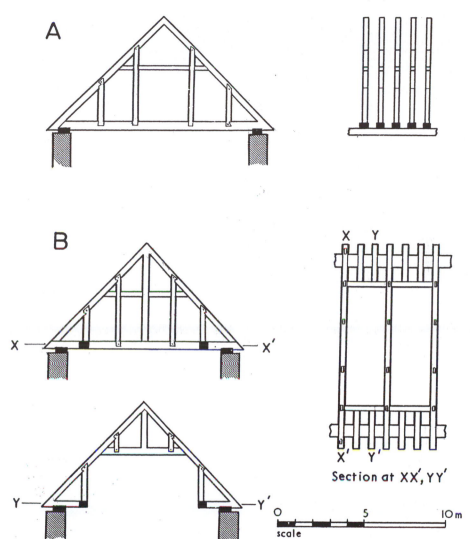

FIG. 4.   12th-century roofs at Soignies Abbey, Belgium. Early (over the nave, A), Late (over the choir, B). After S. Brigode, *Bull. Commission Royale des Monuments Sites*, 1, 1949

   More than eighty trusses over the nave of Ely Cathedral use collar-beams, and straight scissor-braces with ashlar-pieces, to make an open roof of seven-canted profile which was built by Bishop Northwold (*c.* 1240d). Its original vault-like appearance is shown in an engraving made in 1838 (Figs 5A and 8). It was boarded out a few years later after its medieval profile had been rounded into a five-canted one by adding more timbers to the soffit. Tree-ring dating of the pine roof of the Romanesque church at Vaernes, Norway, seems to show that Norse carpenters were already building open roofs of similar design over stone churches at the beginning of the 12th century.[11] The

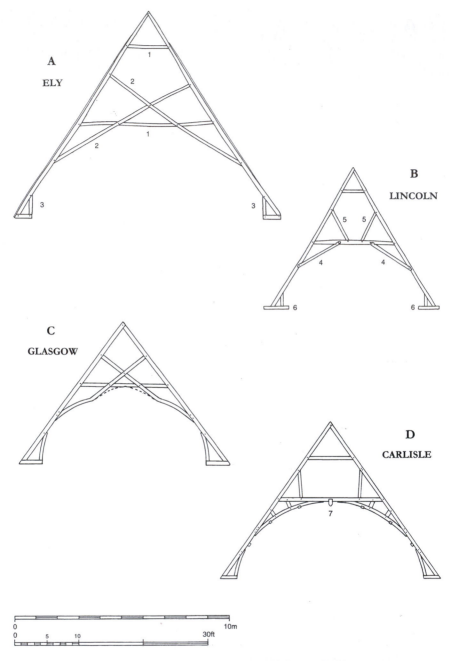

FIG. 5.   A. Ely Cathedral, nave roof-truss, *c.* 1240d. 1, collar beams; 2, scissor braces; 3, ashlar pieces. B. Lincoln Cathedral, chapter-house vestibule roof truss, *c.* 1220d. 4, soulaces; 5, struts; 6, sole pieces. C. Glasgow Cathedral, choir roof truss, *c.* 1260d? D. Carlisle Cathedral, chancel roof truss, *c.* 1355d. 7, ridge beam

Fig. 6.   Greyfriars Church, Lincoln, timber open roof
Photograph: C. R. Salisbury

nave of Peterborough Cathedral is still covered by the remnants of one of the earliest scissor-braced roofs in north-west Europe which recent research has indicated was constructed in the period 1169–89d to cover a stone vault which was never built, but around the middle of the 13th century the soffits of its open roof timbers were boarded out to make a five-canted vault.[12] These examples demonstrate how, by modification of the roof trusses, medieval carpenters were able to create a vaulted profile from the soffits of the timbers which could, if so desired, be lined with boards to make a true barrel-vault or wagon-roof.

Medieval buildings in Britain, which have, or once had timber vaults, have been the subject of recent papers.[13] Timber ribbed-vaults, such as the quadripartite vault over the nave of Warmington Church or the lierne vault over the presbytery of St Albans Cathedral, should be mentioned briefly here.[14] Like their counterparts in stone, they rise from springers set in the walls, are usually no higher than the tops of the walls and not dependent on the roof for their stability. They could be built without centering or much scaffolding and, like timber barrel-vaults, are lighter than stone vaults, so particularly suitable to cover buildings with thin, unbuttressed walls. Moreover, like the St Albans vault, they were often painted to imitate stone.

Quasi-vaults such as those at Branches and Ely and panelled barrel-vaults such as Carlisle are based upon sole-pieces which are seated on wallplates. They rise above the wall-tops and encroach on the roof-space thus giving greater height to the interior of the building and allowing larger windows in the gable walls. Although they form a distinctive group in north-west Europe there are regional variations in the carpentry, and particularly in the decorative treatment of the vault. British examples often tend to be more ornate than those of the Continent. The Carlisle roof has collar-beam trusses, whereas the roof of the vault over the choir of Glasgow Cathedral, 100 miles to the north, has scissor-braced trusses and both vaults have close parallels among the largest group of barrel-vaulted churches, in Cornwall, Devon and Somerset (Figs 5C and D).[15] Banwell Church in Somerset has a series of six transverse panels along the vault defined by moulded ribs and purlins, with sprigged bosses covering the intersections, similar to Carlisle which, however, has eight transverse panels. Glasgow has four transverse panels, with purely decorative diagonal ribs, and the bosses at the intersections are larger and more ornate recalling the vaults of Cullompton or Hennock in Devon.[16]

Examples of panelled vaults are distributed in a broad arc extending from the Frisian coast, through western Holland, Belgium, central and northern France to Brittany. They are particularly common in the Netherlands in regions where stone is not readily available and are not confined to ecclesiastical buildings, although, where found in a secular context they are usually in buildings of high status. Here again there is perhaps more variety in the appearance of the vaults than in the structure of the roofs. They range from unsegmented barrel-vaults to those, like Carlisle, with ribs and purlins defining rectangular panels.[17] The earliest firmly dated examples are in the Netherlands and they are also the plainest, moulded transverse ribs between the bays being the only decorative feature, as in the east range of the cloister of the Cistercian Abbey of Val-Saint-Lambert (c. 1234d — see Fig. 9) and at the churches of Saint-Christophe and Saint-Antoine (c. 1250d) at Liège, Belgium.[18] One of the earliest Dutch roofs is that over St John's Church in Utrecht, which was built about 1280 and originally had a barrel-vault of pine boards which was painted, perhaps a decade or two later. Original early-13th-century barrel-vaulting of conifer also survived until recently in St James's Church in Tournai.[19] The 14th-century choir vault of Kapelle Church, Holland, is constructed much like the Carlisle vault. It has principal trusses in which the ribs and purlins define a series of four transverse panels along the vault.[20] The principal trusses are made up of arched-braces tenoned into the soffits of the lower collars and into the middle of the rafters, which are there moulded to continue the rib-profiles until ashlar-pieces tenoned into the lower soffits of the rafters carry the ribs on to the wall-shafts. The ridge-beam, and purlins tenoned into each principal truss make up the longitudinal plates and help to keep the structure rigid, as do the boards which are nailed to the faces of the intermediate ribs and have their ends slotted into grooves in the sides of the principal ribs and purlins.[21]

Unfortunately, at Carlisle, as at Glasgow, all the web boards were renewed when the vault was restored. However, the use of wainscot oak imported from the Baltic for the decorative sprigs on the bosses provides a link with web boards imported from the same area used in timber vaults at St Albans (c. 1273–99d), the Octagon, Ely (1334/35) and Salisbury (c. 1365–92d) Cathedrals.[22] The boards were usually fitted together using the typical medieval form of the tongue-and-groove joint which is also used in vaults in the Netherlands.[23] In this respect, however, the vaults of Warmington Church, Peterborough Cathedral and Greyfriars', Lincoln are exceptional in that their boards overlap clinker-fashion, the feather-edge of each board resting on the thick edge of its neighbour (Fig. 7). Tree-ring analysis has indicated a north-west German origin for the Peterborough boards and there is also documentary evidence of timber trade across the North Sea with Hamburg around the mid-13th century, before a Hanseatic timber trade with the Baltic had fully developed.[24] Clinkered boards of pine have also been found covering the roofs of medieval churches in Norway, fitted in a way which

Interior of the   Chapel, looking East.

FIG. 7.   Drawing of the boarded vault of the chapel Greyfriars', Lincoln, by Edward Wilson,
c. 1845

© *Lincoln Cathedral Library*

certainly relates them to ship construction.[25] There may be a similar explanation for the English examples, but a connection with German carpentry seems more likely, at least for the Peterborough boards. One category of timber imported from the Baltic was clapboard (*clapholts*) which was probably used to clad buildings in this fashion. It is still part of the architectural vocabulary of the American New England states, but is known as weatherboarding on this side of the Atlantic. The second element of the word is the Low German form of modern *holz* (wood).[26]

Fawcett has noted the use of sprigged bosses in the town hall at Bruges built in 1402. They are also found in 15th-century contexts associated with flat bosses on the barrel-vault over the nave of St Agnes Church, Sint-Truiden, Belgium, and on the apsidal vault of the choir of the 15th-century St Laurence's Church at Alkmaar, Holland. The former is closer to Carlisle in form and date. It has principal trusses in which the ribs, and the purlins between, define a series of six transverse panels along its painted vault.[27] The latter, however, is closer in date and in form to later Scottish choir vaults at King's College Chapel and St Nicholas' Church, Aberdeen.[28]

FIG. 8.   Ely Cathedral,
view of the nave ceiling,
looking east. After
Winkles, 1838

*Photograph: Society of
Antiquaries of London*

   The carpenters' assembly marks at Carlisle are scribed on each truss in Roman numerals, like those of continental church roofs of the 13th and 14th centuries, although the numerals 19, 40, 50 and 60 are represented in slightly different ways. However, like the carpenters' assembly marks in the early-13th-century roofs over the naves of Ely Cathedral and Rouen Cathedral the numerals are not in sequence, and some are even repeated. This is probably an 'early' feature. In the mid-14th-century transept roof of the Oude Kerk, Amsterdam they are in sequence.[29] The assembly marks of the triforium roofs at Carlisle are of the same kind and not in numerical sequence, although I to VIII are on the north side and IX to XVI are on the south side.
   Continental carpenters generally seem to have been reluctant to abandon tie-beams completely in barrel-vaulted roofs and there may be several, widely spaced, along its length to reinforce the stability of the structure. The medieval Hospice de la Comtesse at Lille, rebuilt following a fire in 1468, has a panelled vault like Carlisle over its chapel and the *salle des malades* has a barrel-vault with tie-beams and king-posts (Fig. 10).[30]

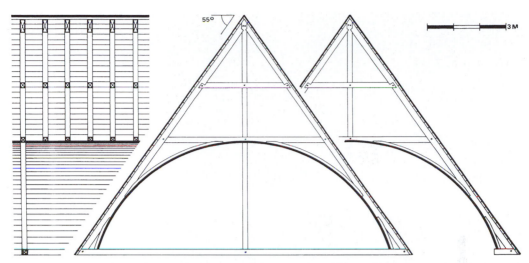

Fig. 9.   The vault over the cloister of the Cistercian Abbey of Val-Saint-Lambert
Thomas Coomans

The most impressive example of the latter type in France, which also covers a medieval hospice, is at Tonnerre, Yonne. It spans 60 ft (18.6 m) and was built at the end of the 13th century.[31] Barrel-vaults with intermittent tie-beams, generally without king-posts, are also common in Holland, except in the south-west of the country. Nothing comparable has been noted in Britain, nevertheless, the most likely explanation for the three curious pairs of brackets at the base of the Carlisle choir vault is that they are the ends of tie-beams that have been sawn out in the 18th century, because they no longer fulfilled any useful purpose.[32] Such tie-beams, supported on decorated brackets, are found beneath contemporary Dutch timber vaults, as for example Amsterdam's Oude Kerk. These vaults also have flat circular bosses and escutcheons, like Carlisle, covering the intersections of the ribs and the purlin plates. Carved decoration is found on the soffits of vaulted ceilings in western Holland.[33]

THE TIMBER TRADE, CARPENTRY AND TRANSMISSION OF IDEAS

CONTINENTAL parallels with medieval architecture in Scotland have been noted and various ways in which ideas might have been transmitted have been suggested in recent publications. One fairly well-documented link is connections by trade and another earlier one is connected to attempts by David I to feudalise his kingdom in the mid-12th century. As part of this process families of French and Flemish origin were granted land and settled, and the post-Reformation writer of the *Rites of Durham* claimed that the king had brought workmen from France and Flanders to work at Holyrood Abbey.[34] Although the impetus towards feudalisation may have slackened by the mid-13th century, connections with the homeland a century later were evidently maintained sufficiently for its architectural traditions still to find a place in the north. As in London, building contracts, not only for royal works, but also in Carlisle for vernacular buildings, were still being drawn up in French in the last decades of the 14th century.[35] A century later, as noted above, close stylistic parallels with Flanders or northern

FIG. 10.   Hospice de la
Comtesse, Lille, *salle des
malades*
Photograph: C. R. Salisbury

France are apparent in the architecture of two Aberdeen churches and a carpenter from
one or other of those regions may have been responsible for the woodwork.[36]

   In historic times the northern Netherlands lacked extensive forests to provide
suitable building timber and increasingly its requirements had to be imported. Oak,
pine and spruce were readily available to the south and could be rafted down the Rhine
and its tributaries.[37] Although there was plenty of oak in England there was neither
pine nor spruce, which had to be imported from Norway, and possibly elsewhere.
Recent research has suggested that there were substantial forests of mature trees in
north-east Scotland in the early second millennium and it is likely that pine (*pinus
sylvestris*) would have been well represented.[38] Documentary and archaeological
evidence suggest that the Norwegian timber trade was already well established before

timber exports by the Hansa from the Baltic began.[39] Like England and Scotland, the Netherlands also benefited from the Baltic timber trade which was developed by Hanseatic merchants from about the mid-13th century. The Hansa commercially exploited the vast reserves of timber from the ancient forests of central and eastern Europe. At first much of it was exported in the form of *estreich* or Eastland boards of oak split or riven from the log.[40]

Conifer timber, probably of German origin, has been found in some of the earliest roofs in the Netherlands as structural timber as well as panelling.[41] In France and Francophone areas of Belgium barrel-vaulted ceilings are still referred to as *charpente lambrissée*, or 'panelled woodwork'. *Lambrissée* is found from the early 12th century in medieval documents of these regions as *lambresche* or *labruscand'* and is said to derive from colloquial Latin meaning 'wild vine' and hence 'to decorate with vine scrolls'. However, doubt about this derivation is expressed in some sources and, as will be demonstrated, documentary evidence from England make a confusion of homophones seem likely.[42] The derivation proposed here is that the first element of the word is Old French *l'ambre* meaning amber, which implies a connection with pine, or generally, conifer timber.[43] Its derivation from Scandinavian language(s) on or close to the Baltic, a major source of the fossilised resin, seems likely for it is also found in Arabic as *'anbar*, which product would have reached Byzantium and the east Mediterranean via documented Viking trade links.[44] Although pine wood is white or cream-coloured when felled, it quickly darkens to become the colour of amber when its sap is exposed to air.[45]

Although documentary sources in England usually state the building or structure where timber was to be used it is often not clear where or how it was to be applied. So, for example, in 1252 Henry III instructed that 200 Norway boards of pine (*sapio*) should be bought at Southampton and delivered to Winchester Castle to panel (*lambrustand'*) the chamber of Prince Edward. Instances where the purpose of the boards is more specifically stated suggest that there was considerable variety in its use. For example, in 1241 the constable of Marlborough Castle was ordered to have the cellar partitioned (or panelled — *lambrusca'*), lined (*lineari*) and whitened — meaning presumably that the timber was to be painted to resemble masonry. In 1244 writs were issued for the great halls of Oxford Castle and Clarendon Palace to be panelled for the space of five rafter couples over the dais and the chancel of the king's chapel in the castle was to be panelled throughout, as well as similar work elsewhere in both places.[46] This discrete panelling over the dais is matched at Hennock Church, Devon, where panelling over the rood is more elaborate than that covering the nave or chancel, and the High Altar of York Minster seems to have received similar treatment in 1371.[47] In 1244 the sheriff of Cumberland had to arrange for the repair, alteration and panelling of the king's chapel in Carlisle Castle, for which purpose the king enjoined Robert de Ros to let him have ten oaks in Inglewood Forest.[48]

In many documentary sources the species of timber is not stated but, as in Carlisle Castle, Hennock and York, oak was often used. The documentary evidence and etymology of *lambr-* as interpreted above implies that a term first used by Scandinavian carpenters and traders exclusively with reference to pine, when Vikings began raiding north-west Europe in the 9th century, came by the 11th century to be applied metaphorically to other species of timber, principally oak, which the Normans used for building in areas they had settled. Oak grows at the northern limit of its natural range in southern Sweden and south-western Norway so that native pine was predominantly used for building and mature oak was probably reserved to make ships, rather than for building or for export.[49]

Archaeological evidence for imported pine and its use for panelling, among other things, seems to be emerging from Viking Age sites in Britain. Waterlogged deposits on Norway's treeless colonies, Orkney and Shetland, have yielded worked conifer timber. In a 9th-century waterlogged pit at Tuquoy, Westray, Orkney, much wood-working debris of imported conifer timber was found, some of which may have been trimmed from riven boards.[50] Excavation at Biggings, Papa Stour, Shetland, of a house thought to be that of Duke Hakon of Norway, has revealed a traditional Viking house (*stofa*), the walls of its principal room panelled and floored with pine boards, which radiocarbon dating has assigned to the late Norse period (A.D. 1013–1156 cal.).[51] The first documentary record of such trade is not until the early 17th century when Shetlanders were buying from Norway 'timber for houses ready framed, deal boards, tar, ships, barks and boats of all sorts'.[52] Two pine boards, evidently from small panels and two pieces of floor-board, of pine and silver fir (*abies alba*), have turned up in late-10th- to mid-11th-century contexts in Coppergate at the heart of Viking *Yorvik*. The former boards are said to have features comparable to those used to panel contemporary and later medieval *minbars* (preaching pulpits) in Muslim mosques which are often made of exotic timber.[53] The tongue-and-groove joints look surprisingly modern and differ in type both from those used in the late-12th-century walls of Kaupanger stave-church and the characteristic V-joints used on imported oak boards, for which northern invention seems most likely.[54] Pine continued to be imported into York and elsewhere throughout the Middle Ages from Norway and the Baltic. For example, the late-13th-century doors of the Minster chapter-house are of pine. Ten ships of Norway whose cargoes included pine boards (*bordis sapineis*) were detained at Grimsby in 1230.[55] A 9th-century cemetery excavated at Barton-on-Humber, just across the river estuary from Hull, one of the major entrepots for Norwegian and Baltic trade, has yielded a coffin made of pine boards.[56]

Early forms of *lambrissé* are also found as *lambruscura* (noun) and *lambruscare* (verb) in English documents written in medieval Latin from the 13th century. They are usually translated as 'wainscot' or 'to wainscot' which is probably anachronistic as there is no documentary evidence for the word, or its German and Dutch (*wagenschot*), Flemish (*wageschot*), or Frisian (*wagenskot*) equivalents around the North Sea before the mid-14th century, although in England, but not in France, it comes to be used in every sense as was the former which it replaces.[57] Some of the earliest manuscript references have '*estrichbord* called *waynescot*', thus confirming it as Baltic oak which dendrochronology has demonstrated to be invariably of the high quality for which wainscot became known.[58] It was close grained, straight grown, often with attractive figure and few knots and carved well to give the sharp lines and detail seen in the sprigs of the Carlisle vault.[59] Etymologists usually acknowledge that the first element has to be 'wagon', which is convincing because Germanic *wagen* translates as English 'wain', but no root has been established for the second, '-scot', which is sometimes found prefixed to '-nail', particularly in documentary sources relating to the north of England.[60] A connection with Dutch *schot*, a partition, has been suggested and it is probable that, like 'room' and 'board', the second elements of both *lambruscura* and 'wainscot' derive from Norse ship construction, a shott being a compartment or 'room' (Old Norse *rum*) partitioned off at the stern of a boat. In its Old Norse form (*skutr*) it probably referred to the partition itself, or partitions generally, which may well have been remarkable for being of pine, in a boat made almost entirely of oak.[61] Of particular significance, therefore, is a reference in which Henry III gives instructions for equipping his galleys at Portsmouth in preparation for a voyage to France in 1242.[62] He specifies that pine boards (*bordum de sap*) should be used in the royal galley to *lambreschura* the queen's cabin (*camera*). In this context 'to make the (partition) walls' would seem to be a better translation of *lambreschura* than 'for panelling' in the sense that the term is now understood, and nicely illustrates a stage in the devolution of the Norse sense of the word into its late medieval meaning. A similar reference to the use of wainscot in royal ship construction at Deptford, is recorded in 1519 with the purchase of 100 wainscot boards and one dozen 'joyned scotes [made-up panels] for the quene is [*sic*] Caban' in the *Katerine Pleasaunce*. The latter were probably of similar construction to the sixteen late-14th-century Baltic oak panels of the ceiling over the crossing of St Albans Cathedral.[63]

The latest use of the term that has been noted relating to an English building is written as *laumbresche* in 1315. The document, which is in French, is an agreement between Sir John Bluet and the Augustinian canonesses for the construction of a Lady Chapel at Lacock Abbey and it is quite clear that a panelled ceiling or barrel-vault was intended.[64] The suffix *-esche* may not relate to *-skutr* or *-'scot'*, but is clearly cognate to modern *lambrissé*. A subtle difference of meaning may be discerned here, the French version literally translating as 'to make the colour of pine' and the English version as 'to make partitions, or to panel, with pine'.

'Wainscot' is first commonly used in English documents towards the end of the 14th century, about the time that negotiations with the Hanse won English merchants the right to import goods from Baltic ports in English ships.[65] Its appearance also coincided with a change in the way the product was marketed, as it became common for boards made for export to be quarter sawn rather than cleft as, for example, those used to panel the ceiling of the late-14th-century guild chapel at St Helen's Church, Abingdon.[66] So it may reflect the need for timber merchants to establish a distinctive brand name for their product. Although a connection with 'wagon roof' seems compelling there is no documentary support for it.[67] On the other hand, there is no way of knowing what length of time might elapse in the Middle Ages between the first use of a word or phrase in speech and its eventual appearance in writing. It is significant that *lambresche* and *lambruscura* which were associated with the architecture of the rich and the powerful in the 12th and 13th centuries, should also survive and develop in the language which was the most fashionable among the cultivated of north-west Europe in the 14th century.[68] The French have also had, since at least the 18th century, their own metaphorical term for the barrel-vaulted roof — *berceau lambrissé*, literally, 'panelled cradle'.[69]

ACKNOWLEDGEMENTS

Thanks are due to Dr David Weston for advice and the loan of books and documents used in the preparation of this paper, and for his help in many other ways; also to the vergers for facilitating access to all parts of the cathedral and for loan of equipment; to Richard Sheppard for his isometric drawing of the Carlisle roof and to Thomas Coomans for allowing me to use his drawing of the Val-Saint-Lambert vault. Jenny Alexander was of great assistance in provision of transport and advice on architectural sources and I am also grateful to her and Chris Salisbury for their help with photography.

GAVIN SIMPSON

Grants from the Society of Antiquaries of London and the Cumberland and Westmorland Antiquarian and Archaeological Society for dendrochronology and for the survey of the roof are gratefully acknowledged.

This paper is dedicated to the memory of Bob Laxton (1933–2002), who died while it was in preparation. He was a founder of the Nottingham University Tree-Ring Dating Laboratory, and he, and our colleague Robert Howard, were responsible for the Carlisle Cathedral dendrochronology.

NOTES

1. R. W. Billings, *Architectural Illustrations, History and Descriptions of Carlisle Cathedral* (London 1840), pl. 7.

2. Browne Willis, *A Survey of the Cathedrals . . .*, 1 (London 1742), 285; D. W. V. Weston, *Carlisle Cathedral History* (Carlisle 2000), 78–79.

3. *Architectural Illustrations*, pl. 36; *Carlisle Cathedral*, 21.

4. E. Christian, 'Report on the Cathedral Church of St Mary, Carlisle - present condition and repairs necessary' (unpublished MS 1852), ff. 10–12. For a recent example of a badly disintegrating medieval timber barrel-vaulted roof see C. de Mérindol, 'Programmes de la décoration des demeures et des chapelles du roi René d'après l'heraldique et emblématique', in *Artistes, Artisans et Production Artistique au Moyen Age*, 2, ed. X. B. I. Altet (Colloque international, CNRS — Université de Renne II, mai 1983, Paris 1987), 253. Although many of the boards have fallen away, as at Carlisle the structural timbers of the roof above seem to have survived in good condition.

5. C. A. Hewett, *English Cathedral and Monastic Carpentry* (Chichester 1985), 93.

6. All dates in this paper followed by 'd' are tree-ring dates. All timber is oak, unless stated otherwise.

7. *The Register of Gilbert Welton, Bishop of Carlisle 1353–1362*, ed. R. L. Storey (Canterbury and York Society, 88, 1999), 231, 534, 599; *Survey of Cathedrals*, 285; C. G. Bulman, 'Carlisle Cathedral and its Development in the Thirteenth and Fourteenth Centuries', *Transactions Cumberland Westmorland Antiquarian Archaeological Society*, ns, XLIX (1949), 87–117. Only shields and sprigs held in store could be sampled for dendrochronology. Though reputedly from the chancel the panelled ceiling of the north transept was similarly decorated and it is just possible that was their original location; see *Carlisle Cathedral History*, 43. It is hoped to publish a fuller account of the carpentry and history of the roof and vault in the *Transactions*.

8. The nave and choir roofs of Soignies Abbey, Belgium illustrate the development and are fairly typical, see J. Fletcher, 'Medieval Timberwork at Ely', in *Medieval Art and Architecture at Ely Cathedral*, ed. N. Coldstream and P. Draper, *BAA Trans.*, II (Leeds 1979), fig. 2.

9. N. D. J. Foot, C. D. Litton and W. G. Simpson, 'The High Roofs of the East End of Lincoln Cathedral', in *Medieval Art and Architecture at Lincoln Cathedral*, ed. T. A. Heslop and V. A. Sekules, *BAA Trans.*, VIII (Leeds 1986), 47–74, fig. 2; R. R. Laxton, C. D. Litton and R. E. Howard, *Timber: dendrochronology of roof timbers at Lincoln Cathedral*, English Heritage Research Transactions, 7 (2001), 48–49; M. Le Port, 'La charpente du xie- xve siècle, aperçu du savoir du charpentier', in *Artistes, Artisans et Production Artistique au Moyen Age*, 2, ed. X. B. I. Altet (Colloque international, CNRS — Université de Renne II, mai 1983, Paris 1987), 365–84 at 378, fig. 4. For similar open roofs in Belgium and Germany see H. Janse, *Houten Kappen in Nederland, 1000–1940* (Delft 1989), 150, 163.

10. A. R. Martin, 'The Greyfriars of Lincoln', *Archaeol. J.*, 92 (1935), 42–64.

11. W. G. Simpson and C. D. Litton, 'Dendrochronology in Cathedrals', in *The Archaeology of Cathedrals*, ed. T. Tatton-Brown and J. Munby, Oxford University Committee for Archaeology, 42 (1996), 189, figs 15.2 and 15.3; B. Winkles, *Illustrations of the Cathedral Churches of England and Wales*, 2 (London 1838), pl. 71; J. Godal, 'Maritime Archaeology beneath Church Roofs', in *Crossroads in Ancient Shipbuilding*, ed. C. Westerdahl, Oxbow Monograph, 40 (1994), 271–78, fig. 2.

12. D. Mackreth, pers. comm.; S. Ware, *A Treatise of the Properties of Arches and their Abutment Piers* (London 1809), pl. 18; I. Tyers and C. Groves, 'List 104: Tree-ring dates from the University of Sheffield Dendrochronology Laboratory', *Vernacular Architecture*, 30 (1999), 114; I. Tyers and C. Groves, 'List 122: Tree-ring dates from the University of Sheffield Dendrochronology Laboratory', *Vernacular Architecture*, 32 (2001), 87–88.

13. M. F. Hearn and M. Thurlby, 'Previously undetected wooden ribbed vaults in medieval Britain', *JBAA*, 150 (1997), 48–58; M. Thurlby, 'Glasgow Cathedral and the Wooden Barrel Vault in Twelfth- and Thirteenth-Century Architecture in Scotland', in *Medieval Art and Architecture in the Diocese of Glasgow*, ed. R. Fawcett, *BAA Trans.*, XXIII (Leeds 1999), 84–87.

14. RCHME, *An Inventory of the Historical Monuments in the County of Northamptonshire*, 6 (London 1984), 157–61; J. Rogers, 'St Albans Abbey Church: the painted wooden vault over the Presbytery and the Saint's Chapel', *Transactions St Albans Hertfordshire Architectural Archaeological Society* (1931), 122–37.

15. 'Dendrochronology in Cathedrals', 191–92; Thurlby, 'Glasgow Cathedral', figs 1, 3 and 15.

16. F. Bond, *English Church Architecture* (London 1913), 822–25.

17. *Houten Kappen*, 390 (English summary).

18. T. Coomans, 'The east range of Val-Saint-Lambert (1233–34)', in *Studies in Cistercian Art and Architecture*, 5, ed. M. Lillich, Cistercian Studies Series, 167 (Kalamazoo 1998); P. Hoffsummer, *Les charpentes de toitures en Wallonie: typologie et dendrochronologie (xie-xixe siècle), Études et Documents, série Monuments et Sites*, I (Namur 1995), 57–58, fig. 59. Later examples of Dutch and Belgian barrel-vaults can be found in T. Coomans, 'L'architecture médiévale des ordres mendiants (Franciscains, Dominicains, Carmes et Augustins) en Belgique et Pays-Bas', *Revue Belge d'Archéologie et d'Histoire de l'Art*, LXX (2001), 76, 82, 86 and 88.

19. *Houten Kappen*, 154, 218–19, 229, n. 5.

20. *Houten Kappen*, 177.

21. *Report on the Cathedral Church*, ff. 10–11; *Houten Kappen*, 167, figs 292–93; Le Port, 'Charpente du xie-xve siècle', 379, fig. 5.

22. R. E. Howard, R. R. Laxton and C. D. Litton, 'Tree-ring Analysis of Timbers from the Presbytery Roof, Abbey Church of St Albans, St Albans, Hertfordshire', *Ancient Monuments Laboratory Report*, 28 (2000); F. Chapman, *The Sacrist Rolls of Ely*, (Cambridge 1907), 72; W. G. Simpson, 'Documentary and Dendrochronological Evidence for the Building of Salisbury Cathedral', in *Medieval Art and Architecture at Salisbury Cathedral*, ed. L. Keen and T. Cocke, BAA Trans., XVII (Leeds 1996), 10–20.

23. *Les charpentes de toitures en Wallonie*, 66, fig. 42; *Houten Kappen*, 202, fig. 387.

24. Willson Collection, Society of Antiquaries, London, Portfolio A2, 41–42; N. Pevsner and P. Metcalf, *The Cathedrals of England*, v2 (Penguin 1985), figs 140–42; Tyers and C. Groves, 'List 122: Tree-ring dates from the University of Sheffield Dendrochronology Laboratory', *Vernacular Architecture*, 32 (2001), 87–88; 'Payment to John Carpenter, travel to Hamburg to buy timber, £4; for shipping boards from Hamburg to Yarmouth, £4 – 17s – 6d; for transport of the same boards from Yarmouth to Norwich, 6s - 6d'. Norwich Record Office, DCN 1/1/3 (Cellarer's Account 1273–74).

25. 'Maritime Archaeology beneath Church Roofs', 274, fig. 6.

26. H. Kurath ed., *The Middle English Dictionary* (Michigan 1959); D. Owen ed., *The Making of Kings Lynn, a Documentary Survey* (British Academy, London 1984), 335, 369–71; F. Charles, *Conservation of Timber Buildings* (London 1984), 131–32; J. A. Simpson and E. S. C. Weiner ed., *The Oxford English Dictionary*, 2nd edn (Oxford 1989).

27. T. Coomans, pers. comm.

28. R. Fawcett, 'Architectural links between Scotland and the Low Countries in the later Middle Ages', in *Utrecht: Britain and the Continent, Archaeology, Art and Architecture*, ed. E. de Bièvre, BAA Trans., XVIII (Leeds 1996), 172–82 at 179; *Houten Kappen*, 192–93, fig. 362; R. Fawcett, 'Late Gothic Architecture in Scotland: considerations on the influence of the Low Countries', *Proceedings Society of Antiquaries of Scotland*, 112 (1982), 477–96; W. Kelly, 'Carved Oak from St Nicholas' Church, Aberdeen', *Proceedings Society of Antiquaries of Scotland*, 68 (1933–34), 355–66, fig. 5.

29. *Houten Kappen*, 30, fig. 9; F. Épaud, 'La charpente de la cathédrale Notre-Dame de Rouen', *Archéologie Médiévale*, 30–31 (2000–01), 133–73; W. G. Simpson, 'Ely Cathedral: archive report on the nave roof' (unpublished, University of Nottingham, 1996), 8.

30. P. Gelis, 'L'hospice Comtesse de Lille', *Congrès archéologique de France: Flandre*, CXX (1962), 186–92; also on the internet: http://europaphe.aphp.org/en/f_npc_lil_com.html, and http://pro.wanadoo.fr/chazaly/html/lille.htm. My thanks to Thomas Coomans for these references.

31. Centre de Recherches sur les Monuments Historiques, *Charpentes*, 2 (Ministère de la Culture, Paris 1982), D6990–91; M. Viollet-le-Duc, *Dictionnaire Raisonné de l'Architecture Française du xie au xvie siècle*, 6 (Paris 1859), 107–14 and 3, 25–33 for other examples of French barrel-vaults.

32. There was originally 'framed work forming struts filling the spandrils' beneath the three pairs of 'hammer-beams'. Christian goes on to record that, 'The ends of these beams have been cut off irregularly, the spandrils have been destroyed'; '*Report on the Cathedral Church*', f. 10. Billings indicates that the iron tie-bars shown in his illustration of the 1764 vault are contemporary with it and were inserted 'in order to secure the walls of the clerestory from being thrust out' — which would have been the function of such tie-beams; see *Architectural Illustrations*, 9 and pls 22 and 36; *Carlisle Cathedral*, 21.

33. *Houten Kappen*, 205–09, 218–19, 390.

34. Fawcett, 'Architectural links between Scotland and the Low Countries', 172–82; G. W. Barrow, *The Anglo-Norman Era in Scottish History* (Oxford 1980), Chapter 2; C. Wilson, 'The Stellar Vaults of Glasgow

Cathedral's Inner Crypt and Villard de Honnecourt's Chapter House Plan: A Conundrum Revisited', in *Medieval Art and Architecture in the Diocese of Glasgow*, ed. R. Fawcett, *BAA Trans.*, XXIII (Leeds 1999), 55–76; H. Summerson, *Medieval Carlisle: City and the Borders from the Late-Eleventh to the Mid-Sixteenth Century*, I, Cumberland Westmorland Antiquarian Archaeological Society, Extra Series, XXV (1993), 26–27.

35. L. F. Salzman, *Building in England down to 1540: a documentary history* (Oxford 1952), 456–57; B. C. Jones, 'House Building in Carlisle in the Middle Ages', *Transactions Cumberland Westmorland Antiquarian Archaeological Society*, ns, LXXXVI (1986), 100–08.

36 See note 28, 'Late Gothic Architecture', 485.

37. R. G. Albion, *Forests and Sea Power*, (Cambridge, Mass. 1926), 156; E. Jansma, 'Dendrochronological methods to determine the origin of oak timber: a case study on wood from 's-Hertogenbosch', *Helinium*, XXXII (1992), 195–214; *Atlas Florae Europaeae: distribution of vascular plants in Europe*, 2: Gymnospermae (Pinaceae to Ephedraceae), maps 152, 158, 168 and 3: Salicaceae to Balanophoraceae, maps 297, 299 and 301, ed. J. Jalas and J. Suominen (Helsinki 1973); *Building in England*, 196.

38. B. E. Crawford, *Earl and Mormaer: Norse-Pictish relationships in Northern Scotland* (Rosemarkie 1995), 11–17; A. Crone, 'Native Tree-ring Chronologies from some Scottish Medieval Burghs', *Med. Archaeol.*, 44 (2000), 201–16; *Atlas Florae Europaeae*, 2.

39. *Building in England*, 247–48, 257; L. F. Salzman, *English Trade in the Middle Ages* (Oxford 1931), 364. In 1186 two hundred *planchis abietinis* (possibly spruce [*picea abies*]) were conveyed up the Thames to Wallingford. Fifty were then distributed as *planchiis de sappo* to each of the royal residences at Clarendon, Ludgershall, Marlborough and Woodstock, see *Pipe Roll, 32 Henry II*, XXI, 116, 199. As a Norwegian origin is not specified in this instance the boards may have been exported from a Rhenish port. See also W. R. Childs, 'Timber for cloth: changing commodities in Anglo-Baltic trade in the fourteenth century', in *Cogs, Cargoes and Commerce: Maritime Bulk Trade in Northern Europe, 1150–1400*, ed. L. Berggren, N. Hybel and A. Landen (Pontifical Institute for Medieval Studies, forthcoming).

40. 'Dendrochronology in Cathedrals', 197–204.

41. *Houten Kappen*, 154, 229, n. 5; D. de Vries, 'Medieval Roof Construction in Utrecht and the Netherlands', in *Utrecht: Britain and the Continent, Archaeology, Art and Architecture*, ed. E. de Bièvre, *BAA Trans.*, XVIII (Leeds 1996), 226–27.

42. *Magnus Rotulus scaccari Normanniae sub regibus Angliae (1180–1201)*, I, ed. T. Stapleton (London 1840–44), 31, 52; D. Du Cange, *Glossarium mediae et infinae latinitatis* (Paris 1937–38); *Building in England*, 256, 258, 379, 382, 384–85; A. Rey ed., *Dictionnaire Historique de la Langue Française* (Le Robert, Paris 1992).

43. R. E. Latham and D. R. Howlett ed., *Dictionary of Medieval Latin from British Sources*, I, A-L (Oxford 1975–97). The editors, however, do not point out the relationship between amber and pine wood in connection with panelling (*lambruscura*).

44. T. S. Noonan, *The Islamic World, Russia and the Vikings, 750–900* (Ashgate, Aldershot 1998); R. A. Hall ed., *Viking Age York* (London 1994), fig. 59, 97. Early medieval confusion of amber with another luxury product, ambergris, is documented in *OED*.

45. J. Holan, *Norwegian Wood: a tradition of building* (Rizzoli NY 1990) for colour photographs and descriptions of Norwegian medieval and vernacular buildings of pine.

46. *Calendar of Liberate Rolls, 1240–45*, 64, 216, 223 — the original roll PRO C62/20 is unfortunately missing and so it has not been possible to establish the exact wording of the last two references; *CLibR*, 1251–60, 86.

47. Bond, *Church Architecture*, 823; S. Brown, 'Our Magnificent Fabrick': An Architectural History of York Minster* (English Heritage, 2003) 140.

48. *CLibR*, 1240–45, 220 — roll missing, see note 46.

49. *Atlas Florae Europaeae*, 3. The export of oak was prohibited in the 17th century, see H. S. K. Kent, 'The Anglo-Norwegian Timber Trade in the Eighteenth Century', *Economic History Review*, series 2, VIII (1955), 62–74, at 65.

50. O. A. Owen, 'Tuquoy, Westray, Orkney: a challenge for the future', in *The Viking Age in Caithness, Orkney and the North Atlantic*, ed. C. E. Batey, J. Jesch and C. D. Morris (Edinburgh 1995), 318–39 at 331–32.

51. B. E. Crawford and B. B. Smith, *The Biggings, Papa Stour, Shetland: the history and excavation of a royal Norwegian farm*, Society of Antiquaries of Scotland Monograph Series, 15 (Edinburgh 1999). A vacant house in Wakefield which had the boards of its internal walls (*de parietibus*) stripped out by thieves in 1297 is mentioned in W. Baildon ed., *Court Rolls of the Manor of Wakefield*, i, Yorkshire Archaeological Society Record Series, XXIX (1900), 261, 269. The case illustrates the value of good quality panelling for resale and reuse.

52. A. Thowsen, 'The Norwegian Export of Boats to Shetland, and its Influence upon Shetland Boatbuilding and Usage', *Sjofarthistorisk Arbok* (1969), 145–208 at 150. I am grateful to Brian Smith of Shetland Archives for this reference.

53. Parts of contemporary casks of pine have also been found, see C. A. Morris, *Craft, Industry and Everyday Life: Wood and Woodworking in Anglo-Scandinavian and Medieval York, The Archaeology of York 17: The Small Finds* (York 2000), 2104, 2372–74, figs 1068 and 1174.

54. K. Bjerknes and H-E. Liden, *The Stave Churches of Kaupanger* (Norwegian Antiquarian Bulletin, I, Oslo 1975), fig. 6; W. G. Simpson, 'A Survey and Dating of the Timber Structures in the Central Tower of the Abbey Church', in *Alban and St Albans: Roman and Medieval Architecture, Art and Archaeology*, ed. M. Henig and P. Lindley, *BAA Trans.*, xxiv (Leeds 2001), 204–12 at 206–07.

55. *Building in England*, 248–49; J. Geddes, *Medieval Decorative Ironwork in England* (The Society of Antiquaries of London 1999), 391; *CClR*, 1227–31, 367.

56. G. Bryant, *The Early History of Barton-on-Humber*, 2nd edn (WEA, Barton-on-Humber 1994), 118.

57. *CLibR*, 1226–40, 405, 407, 453, 456; *CLibR*, 1251–60, 86, cf. PRO, C62/29, m.14; *OED* under 'wainscot'.

58. *Building in England*, 246; R. Hussey ed., 'Fabric Roll of Rochester Castle', *Archaeologia Cantiana*, 2 (1859) at 117 and 130–31 — to make doors, window shutters and roofs in 1367–68.

59. 'Figure' is a term given to the distinctive pattern on the surfaces of oak boards which have been cleft or sawn radially from the log.

60. See *OED* for wainscot and R. E. Lewis ed., *The Middle English Dictionary* (Ann Arbor 1986) for scotnail; *Building in England*, 314.

61. N. Nicolaysen, *The Viking-Ship discovered at Gokstad in Norway* (Christiana 1882 and reprinted, Gregg International Publishers 1971), 16, 27–28; Thowsen, 'The Norwegian Export of Boats to Shetland', 173–84.

62. *CLibR*, 1240–45, 115, 141.

63. I. Friel, *The Good Ship: Ships, Ship building and Technology, 1200–1520* (London 1995), 77–78; Simpson, 'Survey and Dating of Timber Structures', 206–07.

64. *Building in England*, 424–25.

65. T. H. Lloyd, *England and the German Hanse* (Cambridge 1991), 48–49, 108.

66. Caroe & Partners (Architects), *Abingdon — St Helen's: report on the Lady Chapel Ceiling, its history, repair and conservation* (privately printed, Wells, Somerset 1992); A. E. Preston, 'The Fourteenth Century Painted Ceiling at St Helen's Church, Abingdon', *Berkshire Archaeological J.*, XL (1936), 115–45.

67. See *OED* under 'waggon'.

68. H. Orton and N. Wright, *A Word Geography of England* (London 1974), 18.

69. *Dictionnaire Raisonné*, 6, 112.

'The dim shadowing of the things which should be': The Fourteenth-Century Doom in the East Window of Carlisle Cathedral

DAVID O'CONNOR

Although the east window is one of the acknowledged glories of Carlisle Cathedral and one of the few major monuments of medieval glass painting in the North-West, it has received scant attention from historians since Ferguson published his article in 1876. He dated the extensive Doom in the tracery as late as 1380: a date closer to c. 1340–50 is proposed here. Past campaigns to repair, restore and conserve the window are documented, in particular William Wailes's major restoration of the 14th-century tracery lights in 1856, John Hardman's new main-light glazing of 1859–61 and the conservation of the medieval panels carried out by the York Glaziers Trust in 1982–83. The iconography of the Doom is examined in the light of a similar scheme at Selby Abbey, Yorkshire. While general aspects of the style and design point to connections with York, detailed analysis confirms that the cathedral window, unlike glass in St Cuthbert's, Carlisle, is not the work of Master Robert and the glaziers responsible for the York Minster west window or the Selby Abbey east window. The Summary Catalogue which concludes the paper is the first detailed panel-by-panel description of the window to be published and the first account to differentiate between original 14th-century glass and 19th-century restoration.

THE GLAZING AND ITS ARCHITECTURAL SETTING

ANYONE investigating the medieval stained glass of the north-west of England is immediately confronted by problems. The territory covered by modern-day Cumbria was not one of the economically wealthy regions of medieval England and, with few major monuments and comparatively little glass, placing what has survived in context is even less easy than in some other areas of the country.[1] This situation will doubtless improve a little when Dr Penny Hebgin-Barnes's survey for the Corpus Vitrearum of the medieval stained glass of Lancashire and Cheshire and the present writer's researches with Jonathan Cooke and Nigel Neil for the Bowness-on-Windermere East Window Project are completed. The difficulties in Cumbria are further compounded by a lack of documentation, both on medieval glaziers working in the region and on possible centres of production.

What is true of the region in general also applies at the centre. In 1840 Robert Billings wrote that 'Carlisle has perhaps suffered more from spoliation and neglect than any other cathedral church in England.'[2] Given the particularly violent history of the city and its border region, a sequence of regular fires, uprisings, attacks from the Scots, religiously motivated programmes of suppression and destruction in the 16th and 17th centuries, interspersed with long periods of neglect and some over-zealous restoration, it is hardly surprising that only a small portion of the medieval glazing of the cathedral has survived.[3] Neglect of a different kind prompted one writer to conclude that Carlisle 'must surely have the distinction of being the cathedral, or indeed the largest church, about which least has ever been written'.[4] Fortunately, in the quarter of a century since this statement was made, a great deal has been done, particularly locally, to rectify the situation.

Although the east window of the cathedral (Col. Pl. III) is one of the few major monuments of medieval glass painting in the North-West, it too has received scant attention from historians. Little of any substance has been written about it, with the exception of Chancellor Ferguson's pioneering article, published as long ago as 1876.[5] While this paper includes a valuable description of the Doom in the tracery lights, it makes no distinction between Victorian replacement and original 14th-century glass. On the basis of an heraldic border design in what is an entirely restored panel (A2), Ferguson identified one of the resurrected kings as John of Gaunt, thus dating the window to around 1380, some thirty or forty years too late. Although Eeles and others queried Ferguson's dating, and Lowther Bouch concluded that 'the whole story connecting him [John of Gaunt] with the east window of the cathedral is a myth', guidebooks persist with the late date.[6]

Most writers on the cathedral have concentrated on the stonework of the window rather than on its glass. The east façade has long been regarded as the church's most imposing external feature and, in the 18th century, the interior of the choir, viewed from west to east, came to represent everything about the building that was romantic and sublime. Indeed, an early-19th-century topographical work juxtaposed a view of the 'Interior of Carlisle Cathedral', with the east window at its centre, with a prospect of a 'Waterfall, near Sty Head, Cumberland'.[7] The accompanying text runs:

The *coup-d'oeil* presented by the choir of Carlisle Cathedral is eminently beautiful, using that term in a restricted sense: beautiful to those who feel a glow of piety within them, whilst contemplating the sacred fane, rendered venerable by age — made hallowed by its sacred uses, beautiful to those who are willing to admit into the temple a sublime grandeur, suitable to the character, and calculated to impress the mind with awful feeling, 'to calm the troubled breast and woo the weary to profound repose' . . . The subdued and many coloured light that falls from the east window produces a tranquillizing effect, which added to the 'expressive silence' that reigns in the building, may without enthusiasm, be said to render it the dim shadowing of the things which should be.[8]

In his monograph on the cathedral, Billings quoted Thomas Rickman who had praised the nine-light window with its flowing tracery as 'one of the finest, if not the finest, Decorated window in the kingdom', comparing it favourably with the west window at York.[9] More recently Bulman attributed the design to a York man, who John Harvey went on to identify as Ivo de Raghton, Archbishop William de Melton's mason at York in 1331. According to Harvey, Ivo, who became a freeman of York in 1317, hailed from Raughton, near Carlisle, but William Wilson, who sees Lincolnshire influence in the stem and leaf design of the tracery, has suggested Roughton, near Horncastle, the Lincolnshire manor of the bishops of Carlisle, as a plausible alternative.[10]

Harvey's attribution to Ivo of a series of prestigious works with flowing tracery, including the east front of Carlisle, designed soon after 1318, the east window of Selby Abbey of *c.* 1330 and the west window of York Minster, glazed around 1338/9, is challenged by Coldstream and Wilson, both of whom grapple with the problem of

FIG. 1.   1 East window tracery
© D. O'Connor

FIG. 2.   nXII 2a: peasant
© D. O'Connor

dating the window but come to different conclusions.[11] Bulman, who suggested a complex series of campaigns for the rebuild, concluded that the tracery of the east window, although a design of *c*. 1320, was not constructed until *c*. 1354.[12]

One architectural feature in the central section of the tracery (Col. Pl. III, Fig. 1) is the presence of three large and two small encircled quatrefoils in what is otherwise a flowing, curvilinear design. These Geometric oculi stand out against the upward movement of the converging mouchettes and have been used to support an early dating for the window design.[13] Coldstream, however, points to another example, of the 1340s, on the east wall of the Beverley Minster reredos and John Goodall has drawn my attention to what is presumably a conscious reuse of this motif in the lost east window of the chapel of Queen's College, Oxford, founded by Robert of Eglesfeld, between 1340 and 1342, specifically to educate scholars from Cumberland and Westmorland.[14]

The reconstruction and rebuilding of the choir, following the fire of 1292, has been reassessed by Jenny Alexander in an important paper elsewhere in this volume, but in the absence of a detailed study of the architecture of the east window, an attempt to date the stonework precisely is not an issue that can be resolved here. Suffice it to say that the same buildings used by architectural historians to provide a wider context for the stonework of the window — York, Selby and Lincoln — also figure prominently in a discussion of the Carlisle glass. Whereas at York and Selby documentary or heraldic evidence provide reasonably firm dates for the glass, no such evidence exists for Carlisle. As late as 1359 John de Salkeld bequeathed 100s. to the fabric of the cathedral and a further 40s. 'to make a certain window anew in the chancel there' (*ad fabriccacionem cujusdam fenestre de novo in cancello ibidem xl s.*).[15] While Bulman was tempted to link this donation to the east window itself, the document is clearly not that explicit. In the absence of documentary evidence dating the glass depends on the much less reliable stylistic evidence presented later in the paper, which suggests that the east window was probably glazed around the same time as the York window in the period *c*. 1340–50.

CONDITION AND CONSERVATION

FOLLOWING the dissolution of the priory in 1540 the fabric of the cathedral had declined into a desperate state by 1639. The loss of so much of the medieval glazing may have as much to do with long periods of neglect and indifference as with deliberate destruction at the Reformation or at the hands of later Puritan and Scottish troops.

Of the window to which Richard III donated £5 in October 1483, nothing is now identifiable and of the twenty-two armorials recorded in the north nave clerestory and other windows by Sir William Dugdale as late as 1665, not one has survived intact today.[16] Gathered together in 1949 in the Friends Window in the south choir aisle (sVI) are nine shields formerly in a south clerestory window in the choir, but with the exception of one of the quarters in a shield of Richard II impaling Anne of Bohemia (2c) and possibly a few 14th-century pieces in a Neville shield (3a), this material is 19th-century.[17] The heraldry suggests that some choir clerestory glazing was being inserted between 1388 and 1399, the dates of Richard's marriage to Anne and his deposition.

What else survived was gathered together in the Fragments Window in the nave (nXII), a collection of mainly 14th- and 15th-century pieces which were in a box until skilfully arranged by Caroline Townsend and Joan Howson in 1925.[18] The style and condition of some of these pieces, notably a medallion with a peasant in a landscape

(Fig. 2), suggest close links with the glass of the east window. Several late-14th-century quarries, foliage designs and border crowns probably came from the choir clerestory as they are similar to glass recorded there by Billings.[19]

Like the building, the east window glazing is a shadow of its former self. The main lights could have disappeared as early as the 1540s, along with the Augustinian priory, the images, relics and chantries.[20] It is highly unlikely that much was left by 1769 when, following a bequest of £100 from Lady Gower to be 'particularly applied to repairing and beautifying the East Window', the York glass-painter, William Peckitt, supplied '455 panes, 3 inch sq[ua]r[e] each of purple and yellow' at a cost of nine guineas to form a border around the plain quarry glazing.[21] This somewhat garish colour scheme found little favour with later antiquarians. By the end of the century Hutchinson was complaining that the window 'has no cast of solemnity, by means of a border of coloured glass, thrown round it, of yellow, red and green, which looks gaudy'.[22] Billings, writing when the Gothic Revival was well under way, dismissed the scheme as 'modern glazing of the most tasteless description' and reported that 'it is said that even the old stained-glass of the tracery owed its preservation, eighty years back, to the expense and difficulty of reglazing the small and intricate forms'.[23]

It was the architect, Ewan Christian, who alerted the Dean and Chapter to the parlous state of the window's stonework in 1852. 'The glazing,' he wrote, 'is so greatly dilapidated that in bad weather the rain pours in and the wall and floor beneath thereby kept constantly wet. Nothing short of a complete renewal of the mullions, tracery and glass of this window can effectively remedy its present dilapidated condition.'[24]

By the summer of 1855 the old stonework had been removed and an appeal had been launched for 'the cleaning and Repair of the old Stained Glass in the tracery of the Great East Window and the providing if possible of other glass of corresponding character to fill the remainder of the above or any other windows'.[25] In January 1856 Chapter resolved 'That Mr. Wailes of Newcastle be employed to restore the stained glass in the upper part of the East Window at an expense not exceeding one hundred pounds'.[26] Two graffiti scratched on paintwork and glass in panels C3 and R1 record his involvement.

William Wailes, one of the leading exponents of Gothic Revival glass, and conveniently situated at Newcastle, must have been an obvious choice for the work.[27] His firm had already been responsible for two new windows in the cathedral. The east window of the south aisle (sII), a memorial to Dr John Heysham (d. 1834) and his family, despite its Decorated stonework, is in an early-13th-century style.[28] The other window (Fig. 3), in the west wall of the north transept (nXI), is a memorial to a former Chancellor, Canon Walter Fletcher, towards which Chapter donated £15 in 1846.[29] With its combination of foliage panels based on Strasbourg work of c. 1310, and a donor-figure kneeling at a prie-dieu, it is resolutely Puginian in style and design.[30] Both these windows amply demonstrate Wailes's skill in reproducing the different styles of medieval glass-painting, an ability remarked upon in a perceptive critique written by William Bell Scott, the Pre-Raphaelite poet and painter, who visited the Wailes studio, when Master of the Government School of Design in Newcastle, in 1843.

As to my object in visiting him, he wanted no more education among his workmen than they had. He had his artists, and did not find workmen with art knowledge or proclivities desirable. His grand object was to make his pot-metal pictures like the old ones, comparatively rude in execution, and in this he was right. He knew what his customers wanted: restoration was the order of the day.[31]

FIG. 3. nXI: foliage ornament. William Wailes, 1846

© *D. O'Connor*

FIG. 4. I O1: resurrection of two priests, man and woman, mostly William Wailes, 1856

© *D. O'Connor*

Little archival material has survived for the Wailes studio and no detailed documentation has so far come to light on what exactly was done to the Carlisle window. The tracery glazing was not complete when Wailes restored it and this may explain why so many of the panels, especially in the lower part of the tracery, are now Victorian. Of forty-eight large tracery lights containing figurative glazing, ten are entirely Wailes's work (Fig. 4), six are virtually entirely restored by him and, in a further seven, all the figures are Victorian, so that over a third of the glass is now Victorian.

Wailes has little reputation as a conservationist. We know from work he did in 1844 on the 14th-century glass in All Saints North Street, York, or from his work on the contemporary Jesse Tree at Morpeth, Northumberland, that his restorations could be severe.[32] At Carlisle, it is comparatively easy to differentiate between original 14th-century glass and Wailes's replacement. The 19th-century artists did not go to enormous lengths to disguise their work, although they painted a false patina on the exterior surface so that from a distance the new and the old merge quite well.

With the restoration of the tracery lights successfully completed, attention turned, between 1859 and 1861, to the main lights. At a cost of £1190, the 18th-century glass was replaced by the present window, a memorial to Bishop Hugh Percy, designed by John Hardman Powell, Pugin's successor and principal stained glass artist at the

FIG. 5.   I 1a: Annunciation, John Hardman,
1859–61
© D. O'Connor

FIG. 6.   I R1 and U1: exterior in 1982
© D. O'Connor

Hardman Studios in Birmingham.[33] It is an impressive window, illustrating the New Testament narrative from the Annunciation (Fig. 5) to Pentecost, cleverly arranged around a central light depicting the Crucifixion, Resurrection and Ascension.

While there seems to have been little interest in attempting to recover the original subject of the window, most probably a Tree of Jesse, demi-figures of Isaiah and other prophets are included in the leafy canopies of rows 2, 4 and 6. Concern that the new work should harmonise with the old may explain an entry in the Chapter Order Book in June, 1859, when the design was approved, confirming 'that Mr. Hardman be allowed to take away three of the compartments from the upper part of the window to be carefully preserved and replaced when done with'.[34] Arrangements did not go to plan, however, as in September 1859 the Chancellor, C. J. Burton, was writing to Hardman to explain that he had been sent modern, rather than medieval panels in error: 'I was not aware until now, my eyesight not being very good, that the glass in the lower part of the tracery of the East Window is not ancient, there not having been sufficient to fill up the whole. All the upper part is ancient. Although it is most likely that you have, on inspecting what was taken out, discovered this, it is right I should mention it.'[35] While, in the end, the two sections of the window remain quite distinct, the overall effect is not unpleasing. As C. King Ely pointed out, in the Bells Guide to the cathedral, Hardman's work is probably more in tune with Owen Jones's restoration of

FIG. 7.   I Vı: head of trumpeting angel

© D. O'Connor

the ceiling than with the ancient glass.[36] Like most of J. H. Powell's windows at this time, Carlisle probably owes as much to trecento Sienna as it does to 14th-century York, although a few ornamental details, like the rinceaux backgrounds, may have been inspired by the old glass.

Nothing further is heard about the state of the window until towards the end of the century when the Chapter Surveyor reported that 'the lead had been broken and several pieces of stained glass broken by a storm of wind which occurred on Tuesday, September 1st, 1891'.[37] What appear to have been only minor repairs to lead and glass were carried out by the local firm, Messrs R. and W. M. Hill of Castle Street, Carlisle.[38]

The only serious work since Wailes's restoration was the conservation carried out by York Glaziers Trust in 1982–83 as part of a major programme of repairs to the choir. By this date there was concern about the poor physical condition of both glass and lead. An exterior view of two panels (Fig. 6), taken from scaffolding in November 1982 just before the glass was removed for cleaning at York, shows the thick crust of corrosive products which had formed on the exterior. Some glass had also corroded on its inner surface (Fig. 7), causing lack of translucency and badly damaging the paint. With the

153

FIG. 8.   I V2: head of trumpeting angel in 1982
before cleaning
© D. O'Connor

FIG. 9.   I V2: head of trumpeting angel in 1983
after cleaning
© D. O'Connor

potassium rich glasses of the Middle Ages such a breakdown of material is not unusual, but severe corrosion of this kind is far from common in English glass of the mid-14th century. Examining the glass in 1982, I wondered whether Wailes had cleaned it with acid, a theory which was disproved when panels were being releaded and it was possible to see the original surface of the glass preserved beneath the leads.

At that time, Dr Alwyn Cox and Dr Kate Gillies of the Department of Physics at the University of York analysed ten badly weathered pieces of blue, green, pink and yellow glass. They found that all the pieces had remarkably similar chemical compositions, with relatively low levels of magnesia and high levels of lime, suggesting that the glass-painters had purchased their sheets from the same source. What is also worth noting is that while the Carlisle glasses compared with a very few samples that the scientists had taken from contemporary windows in York, their chemical composition was radically different from what was usual in York and neighbouring sites.[39]

Conservation policy in York in the 1980s was to remove weathering crusts from the exterior of badly corroded glass and, when trial cleaning with ultrasonic equipment and glass fibre brushes proved ineffective, it was decided to use airbrasive equipment. The results can be seen by comparing photographs of the head of a trumpeting angel in panel V2, one of the better preserved heads in the window, taken *in situ* in 1982, prior

FIG. 10.   Exterior of east window showing the protective glazing in 1984
© D. O'Connor

to cleaning (Fig. 8), with a photograph of the same glass, taken the following year at York, shortly after airbrasive treatment (Fig. 9).

There is little point in carrying out extensive cleaning of unstable glass, only to fix it back in the window unprotected, where, exposed to high humidity levels, rain water and condensation, the process of corrosion and darkening simply starts afresh. At Carlisle, 3 mm thick protective glazing was cut and leaded to follow the main outlines of the medieval panels and fixed into the same glazing groove (Fig. 10). While the choice of an externally ventilated protective glazing may seem eccentric — usually an isothermal protective glazing ventilated from the interior of the building is preferred — the present system was installed on the advice of Professor Roy Newton, scientific adviser to the York Glaziers Trust who, presumably, found exceptional climatic conditions at Carlisle.[40] Only time will tell how successfully the protective glazing performs, but it should extend the life of the glass considerably and reduce the need for major releadings and extensive repairs.

SUBJECT MATTER AND ICONOGRAPHY

ALTHOUGH there is no firm evidence to confirm the original contents of the main lights of the window, Ferguson's suggestion, that the lower part of the window probably consisted of a Tree of Jesse, is almost certainly correct.[41] The theme of the genealogical tree, showing Christ's earthly ancestors, including the kings of Judah, alongside his spiritual ancestors, the Old Testament patriarchs and prophets, was extremely popular in England in the 14th century.

As a subject linked to the cult of the Virgin, many examples are found in churches and chapels dedicated to Mary, or associated with Marian altars. Given the original dedication of the cathedral to the Virgin Mary and the presence there, by the 14th century, of an altar, lights and cult image, a Jesse in the principal window would make sense.[42] Nothing seems to be known about the liturgical significance of the two bays to the east of the high altar in its original setting. Had this area functioned as a Lady Chapel, as at Beverley, Selby or York, then such a window would have even more specific significance.

The presence of the Doom in the tracery lights lends further support to this theory. The three basic methods of dealing with the tracery lights of English Jesses in the 14th century were to extend the Jesse upwards with kings and prophets, as, for example at Bristol, or to append an Infancy cycle, as in the northern Jesses at Cartmel Priory, Cumbria and St Mary's, Morpeth, Northumberland, or to provide an extensive Doom like that at Carlisle. This last solution was used, for example, at Selby Abbey (Fig. 12), Wells Cathedral, New College, Oxford and Winchester College.[43] It is difficult to come up with a single example of an extensive tracery-light Doom cycle in English 14th-century glass, as opposed to a smaller-scale grouping of Christ as Judge with angels, which does not contain a Jesse Tree below. Unlike the combination of Jesse and Infancy cycle, which probably depended on illuminated manuscripts, the linking of Jesse and Last Judgement reflects the liturgy. Its popularity with designers of large-scale multi-panelled traceries may have had something to do with its flexibility as a theme, but there are good theological reasons for a typological approach based on liturgical texts for Advent which link Christ's first coming to his second coming as judge.

A nine-light Jesse would not be impossible to devise, but there is a precedent at Selby for a seven-light window which combines a Jesse in five central openings with a pair of outer lights containing apostles, evangelists, doctors of the church and other male

FIG. 11. I U1: resurrection of man, priest and king
© D. O'Connor

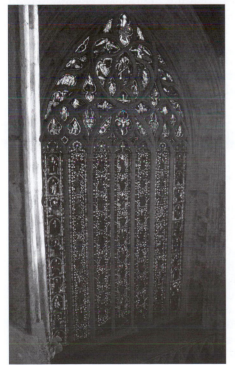

FIG. 12. Selby Abbey, Yorkshire, east window (I):
tree of Jesse and doom, Ward and Hughes, 1906–09
copy of glass of c. 1340
© D. O'Connor

saints.[44] It is not impossible to envisage figures, important to the spiritual life of the cathedral and the diocese, like St Augustine of Hippo or St Cuthbert, who might appear in such a window. Firm evidence may emerge in due course to resolve this matter.

The subject of the tracery, an extensive Doom (Fig. 1) is more straightforward. As arranged at present there are 36 large openings depicting souls rising from their tombs: two smaller openings (W1, W2) also contain heads of souls in winding sheets, but only the first of these is original and it could have wandered from a larger opening. The souls form the largest group of figures in the window, not only taking up virtually all the outer sections of the tracery, but also several openings in the central section of the window, as well as the spandrels near the top. Although many of these panels, especially those at the bottom in rows A and C, are entirely or mostly by Wailes's glaziers, enough original glass remains to show that the present iconography, depicting the souls as representative of all conditions and levels of society, men, women, knights, priests, canons or monks, popes and kings, follows the original format.

Apart from their variously coloured winding sheets the figures are naked, with the exception of clerics (Fig. 11), who were buried in their vestments and kings who are depicted crowned and sometimes robed. The souls usually emerge out of tombs (Col. Pl. IVa), shown with arcading or openings in perspective, and with incised covers showing a wide variety of cross forms, sometimes adorned with chalices or, possibly, weapons, to indicate the occupation of the deceased (Fig. 11). These designs reflect grave forms popular in northern England in the 14th century; indeed, comparisons can be made with recently surveyed local material of this kind.[45]

Ferguson pointed out that many designs for these panels are repeated. As with other big windows of this type, Selby east window or York west window for example, the designer was really only working on about half the window. Full-scale cutlines would have been produced on wooden tables so that a figure on the left of the window could be turned round, and reused, perhaps with some variation in colour and ornament, in the equivalent panel on the right.

While there is no evidence for a figure of St Michael weighing souls in the present window, it is difficult to imagine a Doom without the archangel. A key central opening (N1), now occupied by a Victorian panel with souls, would have been the ideal location for just such an image. Nicely weighted imagery, grouped around a central axis, must have been an important element not only in the design, but in the overall meaning of the window. Pamela Sheingorn has shown how crucial this left-right balance was to the artists who first tried to give visual expression to a confusing series of biblical texts on the Last Judgement.[46] While, at Carlisle, there is no attempt to differentiate between damned and saved, presumably those on Christ's left are hell bound and those to his right are heading for heaven.

Six panels, the four in row J and the two flanking Christ near the apex of the window (V1, V2), contain winged angels with long natural trumpets, sounding the last trump (Fig. 13). Seated on a rainbow, dominating the top of the window (X1), is the much restored figure of Christ, displaying his wounds (Col. Pl. IVb). His original disposition has probably been reversed, as it is more likely that Christ was depicted with his right hand raised in blessing than with his left hand raised as now.

While it is possible that they were deliberately designed in order to give special prominence to heaven and hell, as Bulman suggested, it is highly unusual in a monumental window like this to find heaven and hell positioned on a vertical, rather than a horizontal axis. The Carlisle tracery may simply demonstrate the medieval glazier's skill in adapting designs to awkward and complex tracery openings.

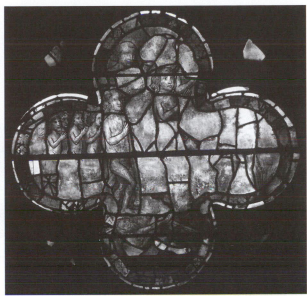

FIG. 14.   I R1: the saved
© D. O'Connor

FIG. 13.   I J1 trumpeting angel
© D. O'Connor

The two upper quatrefoils (R1, R2) represent the Heavenly City with a group of some sixteen saved souls in procession on the left (Fig. 14) and, in a much restored panel on the right (Col. Pl. IVc), more souls welcomed by angels and by St Peter, who stands at the entrance to a city with perspectival architectural forms. Substituting dark coloured backgrounds in these two panels with white glass, enhanced in places with yellow stain, is a simple, but effective means of creating a heavenly ambience.

A third quatrefoil (Col. Pl. Vb), containing hell (D1), also stands out because of its striking red colouring and distinctive shape. This must be the most imaginative, dramatic and visually exciting design in the window, reminiscent of the lively hell scene in the Last Judgement in the Holkham Bible of c. 1320–30.[47] In the lower half, where hell mouth is depicted as a monstrous head with streaky red fur and large multicoloured eye and eyebrow, a naked man, impaled on a spit, is roasted over a container (Col. Pl. Va). Ruby flames extend upwards into the upper half of the panel, engulfing a soul whose hair stands on end. At the top, four damned souls are boiled in a cauldron, while devils, armed with flesh hooks, flank the gallows on which hang two naked figures, one of them (Col. Pl. Vc) a woman with a noose around her neck. Interesting materials are used to enhance dramatic effects. The very uneven, streaky ruby glass gives an almost three-dimensional sense of movement to the flickering flames. A bull's-eye, used on the cauldron, shows that the Carlisle glaziers worked with crown as well as cylinder glass.

159

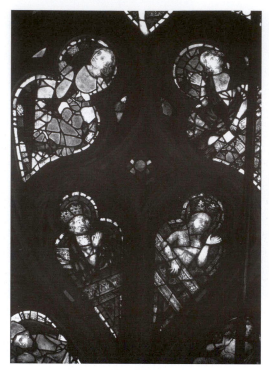

FIG. 15. I I3, I4, K3 and K4: resurrection of
kings and men

© D. O'Connor

FIG. 16. Dorchester Abbey, Oxon. I 5b:
resurrection of king from Selby Abbey, I H1
c. 1340

© the late Dennis King

At York and Beverley, around the same date, such bull's-eyes were used for special effects.[48]

In their general approach to the Doom comparisons can be made between the tracery at Carlisle and the Last Judgement cycles in the south rose at Lincoln Cathedral and the east window at Selby (Fig. 16). The Lincoln window is, unfortunately, very poorly preserved and Selby is now a facsimile of 1906–09, although some original glass has survived elsewhere and there are good reasons for thinking that the present window is a faithful copy of the *c.* 1340 design.[49] While there are fewer panels at Selby, they also show souls rising from tombs with gravecovers, trumpeting angels and angels holding instruments of the passion, flanking the wounded Christ. Like Carlisle, the Selby heaven is an architectural concept and hell also contains a monstrous mouth and cauldron. While the Carlisle designer may have known the Selby window, which is probably, but not necessarily the earlier of the two works, these Dooms, though similar, were not produced from the same designs.

STYLE AND DESIGN

THE Selby east window discussed above is attributed to Master Robert and the glaziers who produced the west window of 1338/9 at York Minster.[50] Comparisons of panels

FIG. 17.   I M1: head of resurrected man
© D. O'Connor

FIG. 18.   York Minster. NV 2a: head of
Jeremiah, *c.* 1330–40

*Photograph: D. O'Connor, by kind permission of the
Dean and Chapter of York*

depicting resurrected kings from Carlisle and Selby (Figs 15 and 16) and of heads from Carlisle and York Minster (Figs 17 and 18) confirm that in general approach to design and figure style the Carlisle window shares many features with the Yorkshire glass. Heads at Carlisle may lack the elegance and control of some York work, but with their narrow, almond shaped eyes, flowing, curly hair and softly modelled features they follow conventions that probably derive from Italian and North French sources that were still fashionable in court circles as late as 1352.[51] More detailed analysis, however, suggests that the windows in York and in Carlisle were produced by different designers and glaziers.

While some of the background designs used at Carlisle, like curling trefoil, kidney and spade leaf rinceaux, are broadly similar to patterns at Selby and York, the border designs are markedly different. At Carlisle these consist mainly of simple, bold geometric patterns with combinations of circles, trefoils, quatrefoils and lozenges (Fig. 19), with a few foliate cross designs (Fig. 20) and a little zigzag, running quatrefoil leaf and running scroll patterns. Heraldic borders, which are such a feature of the York glass, only occur in a few Victorian panels. Many of the smaller panels, higher up the tracery, have plain borders.

Architectural forms, like the simple arcading and openings on tombs or the more elaborate but much restored townscape of heaven (R1, R2), incorporate the kind of three-dimensional effects (Col. Pl. IVc and Fig. 21) that were such features of English

FIG. 19.   I X1: detail of background and
border
© D. O'Connor

FIG. 20.   I K4: detail of background and border
© D. O'Connor

stained glass of the second quarter of the 14th century.[52] These spatial effects are less developed than in the glass associated with York and there is no evidence for a similar obsession with architectural ornament and Decorated tracery designs.

To sum up, there appears to be a marked difference in artistic quality between the Carlisle and the York glass, a feature which might simply reflect the two city's relative status as ecclesiastical and artistic centres or the availability of funds. Archbishop Melton, the donor of the York west window, was one of the great clerical patrons of his day and innovatory iconography, fashionable Parisian styles of painting and an unmatched technical brilliance mark out his window as an exceptional work. These particular qualities are not so evident at Carlisle, where designs are less complex, ornament is less exuberant and painting and staining techniques are less precocious. Comparisons between windows designed for different settings and in different states of preservation may appear invidious, but the Carlisle window was probably a little more saturated and intense in its colouring than the York window, with more restricted use of white glass and yellow stain and probably with less of the brilliance and transparency of the Master Robert work. Perhaps the chemical analysis of the glass, mentioned previously, tends to reinforce the differences in approach.

The differences in style are made clear when comparing the cathedral glass with that in the nearby parish church of St Cuthbert, a building for which the cathedral canons were responsible. In the nave of the present 18th-century church (nIV) are some well

FIG. 21.   I R2: detail
of angel and Heaven
© D. O'Connor

FIG. 22.   Carlisle, St Cuthbert, nIV:
composite window using mainly fragments of
c. 1340
© D. O'Connor

preserved fragments (Fig. 22) of the very highest quality which show all the characteristics of the York west window glazing of *c.* 1340.[53] These remnants of figures, canopies, rinceaux backgrounds and borders were very successfully rearranged by the dean of York, Eric Milner-White and the York Minster glaziers in 1960; 'A miraculous piece of work, though I say it myself,' the dean proclaimed.[54]

While the glass is said to have come from the previous, medieval building on the site, given the church's connections with the cathedral, and because some of the 15th-century pieces replicate designs found in the Fragments Window of the cathedral (nXIII), it is tempting to suggest that the glass could have wandered. Unless the main lights and the tracery lights of the east window were produced by two different workshops, a previous suggestion of mine, tentatively linking this glass with the cathedral east window, now seems unlikely.[55] If nothing else though, St Cuthbert's confirms that some 14th-century patrons in Carlisle, like their Augustinian counterparts at Cartmel, turned to the capital of the Northern Province for stained glass, just as others did for luxury goods and armaments.[56]

If stylistic analysis suggests that the cathedral window is not linked directly with York, the evidence suggests that it is likely to have been produced by craftsmen who may well have been influenced by York work. Virtually nothing is known about medieval glaziers in Carlisle, although their presence in the city is documented in the late 13th century and a Master John the Glazier of Carlisle worked on Edward I's lodgings at Lanercost Priory in association with the king's visit in 1306–07.[57]

During the reconstruction of the cathedral choir a resident glazing team of some sort must have been a necessity, but whether stained glass was produced in Carlisle itself or whether much of it was transported long distances from York, or whether Newcastle glaziers were involved, as they were in the 19th century, remains uncertain.[58] The 14th-century glass of County Durham and Northumberland presents a similar picture to the situation in Cumbria. Windows like those at Morpeth and Ponteland were almost certainly produced by York glaziers, while glass at Bothel, for example, shows stylistic affinities with York glass.[59]

Some outstanding Cumbrian windows, in places like Bowness-on-Windermere, Cartmel Priory and Greystoke, confirm that the relationship with York continued right up to the Reformation.[60] Moreover, there is documentary evidence to link York glaziers like Robert Preston (d. 1506) and John Petty (d. 1508) with such institutions as Wetheral Priory and Furness Abbey.[61] Until the medieval stained glass of Cumbria has been fully recorded and documented it is difficult to be sure whether it was only the rich patrons of the monasteries and the cathedral who forged these links directly or, whether the influence of York glaziers in Cumbria was a much more pervasive phenomenon.

SUMMARY CATALOGUE

The Corpus Vitrearum Medii Aevi window and panel numbering system is used in this article. For the position of panels in the tracery of the east window (window I) see the accompanying diagram (Fig. 23).

EAST WINDOW (I): TRACERY LIGHTS (Col. Pls III and VB, Fig. 1)

THE main lights of the nine-light east window of Carlisle Cathedral contain New Testament scenes from the Annunciation to Pentecost, designed by John Hardman Powell for John Hardman of Birmingham in 1859–61. The flowing tracery above contains a Last Judgement or Doom, probably dating from

FIG. 23.   East window tracery: key to numbering of panels

© *D. O'Connor*

c. 1340–50. The medieval glass was restored by William Wailes of Newcastle in 1856 and was conserved by the York Glaziers Trust in 1982–83, when exterior protective glazing was installed.

A1. Resurrection of Man, h. 0.96 m, w. 0.61 m

Victorian panel with man in green winding sheet rising from tomb. Red rinceau background. Border with rose-stem on alternating blue and red background.

A2. Resurrection of King, h. 0.96 m, w. 0.61 m

Victorian panel with crowned king in pink winding sheet rising from tomb. Blue background. Red and yellow border with heraldic devices of castles or and lions heads gules.

A3. Resurrection of Priest, h. 0.96 m, w. 0.60 m

Bearded and tonsured cleric in yellow winding sheet rising from tomb and holding green grave cover incised with a cross with fleur-de-lys terminals. Blue background. Borders of alternating red and yellow foliate crosses in quatrefoils.

Head by Wailes. This, as well as the dress and the absence of a chalice on grave cover cast doubt on figure's original identity. A few other minor restorations, but most of glass original, if badly corroded and cracked.

A4. Resurrection of Man, h.0.96 m, w.0.61 m

Victorian panel, as A1 reversed, but with pink winding sheet and blue rinceau background.

B1–B4, B7–B10. Tracery Designs

Small modern triangles in blue, red and yellow glass.

B5, B6. Tracery Designs, h. 0.25 m, w. 0.12 m

Two triangular openings. In B5, a modern blue circle on 14th-century red background with white border. In B6, a 14th-century blue and red quatrefoil on white foliage background containing some plain 14th-century glass.

C1. Resurrection of Priest, h. 0.92 m, w. 0.32 m

Victorian panel with tonsured priest in white winding sheet, rising from tomb with grave cover. Blue trefoil rinceau background. Spandrels in modern yellow and blue.

C2. Resurrection of Man, h. 0.87 m, w. 0.35 m

Bearded man, with white winding sheet pulled over head, rising from red tomb with white cover incised with straight-armed cross with

round terminals. Blue rinceau background. Green border with running quatrefoil leaf pattern.

Mainly original but the head, some drapery, most of tomb and a few other pieces by Wailes. Severe corrosion, except in borders. Severe paint loss on blue and red. Spandrels in modern red.

C3. Resurrection of Man, h. 0.86 m, w. 0.37 m

Bearded man in blue winding sheet rising from tomb with square windows in perspective on the side. Red foliate background, changing to blue trefoil-rinceau at top. Border with running scroll motif in white and yellow stain, changing to green with running band of alternating circle and quatrefoil ornament at top.

Figure and part of tomb by Wailes. Remainder mostly 14th century but, presumably, incorporating glass originally in separate panels. Bottom right border patched with architectural fragment from 15th-century canopy. Severe corrosion and paint loss. Graffito scratched out of paint on restored piece of tomb top: 'Restored by W Wailes Newcastle on T[yne].' The end now obscured by mending lead inserted in 1983. Spandrels in modern white.

C4. Resurrection of Priest, h. 0.86 m, w. 0.26 m

Victorian panel, as C1 in reverse, except for a few 14th-century pieces in border. Spandrels in modern white on left and blue on right.

C5. Resurrection of Priest, h. 0.89 m, w. 0.31 m

Victorian panel, as C1, but with blue winding sheet and red background. Spandrels modern.

C6. Resurrection of Soul, h. 0.87 m, w. 0.36 m

As C3 in reverse, but with blue winding sheet pulled over head and with entirely red background and white border.

Head and a few other pieces by Wailes. The panel was inside out and did not fit stonework in 1982, when the leading was buckling. Spandrels red.

C7. Resurrection of Man, h. 0.87 m, w. 0.35 m

Much as C2, but tomb has bold quatrefoil pattern, background is red and border white with running scroll motif.

Figure and a few other pieces by Wailes. Severe corrosion has virtually removed the flashed surface of the red. Spandrels modern, red on left and blue on right.

C8. Resurrection of Priest, h. 0.92 m, w. 0.33 m

Victorian panel, as C1, but with 14th-century architectural fragment patching grave cover and other fragments in border.

D1. Hell, h. 1.06 m, w. 1.06 m (Col. Pls Va, b, and c)

The panel is divided in half by a horizontal leadline. In the lower half, hell mouth is represented by a monstrous head with streaky, flame-like red fur, a large eye with blue pupil and white and yellow stained iris, and a green eyebrow. In the bottom foil, tormented by flames, is a group of some eight naked souls with a devil. Above, roasted over a yellow container by two green devils, is a naked man with hands and feet bound, impaled on a spit. Streaky red flames extend into the upper half of the panel where, on the left, they engulf a naked soul whose hair stands on end and, on the right, a group of three naked souls in torment. In the top foil, four damned souls are boiled in a pale blue cauldron, the third figure wringing his hands in sorrow. Standing on the left of the cauldron is a pale yellow devil holding an implement by the shaft and on the right is a hairy blue devil with furry tail, holding a flesh hook. They flank a pair of gallows on which hang two naked figures, the one on the left a woman with a noose around her neck. Blue rinceau background, but green in top foil.

The panel is a mixture of original glass and restoration by Wailes. Nearly all the figures in the bottom foil are restored and there is some ruby replacement in the left foil. The two green devils in the central section are restorations, as is the group of figures in the right foil. The top foil is original apart from the second figure in the cauldron, in pink glass, and the gallows at top right. Prior to 1983, when a few

areas were releaded, the panel was buckling and the original glass which, apart from the cauldron is mostly heavily corroded, was badly cracked in places. Graffito scratched on exterior of 19th-century insertion: 'W[illia]m Baty, 20 C[ar]rock Square, Carlisle, Nov[ember] 21st 1891.'

Some of the streaky ruby glass used for fur and flames is very uneven and was probably chosen deliberately to enhance the visual effect. A large bump on the cauldron looks like a bull's-eye from the centre of a sheet of crown glass.

Spandrels with four small triangles in 14th-century blue, pink and white glass.

E1–E4. Tracery Designs

Four small triangles in modern red glass.

F1. Resurrection of Soul, h. 0.37 m, w. 0.72 m

Half-length figure in white winding sheet, rising from tomb. Blue background. Blue border with yellow foliate crosses in quatrefoils.

Piece of hair, right shoulder and hand, and most of tomb by Wailes. Remainder suffering severe corrosion and paint loss, with one piece virtually eaten through. Buckling badly in 1982. Some plating in 1983.

F2. Resurrection of Bishop, h. 0.37 m, w. 0.71 m

Half-length mitred cleric wearing pink chasuble and holding yellow crozier, rising from tomb. Blue trefoil-rinceau background. Border with quatrefoil band in white and yellow stain.

Figure by Wailes, with exception of lighter pieces of chasuble and stem of crozier. Rest mainly original, but central background and top and right of border restored. Very severe corrosion and paint loss.

F3. Resurrection of Bishop, h. 0.37 m, w. 0.72 m

As F2 in reverse, but fixed inside out.

About half the glass is original with head, hands, background and most of left part of border by Wailes. Severe corrosion, cracking and paint loss.

F4. Resurrection of Man, h. 0.37 m, w. 0.71 m

Similar to F1, in reverse. Half-length figure, in pink winding sheet, rising from tomb with blue grave cover incised with a cross. Red background. Borders of mainly blue, green and yellow lozenges in quatrefoils.

Figure and surrounding glass on left of panel by Wailes. Largely original, very corroded glass to right of figure. Spandrels in modern blue and purple.

G1, G8. Tracery Designs

Two small triangular openings in mainly 14th-century glass. In G1 is a red circle on pink with white border and in G8, red glass on blue within a white border.

G2, G3, G6, G7. Tracery Designs

Four small modern triangles in red and purple glass.

G4, G5. Tracery Designs

Two small triangular openings. In G4 is a 14th-century medallion containing a red lozenge with blue and yellow glass on a modern blue and white background. G5 also contains old glass.

H1. Resurrection of Two Men and Woman, h. 1.16 m, w. 0.64 m

Almost entirely restored panel depicting three figures rising from tombs with grave covers. Original glass includes a few blue and red pieces of tomb and the upper part of the green grave cover, as well as the top section of red rinceau background. Spandrels in modern red on left and medieval blue, pink and white on right.

H2. Resurrection of Two Men and Woman, h. 1.16 m, w. 0.64 m

Almost entirely restored panel, as H1 reversed. Blue rinceau background mostly original.

Spandrels in medieval green and white on left and modern white on right.

I1. Resurrection of King, h. 0.85 m, w. 0.36 m

Victorian panel with figure in blue robe on red background.

I2. Resurrection of King, h. 0.86 m, w. 0.38 m

Victorian panel with naked figure on blue background.

I3. Resurrection of King, h. 0.82 m, w. 0.37 m
(Fig. 15)

Virtually entirely Victorian panel with king in green winding sheet, rising from tomb with incised grave cover. Blue background. Red and white border.

Three pieces of 14th-century white glass in border; two fragments of stem from foliage grisaille and a piece with yellow stain.

I4. Resurrection of King, h. 0.86 m, w. 0.39 m
(Fig. 15)

Victorian panel with naked king rising from tomb. Red background. Blue and white border.

J1. Trumpeting Angel, h. 0.91 m, w. 0.31 m
(Fig. 13)

Barefooted angel, in pink robe and yellow wings, standing to right blowing a long white trumpet. Blue kidney-rinceau background. Plain white border.

Mainly original, very corroded glass. Minor restorations to hair, robe, trumpet and background. Panel was buckling, prior to 1983, when some shattered glass was about to fall out.

J2. Trumpeting Angel, h. 0.92 m, w. 0.30 m

Copy of J3, in reverse, by Wailes, but with blue robe, green wings and red background. Piece inserted in robe in 1983.

J3. Trumpeting Angel, h. 0.92 m, w. 0.32 m

Barefooted white angel, with pink robe and yellow wings, standing to right blowing a long yellow stained trumpet. Blue rinceau background. Plain white border.

Foot and lower half of robe are original, but rest of figure and trumpet by Wailes.

J4. Trumpeting Angel, h. 0.88 m, w. 0.31 m

As J1 in reverse, but angel in pale blue robe, trumpet yellow and background red.

Head and bell of trumpet, as well as some pieces of ground and border by Wailes. Severe corrosion and paint loss on original.

K1. Resurrection of Man, h. 0.88 m, w. 0.51 m (Col. Pl. IVA)

Man in murrey winding sheet rising from tomb with pale-blue grave cover engraved with a bracelet cross and, possibly, a spear shaft in yellow stain. Blue rinceau background patched in places with alien red diaper. Red border with white foliate crosses in quatrefoils.

Original except for the figure which, with the exception of the left hand and main central section of mantle, is by Wailes, who also restored top left of grave cover. Most original glass is severely corroded, but the grave cover is unusually well preserved. Spandrels red with medieval glass on left and modern on right.

K2. Resurrection of Man, h. 0.89 m, w. 0.48 m

Victorian panel with a man in green winding sheet rising from tomb with grave cover. Blue background. Spandrels with medieval white to left and modern red to right.

K3. Resurrection of Man. h. 0.89 m, w. 0.45 m (Fig. 15)

Probably originally much as K1, with man in pink winding sheet rising from tomb with a white cover incised with cross. Blue trefoil rinceau background. Border as K1.

Head, a few pieces of the mantle, background and border by Wailes. Original in very poor condition, with severe paint loss and cracking. Spandrels in medieval white on left and pink, red and white on right. One piece of streaky ruby painted with curving lines may come from hell in D1.

K4. Resurrection of Man, h. 0.89 m, w. 0.49 m (Figs 15 and 20)

Largely original panel with man in green winding sheet rising from a tomb, with quatrefoil base, arcading in perspective and white and yellow stained cover. Blue trefoil rinceau background. Red border with yellow foliate crosses in quatrefoils.

Head, right wrist and parts of upper left arm by Wailes with minor patches and restoration elsewhere. Spandrels in medieval blue and white on left and modern white on right. One 14th-c. piece, set inside out, has a band of round-armed cross ornament.

L1, L2. Tracery Designs, h. 0.17 m, w. 0.17 m

Two small 14th-century lozenges. In L1, blue, green, yellow and white glass, including two green painted pieces set inside out. One of them, with a cross moline, probably comes from a grave cover. In L2 a white circle on blue background.

M1. Resurrection of Two Men, h. 0.87 m, w. 0.37 m (Fig. 17)

Two bearded figures rising from a tomb with grave cover. The man below wears a blue winding sheet, and the upper figure, whose hand supports his cheek in an attitude of sorrow, is in green. Red rinceau background. White border with band of quatrefoils.

Only the leg of the lower figure is original, but the upper figure is authentic except for the lower part of hand. Severe exterior corrosion, especially at top.

M2. Resurrection of Pope, h. 0.89 m, w. 0.34 m

Bearded cleric wearing papal tiara and holding papal cross-staff, rising from tomb with grave cover. White patterned border.

Figure restored by Wailes. Remainder original, except for a few recycled 14th-century pieces and minor restorations. Severe exterior corrosion, but back-painting has preserved the raised surface of the cross, and what looks like a crozier, on the grave cover.

Tiny spandrels to left and right in 14th-century pink, red and white glass. Some streaky ruby painted with curling lines, may have come from hell in D1.

N1. Resurrection of Souls, h. 1.19 m, w. 0.90 m

Victorian panel with a group of five figures rising from tombs with grave covers. Red background. Four tiny spandrels in blue and yellow glass.

O1. Resurrection of Two Priests, Man and Woman, h. 1.14 m, w. 0.68 m (Fig. 4)

A virtually entirely Victorian panel with four figures rising from tomb with grave covers. Only top pieces of red background are original.

O2. Resurrection of Two Priests, Man and Woman, h. 1.14 m, w. 0.68 m

As O1, in reverse, but with a little more original glass, including the upper priest's purple chasuble, the woman's purple winding sheet and some blue trefoil-rinceau background. Some very severe corrosion.

P1, P2. Tracery Designs

Two small modern triangles with white cinquefoil flower on white foliage.

P3, P4. Tracery Designs

Two tiny triangles in modern glass.

P5, P6. Tracery Designs

Two small triangles with green cinquefoil flower on white foliage. In P3, one petal is original and in P4, some of the white background.

Q1. Resurrection of Archbishop. h. 0.59 m, w. 0.34 m

Cleric in green amice, pink chasuble and patterned yellow pallium rising from a tomb with incised cross on grave cover. Blue spade-leaf rinceau background. White border. Side of tomb pierced with little round-headed windows in perspective.

Head, right hand and top of grave cover by Wailes. Original severely corroded and cracked.

Q2. Resurrection of King, h. 0.59 m, w. 0.34 m

Heavily restored panel with king in yellow winding sheet rising from tomb. Blue trefoil rinceau background. White border.

Figure, apart from drapery, by Wailes who replaced part of tomb with green drapery and much of background with spade-leaf rinceau. Severe corrosion except towards bottom of panel.

R1. The Saved, h. 1.00 m, w. 1.02 m (Figs 6 and 14)

Above a tomb-like architectural form at bottom centre, a group of some sixteen naked men and women, in white glass, stand to the right in prayer. No coloured background. Border of yellow lozenges and quatrefoils on blue background.

Mostly 14th-century, but one entire figure, the heads and shoulders of some six others, and a few pieces of architecture and border are by Wailes. Exterior graffiti on modern glass: 'W[illia]m Graham, Glazer, Newcastle u/[pon] Tyne, May 26, 1856' and 'R. Hill, Plumber, Castle St[reet], November 19th, 1891'. Severe paint loss on original glass due to corrosion. Prior to 1983, the panel did not fit the stonework properly, leaving gaps around the edge.

The four spandrels contain corroded 14th-century blue, yellow and white glass.

R2. Heaven, h. 1.00 m, w. 1.01 m (Col. Pl. IVc, Fig. 21)

A group of some four naked souls are greeted by St Peter who stands in the gateway of an elaborate city with perspectival windows, gables turrets and roofs. Two nimbed and winged angels point down at souls from battlements. All in white glass, but with traces of yellow stain on architecture to right. No coloured background. Borders of green and yellow lozenges on red backgrounds.

About half the panel is 19th-century restoration, including parts of bodies and a head of a soul, St Peter and upper half of gateway, a large piece of architecture on right and much of border. As in A5, most of the original suffers from severe corrosion and paint loss.

The four spandrels contain modern blue, red and white glass.

S1. Resurrection of Man, h. 0.73 m, w. 0.73 m

Figure in purple winding sheet rising from a multi-coloured tomb with incised cross on cover. Use of pink glass for flesh tones, rather than white, suggests figure is probably male. Green spade-leaf rinceau background. Border of white and yellow lozenges on blue background.

Mostly original, except for figure which is heavily restored. Only left arm and hand and right leg and knee are 14th-century. Severe corrosion, causing cracking and paint loss on original glass. Panel was buckling prior to 1983, perhaps because of two different types of leading.

S2. Resurrection of Man, h. 0.70 m, w. 0.70 m

As S1 in reverse, but figure wears green winding sheet. Blue background. Border with yellow lozenges on red background. The tomb base is pierced by small round-headed windows in perspective and there is a band of quatrefoils on the side.

Mostly original but, head, part of left leg and a few other pieces by Wailes. Severe corrosion and cracking on original glass. Heavy paint loss. Buckling a little before 1983. The four spandrels contain modern red above and blue below.

T1, T4. Tracery Designs

Two tiny triangles in modern red glass.

T2, T3. Tracery Designs

Two small triangles, mainly in 14th-century glass. In T3 a yellow piece painted with a quatrefoil is inside out.

U1. Resurrection of Man, Priest and King, h. 0.32 m, w. 0.90 m (Figs 6 and 11)

Three figures rising from tombs with incised crosses on covers. In the centre is a tonsured priest in yellow chasuble and green amice; on his grave cover is a chalice as well as a cross. He is flanked by two smaller figures of a man in white robe and a crowned king in green robe. Blue, probably trefoil rinceau, background. White border.

Mostly original. Head of man by Wailes and part of amice patched with 14th-century wing. Original glass severely corroded, broken and with heavy paint loss.

U2. Resurrection of Man, Priest and King, h. 0.32 m, w. 0.90 m

Modern copy of U1, in reverse, by Wailes, but king in yellow robe, chasuble green and man in red winding sheet. Blue trefoil rinceau background.

V1. Trumpeting Angel, h. 1.03 m, w. 0.23 m (Fig. 7)

Angel in yellow robe and green wings, standing in profile to left, blowing trumpet. Red background. White zig-zag and trefoil border.

Heavily restored. Only the head, wings and a few pieces of background and border are original. Severe corrosion and paint loss on original glass.

V2. Trumpeting Angel, h. 1.03 m, w. 0.23 m (Figs 8 and 9)

As V1 in reverse, but with quatrefoil and circle ornament in border. Yellow stain on hair, mouthpiece and decoration in border.

Mainly original, apart from upper half of robe and some wing. Severe corrosion, especially on yellow glass.

W1. Resurrection of Soul, h. 0.25 m, w. 0.24 m

Head in white winding sheet, tied at top. Plain blue background and white border.

Glass is 14th-century and very corroded.

W2. Resurrection of Soul, h. 0.25 m, w. 0.24 m

As W1, but head by Wailes and background yellow.

DAVID O'CONNOR

XI. *Christ in Judgement with Angels holding Instruments of the Passion, h. 1.43 m, w. 1.00 m* (Col. Pl. IVB)

Cross-nimbed and bearded Christ in blue mantle with yellow hem, sitting on multi-coloured rainbow, displaying wounds. He is flanked by two winged angels in albs, one holding a white spear and three nails and the other holding a green cross and crown of thorns. Red spade-leaf rinceau background. Border with white lozenges on blue background.

Christ mostly restored, apart from nimbus and upper half of mantle. Head of left angel by Wailes. Severe corrosion and paint loss on original glass. Four spandrels in modern blue, pink and red glass.

ACKNOWLEDGEMENTS

I am indebted to a former Dean of Carlisle, the Very Revd John Howard Churchill and to a former Surveyor of the Fabric, Mr Norman Phillips, for allowing me access to the east window scaffolding in 1982. Peter Gibson kindly arranged for me to see some of the glass at the York Glaziers Trust during conservation the following year. More recently, I have received most generous help and encouragement from the Canon Librarian, the Reverend Dr David Weston.

For help with archival material I am grateful to David Bowcock and the staff of the Cumbria Record Office in Carlisle and to Roy Albutt and Glynnis Wild for some preliminary research in the Hardman Glass Archive at Birmingham Reference Library and Birmingham City Museum and Art Gallery. I should also like to thank Dr Nicola Coldstream, Dr Alwyn Cox, Dr John Goodall and Lucy Rutherford. The British Academy's Corpus Vitrearum Medii Aevi Committee has generously given a grant for the colour plates.

NOTES

1. Most medieval glass from Cumbria is included in L. Smith, 'A survey of the surviving medieval stained glass in the churches of the Anglican Diocese of Carlisle, together with the few examples of painted glass of the seventeenth and eighteenth centuries, and of the first decade of the nineteenth century', *Transactions Cumberland Westmorland Antiquarian Archaeological Society*, 96 (1996), 87–104 and colour pls 1–17.

2. R. W. Billings, *Architectural Illustrations History and Description of Carlisle Cathedral* (London 1840), 8.

3. For a brilliant survey of the economic and political history of the region in the Middle Ages, see Henry Summerson, *Medieval Carlisle: The City and the Borders from the Late Eleventh to the Mid-Sixteenth Century*, Cumberland Westmorland Antiquarian Archaeological Society Extra Series, 25, 2 vols (Kendal 1993).

4. William Wilson, 'The East Window of Carlisle Cathedral' (unpublished B.A. thesis, History of Art Department, University of Manchester 1976), I.

5. R. S. Ferguson, 'The East Window, Carlisle Cathedral: Its Ancient Stained Glass', *Transactions Cumberland Westmorland Antiquarian Archaeological Society*, 2 (1876), 296–312.

6. F. C. Eeles, 'Ancient Glass at Carlisle Cathedral', *Transactions Cumberland Westmorland Antiquarian Archaeological Society*, 26 (1926), 312–17; C. M. Lowther Bouch, 'Notes on Carlisle Cathedral. 1. John of Gaunt and the East Window', *Transactions Cumberland Westmorland Antiquarian Archaeological Society*, 45 (1945), 122–25. The glass is dated *c.* 1380 in Arthur Penn and Edna Mallett, *Carlisle Cathedral: The Stained Glass and the Carved Capitals* (Carlisle 1996), 5.

7. Thomas Allen, G. Pickering and T. Rose, *Westmorland, Cumberland, Durham and Northumberland Illustrated*, 2 vols, II (London, n.d. 1835), opposite 141.

8. ibid., 143.

9. Quoted in Billings, 30; William Whelan, *The History and Topography of the Counties of Cumberland and Westmorland* (Pontefract 1860), 101; C. King Ely, *The Cathedral Church of Carlisle: A Description of the Fabric & a Brief History of the Episcopal See* (London 1900), 46.

10. Wilson, 38–41.

11. J. Harvey, 'Architectural History from 1291 to 1558', in *A History of York Minster*, ed. G. Aylmer and R. Cant (Oxford 1977), 149–92; Nicola Coldstream, 'The Development of Flowing Tracery in Yorkshire 1300–1374' (unpublished Ph.D. thesis, University of London, 1973), 87–89; Wilson, ch. 3.

12. C. G. Bulman, 'Carlisle Cathedral and its Development in the thirteenth and fourteenth centuries', *Transactions Cumberland Westmorland Antiquarian Archaeological Society*, ns, XLIX (1949), 11–12.

13. Wilson, 22–23; Coldstream, 89.

14. J. Goodall, 'The Lost Chapel of Queen's College, Oxford, and the Design of its East Window', *The Queen's Journal*, VII/2 (1996), 22–33.

15. R. S. Ferguson ed., *Testamenta Karleolensis, Transactions Cumberland Westmorland Antiquarian Archaeological Society*, Extra Series, 9 (Kendal 1893), no. 19. For this donor see Summerson, I, 355.

16. For the royal window see Summerson, II, 465. Dugdale's notes are published as an appendix in C. M. Lowther Bouch, *Prelates and People of the Lake Counties* (Kendal 1948), 166–68.

17. Penn and Mallett, 8–9 and colour pl. 17. The glass had been restored by 1875; see Ferguson, 309–10.

18. Eeles, 312–27 and colour illustration in Penn and Mallett, 14. Joan Howson's design for the window is in the author's possession.

19. Billings, 39 and pls XIV and XV.

20. David Weston, *Carlisle Cathedral History* (Carlisle 2000), 18–20.

21. Carlisle CRO, D. & C., 1/11 Chapter Act Books 1752–92, p. 151, Letter of 2 July 1786 from Dean and Chapter to Lady Gower; J. T. Brighton, 'William Peckitt's Commission Book', *The Walpole Society*, 54 (1988), 334–453 (p. 384).

22. William Hutchinson, *The History of the County of Cumberland*, 2 vols (Carlisle 1794–97 and 1974 reprint), II, 599.

23. Billings, 64.

24. Weston, 26.

25. Carlisle, CRO, D. & C., Chapter Order Book 1855–74, p. 4. Very similar wording is used in *Restoration of Carlisle Cathedral*, a leaflet issued by Dean Tate on 21 July, 1855; CRO, D. & C., Box CF2c 1–15, Cathedral Restoration and Repairs 1668–1892.

26. Carlisle, CRO, D. & C., Chapter Order Book 1855–74, p. 4.

27. For Wailes see Martin Harrison, *Victorian Stained Glass* (London 1980), especially 18–19 and 83; and F. Skeat, 'The Family of William Wailes of Newcastle-on-Tyne', *Family History*, 11, nos 79/80 (1980), 184–205.

28. Penn and Mallett, 6–7 with colour illustration.

29. ibid., 14–15 and illustrated in Weston, 41.

30. Like, for example, Wailes's west window of 1848 at Bradfield, Berkshire; D. O'Connor, 'Pre-Raphaelite Stained Glass: The Early Work of Edward Burne-Jones and William Morris', in *William Morris: Art and Kelmscott*, ed. Linda Parry (London 1996), 38–56 (p. 38 and fig. 3.1).

31. W. Bell Scott, *Autobiographical Writings of William Bell Scott*, ed. W. Minto, 2 vols (1892), I, 188–91. For Scott see Jane Vickers ed., *Pre-Raphaelites: Painters and Patrons in the North East*, Laing Art Gallery exhibition catalogue (Newcastle upon Tyne 1989).

32. For comments on his restoration of the east windows of All Saints see D. O'Connor, 'Morris stained glass: "an art of the Middle Ages"', in *William Morris and the Middle Ages*, ed. Joanna Banham and Jennifer Harris, Whitworth Art Gallery exhibition catalogue (Manchester 1984), 31–46 (p. 43).

33. For Powell and Hardman see Harrison, 18–28 and 78; and S. Shepherd, 'Stained Glass', in *Pugin: A Gothic Passion*, ed. P. Atterbury and C. Wainwright (London 1994), 195–206. There is a brief description of the Hardman glass with colour illustrations in Penn and Mallett, 1 and 4–5.

34. Carlisle, CRO, D. & C., Chapter Order Book 1855–74, p. 100.

35. Letter from C. J. Burton to Hardman, 20 September 1859 in Birmingham Reference Library Archives Department.

36. King Ely, 46.

37. Carlisle, CRO, D. & C., 1/15, Chapter Order Book Vol. XV 1874–1901, 23 November 1891, p. 274.

38. The glazier's bill only came to £3 8s. 11d.: Carlisle, CRO, D. & C., Treasurer's Accounts 1892. There is a Hills graffito in panel R1 and that of the builder who scaffolded and repointed the window in D1.

39. I am grateful to Dr Cox for providing me with a copy of G.A. Cox and K. Gillies, 'Report on the Weathering of 14th Century Glass from the East Window of Carlisle Cathedral', produced for the Dean and Chapter in 1983. The analyses are placed in a wider context in K. Gillies and A. Cox, 'Decay of Medieval Stained Glass at York, Canterbury and Carlisle', Part 1: 'Composition of the Glass and its Weathering Products, *Glastechnische Berichte*, 61, no. 3 (1988), 75–84 and Part 2: 'Relationship between the Composition of the Glass, its Durability and the Weathering Products', ibid., 61, no. 4 (1988), 101–07.

40. I have been unable to locate conservation records from 1983 either in Carlisle or in York but am grateful to Lucy Rutherford of York Glaziers Trust for providing me with copies of some correspondence about the work.

41. Ferguson, 311.

42. For the importance of her cult at Carlisle see Summerson, I, 359 and II, 415 and 603.

43. For literature on these windows see D. O'Connor & H. Harris, 'The East Window of Selby Abbey, Yorkshire', in *Yorkshire Monasticism: Archaeology, Art and Architecture from the 7th to 16th Centuries*, ed. Lawrence Hoey, *BAA Trans.*, XVI (Leeds 1995), 117–44 (pp. 122–23).

44. ibid., p. 122.

45. Peter Ryder, *The Cross Slab Grave Covers of Cumbria* (Carlisle 2001).

46. P. Scheingorn, ' "For God is Such a Doomsman": Origins and Development of the Theme of the Last Judgment', in David Bevington et al., *Homo Memento Finis: The Iconography of Just Judgment in Medieval Art and Drama* (Kalamazoo 1985), 15–58.

47. London, British Library, Add. MS 47682, f. 25v; W. O. Hassall, *The Holkham Bible Picture Book* (1954), illustrated in W. O. Hassall f. 25v.

48. Thomas French and David O'Connor, *York Minster: A Catalogue of Medieval Stained Glass: The West Windows of the Nave*, Corpus Vitrearum Medii Aevi Great Britain, III/1 (Oxford 1987), 14; and D. O'Connor, 'The Medieval Stained Glass of Beverley Minster', in *Medieval Art and Architecture in the East Riding of Yorkshire*, ed. C. Wilson, *BAA Trans.*, IX (Leeds 1987), 62–90 (p. 79).

49. D. J. King, 'The Glazing of the South Rose of Lincoln Cathedral', in *Medieval Art and Architecture in Lincoln Cathedral*, *BAA Trans.*, VIII (Leeds 1986), 132–45; O'Connor and Harris.

50. ibid., 123–25.

51. For comparisons between York glass and windows at St Stephen's Chapel, Westminster see French and O'Connor, 22 and pls 31c and d.

52. Richard Marks, *Stained Glass in England during the Middle Ages* (London 1993), 157–65.

53. French and O'Connor, 22 and pl. 29 (a); Smith, 91 and colour pl. 5.

54. Carlisle, CRO, Faculty Papers: St Cuthbert's, Carlisle, PR/79/161, letter from Dean Eric Milner-White to Canon G. T. Berwick, 25 March 1961.

55. French and O'Connor, 22.

56. For Carlisle's continuing economic and administrative links with York see Summerson, II, 584–86.

57. Summerson, I, 158 and 206.

58. For Carlisle's close commercial ties with Newcastle see Summerson, I, 137–39 and II, 579–81.

59. French and O'Connor, 21–22.

60. J. C. Dickinson, *The Priory of Cartmel* (Milnthorpe 1991), 46–55, 74–75 and 87; Daniel Chadwick, 'The Ancient Glass in the East Window of the Church of St Andrew, Greystoke, Cumbria' (unpublished B.Phil. thesis, University of York, 1974).

61. J. A. Knowles, *Essays in the History of the York School of Glass-Painting* (London 1936), 149; and J. A Knowles, 'Glass-Painters of York: VI. The Preston Family', *Notes and Queries*, VIII (18 June 1921), 485–87 (p. 486).

The Stylistic Antecedents of the Gondibour Screen at Carlisle Cathedral

CHARLES TRACY

The Gondibour screenwork was an important element in the refurbishment of Carlisle Cathedral undertaken by Prior Thomas Gondibour (1465–1500). It has long been recognised by specialists as an important monument of late-15th- or early-16th-century craftsmanship. At least one theory has been put forward relating to its stylistic provenance, but no serious work on this intriguing question has ever been undertaken. Moreover, virtually nothing was known, beyond the confines of Carlisle, about the history of the woodwork after its expulsion from its medieval situation in the cathedral presbytery by Bishop Lyttleton in 1764. In this paper the lamentable fortunes of the medieval screenwork are related, as far as is known, but attention is also concentrated on its probable medieval appearance and location. Finally, an attempt has been made to locate the Gondibour Screen stylistically within the context, not only of contemporary English and Scottish art of the period, but also of developments at that time in both France and Flanders.

DESCRIPTION

THE two surviving oak screens enclose the north and west sides of the former St Catherine's Chapel, off the south transept (Figs 1 and 2). The north screen is 3.62 m long, and the west screen 2.69 m long. Their height is 3.14 m. They comprise a deep cornice with curvilinear tracery and cresting at the top, a soffit with carved bosses, and a zone of open panelling sub-divided by buttresses with Flamboyant-type tracery in the heads. Above the dado rail there is curvilinear brattishing. The dado panels are decorated with a simple chamfered ornament, with one wide leaf and a single arris each side, and a spreading and curving profile at the top and bottom. Above is a zone of framed and pierced tracery. A mutilated heraldic shield is positioned on the cornice on each side, which may well be an addition. There is a door in the centre of the western screen which has been cut in later. It bears the initials of Prior Thomas Gondibour (1465–1500), the last of the cathedral's medieval patrons. The screens are usually dated *c.* 1500, although they are possibly up to a generation earlier than this.

Over the years this screenwork has received generous accolades from distinguished antiquaries. J. C. Buckler described it as having: 'various panels of the richest and most minute patterns, and compartments intricately intersecting each other. The execution of this tracery is exquisite; and, excepting the famous rood-loft at Hexham Abbey church, I have seen none more elegant.'[1] Later Aylmer Vallance wrote of it that 'in spite of all (the mutilation) it remains a most exquisite monument, and with its rich and varied tracery patterns fitly demonstrates the inexhaustible resourcefulness of late Gothic design'.[2] Whereas the choirs of English greater churches are almost invariably

FIG. 1. Cathedral: Gondibour
screen, west section
© *Crown copyright NMR*

FIG. 2. Carlisle Cathedral:
Gondibour screen, north section
© *Crown copyright NMR*

screened off, either by tombs, as at Tewkesbury Abbey, for instance, or by stone or wooden screens, there no longer exists a complete set of matching screens, as existed at Carlisle. Exeter Cathedral and Beverley Minster have fine 14th-century wooden screens across their *ostia chori*. York Minster has wooden screenwork through two bays east of the choir, but the most extensive set are those at Ripon Minster, where there are four screens on the north and three on the south sides of the presbytery (Fig. 3).[3] Sadly they are only today in a heavily 'restored' state and, strictly speaking, although of about the same date, they are not a set.

Although displaced and mostly lost, the Gondibour screenwork still occupies a unique place in English medieval woodwork, on account of its highly original tracery. Because it is so unusual, no convincing attempt has been made so far to provide a stylistic context for it. As we know from the remarkable decorative vocabulary of the mid-14th-century choir-stalls at Lancaster Priory, north-country English medieval craftsmen could be defiantly independent and innovative. This paper will attempt to explore similar obscure territory at the close of the Middle Ages.

LOCATION

ACCORDING to Billings, who looked into the subject at least as early as 1839, until the 1760s similar screenwork enclosed the chancel at Carlisle. The only plan of the cathedral to record these medieval screens is provided by Browne Willis in 1727 (Fig. 4).[4] From this it can be deduced that they enclosed the *ostia chori* and the next two bays to the east. We do not know if they extended behind the high altar, which in the Middle Ages stood immediately west of the second pair of piers from the east, but altar screens in greater English churches were almost invariably in stone. We can be almost certain that our screens stood on the low plinth walls between the chancel piers, many of which survive from both the early 15th century or Prior Gondibour's time (Figs 5 and 6).[5] The screens, in some form probably crossed both of the *ostium chori* bays, as at Ripon, for instance, although there is only evidence for the plinth walls crossing on the north side. The jointing scars in the bases of the piers on either side of these bays are clearly visible. A plinth wall similarly placed on the south side would have been an encumbrance, as this would have been the most important entrance to the choir. If we assume that the early-16th-century Salkeld screen across the north *ostium chori* was intended to align as nearly as possible with the earlier furniture, a tentative reconstruction of the late-15th-century arrangements in the chancel becomes possible. Confirmation that the screens were placed above the plinth walls is provided by the three square-sided holes, 76 mm wide and 51 mm deep, placed equidistantly on their top surface, which probably would have housed the dowels, which fitted into matching holes in the foot-rail. They would have ensured that the sill stayed in line and did not twist. The scars of consistent excavations on the inside faces of the appropriate piers are not likely to be connected with the fixing of the Gondibour woodwork, which was probably secured to the masonry by means of iron bands, as used on the Salkeld Screen. One of these has recently been opened up, and the shallowness of the mortises on the inside has ruled out any serious structural purpose.[6] Unfortunately, we still have no precise indication of the height of the screens, but they are unlikely to have reached more than about 4 m from floor level.

An unusual, and un-English, characteristic of the screenwork at Carlisle is that it only carries decoration on one side. It is probable, therefore, that some form of covering

FIG. 3.   Ripon Minster, West Riding, Yorkshire: view of presbytery parclose screens, north side

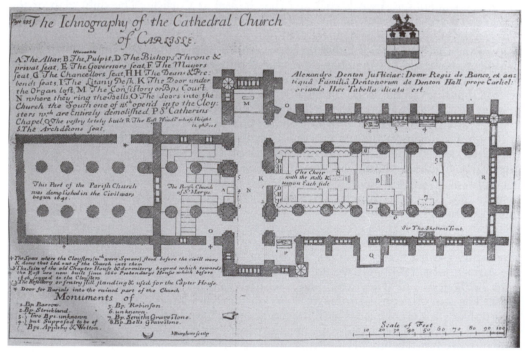

FIG. 4.   Carlisle Cathedral: ground plan from Browne Willis, *A Survey of the Cathedrals*,
I (1727), 285

FIG. 5.   Carlisle Cathedral: plinth wall, early-15th-century type

FIG. 6.   Carlisle Cathedral: plinth wall, late-15th-century type

was placed against the blind side, such as a tapestry, which would have been appropriate in terms of both location and period.

RETROSPECT

UNFORTUNATELY, Prior Gondibour's woodwork was entirely swept away at the time of Bishop Lyttleton's comprehensive restoration of the cathedral in 1764. Subsequently there remained only enough material to reconstruct the surviving screens now surrounding the St Catherine's Chapel in the south transept, which was drawn by Billings much later (Figs 7 and 8). Three refugee panels found their way to Featherstone Castle, between Carlisle and Hexham, where they were built into the Dining Room sideboard (Fig. 9). Of Lyttleton's doubtless well-meant artistic vandalism, Billings writes:

The whole of the choir screens were removed, and their place occupied by a high stone wall, covered in the Choir by a wooden arcade in the true Gothic style of that period, and in the aisles by a carefully-executed coat of plaster. The old and useless panelling was removed to some of the outbuildings, and by far the greater part either lost or destroyed.[7]

He tells us that a few of the more desirable components of the screenwork were:

broken up and altered to enrich the door of the quire near the Bishop's throne. The great mass, however, was removed from the cathedral either into the fratry or the crypt beneath it, and much

FIG. 7.   Carlisle Cathedral: Gondibour screen, west section. Drawing by R. W. Billings, from
R. W. Billings, *Illustrations of Geometric Tracery from the panelling belonging to Carlisle
Cathedral* (London 1842), Pl. i

FIG. 8. Carlisle Cathedral:
Gondibour screen, north section.
Drawing by R. W. Billings, from
R. W. Billings, *Illustrations of
Geometric Tracery from the
panelling belonging to Carlisle
Cathedral* (London 1842), Pl. xxxiii

FIG. 9. Featherstone Castle,
Haltwhistle, Northumberland:
dining room. View of early-19th-
century sideboard

By kind permission of Mr J. M. Clark

of it, it is said, was actually used for firewood. Some of it came into the hands of Lord Wallace, in whose castle at Featherstone, Northumberland, are three beautiful specimens of these panels.[8]

Billings's description of Bishop Lyttleton's furnishings is the only one to be recorded before this Georgian material, in its turn, was swept away in the re-ordering of 1853–56. The designer of this new woodwork was the bishop's nephew Thomas Pitt, first Baron Camelford, an amateur architect. Apart from the new screenwork between the presbytery piers, Pitt also designed a bishop's throne, reredos, pulpit, communion rails, and box pews with traceried panelled fronts. The joiner who made this work was one Thomas Carlyle. The later history of this material will be discussed below.

The screens that now surround the former St Catherine's Chapel seem to be a later quarry of panels and stiles from the former presbytery furniture. Their overall widths bear little relation to those of the chancel bays, and the woodwork has clearly been cut to fit. Evidence on the stonework of the chancel piers for the original placement of screens mid-way between the columns is lacking. This also goes for the St Catherine's Chapel, where, in any case, the screen is not placed in the centre of the pier, but at the front of the bay.[9] In Pitt's re-ordering there were stone walls filling the bays of the east end on either side, which were plastered on the aisle sides, and fronted by a wooden arcade, as Billings remarked, 'in the true gothic style of that period' (Figs 10 and 11).[10] These must have been positioned above the medieval stone plinth.

Billings's drawings show that before the Ewan Christian restoration of 1853–56 the Gondibour screens were even more of a puzzle than they are now. At that time two of the tracery panels had been fitted in sideways and another, above the door in the south screen, upside-down. Also the spacing of the stiles above the dado is inconsistent. The stiles on the west screen are all of the type with the forward-projecting buttresses, whilst on the north side the latter type is alternated with plain stiles. These refugee components could have been cobbled together in this position at any time from the late 18th century. However, the screens cannot have been fitted up any later than 1839, if Billings was correct in alleging that the centre panel on the west screen, initialled TG, 'was unfortunately pulled out and taken away by some mischievous person' in the winter of 1839.[11] Although some repairs in new wood were inserted in the mid-19th century, and this probably includes the whole of the foot-rail, most of the decorative elements, including the 'linenfold' panelling, seem to be ancient. The screens would have been made up from the fragments, which are known to have been stored, since their dismantling, in various places, including the undercroft of the fratry.[12]

Billings also stated that there was another TG monogram, 'forming the cusps of a trefoil from Carlisle (and) may be taken from Prior Gondibour's. It is among the remains at Carlton Hall'.[13] Moreover, he writes: 'The whole of the frame-work of the mutilated screen at that house, was ornamented with the bordering, shewn in Plate XVIII. Fig.B (of his book).'[14] Carlton Hall, better known for its important collection of early-19th-century fitted furniture by Gillow, is situated near Penrith. It was formerly the home of Thomas Wallace, later Lord Wallace, who moved to Featherstone Castle in the 1820s. He probably acquired these ecclesiastical fragments before he sold Carlton Hall to William Cowper, the owner at the time that Billings was writing. There is no longer any trace of this material in the house.

The Dining Room sideboard at Featherstone Castle, topped by a tripartite canopy, with deeply-excavated cusped cells in the interstices of the vaults, is an early Gothic-Revival fantasy, which could have been transported from Carlton Hall. It was in keeping with Wallace's ambitious Gothic-Revival extension to the castle. The canopy

FIG. 10.   Carlisle Cathedral: Gondibour screen. Drawing of 'The choir looking East', by R. W. Billings, from R. W. Billings, *Architectural Illustrations, history and description of Carlisle Cathedral* (London 1840), Pl. xxxvi

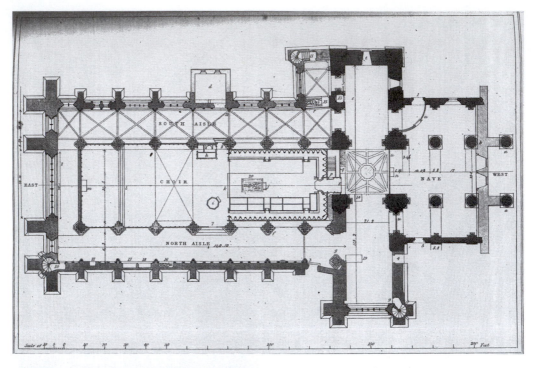

FIG. 11.   Carlisle Cathedral: ground plan
drawn by R. W. Billings, from R. W. Billings,
*Architectural Illustrations, history and
description of Carlisle Cathedral* (London
1840), Pl. ii

FIG. 12.   Carlisle Cathedral: drawing of 18th-
century arrangement of south *Ostium Chori*, by
R. Carlyle, from J. Storer, *Cathedral Churches
of Great Britain*, I (London 1814), Pl. 4

is carved in the solid from a substantial piece of oak 2.69 m wide by 0.5 m deep. It has been stated, on no particular authority, that this feature belonged to Thomas Pitt's high-altar reredos. But if that were so, one would have expected Billings to have mentioned the fact in 1842. Besides, it seems unlikely that Bishop Lyttleton's furnishings would have been removed piece by piece in advance of the subsequent chancel re-ordering a generation later. In any case the canopy could well be a re-used medieval object, probably of the 15th century. Importantly it exemplifes a procedure one would not expect in the 18th century. Could this, along with the castle's three Gondibour panels, have been removed from the cathedral? We know when the side-board at Featherstone Castle was set up from the pencil inscription '1833', which has been found underneath the table-top of the buffet.[15]

Some of the smaller panels from the presbytery screen, including the primitive linenfold ones, were in fact re-used by the cathedral within Bishop Lyttleton's Georgian 'Gothick' replacement fittings. Up to eleven Gondibour panels, including three with linenfold ornament, seem to have been placed on the door on the south side of the chancel adjacent to the new bishop's throne (Fig. 12). The extant panel on the door of the bishop's stall, on the south side of the return stalls, has had Gondibour panels attached to it (Fig. 13).

In 1853, with the appointment of Ewan Christian, the Lyttleton fittings were removed. The ejected woodwork, both Gothic and Georgian, was taken into the custody of the diocese, from whence the Secretary, and Clerk to the Dean and Chapter, Charles Saul, acquired it to furnish his house at Brunstock, just outside the city. This material was sold after his death, probably at the house contents sale in 1906. It was acquired by the brothers J. and T. Minns, who owned the Golden Lion Hotel in Botchergate, at which they displayed a large collection of stained glass. They also owned the Wellington Hotel in Carlisle, and the brother John decided to install the woodwork in an upper room there, along with assorted armour and weapons, stained glass, antlers, stuffed animal heads, and paintings. In the spirit of the 'themed' public houses of today, he dubbed it 'Ye Olde English Baronial Hall — Inglewood' (Figs 14 and 15). The Inglewood Forest had been not only a local, but also a national source of suppy of oak for architectural purposes in the Middle Ages.[16] However, in the case of Carlisle Cathedral's Gondibour screen, a work of joinery, it is probable that the timber, for the panels at least, would have been obtained from the Baltic region.

In 1916 the Wellington Hotel was closed, and the fittings were removed to storage. The material was then left in the open air in a brewery yard, but after a public outcry, in 1920, it was given over to the care of the former Victorian parish church of St Mary's in the cathedral precinct. The latter, with its woodwork still intact, was closed in 1938, and converted into a grain store. It was demolished in 1954, and the woodwork was then dispersed to various churches in the city, but mainly to St Paul's. In its turn, St Paul's Church closed in 1976, and the remaining woodwork has been scattered.

Judging from two surviving photographs of the Baronial Hall, little if any of the woodwork bears much stylistic relationship to the extant work of the Gondibour screen. A notable exception was the door, originally adjacent to Thomas Pitt's bishop's throne on the south side of the chancel, already mentioned.[17] Part of the door head seems to have been Georgian, as do the two traceried, crocketted and finialled arches, and the overmantel. In 1951 C. B. Martindale, the Carlisle architect, who examined the residue of this material, then in St Mary's Church, suggested that the canopy, which at the Baronial Hall had been used as an overmantel, was the canopy of Bishop Lyttleton's throne.[18]

Fig. 13.   Carlisle Cathedral: choir-stalls. Door panel of bishop's stall at south end of return stalls

STYLISTIC SIGNIFICANCE

THE tracery designs on this monument were the subject of a comprehensive study by Robert Billings's in 1842, and published in his *Illustrations of Geometric Tracery from the panelling belonging to Carlisle Cathedral*. Billings illustrated eighteen of his own drawings of the different tracery designs in the Gondibour screenwork. He described the screens as follows:

The two screens . . . consisting of a basement of draped panels (with linenfold), and immediately above them a series of perforated Geometric Panels. Above these is a plain string, surmounted (on the west side) by a series of smaller Panels, and (on the north side) by the running border . . . The upper portion of the screen in a series of detached piers, all ornamented (on the west screen) by flying buttresses, and (on the north screen) a buttress on each alternate pier. Above the buttresses is a square-headed capital, and the space between this and the upper string (ornamented alternately

FIG. 14.   Former Wellington Hotel, Carlisle: 'Ye Olde Baronial Hall. View towards minstrel's gallery'

Cumbria County Council Carlisle Library

over each pier with a head and leaves) is filled with tracery, the cusps of the lower arch being ornamented with leaves.

The string is surmounted by a richly decorated parapet, with a border of leaves connected at the top by a bead. In the centre of each parapet is a shield, the armorial bearings of which have disappeared.[19]

He intended to show how the different designs were set out (Figs 16–18), and remarked that:

Some of the specimens are perhaps not so interesting in themselves for elegance of design, as from the circumstance of their proving that the majority were designed on the same ground-work, namely, the division of a square into four parts each way, or sixteen squares. Upon the lines of these squares the centres of all the curves are worked, and upon such a simple calculation of parts, as to render their construction perfectly easy. It is of essential importance to have a ready means, well known, of re-producing the beautiful forms displayed in many of these and other specimens, and the author trusts that the means he has adopted will effect this, for no workman, following the descriptions given of each Plate, can possibly err in any of the leading features'.[20]

Billings illustrates a large number of different designs, and it is difficult to imagine how they could have all been utilised within the rather conventional framework we are left with. One can only speculate that they may have been employed to fence off shrines, although, unfortunately, at Carlisle we have virtually no evidence for the existence of any such. Also the chancel aisles are comparatively narrow, and the positioning of shrines in this area would have obstructed the flow of pilgrims through the church.

FIG. 15.   Former Wellington Hotel, Carlisle: 'Ye Olde Baronial Hall. View with window on left'
Cumbria County Council Carlisle Library

Even after the exhaustive efforts that have been made to tease out the original design of the parclose elements, the monument is still far from yielding up its secrets. Billings was certainly one of the first of the 19th-century antiquaries to study the problems of setting-out, in either wood or stone, with the possible exception of the Reverend Thomas Kerrick, who travelled through England in the same period recording window tracery.[21]

Billings goes on to claim that the tracery on the wooden pulpitum at Hexham Abbey was 'produced under the same geometrical principles' (Figs 19 and 20).[22] To support this technical as well as stylistic cousinage, he stresses that Richard Bell, who was prior of Durham Cathedral at the time that the pulpitum was erected, became Bishop of Carlisle in 1478.

Billings was not the last to draw parallels with Carlisle's overlapping arcs in the tracery of the Gondibour screens with the Hexham pulpitum, and the parclose screen around Prior Leschman's chantry in that place. Hexham Abbey was another Augustinian foundation. Bulman suggested that the Carlisle and Hexham woodwork could even have been the product of the same workshop.[23] Certainly, the ascending heart-shaped design on the main panels of the Hexham pulpitum, and the Leschman Chantry screen (Fig. 21), is similar to that on the Gondibour woodwork. The tracery heads on the veranda of the Hexham pulpitum are also close to those at Carlisle. The use of miniature flying buttresses, on the Leschman chantry, which in both places are also carved in the solid with the stiles, is close to the same motif on the Carlisle screen. Hexham's rood-screen probably dates from the time of Prior Thomas Smithson (1491–1524), and the date of the Leschman chantry is 1491.

188

FIG. 16. Carlisle Cathedral: Gondibour screen. Drawing by R. W. Billings of tracery detail, from R. W. Billings, *Illustration of Geometrical Tracery from the panelling belonging to Carlisle Cathedral* (London 1842), Pl. xiii

In view of the political situation at the time, when, for instance, in 1491 Henry VII was at war with France, it seems likely that the craftsmen in both places would have come from the north of England or the Lowlands of Scotland, rather than metropolitan England. The style of the surviving tracery panels at Carlisle is certainly not English, and seems ultimately to come from Flanders. The possibility that some of the craftsmen, here and at Hexham, were immigrants or first-generation foreigners cannot be dismissed.

In Brittany there are fully-fledged linenfold panels at St Fiacre du Faöuet, dated to 1480, and at Colebrooke, Coldridge and Brushford in Devon, all again *c.* 1480, although the style of both the Breton and Devon screens, is quite different to that at Carlisle (Fig. 22).[24] The Gondibour screen tracery is probably earlier than the northern French panels on the prior's stall door (Fig. 23). Nor does it relate to the more Flamboyant mode of the early-16th-century panels from the Palais de Justice in Rouen.[25] Linenfold panels, similar to the primitive type at Carlisle, do occur elsewhere in England at this time, although it is not possible to be precise about their dating. The screen from

FIG. 17. Carlisle Cathedral: Gondibour screen. Drawing by R. W. Billings of tracery detail, from R. W. Billings, *Illustration of Geometrical Tracery from the panelling belonging to Carlisle Cathedral* (London 1842), Pl. iii

FIG. 18. Carlisle Cathedral: Gondibour screen. Drawing by R. W. Billings of tracery detail, from R. W. Billings, *Illustration of Geometrical Tracery from the panelling belonging to Carlisle Cathedral* (London 1842), Pl. xiv

FIG. 19.   Hexham Abbey:
pulpitum, west side. Detail of
tracery. From C. C. Hodges,
*The Abbey of St Andrew,
Hexham* (privately printed
1888), Pl. 52

Brightleigh, Devon, in the Victoria and Albert Museum, which can be dated on style between 1490–1510 has them.[26] Another example is the extant settle in the abbot's parlour at Muchelney Abbey, Somerset, which is probably from the last quarter of the 15th century.[27]

The tracery style at Carlisle has distinct Flamboyant tendencies, but possibly with the exception of the heart-shaped design in the door of the St Catherine's Chapel and that used for all the tracery heads in the long panels, it is too dense and convoluted to rival the flickering incandescence of the Northern French Flamboyant, typified by the early-16th-century central portion of the west front at Rouen Cathedral (Fig. 24).[28] In the late 15th century the Flemish were more restrained in their use of traceried decoration. Whereas their buildings were often encrusted with canopies and sculpture, only small-scale intricate tracery was used selectively for such elements as balustrades and friezes. Another example of Flemish decorative selectivity can be seen on the stone model by Joos Massys and Jan Beyaert for a triple-tower west façade for St Peter's,

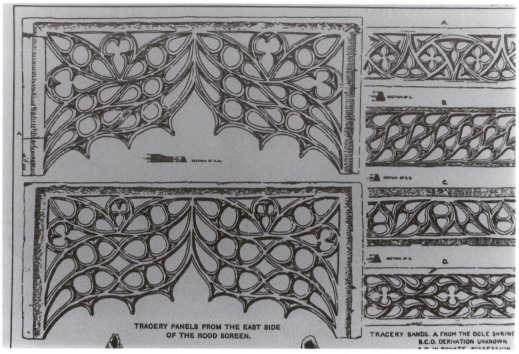

FIG. 20.   Hexham Abbey: pulpitum. Details of tracery heads on east side veranda. From Hodges, *Abbey of St Andrew*, Pl. 46

Leuven, which is still kept at the church. The building of this was only partly completed.[29] Better-known monuments, displaying the same characteristics, would be the Brussels and Leuven town halls, both completed in the second half of the 15th century.[30] By the third decade of the next century the Flemish had caught up with the Flamboyant, in their 'Renaissance-Gothic' phase[31] with a proliferation of tracery, used on a large scale, especially on stone furniture, such as the jubé at the Gummaruskerk, Lier, of 1536–40.[32] This extreme tendency of *horror vacui* was perhaps more influenced by contemporary German than French art.

The selective use of tracery patterns in late-15th-century Flanders is also seen widely on wooden furniture. For instance, the two-tier undulating and cusped running ornament on the dado rail of the north section of the Gondibour screen can be paralleled with the small-scale decorative ornament on late-15th-century Flemish altarpieces, such as that at Strängnäs, Sweden, or with the Passion retable in the Musée des Beaux Arts, Dijon. As we have already seen in architecture, running ornament is a common decorative feature at this time in Flanders in all media, and we see it again, for instance, on the Flemish chest at Southwold church in Suffolk.

Perhaps the best Flemish comparison with the tracery style on the Gondibour screen, is with that on the choir-stalls at St Salvator, Bruges, which although undated, are generally thought to be of the second quarter of the 15th century.[33] Here the tracery is typically Flemish, that is restrained and firmly rooted in the Gothic tradition, but arranged in an unusual way (Fig. 25).

Fig. 21. Hexham Abbey: Leschman Chantry screen. Detail of tracery
© *Courtauld Institute of Art*

Fig. 22. Colebrooke Church, Devon: tracery details of parclose screens
© *Courtauld Institute of Art*

FIG. 23. Carlisle Cathedral: French wainscot panel on Prior's stall door

FIG. 24. Rouen Cathedral: West front. Stone tracery, detail

© Courtauld Institute of Art

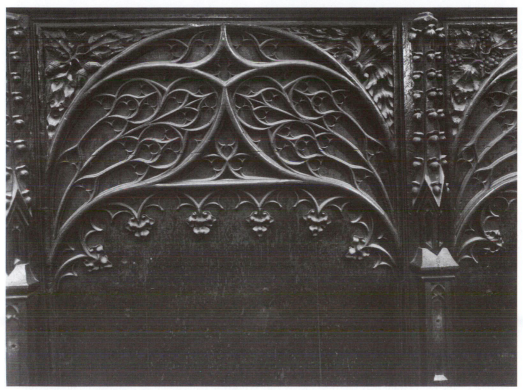

FIG. 25.   St Salvator, Bruges: choir-stalls. Detail of traceried panelling on seat backs, second quarter 15th century
IRPA-KIK, Brussels

Ecclesiastical and trading links between Carlisle and Scotland certainly existed at the end of the 15th century. Indeed, Bulman posited the connection between Melrose and Holm Cultram, both Cistercian houses, and with direct relations with France, and cited the visit of the abbot of the latter house to Rose Castle to receive the episcopal benediction from Bishop Bell of Carlisle around 1480.[34] The second phase of the building at Melrose Abbey, after the fire of 1395, was under the direction of a French master-mason.[35] The restrained 'Decorated'-type tracery of the windows reminds one a little of the more elegant proto-Flamboyant designs in the south nave aisle at St Ouen, Rouen, for instance, although its roots are in the late 14th century. It also serves to distinguish the tracery on the Gondibour screen as something quite different.

The choir-stalls at King's College, Aberdeen, 1506–09, have quite correctly been invoked in a Flemish context[36] but their style is distinctly *retardataire*, and poorly executed. One clear distinction between the two monuments is the absence at Carlisle of any small-scale sub-tracery. This is typically found in Flanders at the end of the 15th century, and in Brittany.

There were plenty of links in Scottish ecclesiastical circles with Flanders, exemplified as early as the 1440s at Melrose Abbey, with the commissioning of a complete set of choir-stalls from Bruges.[37] Indeed that monument must have radiated stylistic influence in all directions. Quite possibly it might have had much in common with the approximately coeval stallwork at St Salvator. As such it could have supplied a missing link, which could explain the appearance of Flemish Flamboyant-type tracery at the end of the century in a swathe across northern England, at Carlisle, Hexham and Brancepeth.[38] Carlisle at that time was probably much more exposed to continental cultural influence, via France and Flanders, directly and indirectly, than to that from metropolitan England.

ACKNOWLEDGEMENTS

I am grateful to the Dean and Chapter for giving me access to the monument and allowing photography. Roy Thompson, the Carlisle wood sculptor, has generously shared his thoughts on the screenwork. Moreover, having painstakingly pieced together the later history of the Gothic and Georgian fittings at the cathedral over several years, he has made available the fruits of his labours in the interests of scholarship. Finally my thanks to The Reverend Canon David Weston, who has exhibited a resolute dedication to the cathedral woodwork by cheerfully facilitating the production of this paper in any way he could.

NOTES

1. A. Vallance, *Greater English Church Screens* (London 1947), 37.

2. ibid., 3.

3. Vallance, *Greater Screens*, 169.

4. Browne Willis, *A Survey of the Cathedrals*, 1 (1727), 285.

5. The earlier plinth walls may very well be late 14th century in date, if one accepts that the substructure of the choir-stalls pre-dates the early-15th-century furniture. This argument is currently too novel to have yet been developed.

6. I am grateful to Roy Thompson for this information.

7. R. W. Billings, *Illustrations of Geometric Tracery for the panelling belonging to Carlisle Cathedral* (London 1842), 4.

8. R. W. Billings, *Architectural Illustrations; history and description of Carlisle Cathedral* (London 1840), 70.

9. The base and plinth at the foot of the attached column on the north side of the west screen is not shown in the Billings elevation. It is curtailed in an east-west direction and the screen has been tucked in behind it.

10. Billings, *Geometric Tracery*, 3.

11. Billings, *Geometric Tracery*, 4.

12. The considerable restoration work that was done in 1853–56 can be made out by comparing the Billings drawings with the present screens. The centre portion of the running dado ornament on the north side is modern, and replaces the inappropriate 18th-century foliate brattishing shown in the Billings drawing (Fig. 8). By the same token, the identical running ornament in the same place on the west screen is entirely Victorian. The prior's monogram on the door of this screen, which, according to Billings, was stolen in 1839, was replaced in the 19th century.

13. Billings, *Geometric Tracery*, pl. xx.

14. ibid., 4.

15. An excellent piece of detective work by Roy Thompson.

16. Inglewood Forest was specified in the records at Ely Cathedral as the source of timber used in the construction of the choir roof. I am grateful to Gavin Simpson for this information.

17. This is confirmed by the report of J. H. Martindale & Son, Chartered Architects, dated 22 November 1951, on the subject of the fittings and woodwork in St Mary's Church, Carlisle. The report opens:

> Some of the fittings and woodwork in this church are of considerable historical interest. They are made up from woodwork which was ejected from the choir of the Cathedral in the middle of last century. This woodwork was installed by Bishop Lyttleton (1762–68) and was designed by his nephew Viscount Camelford, a member of the

great Pitt family. In fitting up the choir with this new woodwork, Lyttleton most unfortunately destroyed a great deal of mediaeval screenwork etc. but a few fragments of this mediaeval work still remain at St Mary's in one of the doors. Lyttleton's woodwork had some wanderings after it was removed from the Cathedral and it was finally presented to St Mary's about thirty years ago and worked up into the various fittings etc. as Memorial to the Great World War 1914–18.

Chancel

Oak communion rails. Two lengths each 10′–3″ long. the(y) are of 'Gothick' design and are of Bishop Lyttleton's time.

Panelling and reredos to apse. Panelling is made up partly of the remains of Lyttleton's 'box-pews', and the tracery panels are from the fronts of the box pews. There is some additional modern work such as the front of the canopy, but the 'groined' ceiling of the canopy, in carved oak, formed the ceiling of Lyttleton's Bishop's throne.

Wooden top to pulpit, Five-sided and of 'Gothic' design. This is modern and fits onto the stone base of the pulpit which is built up solid, with stone steps, at the front of the chancel.

Oak Communion Table, 2′–8″ wide x 7′–6″ long x 3′–2″ high. Modern.

2 Choir stalls 12′–0″ long with carved bench ends. Several smaller lengths with carved ends.

Front to Clergy seat, with Gothic tracery front.

Oak Clergy seat in chancel.

Oak lectern of poor 'Gothic' quality design. It is very low, only 3′–9″ high and formely [*sic*] fitted on to a stone base next to the pulpit at front of chancel.

Oak parclose screen between chancel and vestry, 11′–7″ long and 7′–0″ high. Open tracery panels in upper part and a door 2′–6″ wide at east end.

Oak parclose screen to west side of Vestry, 9′–6″ wide by 8′–9″ high, with open tracery panels in upper part. Door in centre 2′–9″ high, with fine mediaeval traceried panels in upper part. Door in centre 2′–9″, with open tracery panels in linen-fold panelling. The traceried panels are relics of Prior Gondibour's screens in the Cathedral *c.* 1490. similar to those now round St Catherine's Chapel. These panels were made up into this door and in Bishop Lyttleton's time this door formed the only access from the south aisle into the choir. There is a little ancient wooden cresting over this door.

Massive oak seat with arms, in Vestry. Probably formerly in Chancel.

Deal cupboards in Vestry, 8′–0″ long x 4′ 2″ high x 1′–3″ wide.

Stone font, modern, circular and carried on four columns with foliated capitals. Inscription round outside of bowl.

Oak panelling to Baptistery at west end, with two carved bench ends. At the back, of the west wall, is a 'Gothick' wooden head of 'ogee' shape, with crockets and tracery work. Part of Lyttleton's work.

At west end, near porch door, there is a large piece of carved oak, 9′–0″ x 5′–3″ high, with carved intersecting arches on the front, and applied wooden shafts. This formed the front of Bishop Lyttleton's Throne. Above are three large 'ogee' heads, carved and crocketted. These originally belonged to the top of the Throne.

Interior porch of oak, 7′–0″ x 9′–6″. Tracery panels and heads are incorporated, using up some of Lyttleton's woodwork. The main west doors have been removed (of porch) but are probably those lying in the chancel. South porch door of 18th cent. woodwork.

Parclose screen to west of organ chamber, with open tracery panels in upper part. 9′–6″ long x 7′–3″ high.

18. ibid.

19. Billings, *Geometric Tracery*, 5.

20. ibid., 4.

21. See, for example, his drawings of the windows at Sleaford, Lincolnshire in BL, MS Add. 6754, from just one of many sketchbooks.

22. R. W. Billings, *The Geometric Tracery of Brancepeth Church in the County of Durham* (London 1845), 4.

23. C. G. Bulman, 'The Gondibour and Salkeld screens in Carlisle Cathedral', *Transactions Cumberland Westmorland Antiquarian Archaeological Society*, ns, LVI (1955), 109.

24. C. Tracy, *Continental Church Furniture in England: A Traffic in Piety* (Woodbridge 2001), L/1, L/4 and L/5.

25. Displayed in the Musée des Antiquités de la Seine Maritime, Rouen.

26. C. Tracy, *Medieval Furniture and Woodwork, Victoria and Albert Museum* (London 1988), Cat. 266.

27. ibid., fig. 57.

28. The tall gabled arches and the work at the upper level of the west front at Rouen Cathedral are a very early example of the French Flamboyant style, having been erected between 1370 and 1420. The central door and the portion above it was made between 1509–14.

29. E. M. Kavaler, 'Renaissance Gothic in the Netherlands: The Uses of Ornament', *Art Bulletin*, LXXXII, 2 (June 2000), fig. 23.

30. C. Tracy, *English Gothic Choir-Stalls: 1400–1540* (Woodbridge 1990), pls 190, 192.

31. Kavaler, 'Renaissance Gothic in the Netherlands, 226–51.

32. ibid., pl. 8.

33. N. Debergh, *Koorgestoelten in West-Vlaanderen* (Tielt en Bussum 1982), 19, pls 2, 23–27.

34. Bulman, 'The Gondibour and Salkeld screens', 111–12.

35. For the work of John Morow at Melrose, see R. Fawcett, *The Architectural History of Scotland* (Edinburgh 1994), 42–50, 99–100.

36. Bulman, 'The Gondibour and Salkeld screens', 110–11; S. Simpson, 'The Choir Stalls and Rood Screen', from *King's College Chapel, Aberdeen, 1500–2000*, ed. J. Geddes (Aberdeen 2000), 74–97.

37. Tracy, *Continental Church Furniture*, 12–13.

38. See R. W. Billings, *Brancepeth Church* (London 1845). Lamentably, the highly original woodwork in this church, which was made for Durham Cathedral, *c.* 1500, was destroyed by fire on 16 September 1998.

Carlisle Cathedral Misericords: Style and Iconography

CHRISTA GRÖSSINGER

In this article I will attempt to present the latest thoughts on the misericords at Carlisle Cathedral. The style of the misericords is characterised, and comparisons are made with others in the north of England, in order to discover influences and similarities. The iconography, with its dependency on the Bestiary, is examined; the meaning of other scenes is commented on, and they are interpreted in relationship to their audience in the choir.

NOTHING is known for certain about the choir-stalls at Carlisle Cathedral; it is thought that they were installed under William Strickland, bishop of Carlisle 1400–19, and the tabernacle work over the stalls may date from the time of Prior Haythwaite, *c.* 1430.[1] Although the fire of 1292 would have destroyed the early stalls, the 14th-century Augustinian canons must have had misericords to rest on, raising the question of why there was a need for forty-six new misericords at the beginning of the 15th century. William Strickland did a great deal of repair work to the cathedral after a severe storm in March 1380 had brought down the upper portion of the central tower on to the north transept. There is no mention of any damage to the choir. Bishop Strickland was a northerner who had not arrived in Carlisle from any major artistic centre with the compulsion to emulate new creations, yet the misericords are of superior craftsmanship. The existing misericords may have been considered old-fashioned and crude, and the motifs needed to be updated. The choir of canons was also enlarged at the beginning of the 15th century from approximately sixteen to twenty in number. This would have brought in extra money, and therewith the opportunity to have new misericords carved.[2] In contrast to the misericords, the present desks are of heavy, thick and deeply grained wood, and may be the remnants of the old stalls.[3] The bases, too, seem to be made of different wood. These parts may have been considered adequate at the time, requiring only the more decorative misericords to be modernised. Assembly marks, which would have helped with the dating, were not found on the heavy desks after careful examination by Gavin Simpson. What Simpson did find, however, were candle marks on the dividing pillarets between the monks' seats, so that the question arises as to whether there were fittings to hold the candles.

A recent discovery by the cathedral conservator revealed that under strong light all the misericords were originally covered with a watery gold wash, the paint seemingly having been sloshed on. Streaks of runny paint are still visible on all the bases. Any signs of colour on misericords are extremely rare, and not necessarily original, whereas the upper tabernacle work and side panels of stalls can be quite colourful. The gold is especially strong in the deeper recesses of the misericords, but there was certainly no care taken with its application. One of the restorations of the cathedral remembered

FIG. 1.   Carlisle Cathedral:
St Michael fighting the
Dragon.

*Photograph: School of Art
History and Archaeology,
University of Manchester*

FIG. 2.   Greystoke, St
Andrews: St Michael fighting
the Dragon

*Photograph: School of Art
History and Archaeology,
University of Manchester*

FIG. 3.   Wyvern with tongue
out

*Photograph: School of Art
History and Archaeology,
University of Manchester*

for its sloppiness and thoughtlessness was that of Bishop Lyttelton in 1764, but it is
more likely that the gold paint reflects Bishop Thomas Gondibour's love of colourful
decoration. He was prior 1465–1500, and had the wooden screens built; most of his
colouring in the cathedral was later removed, but there are still remnants of gold, red
and blue on the woodwork around the organ screen. A cupboard (armoire) in the north
choir aisle, dated *c.* 1500, is covered in the same sort of a yellow-gold paint wash as on
the misericords, ornamented with green plants and petalled flowers, and is still extant
in the north choir aisle.[4]
    The central carvings of the misericords bulge outwards, making full use of the space
underneath the seat; they are deeply undercarved, giving three-dimensionality to the
motifs. Feathers seem to have been the speciality of the carvers, as seen on powerfully

FIG. 4.   Angel with Gittern
Photograph: School of Art History and Archaeology, University of Manchester

FIG. 5.   Angel with Gittern
Photograph: School of Art History and Archaeology, University of Manchester

winged birds, angels, St Michael (Figs 4–6) and hybrids. There are many knobbly wyverns, and dragons, some of which have extra long ears (Fig. 3). The eyes are very expressive, with the small pupils drilled between pronounced eyelids and bags under the eyes. Some of the figures have a knot in the central parting of the hair. All the creatures and human figures curve rhythmically underneath the ledge; the wyverns' tails are often given an extra spiralling twist at their ends, and tails wriggle along the bracket towards the supporters. This curving style is especially noticeable in St Michael's spear (S. side 13), and one of the angels' gittern, or the washing beetle the woman lifts to beat her husband with (S. side 8), and which curves parallel to the edge of the bracket (Figs 1, 4 and 9).

Four of the central motifs have been repeated, although the supporters are different: the *Angel Plucking a Gittern* (S. side 16 + N. side 16; Figs 4 and 5), where the misericords face each other across the choir aisle, at the point where steps lead up to them; the *Pelican Plucking its Breast* to feed its young (S. side 17 + N. side 10); the *Lion and Wyvern Fighting* (S. side 23 + N. side 11); and the *Fox* who has just bitten a goose in the neck (S. side 112 + N. side 10). The last two are copies in reverse, something that tends to happen with engravings, but in the case of these carvings there must have been a conscious attempt to create variations on a theme, possibly having run out of suitable workshop models.

Although more than one carver must have been at work, the style of the carvers is very close, making it very difficult to differentiate hands. Nevertheless, when examining those misericords that use the same patterns in reverse slight differences can be detected, for example in the *Lion and Wyvern Fighting*, the wyvern's body has scales in one case,

Fig. 6.   A winged Hybrid with a man's face

Photograph: School of Art History and Archaeology, University of Manchester

Fig. 7.   Darlington, St Cuthbert: a winged Hybrid with a man's face

Photograph: School of Art History and Archaeology, University of Manchester

Fig. 8.   A hyena devouring a corpse

Photograph: School of Art History and Archaeology, University of Manchester

and knobbles in the other, and the wings are different; also, the carving of the one with the knobbly body is cut off by the ledge, diminishing the size and power of the lion's body. As for the *Fox killing the Goose*, the differences, such as the fox's paws which has sharp claws in the example on the north side, but not on the south side, are negligible. The *Pelican* whose one young has been destroyed (north side) has more feathers, and a more intricately constructed nest, whereas the detail in the other looks flatter. Apart from their musical instruments, the angels look like twins, including the knot on their forehead. This is a characteristic of all the other half-length angels. In contrast, a plain parting of the hair with a high forehead is found on *St Michael killing the Dragon* (Fig. 1) and on the *Wild Man killing a Winged Dragon* (S. side Fig. 19). The wild man's dragon has scales, as in one of the dragons fighting a lion, and the face of St Michael's dragon looks like the single *Winged Wyvern* with its tongue out that has both scales and knobbles (S. side 5; Fig. 3). Taking the parting of the hair as criteria, the wild man with wings also has a knob and can be added to the angels, whereas the man pecked at by birds (N. side 22), the winged hybrid with a man's face (N. side 4; Fig 6), the head of the corpse devoured by the hyena (S. side 18; Fig. 8), and the mermaid have a plain, high forehead (S. side 22). To this group can be added those carvings with narrative scenes, such as the Woman beating the Man (S. side 8; Fig. 9). As for the birds, it is most difficult to differentiate between the feathers, but those with better defined feathers might fit the last group. The others, and those carvings that have more simplified, large motifs in the centre, would go with the group of half-length angels. This division of hands is very hypothetical and shows the difficulties experienced when trying to do so because of the close adherence to a workshop style, and the use of common models, typical of medieval workshops.

Bishop Strickland fitted up the choir for cathedral services in 1401,[5] and when considering the date of the misericords, apart from the rounded shapes, and extensions of curved lines that point to the period of the International Gothic Style around 1400, the fashion exhibited by the figures also indicates that period. The wide sleeves of the *Man attacked by a Griffin* (S. side 19), and the dagged edges of the gown of the man attacked by the woman (Fig 9) point to *c.* 1410–30. They can be compared, for example, with the dress in the *Très Riches Heures* of the Duc de Berry (Chantilly), dated to *c.* 1416. Similarly, the baggy headdress of the latter and the man holding down two dragons, as well as his low, decorative belt are typical of these dates (S. side 20; Fig. 11). Jewellery on the headdress was also popular, as seen on manuscripts of the time of the Duc de Berry, or in a painting of Jean sans Peur (Louvre) who died in 1419. Comparisons of fashion, however, cannot be pinned down to a specific date, and so too, the misericords can only be dated approximately. Bond, Billings and Henderson date the misericords to *c.* 1401; Cox and Harvey date them to *c.* 1400–15; Tracy to *c.* 1410–20; Remnant to the time of Bishop Strickland (1400–19); and Weston to *c.* 1410. Taking into account the northern position of Carlisle, away from the most up-to-date developments, a date between 1415 and 1420 seems appropriate.

Close comparisons in style and date to the Carlisle Cathedral misericords are difficult to find, and one must not forget possible destruction of many stalls, especially in the north as a result of political upheavals and accidents. The carvers of the geographically not too distant misericords in St Cuthbert's church Darlington, must have known the misericords in Carlisle Cathedral, although their work of *c.* 1430 is much cruder and heavier.[6] The shape of the supporting tendrils with a protrusion is the same, and there is a similar tendency for the central carvings to spread out horizontally. Furthermore, there is the same evidence for powerful wings in birds and winged beasts, and the carving that comes closest is that of the *Winged Hybrid with Human Face*, although, in contrast to the Carlisle example (N. side 4) it is obviously flat, stiff, and roughly cut in the face, with rather blank, goggly eyes, and no neck. The Carlisle example is beautifully curved with creases in the skin (Figs 6 and 7). Another comparison, at the same time stressing the contrasts with examples of half-length angels in Carlisle, is a half-length *Angel holding a Book*. All the figures in Darlington have bulging bodies and there is no indication of textures of body or dress.

Of finer quality, and of the same period as the Carlisle misericords, are those in Greystoke, St Andrew's, dated to the late 14th to early 15th century.[7] Here, *St Michael fighting the Dragon* (Figs 1 and 2) and the *Pelican Pecking its Breast* to feed its young

FIG. 9.   A woman beating a man with a washing beetle

Photograph: School of Art History and Archaeology, University of Manchester

FIG. 10.   York Minster: a woman beating a man with a washing beetle

Photograph: School of Art History and Archaeology, University of Manchester

FIG. 11. Fashionably dressed man holding down two dragons

Photograph: School of Art History and Archaeology, University of Manchester

can be compared. The image of St Michael at Greystoke wears a headband with cross and has powerful wings. In both examples the figures and spears curve around the base of the misericord. At Carlisle the dragon lies on its back with its paws up in the air looking quite helpless, and we are able to look right up its jaws pierced by the spear, thereby, increasing the sense of illusion. The Pelican in Greystoke has really strong claws with very pointed, horny ends that are able to dig deep into any flesh. There is the same curving composition, but the figures and feathers are daintier in Greystoke, and the protuberances not articulated as much. Nevertheless, of all the comparisons in the region these come closest, and although it is difficult to come to a conclusion on the basis of two misericords, Greystoke is the most likely place to have shared a carver with Carlisle, perhaps slightly preceding it.

Of the great northern centres that could have exerted an influence on the Carlisle workshop Durham Cathedral has misericords from the time of Bishop Cosin, after the medieval ones were destroyed in 1650, and those in York Minster were destroyed by fire in 1819. Two, however, remain in the Zouche Chapel dated to *c.* 1425: a *Man Supporting the Seat*, and the *Eagle of St John* holding a scroll. The misericord seats can be compared in general, and the dress of the figure holding up the seat is of the same period, although simpler than in Carlisle. The eagle is of a more compact shape. Two additional misericords, published by Joseph Halfpenny in 1795, reprinted in 1895, represent a *Schoolmaster birching a Boy*, and a *Woman beating the Man.*[8] The last is very close to the Carlisle misericord with the same subject matter (Figs 9 and 10); the woman grabs the man by the beard, and is about to belabour him with a washing beetle which Halfpenny has interpreted as a spearhead; she holds it in the same manner; the man has lowered his hand to support himself from falling down flat on the ground, and both are facing the spectator. The clothes worn seem plainer in York, but again, are of the same period. In the scene of the *Schoolmaster spanking the Schoolboy*, the winged dragon in the left supporter is similar to such in Carlisle, as are the lions' heads in the supporters of the *Woman beating the Man*. There is the possibility, therefore, that the York carvers influenced the Carlisle workshop, but in the iconography rather than the style for, as illustrated by the eagle of St John, there is none of the sweep of the wings, and all is more tightly carved.

One of the closest comparisons with a misericord can be found under the organ screen in Carlisle Cathedral itself. An extension of the stall work, the screen incorporates a boss representing a *Coronation* scene which must have been modelled on the misericord of the same scene (N. side 8). In both cases it is not a straightforward *Coronation of the Virgin*, but a half-length figure floating above a ring of clouds, crowned by two angels wearing albs with amices identical to the central figure; all have short hair (Figs 12 and 13).

ICONOGRAPHY

THE iconography of the Carlisle misericords is the usual one of half-length angels, beasts deriving from the Bestiary, hybrid creatures, and narrative scenes, including the inverted world theme of the Woman beating a Man that no decent set of misericords could be without.

The half-length angels all wear albs with amices; some play musical instruments, one has a blank shield strapped around his shoulders, one seems to wave, and two angels together hold up between them what may be a host or a relic.

FIG. 12.   Coronation

Photograph: School of Art History and Archaeology, University of Manchester

FIG. 13.   Carlisle Cathedral under the organ screen: Coronation

Photograph: School of Art History and Archaeology, University of Manchester

English manuscripts of the Bestiary were popular in the 13th century, in particular, although, as Baxter says, there is strong circumstantial evidence of a lack of interest in bestiaries in secular cathedrals in general, and that no surviving bestiary has been localised in such a foundation.[9] Nevertheless, they formed an important repertory for misericords, combining the necessity for a large number of carvings required for choir-stalls with the desire to tell moral tales. Typical of many choir-stalls the *Pelican Pecking its Breast* to feed its young is present in Carlisle in two places, together with two more possible pelicans preening their feathers. These are found in the supporters of the one with three chicks (S. side 17) and the other with flowers in the supporters has lost one chick (N. side 10). *The Pelican* is symbolic of Christ suffering for humanity and shedding his blood on the cross for mankind's salvation, as experienced in the sacraments of the eucharist and baptism. A similar bird, pecked at by three chicks (N. side 2), may represent the preceding part of the narrative, as told in the *Physiologus*. Here the chicks attack the parents who punish them by killing them, before reviving them on the third day with their own blood.[10] The scene of the rebellious chicks is rarely portrayed, and another suggestion is that the bird is a *Hoopoe*, which, when growing old, has its feathers preened by its young, thus giving a good example of mutual care.

Forming the supporters to a serpent-type wyvern biting its own tail are two *Basilisks* or *Cockatrices* (S. side 6). The cockatrice is hatched from the egg of a seven-year old cock, laid in a dungheap and fertilised by a serpent or toad. Thus, the offspring is half cock and half reptile. Any human or bird it casts its eyes upon first, before being seen by them, will fall down dead, and vice-versa. The only antidote to this was to set up a mirror which would reflect the creature's poisonous gaze back at it. The cockatrice, thus, stands for the devil, only to be combated by Christ entering the crystal clear vessel that is the body of the Virgin.

In the left supporter of the *Fox Catching a Goose* there is a goose with an eel in its beak. This can be compared to illuminations of the *Creation of Animals* as, for example, in the full-page *Christ Creating the Birds and Fishes* in the Aberdeen Bestiary (Aberdeen University Library MS 24, fol. 2). Here a stork stands at the edge of the water with a snake in its beak.[11]

The *Hyena devouring a Corpse* (Fig. 8) is the only example I know of on a misericord, and it represents vice feeding on corruption, Christians having turned away from their faith and succumbed to a life of greed and lust, enabling the hyena to become well fed.

The story of the *Fox* as told on misericords largely derives from the Bestiary, and only those at Bristol Cathedral tell it according to the Romance of Reynard the Fox. The *Fox catching the Goose*, and making off with it, was a well-known occurrence in country life where it was both feared and admired for its cunning and craftiness. It is associated with the Devil, catching the unsuspecting human soul that has failed to be constantly on the lookout for the Devil and his temptations. Any inattentiveness to matters spiritual will be taken advantage of by the Devil. In Carlisle, the moment of the goose being caught is shown twice, followed by the fox with lion-like paws making off with an enormous goose which was bigger than itself (N. side 7). Another episode is of the *Fox feigning death*: it rolls in red soil, so as to look bloody, and lies on its back, mouth gaping; the birds come to peck at this supposedly lifeless body, whereupon the fox leaps up and catches its dinner. The bird on the Carlisle misericord (S. side 3; Fig. 14), however, looks like a powerful eagle against which the fox is struggling in vain. Although there are Bestiaries with illuminations of large birds sitting near the pretending fox, they are more placid and there are usually several of them as, for example, in St John's College Oxford, MS. 178, fol. 168.[12] In Carlisle by contrast, the odds seem to be against the fox.

Also known for its deceptiveness is the *Amphisbaena* on the left supporter of the human-headed quadruped (Fig. 6): it is a serpent with two heads, one at either end, thus, doubly evil, allowing it to move backwards and forwards without warning.

Dragons on the Carlisle misericords come in a great variety of shapes, mostly as wyverns with two legs, not the four legs of dragons, or resembling a serpent. There is one with its tail wound around a fleeing quadruped with a beaked nose; here too, the same composition is used again, except that the coiling dragon has become feathery.

One of the *Wyverns* in Carlisle Cathedral (S. side 2) with outspread wings and squarish face can be compared to the same in Cartmel, except that the Carlisle species faces backwards, biting its wing. According to the Bestiary, its tail was more dangerous than its bite, and in Carlisle they are often extended into spirals, and curls. One example in Carlisle looks especially cheerful with its tongue out, possibly because it has

just poisoned someone with its breath (S. side 5; Fig. 3). The wyvern and dragon represent the serpent from the Garden of Eden, the Devil, and in the example of the *Lion and Wyvern Fighting* (S. side 23), it is Christ (the lion) fighting the Devil, or Good battling against Evil. This last scene was very popular with carvers, for the interlocking beasts gave themselves to strong and satisfying composition that fitted well underneath the misericords, and it represented a simple moral message in a powerful manner.

The *Griffin* was also greatly feared, for it was known to tear human beings and horses apart, and on the misericord a well-dressed man's sword is of no avail to him when attacked by such a ferocious beast; his defence is rather listless, and the lions masks in the supporters put their tongues out in gleeful derision (S. side 19). Griffins are the birds that lift Alexander the Great into the skies, as carved on a misericord in Darlington, but in Carlisle it tears apart human beings. A griffin standing victorious over a dead knight in armour is also found on a misericord in Nantwich, Cheshire, illustrating its destructive power over armed men.

The *Mermaid* in Carlisle is truly a *Siren*, for, most unusually, she is both bird and fish. Like a bird it causes the sailors to fall asleep charmed by her dulcet song (S. side 22; Fig. 15). Once asleep, the sailors are ripped apart by the sirens. Objects of vanity, such as the mirror and comb, are the symbols of these representatives of lust and pride, and men fall for the temptations of worldly pleasures and are consequently doomed. The Lorelei, on one of the narrowest parts of the Rhine flanked by precipitous, treacherous rocks, is well known for the Mermaid that sits on top of the rock, combing her hair and singing. The sailors down below are lulled into admiration of her and disregard the rocks under the water, resulting in shipwreck.

FIG. 16. Two wyvern's bodies with one head

Photograph: School of Art History and Archaeology, University of Manchester

FIG. 17. A winged furry man on his haunches

Photograph: School of Art History and Archaeology, University of Manchester

Apart from birds arranged in symmetrical compositions, there are several carvings of composite beasts, some with human faces. These cannot be traced back to the Bestiary, for even the winged, human-headed quadruped is not quite a *Manticora* (N. side 4; Fig. 6), because it has human hands and wings, and no scorpion's tail, or rows of teeth, as described in the Bestiary. Are these the types of creatures that annoyed St Bernard, when he raved against them in his letter in the 'Apologia' to William, abbot of St Thierry in *c.* 1125? There he speaks of 'those monstrous centaurs, those half-men', saying 'Many bodies are there seen under one head, or again, many heads to a single body. Here is a four-footed beast with a serpent's tail; there, a fish with a beast's head'. These are the half-human and half-animal creatures so familiar in Romanesque sculptures, continuing into the 14th century, as seen around the capitals illustrating the Labours of the Months from the first half of the 14th century in Carlisle Cathedral, and then on the 15th-century misericords. There is a human face with beard and sideburns wearing a soft hat attached to two wyverns' bodies (N. side 20; Fig. 16); a combination of a lion's head with two bodies that have eagle's claws (S. side 7); a grotesque lion mask whose protruding lip is pecked at by two birds (S. side 11); or a furry man with lions' paws and wings hunched up, facing (N. side 15; Fig. 17); the protrusion from the bottom of his belly has been cut away, possibly having shown some genital component. Generally the half-human and half-animal creatures are associated with the animal nature of humankind, warning against all carnal passions. The hairy winged man represents a 'fallen angel', having turned away from God, and become a devil, just as Hieronymus Bosch has his Falling Angels turn into winged insects. Some of the devils presiding in Hell in the *Last Judgement* (Vienna, Akademie der Künste) are grotesque creatures with wings, like one devil reading out a soul's sins before Satan enthroned. St Bernard, however, could see no meaning in them, and asked: 'What profit is there in these ridiculous monsters, in that marvellous and deformed comeliness, that comely deformity?' He saw these 'curious carvings' as pagan, as abominations, for after all many of them can be traced back to the satyr and the centaur of Greek mythology. His main concern was that they would divert the attention of his monks who would be more interested in these grotesques than in their serious reading. Would he have been so offended if he had recognised them as Bestiary beasts telling a moral? St Bernard was, however, prepared to allow such monstrosities in secular churches for the edification of lay people, as he says; 'to excite the devotion of carnal folk'. The grotesques so feared by him became most prevalent in the margins of 14th-century manuscripts which are full of such diverting subject matter. The carvings on misericords can be likened to this type of marginalia, for the margins of East Anglian manuscripts, and the *Luttrell* and *Queen Mary* Psalters are full of monstrous creatures, more animal than human in their combinations, as found in Carlisle. With the introduction of marginal subject matter an element of playfulness is introduced, and therewith a new secular element. In contrast to the bestiaries of the 12th and 13th centuries written for a monastic audience, misericords, although positioned in the sanctuary, were carved by laymen from without the cloister walls. Considering the advance in time one must ask whether the Bestiary subjects on the misericords have preserved their original meaning, or whether some of the beasts not precisely identifiable were already misunderstood by the 15th-century carvers; for example, were human hands added to the *Manticora* in Carlisle because of a misinterpretation, or is it just supposed to be a hybrid quadruped (Fig. 6)? It is known that medieval artists used patterns, and as misericords demonstrate, there rarely seems to have been a specifically planned programme. Only when working at a very important artistic centre such as at court, would artists have had access to manuscripts from which they could derive inspiration. When the Carlisle stalls were being constructed pattern books and travelling artists would have transmitted motifs, to be replaced in the second half of the 15th century by cheaper and more easily available prints. The Ripon Cathedral misericords were the first to benefit from this new technique.[13] There is a need, therefore, to be careful about giving meaning to every single misericord, especially if a large number of seats had to be carved. However, as explained by Randall, marginalia can be compared to exempla used by preachers in their sermons to drive home a moral message. The Bestiary themes formed a very popular and suitable source for such, especially the story of the Fox who was identified with the Devil.[14] On a Carlisle misericord the most fashionably dressed young man who holds down two wyverns, thereby making the carving into a symmetrical composition, could be interpreted as an admonishment to him for his vanity and pride, and an injunction to keep these deadly sins under control, to stamp them out (Fig. 11).

One of the most popular exempla of the world upside-down found on misericords is that of the *Woman as Virago* beating her husband (Fig. 9). As in the case of the man attacked by the griffin, the husband's weapon is no match for the woman's washing beetle, and he has gone down on the ground, vainly trying to keep his torso upright. Worst of all, the woman has grabbed his beard, thus causing him to lose all honour and power, and to become the subservient husband. He who should have been bossing his wife about has become her plaything, the tables have been turned, and he will be asked to do women's work.

According to medieval medical opinion, a person's physical and mental qualities were determined by the four humours, resulting in the four temperaments: sanguine, phlegmatic, choleric and melancholic. Women's dominant humour had the qualities of coldness and dampness, making them weak and pliant, especially susceptible to the influence of the devil. Waxing and waning like the moon they could never be trusted, they were unstable, prone to lose their tempers, and to be gossips. The early Church Fathers characterised them as being insatiable in their sexual appetites. The woman doing battle with her husband is already found on misericords of the 1340s, as at Hereford Cathedral, where she kicks him and throws a bowl at him. From the 1370s at Lincoln Cathedral, the woman beating up her husband spreads like wild-fire. On the Continent, on misericords and in manuscripts, and in particular in later 15th-century prints, the scene is more likely to be depicted as the *Battle for the Trousers*, or the *Henpecked Husband*, where he has to do the spinning. On English misericords, the cause of the trouble is often depicted as the husband who has been meddling in the kitchen which is the woman's domain. Here he is usually belaboured with a ladle or a washing beetle. Honour forbids the husband to shout about his treatment, and a large number of obedient husbands suffer patiently. There are so many that the mythical beast called *Bigorne* (Fillgut)(N. side 1; Fig. 18) gets obese on a diet of good, patient husbands.[15] This is what is shown on the misericord of an enormous wyvern swallowing up a man. There is another example on a misericord in Worcester Cathedral. Bigorne's opposite is *Chichefache* (Pinch Belly) who feeds on obedient wives, but as there are none, it is haggard and starving, and certainly not found on misericords!

A *Nude Man* (N. side 22) in pants and showing his belly-button sits on his haunches, while eagles nibble at his beard. They do not seem too aggressive, but the beard and hair is a man's seat of strength and virility. If he was a *Wild Man*, he could become master of the animals, as is illustrated by the carving of a *Wild Man tearing open the Jaws of a scaly Dragon* (S. side 14; Fig. 19). The wild man's body was covered in fur, except for his hands and feet, and being so hairy he was extremely strong, and able to pull out whole tree trunks to use as a weapon.[16] His abode was the forest and he was master and keeper of the wild animals. Although he did not believe in God he was considered human by St Augustine. The wild man was popular, especially in the Age of Chivalry, when, after having started life as a fierce giant, he became civilised. Although he would kidnap fair ladies, they had the ability to tame him through chivalrous love. Thus, he is depicted on many love caskets as at Cologne, Kunstgewerbe Museum. The misericords in Lincoln and Chester Cathedrals have several depictions of the Wild Man, fighting, or riding on wild beasts, such as lions, and holding them on chains. This is one way he is depicted in Darlington, where he swings a knobbly club and holds the lion on a heavy chain (Fig. 20). Although the *Wild Man* in Darlington has no visible tufts of fur, but looks nude, apart from sporting a dainty pair of boots which give him an air of civilisation and chivalry. Another misericord in Darlington shows him holding bunches of roses, thus associating him with May as the month of love, and his prowess in love; for this reason, as a symbol of fertility, both wild men and wild women were seen as mascots and used in coats of arms of families desirous to ensure their propagation into the future. At the end of the 15th century the wild man and wild woman were most popular on Swiss and South German tapestries, where they are shown as leading an idyllic family life, the wild woman usually carrying a baby in her arms.

No theme could be more apt for choir-stalls than the woman possessed by the devil, for it must have been the perfect warning for the clergy to beware of matrimony, or any crack in their oath of celibacy. That is probably why these misogynistic scenes were so popular on misericords. Equally, the *Mermaid* or *Siren* was the temptress incarnate,

FIG. 18. Bigorne swallowing up a good husband

Photograph: School of Art History and Archaeology, University of Manchester

FIG. 19. Wild man seizing a dragon

Photograph: School of Art History and Archaeology, University of Manchester

FIG. 20. Darlington, St Cuthbert: Wild man with chained lion

Photograph: School of Art History and Archaeology, University of Manchester

beguiling any unsuspecting man, but especially one of the Church (Fig. 15). Already, Tertullian (*c.* 160–*c.* 225) criticised early Christian converts for their pagan attitudes towards dress and appearance, and medieval preachers chastised women for their constant endeavours to look enticing to men. Then there are the misericords of the fox, and although the fox is not shown preaching in friar's clothing, foxyness was equated with deviousness, and with the clergy, especially the mendicant friars. By extension, the fox catching the goose may have been a warning to the Augustinian canons, for in their preaching they had the power to deceive, to mislead, and thus, to lead others and themselves into sin and consequent hellfire. The Church also had to keep a constant watch on corruption, represented by the hyena feeding on corruption, and it was criticised throughout for getting fat by evil means, thus being in league with the devil; there are numerous pictures of the clergy at the Last Judgement being the first to enter the jaws of hell. Many of the misericords concentrate on the battles to be fought between good and evil, of the animal nature in humans to be kept at bay. This, of course, was a problem for the clergy who had to fight a continuous battle with chastity, and who had to renounce all the trappings of life. The grotesque creatures on the misericords might well represent the inner demons that afflicted monks. Often these demons would change into tempting women. Women were also known for giving in to their lust, but monks were men with human emotions who had to control their bodies and discipline their carnal desires. Some of the grotesques seem to be combinations created by the artists for amusement, and it must be remembered that medieval sermons were famous for the inclusion of humorous anecdotes, with the intent of keeping the attention of the congregation, and of making the sermon memorable. St Bernard chastised his monks for their lack of proper attention, but he did not place the same conditions on lay people outside the cloister walls. In the Middle Ages the sacred and profane was closely allied, as illustrated most successfully by misericords themselves. They were placed in the most sacred space of a church, yet they contained little religious subject matter, and supported the basest part of the human anatomy of those humans concerned with the most spiritual. St Bernard's concern for the soul of his monks also illustrates the power of images on the minds of people, and I believe that the purpose of misericords was to inspire the clergy with the fear of indulging in carnal pleasures with the help of humour and understanding of the human psyche.[17]

NOTES

1. D. V. W. Weston, *Carlisle Cathedral History* (Carlisle 2000), 44; C. Tracy, *English Gothic Choir-Stalls* (Woodbridge 1990), 2 and 6.

2. Information, Dr Henry Summerson.

3. Information, Dr David Weston.

4. Pointed out to me by Jane Geddes. See also Weston, 53.

5. R. W. Billings, *Architectural Illustrations, History and Descriptions of Carlisle Cathedral* (London 1842), 3.

6. Made under Cardinal Langley (1406–47); they have his device of an *eagle regardant* and his coat of arms.

7. The misericords in Greystoke are of two dates: six from the late 14th/early 15th century and the remaining fourteen from the 17th century.

8. J. Halfpenny, *Gothic Ornaments in the Cathedral Church of York* (York 1795), pls 54 and 69.

9. Ron Baxter, *Bestiaries and Their Users in the Middle Ages* (Stroud 1998), 154.

10. Ron Baxter, ibid., 40; a prophesy from Isaiah relates the chicks' attack on their parents to the rejection of Christ by the Jewish nation.

11. W. George and B. Yapp, *The Naming of the Beasts. Natural History in the Medieval Bestiary* (London 1991), 32, fig. 16.

12. W. George and B. Yapp, ibid., 13, fig. 4.

13. J. S. Purvis, 'The Use of Continental Woodcuts and Prints by the Ripon School of Woodcarvers', *Archaeologia*, LXXXV (1935), 107–28.

14. L. Randall, 'Exempla as a Source of Gothic Marginal Illumination', *Art Bulletin*, 39 (1957), 97–107.

15. S. M. Taylor, 'Monster of misogyny', *Allegorica*, 5 (1980), 98–124.

16. R. Bernheimer, *Wild Men in the Middle Ages* (Cambridge, Mass. 1952).

17. These last thoughts may be problematic in connection with Bishop Strickland's private situation, for as I was informed by Henry Summerson, the bishop, while in minor orders, had a wife and daughter, and his son-in-law later donated money to the cathedral.

Late Medieval Paintings at Carlisle

DAVID PARK AND SHARON CATHER

Carlisle Cathedral is distinguished by an exceptional amount of late medieval painting, notably the extensive figurative programme associated with Prior Thomas Gondibour (c. 1465–c. 1500) on the reverse of the choir-stalls, and the strikingly sophisticated decoration of the ceiling executed for Prior Senhouse (c. 1500–c. 1520) in the Prior's Tower. In discussing the choir-stall paintings, which include cycles of St Augustine of Hippo, St Cuthbert and St Anthony of Egypt, the present paper considers their dating attribution and patronage, as well as their technique and physical history, and demonstrates that they were painted in situ *rather than relocated from elsewhere. The complex design of the Prior's Tower ceiling is analysed, as well as the significance of its extensive inscriptions and unusual carved bosses, and it is discussed within the context of other painted ceilings of similar date especially in the north of England.*

AN extraordinary amount of late medieval painting survives at Carlisle Cathedral. By far the most important examples are the paintings on the backs of the choir-stalls, and the decoration of the ceiling in the Prior's Tower, which together will form the focus of this paper. In addition, there is an armoire with painted foliate decoration now in the north choir aisle, which almost certainly dates from the time of Prior Thomas Gondibour (*c.* 1465–*c.* 1500); his initials were incorporated in the polychromy of a second armoire, now lost but recorded in the 19th century.[1] Unfortunately, however, a great deal of painting uncovered during the restoration of the cathedral in the 1850s was destroyed at that time: the St Cuthbert scene depicted on the north-east pier of the crossing (Fig. 4), which is discussed further below, and also the decoration of the choir piers. These were found to be 'painted white, and diapered with red roses nearly a foot in diameter, with a gold monogram, I.H.C. or J. M.'.[2] This scheme, thought also perhaps to date from Gondibour's time, was doubtless a product of the increasingly popular cult of the Holy Name of Jesus in the late 15th century.[3] Also recorded in the 1850s was the medieval colouring of the choir ceiling, described as 'principally red and green upon a white ground, the bosses gilt'.[4] Following extensive structural restoration, however, the ceiling was provided with a new scheme of gold stars on a blue ground, itself repainted in 1969–70.[5] Consequently, the main survival of medieval polychromy to be seen in the cathedral today is the painting on the choir-stalls.

THE CHOIR-STALLS

FOUR sets of painting appear on the backs of the choir-stalls (Fig. 1). On the south side is a cycle of scenes from the life of St Augustine of Hippo (Col. Pl. VI), while on the north, a series of St Cuthbert scenes at the east end is followed by full-length figures of the twelve apostles, and at the west end by a cycle of the life of St Anthony of Egypt (Col. Pl. VII). Overall, there are no fewer than fifty-six scenes, as well as the figures of

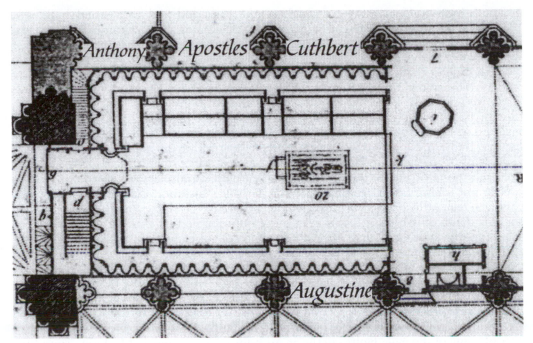

FIG. 1.   Choir-stalls: plan locating paintings

apostles, and with the exception of parts of the St Cuthbert cycle the painting is generally well preserved. Each of the scenes is accompanied by an explanatory inscription in English, and each of the apostles by a phrase in Latin from the Apostles' Creed. Regarding the choice of subjects, St Augustine is obviously appropriate in this Augustinian house, St Anthony as the founder of monasticism, and St Cuthbert as the premier saint of the north of England.

Following the Reformation, the paintings were whitewashed with the rest of the choir, but by 1703 they were at least partly visible due to the degradation of the limewash, and in 1778 all the paintings were fully exposed.[6] Various antiquarian publications followed, of which the most important was Harcourt's of 1868, which remains — with its crude line-drawings — the only fully-illustrated account of the paintings.[7] The only significant art-historical analysis of any aspect of the paintings has been Colgrave's article on the St Cuthbert cycle, published in 1938, with black and white photographs of about half the scenes.[8] Given this lack of adequate reproductions, the paintings have been extraordinarily difficult to study, and it is only now through the superb set of colour photographs taken by English Heritage in connection with the present conference that this situation can begin to be rectified.[9]

It has always been recognised that the paintings are later in date than the stalls themselves, which are essentially of *c.* 1410, though the canopies may date from about the 1430s.[10] Clear dating evidence is provided by the background of the scene of St Augustine and the devil (Col. Pl. VIII), which is scattered with a stencilled white floral device enclosing the TGP monogram of Prior Thomas Gondibour (*c.* 1465–*c.* 1500).[11] As already noted, Gondibour's initials also occurred on one of the painted armoires in the cathedral, and they still appear on the stone bench below the St Cuthbert scenes and in various other contexts throughout the cathedral and conventual buildings. Whether their appearance in the St Augustine cycle dates all the choir-stall paintings, however, is complicated by the stylistic evidence that at least two artists or workshops were involved. Overall, the style of the Cuthbert and Augustine cycles is sufficiently close to suggest that they are by a single hand or workshop, despite the different taste displayed for stencilled designs and textile patterns in the backgrounds (Col. Pls IX-X). Radically different, however, is the style of the Anthony series: much more crude, though no less vigorous, this is also the only one of the three cycles in which the inscriptions have been set out on ruled lines (Col. Pl. XI).[12] Despite their inferior quality, the St Anthony paintings nevertheless incorporate the most 'advanced' feature stylistically: the column separating the two scenes at upper right (Col. Pl. XIII),[13] which preserves none of the Gothic flavour of the architectural elements in the other two cycles, but seems rather to anticipate the early Renaissance style of Prior Salkeld's carved screen (after 1541).[14] Although a dating as early as *c.* 1500 might seem unlikely for this detail, however, it seems even more improbable that the Anthony cycle is of substantially later date than the other paintings. Certainly, the costume evidence throughout the paintings indicates a dating in or around the closing years of the 15th century, as illustrated in the scene of St Anthony resisting the Spirit of Fornication (Col. Pl. XIVA). Here, Fornication's long sleeves with large cuffs covering her hands, as well as her headdress with its projection at the back and long lappets hanging at the sides, may all be compared with, for example, the dress of the wife of Sir Walter Mauntell (d. 1487) on their brass at Nether Heyford (Northants).[15] Likewise, the shoulder-length hair of some of the male figures in the St Anthony cycle is typical of fashion around the end of the 15th century, and is paralleled by the figure of Sir Walter on the Nether Heyford brass.[16] Perhaps the most likely solution, given the clear evidence of at least two different hands or workshops, is that the Anthony cycle (and the apostles) are slightly later than the other paintings located more prominently to the east.

The technique of the paintings has never been investigated, but a fine, overall craquelure strongly indicates that they were executed in oil.[17] The paint layer is surprisingly thick, with considerable impasto employed for decorative details such as the scrollwork on the bed-cover in the scene of St Augustine healing the prior. In general, the materials of the paintings seem to be fairly inexpensive, with, apparently, no use of metal foils; thus details which might have been gilded, such as mitres or crosiers, are merely painted yellow. The one relatively expensive 'pigment' which *is* employed extensively — at least in the St Augustine cycle — is the readily recognisable red lake, a dye derived from plants or insects, that is subject to fading.[18] In the scene of St Augustine and the devil (Col. Pl. VIII), the red lake is almost perfectly preserved in the background behind the saint, whereas in the scene of his Baptism the lake has faded to produce mauve.[19] In other respects, as already mentioned, the condition of the paintings is surprisingly good. Waxed by Tristram in 1936, the paintings were treated again by Pauline Plummer in the 1970s, when a wax-resin mixture was driven into the surface with a hot air blower and heated spatula.[20] Little, if any, modern retouching is discernible.

In addition to issues of dating, attribution and patronage, the paintings pose a number of further questions: whether they have been relocated from elsewhere; why the southern side has only a single painting cycle, whereas the northern side is completely painted; and why each of the four paintings terminates along its eastern edge in an unpainted area.

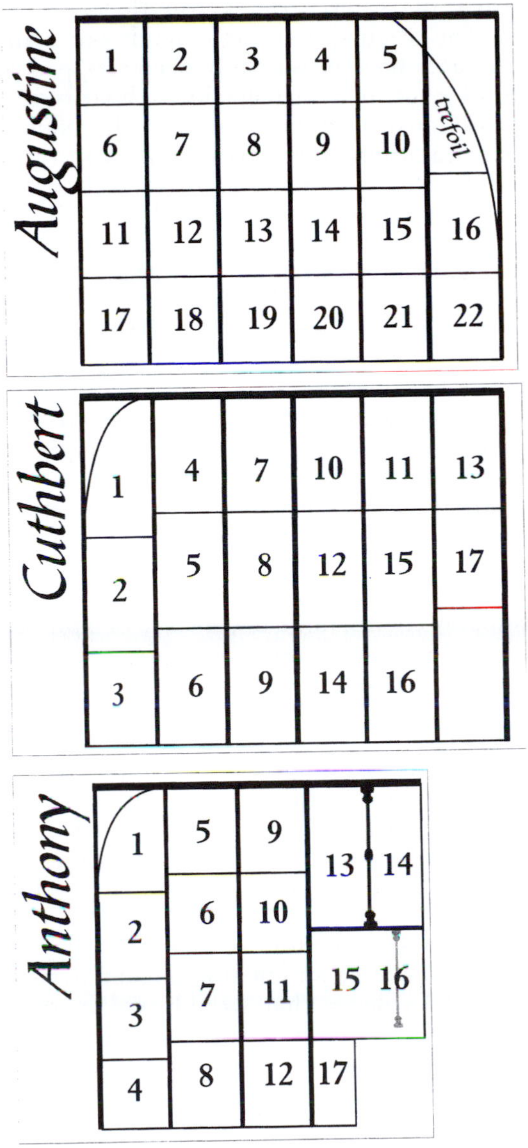

FIG. 2.   Choir-stalls: sequence of scenes in the saints' cycles

© *Courtauld Institute*

Of crucial significance is whether the panels have been relocated since they were painted. A range of physical evidence can be adduced to demonstrate that they *were* painted *in situ*, and that, apart from a few boards in the St Anthony cycle, they remain undisturbed. The support for the paintings forms, simultaneously, the back of the choir-stalls (Fig. 3). Only a single plank in thickness, this wooden screen consists of butt-joined, vertically aligned boards secured by muntins; in some areas the edges of the planks have been chamfered to fit the muntins. The muntins are carved on their inner faces and fastened to the pinnacles of the choir-stalls by brackets and braces. This structure presumably formed part of the choir-stall design, perhaps from the period of later alteration, and predates the paintings. The original painting extends on to the sides of the muntins (although the now-bare faces have presumably been stripped of their original painting), into numerous areas of mechanical damage in the boards, and across deformations caused by shrinkage and consequent movement of the planks, providing unequivocal evidence both that the paintings were carried out *in situ* and that they have not since been moved. The only exception is in the St Anthony cycle, where several of the westernmost boards have been removed and replaced in the wrong order. This is easily explicable by the fact that this area extends across the void which gives access to the area of the pulpitum stair (Fig. 1). It is wider than the normal spacing between the muntins, and therefore scenes 13–14 (Col. Pl. XIII) and 15–16 (as shown in the 19th-century drawings) were both originally divided vertically by a fictive column rather than a structural muntin. Scenes 15 and 16 (the saint's Death and Burial) have since been haphazardly reassembled so that the dividing column now appears near the right. Presumably, at some time after the drawings were made, greater access to this void was required, perhaps to construct a new stair, and the panels were then replaced in the wrong order. [21]

It seems odd that on the north side there are three sets of painting, whereas on the south only one. However, this issue has already been partly addressed in considering the authorship of the different cycles. Since the Augustine and Cuthbert cycles occupy the liturgically more significant eastern bays of the choir screen, and they are by the same artist or workshop and therefore presumably coeval, one can conceive of a phased programme of decoration beginning from the east. Phasing of this ambitious programme would account both for a pause — explaining the different style of the apostles and Anthony paintings — and, indeed, the eventual abandonment of the project.

All four sets of painting share a curious feature: the easternmost area is unpainted. In all cases, it terminates in an arc, although that of the southern (Augustine) cycle differs from those on the north in being larger and more disruptive of the narrative scenes. These unpainted areas and their arcs must be original since in all cases the painting and inscriptions accommodate them (Col. Pl. XI). This is best seen in the second register of the St Augustine cycle, where the easternmost compartment has been reduced to a triangle and infilled with the expedient of a trefoil design and four-line inscription (Col. Pl. VI). Additionally, all the sets on the north side include an unpainted compartment at lower right. There seems to be no surviving evidence that would explain these features: the unpainted boards are original (many retaining carpenters' marks), the boards appear never to have been painted, and the paintings simply end without an indication that they were painted up to a fixed element. A possible explanation is that altars were situated on the western sides of the piers, though this must remain purely speculative.

Compartmentalisation of the narratives was predetermined by the pre-existing muntins, adamantly defining the vertical pictorial fields. However, within this constraint, disposition of the narrative sequence differed. The Augustine narrative is disposed in 22 rigorously regular compartments, reading horizontally from upper left to lower right in four registers. The Cuthbert cycle is only somewhat less regular in arrangement, but with fewer subjects (17) each scene is taller, resulting in only three registers. It differs, however, in the sequence of the narrative: although it too begins at upper left, it reads from top to bottom, and then appears to end in disarray, with the last seven scenes in a confusing order (Fig. 2).[22] This might suggest that the boards had

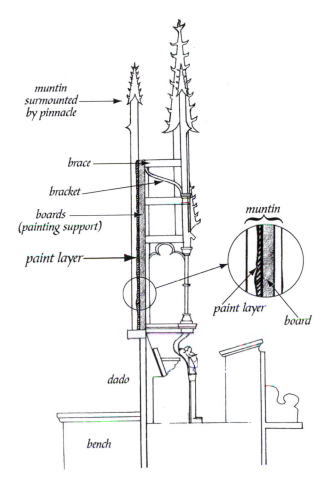

muntin
surmounted
by pinnacle

brace

bracket

boards
(painting support)

paint layer

muntin

paint layer

board

dado

bench

FIG. 3.   Choir-stalls: diagram
showing construction
© *Courtauld Institute*

been rearranged, but it is clear from the evidence of the horizontal joins that this is not the case; for example, scenes 13 and 17 share the same vertical planks. Perhaps the apparent disarray can be explained by reference to the scenes which have been moved from their proper narrative sequence and placed in the bottom register — the Consecration and Last Sacrament (scenes 14 and 16) — suggesting the overriding concern was for visibility.

The inscriptions accompanying the saints' scenes have been the subject of a useful study by Andrew Hamer, who has shown that they are in a mixed dialect incorporating northern English as well as standard forms.[23] For instance, for the third person plural, both northern and standardising spellings are employed: 'thai' and 'yam' on the one hand, and 'They' and 'them' on the other. Two words are certainly of northern origin: 'kyrk' and 'layks' (the latter in the scene of Cuthbert's childhood: 'Her Cuthbert was forbid layks and plays'). In the scene of crows removing thatch from Cuthbert's 'hous', the spelling of 'unthek' (= unthatch) 'indicates a Northern, unpalatalised pronunciation, quite possibly influenced by Norse'. Hamer concludes that 'the writer of these verses were certainly a Northerner, although he cannot be localised more closely than that, and that his dialect was considerably influenced by the emerging standard' in the late 15th century.[24]

The extraordinarily extensive programme of paintings on the choir-stalls at Carlisle is now unparalleled in England, but this was not the case originally. In a sense, the great 'wooden walls' formed by the backs of the stalls function in the same way as stone choir enclosures, so the programme may be compared in a general way with such programmes as the scenes of St John the Baptist and St Firmin carved on the exterior of the choir enclosure of Amiens Cathedral at the end of the 15th century,[25] or with the Old Testament cycle provided *in choro et circa* at Bury St Edmunds Abbey in the late 12th century, which M. R. James argued was likewise painted on the outside of the choir enclosure.[26] While the series of apostles with phrases of the Creed on the Carlisle stalls may now be most readily compared, in an English context, with contemporary rood-screens, a group of no fewer than 13 late medieval stalls in Switzerland and north Italy feature the same theme (albeit on the front).[27] In England, the choir-stalls of Peterborough Abbey were painted in the mid-13th century with an extensive typological cycle with accompanying verses, although it is uncertain whether on the front or the back.[28] Two other sets of choir-stalls, however, still retain painted figure-subjects on the back: at Gloucester Cathedral, late-14th-century(?) figures of standing saints — including St Anthony — as well as small-scale scenes of Reynard the Fox;[29] and, in St George's Chapel at Windsor, figures of kings dating from *c.* 1493, and therefore almost exactly contemporary with the Carlisle paintings.[30]

Of the individual series of paintings on the Carlisle stalls, it has already been noted that the St Cuthbert cycle is the only one so far to have received serious art-historical study, though there is also a useful discussion of the St Augustine subjects by Colledge.[31] While single figures of Augustine and Anthony commonly occur in late medieval art — Augustine typically as one of the Four Latin Doctors — the Carlisle paintings appear to represent the only surviving cycles of these saints in England. Of St Anthony, we know that another existed on painted cloths in the London church of St Anthony, Threadneedle Street, for which an inventory of 1499 records 'ij stenyd clothys to hange abowte the church, on of the lyffe of Seynt Antonye. And another of the Invencion' (the latter probably depicting the discovery of the saint's grave in Egypt and his translation to Constantinople).[32] Clearly, there is ample scope for future research on the relationship between the Carlisle cycles and those still existing in late medieval art elsewhere in Europe.[33]

In 1938 Bertram Colgrave convincingly demonstrated that the St Cuthbert cycle must have been derived from the Durham illuminated *Life* of *c.* 1200 now in the British Library.[34] The similarity of the compositions is too great to be coincidental, though a plethora of landscape and architectural detail has been added in the late medieval version (Col. Pl. X). Colgrave observed that the manuscript might well have been available for copying through the good offices of Bishop Bell (1478–95), who had previously been prior of Durham (and whose great brass occupies the floor-space between the choir-stalls). However, the variations from the source are sufficiently significant and the derived elements sufficiently simple that an intermediary in the form of a sketchbook can be readily imagined; this would, in any case, be closer to what we now understand of medieval workshop practice. Moreover, the artist of the Cuthbert cycle chose to represent only 17 scenes in three registers — in contrast to the 22 in four registers of the Augustine cycle — while the *Life* has more than twice that number.

Several other St Cuthbert cycles still exist, including an early 12th-century *Life* now in Oxford, and a window probably of the early 1440s in the south choir aisle of York

FIG. 4.   Vision of St
Cuthbert, formerly on the
north-east crossing pier

*Copy by E. Towry Whyte of a
drawing by Matthew Nutter*

Minster. In 1978 Malcolm Baker devoted a celebrated article to the relationship of the
various cycles, positing a lost original of the late 11th century, and another lost cycle
dating perhaps from the mid 12th century.[35] However, many problems remain; for
instance, how do the *c.* 1200 *Life* and the Carlisle stalls relate to the two scenes of the
saint painted in the late 12th century on the splays of a window at Pittington, near
Durham, and which presumably once formed part of a much longer cycle?[36] The
Pittington scene of the Consecration of St Cuthbert is close in composition to its very
damaged counterpart at Carlisle — in both, Archbishop Theodore is depicted anointing
the saint's head, and King Ecgfrith is shown to the right — so it might be assumed that
the (now missing) illustration of this scene in the *c.* 1200 *Life* was also similar. On the
other hand, the second scene at Pittington, St Cuthbert's vision at the table of the
Abbess of Whitby, does not occur in the Carlisle cycle, and is sufficiently different from
its counterpart in the *c.* 1200 *Life* to suggest that they depend from different models.
   Finally, how do the choir-stall paintings relate to the wall-painting formerly on the
north-east pier of the tower of the Cathedral, recorded in a drawing by Nutter (Fig. 4),
and interpreted as St Cuthbert's vision of St Aidan's soul taken to heaven?[37] This does

seem to be the correct identification, despite various inaccuracies in the copy (for instance, the reclining figure with a staff appears merely to be an accompanying shepherd, so the figure of Cuthbert himself is missing; it is also most unlikely that a unicorn appeared in the original painting!). This scene is absent from the *c.* 1200 *Life*, but at least two other surviving depictions show St Aidan's soul carried to heaven by two angels,[38] as described in the label of this subject on the choir-stalls:

> Her saw he Aydan's sawl upgo
> To hevyns bliss w[t] angels two.

Damaged though it is, this scene on the stalls strangely but unmistakably shows not Aidan's soul supported by angels, but a robed figure of Christ in Majesty, seated on a rainbow in a rayed mandorla. The wall-painting appears to have been basically similar, with a bearded figure of God flanked by angels appearing in the sky. Does this iconography derive from a lost scene in the *c.* 1200 *Life*? Much further research needs to be done on the Cuthbert cycle, as on other aspects of the choir-stalls.

CEILING OF THE PRIOR'S TOWER

UNTIL recently part of the Deanery, the Prior's Tower originally formed part of a more extensive range of buildings along the southern boundary of the priory, their backs toward West Walls. A three-storey crenellated building, it probably dates in its entirety from the time of Prior Senhouse (*c.* 1500–*c.* 1520), whose patronage of the painted ceiling (Col. Pl. XIVB) on the first floor is recorded in one of its inscriptions.[39] This first-floor room has oriel windows in the north and south walls, of two and three lights respectively, and features a large fireplace in the east wall. The traceried wooden panelling above the fireplace is later (perhaps 16th-century French work),[40] and the panelling around the walls probably dates from the time of Dean Smith (1671–84). It is likely that it was also at this period that a plaster ceiling was inserted below the original ceiling,[41] but this was removed at some point after the rediscovery of the original in 1792. In the 19th century, the original painted ceiling was restored, including varnishing and some retouching and re-gilding, and in 1976 a comprehensive conservation programme was carried out by Pauline Plummer, when some further retouching was undertaken.[42]

The overall ceiling design is best understood from a watercolour painting dating to 1890 (Col. Pl. XVA).[43] Structurally, the ceiling is divided into nine compartments by two principal beams running east to west, and by two secondary beams (arched underneath) running north to south. The disposition of the painting, however, ignores the divisions created by the secondary beams, and is composed of three, sequentially repeated elements (Col. Pl. XVB):

(1) the scallop badge of the Dacre family interlaced with the ragged staff of the Greystokes against a dark green ground, commemorating the union of these major local families as a result of Sir Thomas Dacre's marriage to Elizabeth Greystoke in 1488;

(2) Senhouse's popinjays with scrolls inscribed either 'symon senus pryor whose soul God have mercy' or 'Soli deo honor et gloria. Deo gracias', and with Senhouse's motto 'symon lothe to offend', against a red ground; and

(3) Senhouse's popinjay crest with roses and the inscription 'senus pryor', against a white ground.

These elements are viewed correctly when entering the room from the stair and facing the fireplace, and are disposed in the three principal fields in the sequence 1-2-3-1 . . ., 3-1-2-3 . . . and 1-2-3-1 . . . The only exception is that closest to the entrance to the stair where the popinjays on their white ground (element 3) have been rotated 180°, allowing this design to be read correctly on exiting the room. The undersides of the main beams are again decorated with the Senhouse popinjays and with roses, while the sides of the beams (shown splayed out in the watercolour) are painted with further badges of local families — choughs for Scrope, and eagle legs for Stanley — and with long inscriptions. That on the northern beam is an eight-line hortatory verse:

> Remember man ye gret pre-emynance
> Geven unto ye by God omnipotente.
> Between ye and angels is little difference,
> And all thinge earthly to thee obediente.
> By the byrde and beist under ye fyrmamente
> Say what excuse mayest thou lay or finde.
> Thus you art maid by God so excellente
> Butte that you aughteste again to hym be kinde.
> Soli Deo honor et gloria. DEO GRACIAS.

On the south beam, the following inscription — comprising Senhouse's motto, and a firm statement of his patronage and intent — is painted on both sides:

> Senus Pryor, lothe to offend. Simon Sennus
> sette yis Roofe and Scallope here, To the intent
> wythin thys place they shall have prayers every
> day of the yere.

Finally, at the edge of the ceiling, above the south window:

> Love God and thy prynce and you
> neydis not dreid they enimys.

Despite the severely limited design vocabulary — essentially only three elements — the artist has contrived to enliven the ceiling decoration by avoiding the use of stencils and, indeed, by varying the repeated elements sufficiently to individualise them, indicating that he was aware of the deadening effect of mechanical repetition. This variation is most conspicuous in the treatment of the ribands in element 2. No two are alike; there is an insistent playfulness in the invention, producing an astonishing diversity of knots and folds. Other subtleties of execution are less readily discernible in the now darkened paintings, such as the careful modelling to produce three-dimensionality, still visible in the Dacre and Greystoke badges and in some of the ribands.

The painting of 1890 also shows very clearly the curious mixture of different types of boss, of several different formats, and — like the ceiling painting — including both religious and secular themes. In the centre, four angels, facing inward, hold shields of the *Arma Christi* (Col. Pl. XVIA). Around the edges, there are three types of boss: semicircles, and large and small roundels. The former display the Dacre scallop (at the end of the beam referring to Senhouse having 'sette yis . . . Scallope here'), a vine, and the crescent and fetterlock of Percy.[44] The smaller roundels bear a rose, and two enigmatic figures to be discussed below, while the larger roundels, both on the west side, show a mermaid and a pelican in her piety.[45]

Most of these carvings are not unusual. For instance, bosses of angels holding the emblems of the Passion occur in England from the 14th century onward, while the particular form employed on the ceiling, with the emblems displayed on shields like heraldic charges, is standard in the later Middle Ages.[46] The mermaid holding a comb and mirror (symbol of vanity and lust) and the pelican in her piety (symbol of Christ's Passion) are extremely common motifs in Gothic art, and both occur elsewhere at Carlisle on the cathedral's misericords.[47]

Two of the 'marginal' bosses, however, are of particular interest. One, showing a jovial figure sticking his tongue out (Col. Pl. XVIB) has always been interpreted as a jester, but this cannot be the case since he is holding a sword and buckler. His dress is deliberately nonsensical, combining up-to-date fashion with that of a century or more earlier: although the flowing plume of his headgear is typically early Tudor, the large buttons down his tunic are characteristic of late 14th-century dress, while the dagging of his sleeves is typical of 'International Gothic' fashion of the early 15th century.[48] A clue to interpreting this figure is provided by the snail shell from which he emerges. The figure is, in fact, a variant of a motif found on no fewer than eight misericords in England — at Chester, Durham and elsewhere — typically comprising a small naked figure (sometimes winged) emerging from a shell and fighting one or more dragons.[49] In the example at Beverley, the figure is clothed, and from the supporters of that misericord — one of which shows a figure attempting to hide in a sack — Malcolm Jones has interpreted the snail-warrior as representing, by contrast, the virtue Courage.[50] However, this can hardly be a satisfactory interpretation of the grotesque figure at Carlisle, which, in its humorous intent, is closer to the 'couple in whelk shells' on a misericord at Stratford-on-Avon; here, though not armed with conventional weapons, the man and woman are shown brandishing a flesh-fork and a spindle respectively.[51]

It is unlikely to be coincidental that, on the Carlisle ceiling, the boss forming a 'pair' to the snail-warrior above the south window shows a female figure. Depicted with long flowing hair, and gazing out over a crenellated corbel (Col. Pl. XVIc), it has been suggested that she represents St Barbara,[52] or, alternatively, Elizabeth Greystoke, famously abducted at the age of sixteen by Sir Thomas Dacre (their intertwined badges, as we have seen, figure prominently in the painting of the ceiling).[53] Again, however, this is not a 'real' figure: although her long hair may indicate that she is a virgin, she is depicted with a broad hat of a kind not worn by women at this period (and which would certainly not be associated with St Barbara).[54] This type of image, of a demi-figure looking down from a crenellated corbel, can be traced back in English sculpture to the first half of the 14th century; perhaps the earliest examples were provided by the corbels supporting the roof of the Guesten Hall of Worcester Cathedral Priory, dating from the 1330s.[55] By the 15th century, the motif had migrated to the less appropriate context of a misericord at Hexham, where the scowling bearded figure is less likely to represent the pope, as has been suggested, than some grotesque figure as yet unidentified.[56] The most likely interpretation of the Carlisle figure, therefore, is as a woman being threatened, though not very seriously, by a comic variant of an image normally representing courage. This is an attacker she 'neydis not dreid', if the inscription between them may be so adapted.

This inscription, which begins 'Love God and thy prynce', obviously refers not to some local lord such as Sir Thomas Dacre, but to the king himself.[57] This signalling of allegiance to the king, although not heavily emphasised on the ceiling, is one of a number of ways in which it fits neatly into what is known of the decoration of other priors' lodgings and bishops' apartments of the period. Although more restrained in its design, probably the closest parallel is provided by Bishop Sherburne's painted ceiling in the hall of his palace at Chichester, dateable to the 1520s, and which features

Sherburne's own arms, initials and badges; Tudor roses, and the initials of Henry VIII and his queen; and the heraldry of local grandees such as the earl of Arundel.[58] At Worcester, a large first-floor chamber of the prior's lodging (demolished in 1845) had a painted ceiling of *c.* 1520 decorated with panels of large Tudor roses alternating with panels of smaller roses,[59] whilst a surviving early 16th-century ceiling in the prior's chamber at Castle Acre (Norfolk) is decorated with a diaper of small roses.[60] None of these example shows the wealth of detail or the lengthy inscriptions of the Carlisle ceiling, though the great oriel window of the chamber at Castle Acre once contained armorial glass and the prior's initials and motto: *Spi(ri)tu principali confirma me* (with original breath strengthen me).[61] A further parallel for the mottoes at Carlisle is provided by wall-paintings in the magnificent abbot's lodging at Forde Abbey (Dorset), built by the last abbot of this Cistercian house, Thomas Chard (1521–39) 'on a scale to justify the Reformation and the Dissolution'.[62] In the Saloon of what became a private house after the Dissolution, and now hidden by 17th-century work, the Forde paintings include foliage, an elaborate jewelled crown, and the motto 'Thinke and Thanke' in splendid Renaissance lettering.[63]

In northern England, no painted decoration closely comparable to the Carlisle ceiling survives in monastic or episcopal contexts, though it doubtless once existed. Perhaps the best parallel is provided by the early 16th-century decoration of a domestic chamber in the Dominican Friary at Beverley, which includes a pattern of ermine, intertwining branches, and black birds (symbolising the Black Friars?) with scrolls inscribed *Jhu mercy*.[64] Even closer, however, is the carved decoration of the great tower erected at Fountains Abbey by Abbot Huby (1495–1526), featuring lengthy bands of inscription, Huby's own arms and initials as well as other local heraldry, and his repeated motto *Soli Deo honor et gloria* — this last derived from Paul's first epistle to Timothy, and also employed by Prior Senhouse at Carlisle.[65]

All such decoration is, of course, a reminder that there was often little difference between the ornament of religious and purely secular buildings in the late Middle Ages. Thus, birds with inscribed scrolls or other attributes were a commonplace in both contexts, especially in stained glass.[66] Of decorative ceilings, there are several secular examples in the north of England, either surviving or recorded, which provide further valuable context for Senhouse's ceiling at Carlisle. Two purely heraldic examples, at Haddon Hall (Derbyshire) and Belsay Castle (Northumberland), may be mentioned first. At Haddon, the ceiling of the ground-floor parlour is decorated with shields and badges, including the Tudor rose, depicted on a large scale in square compartments set against a chequered ground. It was probably executed in the early 16th century for Sir Henry Vernon (1467–1515), and includes the talbot badge of his wife Anne (d. 1494).[67] In the Middleton stronghold at Belsay, the ceiling of the Great Hall is now lost, though fragments still remain of the associated wall-paintings of late 15th- or early 16th-century date, showing a naval scene, and a display of shields hanging from lopped trees against a flowered ground (a design based on contemporary *millefleurs* tapestries).[68] The arms on the ceiling were recorded by Dugdale in the 1660s, and comprised twelve shields of the Middleton and other local families.[69]

Closer to Carlisle were the two elaborately painted early 16th-century ceilings at Naworth, the chief stronghold of Sir Thomas Dacre himself. Destroyed in the disastrous fire at Naworth in 1844, they are known from 19th-century watercolours and from antiquarian and other early references, and have recently been discussed in relation to contemporary carvings from Naworth by Emily Chappell.[70] In the Great Hall, the ceiling showed the genealogy of the kings of England — from 'Brute' to Henry VII —

as a series of bust-length figures in contemporary dress, while on the chapel ceiling the Tree of Jesse was represented by another series of busts depicted in Tudor costume. Both ceilings were further adorned with carved heraldic bosses; the Dacre scallop, among other devices, seems discernible in the watercolour of the chapel ceiling. In fact, both ceilings originally adorned another of Sir Thomas's Cumberland residences, Kirkoswald Castle, and were only transferred to Naworth in the 17th century. Four large wooden carvings of heraldic supporters, including the salmon device of Elizabeth Greystoke, were also transferred from Kirkoswald to Naworth, and Chappell argues convincingly that these and several other wooden sculptures (all recently acquired by the Victoria and Albert Museum) would originally have formed part of a single decorative scheme in the Great Hall at Kirkoswald, the bosses and paintings of the ceiling 'representing Thomas's own ancestry interwoven with that of the Kings of England in a powerful display of legitimacy'.[71] Despite its very different format and painted scheme, much the same intentions can be discerned in Prior Senhouse's ceiling at Carlisle, with its combination of heraldry, mottoes, and invocation to 'Love God and thy prynce'.

None of the contemporary ceilings so far adduced in comparison, however, provides a parallel for the inscriptions on Senhouse's ceiling. Of these, the longest is the eight-line poem on the northern beam, beginning 'Remember man ye gret pre-emynance'. Although this poem has yet to be identified, it belongs to a common class of verse beginning 'Remember man' or 'Memento, homo', though such verses normally dwell on man's mortality. At Carlisle, by contrast, the poem stresses his excellence (only just below the angels) and exhorts him to be 'kinde' (ie loving or grateful) to his Maker.[72] Moralising inscriptions were clearly very commonly employed in domestic decoration throughout the 16th century; thus, Thomas Tusser's *Five Hundreth Points of Good Husbandry. . .* (1573) provides a series of 'Poesies' for, *inter alia*, the parlour and guest chamber, several of which appear in surviving late-16th-century wall-paintings.[73] Very few examples, however, remain from earlier in the century. At Acton Court (Gloucestershire), two sets of admonitory inscriptions in elaborate display in the long gallery of the north range — one series taken from scripture, and the other with moralising verses expressing such sentiments as 'The wise man, when he cannot overcome, gives way for the time being' — both apparently dating from the 1550s.[74]

Closer in date to the Carlisle ceiling are the splendid wall-paintings of *c.* 1520 in the solar of Bramall Hall (Cheshire), where figures of a musician and his lady, as well as various grotesques, are set against a dense foliage background in imitation of contemporary *verdure* tapestries, and two-line black letter inscriptions appear on fictive scrolls at the top of the walls. These have yet to be fully deciphered, but again seem to comprise a mixture of religious and straightforwardly moralising verses.[75] But, in decorative schemes of the early 16th century, by far the most extensive series of moralising verses of which evidence survives were those employed in the great Percy houses of Leconfield and Wressle in the East Riding. These were recorded, and most likely composed, by William Peeris, 'clerke & preste secretary' to Henry Percy, fifth earl of Northumberland (1478–1527).[76] At Wressle, two chambers of the garden house were inscribed with proverbs, and another with Aristotle's advice to the young Alexander. Aristotle's advice also appeared in verses at Leconfield, where the walls or ceilings of no fewer than six rooms were inscribed with proverbs or moralising verses, such as the 150 lines of debate between the parts 'sensatyue' and 'intellectyue' in the garret over the bath. Many of these texts were concerned with youth, and must have been directed at the fifth earl's heir, Henry (born *c.* 1502).[77] Nothing now survives of the house at Leconfield, and only the gutted south range of Wressle Castle, of which however a late 18th-century account records that 'The ceilings still appear richly carved, and the sides of the rooms are ornamented with a great profusion of ancient sculpture, finely executed in wood, exhibiting the ancient bearings, crests, badges, and devices of the Percy family, in a great variety of forms, set off with all the advantages of painting, gilding, and imagery'.[78] Now, only in the carved and painted ceiling of the Prior's Tower at Carlisle, do we find a combination of the lavish heraldic display and the moralising texts which were both evidently so characteristic of grand domestic interiors in the early 16th century.

ACKNOWLEDGEMENTS

David Weston's enthusiasm and generosity in sharing his unparalleled knowledge of the cathedral has made the research for this paper a particular pleasure. We are also much indebted to our Courtauld colleague Dr Margaret Scott for her expert comments on the dress depicted on the stalls and prior's ceiling. Detailed study of the stall paintings would not have been possible without the splendid photographs taken by Alun Bull of English Heritage, and we are most grateful to him and to Anna Eavis who arranged the photography. Emily Chappell kindly allowed us to refer to her valuable recent research on Thomas Dacre's ceilings and sculptures, while help of other kinds was generously provided by Dr Christa Grössinger, Emily Howe, David O'Connor, Pauline Plummer, the Very Revd Henry Stapleton, and Sophie Stewart.

NOTES

1. W. B. Scott, *Antiquarian Gleanings in the North of England* (London 1851), 15, pl. xxxii; J. Geddes, *Medieval Decorative Ironwork in England* (London 1999), 311; D. W. V. Weston, *Carlisle Cathedral History* (Carlisle 2000), 53. See also P. Plummer, 'Treatment of the mediaeval armoire, Carlisle Cathedral' (unpublished report, 2001).

2. *Archaeol. J.*, 16 (1859), 374; R. Bower, 'Mural and other painted decoration in the diocese of Carlisle', *Transactions Cumberland Westmorland Antiquarian Archaeological Society*, XV (1897–99), 14; Weston 2000, 24, 67.

3. For a discussion of other 15th-century schemes featuring the Sacred Monogram, see J. A. A. Goodall, *God's House at Ewelme: Life, Devotion and Architecture in a Fifteenth-century Almshouse* (Aldershot 2001), 159–69.

4. *Archaeol. J.*, 16 (1859), 374.

5. Simpson, this volume; see also Weston 2000, 24, 42–43, 72.

6. For the physical history of the paintings, see Weston 2000, 67, who quotes Bishop Nicolson in 1703 as referring to paintings of 'Cuthbert and other saints'.

7. C. G. V. Harcourt, *Legends of St Augustine, St Anthony, and St Cuthbert, Painted on the Back of the Stalls in Carlisle Cathedral* (Carlisle 1868); many of the drawings (by Lady Harcourt) were based on originals by Matthew Nutter, and drawings by both are still displayed beneath the choir-stall paintings. For other antiquarian literature and copies, see Weston 2000, 67–71, and accompanying illustrations.

8. B. Colgrave, 'The St. Cuthbert paintings on the Carlisle Cathedral stalls', *Burlington Magazine*, 73 (1938), 17–21.

9. Taken in 2001, the photographs provide detailed coverage of all the paintings except the apostles.

10. Tracy, this volume.

11. Harcourt, *Legends*, iii. Two of these monograms are particularly clear against the red background immediately to the left of the devil's club. For Prior Gondibour's dates, see Weston 2000, 143.

12. Such lines also appear, however, in the inscriptions of the apostles series.

13. A further such column in the St Anthony cycle is illustrated by Harcourt, *Legends*, between scenes 15 and 16; it has since been moved to the right, and its detail is lost.

14. C. G. Bulman, 'The Gondibour and Salkeld screens in Carlisle Cathedral', *Transactions Cumberland Westmorland Antiquarian Archaeological Series*, ns, LXI (1956), 112–27; Weston 2000, 51.

15. M. Clayton, *Catalogue of Rubbings of Brasses and Incised Slabs* (Victoria and Albert Museum), 2nd edn (London 1929), pl. 25. Here, the long cuffs have been turned back so that she can hold her husband's hand.

16. We are very grateful to Dr Margaret Scott for her observations on the costume depicted in the paintings. She also points out that, relatively crude and provincial though they are, the paintings are sufficiently sophisticated to include one deliberately historicising example of dress: that of St Anthony's father, in the scene of the saint's baptism (Col. Pl. XII). Here, the long fur-lined slits through which his arms emerge were fashionable in the second half of the 14th century; see the examples of *c.* 1370 in L. F. Sandler, *Gothic Manuscript Illumination 1285–1385* (A Survey of Manuscripts Illuminated in the British Isles, 5) (London 1986), ill. 363.

17. Colgrave, 'St Cuthbert paintings', 17, quotes a brief unpublished account of the stalls by E. W. Tristram to the effect that the paintings are 'executed in oil', though no evidence is adduced. In the same account (of which there is a copy in the Tristram Archive at the Courtauld Institute), Tristram observes that the St Anthony cycle is by a 'poorer and coarser craftsman' than the other paintings.

18. For the preparation and use of red lake, see H. Howard, 'The Pigments of English Medieval Wall Painting' (unpublished Ph.D. thesis, Courtauld Institute of Art, University of London, 2000), 196–218.

19. This fading may well continue unless ultraviolet light filters are provided for adjacent windows.

20. P. Plummer, 'Treatment of the paintings on the backs of the choir stalls: Carlisle Cathedral' (unpublished report, 1978).

21. At present, access to the electrical wiring in this area is through a loose board in the dado.

22. The sequence of the scenes shown in Fig. 2 is based on Baker's concordance of the narrative subjects in surviving lives of Cuthbert. See M. Baker, 'Medieval illustrations of Bede's *Life of St Cuthbert*', *J. Warburg and Courtauld Institutes*, 41 (1978), 40–42).

23. A. Hamer, 'The verses on the screens in Carlisle Cathedral' (unpublished report (1995) in the Cathedral archive (CCA F15)).

24. As John Goodall has kindly pointed out to us, the English inscriptions over the St Andrew scenes in the stained glass of nearby Greystoke Church are somewhat similar. These have likewise been shown to be in a northern dialect, and the glass itself to be late 15th-century and the product of a York atelier; see D. J. Chadwick, 'The Ancient Glass in the East Window of the Church of Saint Andrew, Greystoke, Cumbria' (unpublished B.Phil. dissertation, University of York, 1974).

25. D. Knipping, *Die Chorschranke der Kathedrale von Amiens: Funktion und Krise eines Mittelalterlichen Ausstattungstypus* (Munich 2001).

26. M. R. James, *On the Abbey of St. Edmund at Bury* (Cambridge 1895), 131.

27. C. Lapaire, S. Aballéa et al., *Stalles de la Savoie médiévale* (Geneva 1991); P. Lacroix, A. Rebon et al., *Pensée, image et communication en Europe médiévale: à propos des stalles de Saint-Claude* (Besançon 1993), esp. 83–99.

28. These paintings and verses were copied in the Peterborough Psalter of *c.* 1300–18 (Brussels, Bibliothèque Royale MS 9961–62); see L. F. Sandler, 'Peterborough Abbey and the Peterborough Psalter in Brussels', *JBAA*, 3rd ser., 33 (1970), 36–49; C. Tracy, *English Gothic Choir-stalls* (Woodbridge 1987), 2–4, 22.

29. E. C. Rouse and K. Varty, 'Medieval paintings of Reynard the Fox in Gloucester Cathedral and some other related examples', *Archaeol. J.*, 133 (1976), 104–17.

30. E. Croft-Murray, *Decorative Painting in England 1537–1837*, I, *Early Tudor to Sir James Thornhill* (London 1962), 14, 174, pl. 7. See also the damaged painted figure on the back of the choir-stalls from Lincluden Collegiate Church (now in the National Museums of Scotland), for which dendrochronological analysis has provided a date of 1477; R. Fawcett, *Scottish Medieval Churches: Architecture and Fittings* (Stroud 2002), 288, 326, 339, ill. 4.55.

31. E. Colledge, *The Augustine Screen in Carlisle Cathedral* (Brampton n.d.).

32. R. Graham, 'The Order of St Antoine de Viennois and its English Commandery, St Anthony's, Threadneedle Street', *Archaeol. J.*, 84 (1927), 398. The inventory also mentions a painted cloth of 'Seynt Antonye and Seynt Paule the hermyte' for the high altar (ibid., 397), while account-books of 1501–03 record '3 dosyn hokes grette and smalle to faste the wyre with to hange the clothys of Saint Antoni's lyffe and the tabulls in the churche' (ibid., 378). See also R. Graham, 'A picture-book of the Life of St Anthony the Abbot, executed for the monastery of Saint-Antoine de Viennois in 1426', *Archaeologia*, 83 (1933), 4.

33. See, for example, R. Graham, *A Picture Book of the Life of St Anthony the Abbot*, Roxburghe Club (London 1937); J. Courcelle and P. Courcelle, *Iconographie de St Augustin — les cycles du XV siècle*, Etudes Augustiniennes (Paris 1969).

34. London, British Library MS Yates Thompson 26 (Add. 39943); Colgrave, 'St Cuthbert paintings'. For good colour reproductions of the manuscript, see D. Marner, *St Cuthbert: His Life and Cult in Medieval Durham* (London 2000).

35. M. Baker, 'Medieval illustrations of Bede's *Life of St Cuthbert*', *J. Warburg and Courtauld Institutes*, 41 (1978), 16–49. Among more recent literature, see C. M. Barnett, 'The St Cuthbert Window of York Minster and the Iconography of St Cuthbert in the Late Middle Ages' (unpublished M.A. dissertation, Centre for Medieval Studies, University of York, 1991); M. E. Carrasco, 'The construction of sanctity: pictorial hagiography and monastic reform in the first illustrated *Life of St Cuthbert* (Oxford, University College MS 165)', *Studies in Iconography*, 21 (2000), 47–89.

36. E. W. Tristram, *English Medieval Wall Painting: The Twelfth Century* (Oxford 1944), 60, 142, supp. pl. 13a, b. We hope to consider the Pittington paintings in more detail in a forthcoming paper.

37. The painting was discovered but then destroyed during Ewan Christian's restoration work of the 1850s: see *Proceedings Society of Antiquaries*, 3 (1853–6), 86; E. T. Whyte, 'A wall painting formerly in Carlisle Cathedral. With notes by the Bishop of Barrow-in-Furness', *Transactions Cumberland Westmorland Antiquarian Archaeological Society*, ns, VIII (1908), 234–35, pl. opp. 234; Weston 2000, 24, 67, 69. In its reference to paintings discovered in the 1850s, *Archaeol. J.*, 16 (1859), 374, mentions that 'On the tower piers were subjects of legendary history', which seems to suggest that further scenes existed; there is, however, no other evidence to this effect.

38. In the early 12th-century *Life*, and in the early-15th-century Salisbury Breviary; Baker, 'Medieval illustrations', 45–46, pls 9e-f.

39. The most valuable accounts of the Tower are J. H. Martindale, 'Notes on the Deanery, Carlisle', *Transactions Cumberland Westmorland Antiquarian Archaeological Society*, ns, VII (1907), 185–204, and Weston 2000, 98–100; for the dates of Senhouse's priorate, see ibid., 98.

40. Although the building is in fact oriented toward the north-east, for convenience the north-east wall will here be called 'north', and the other walls accordingly.

41. The earliest reference to the painted ceiling is of 1686 (Weston 2000, 99), but this seems likely to be retrospective and associated with the renovation works.

42. P. Plummer, 'Treatment of the painted ceiling of the Prior's dayroom' (unpublished report, 1976); Weston 2000, 100.

43. In the Cathedral Library past literature on the ceiling includes Martindale, 'Notes on the Deanery', 188–92; N. M. Phillips, 'The Prior's Room, Deanery Tower, Carlisle' (typescript, n.d.); M. E. Burkett, 'Cumbrian wall paintings', *Transactions Cumberland Westmorland Antiquarian Archaeological Society*, ns, XCIX (1999), 159–60; I. Harkness, 'The Pele Tower within the Deanery: heraldic decoration on the ceiling in the Prior's Room' (unpublished report, n.d.); Weston 2000, 79, 99–100. We have not consulted Samantha Riches's unpublished M.A. dissertation on the ceiling (University of Keele).

44. Martindale, 'Notes on the Deanery', 191, refers to the carving of the scallop and vine bosses as 'renewed', but on what evidence is unclear. Pauline Plummer's conservation report of 1976 mentions the discovery of two pencil inscriptions 'found beneath the bosses' (though which bosses is not recorded) reading 'Repaired 1828' and 'Bosses refixed 1888'.

45. David Weston has kindly drawn our attention to another series of carved wooden bosses, formerly hung on the walls just below Senhouse's ceiling (Martindale, 'Notes', pl. IV; Weston 2000, ill. on 99) but now exhibited in the Treasury. These are very close in style to the ceiling bosses, and may well be by the same hand. Perhaps they are survivors of the original ceiling of the upper room of the Prior's Tower.

46. C. J. P. Cave, *Roof Bosses in Medieval Churches* (Cambridge 1948), 36–38, ills 113–14, 239–46.

47. Grössinger, this volume.

48. Spectacular examples of such dagging occur in the *Très Riches Heures*; see M. Scott, *Late Gothic Europe, 1400–1500* (The History of Dress) (London 1980), ills 6, 43–44, col. pl. 1.

49. G. L. Remnant, *A Catalogue of Misericords in Great Britain* (Oxford 1969), 25, 27, 41, 64, 81, 89, 210; J. Cherry, 'Good and evil in the British Museum', *The Profane Arts of the Middle Ages*, 6 (1997), 316–17; C. Grössinger, *The World Upside-down: English Misericords* (London 1997), 82, pl. 118; idem, 'Chester Cathedral misericords: iconography and sources', in *Medieval Archaeology, Art and Architecture at Chester*, ed. A. Thacker, *BAA Trans.*, XXII (2000), 104, pl. XXVIB. The example in the chapel of Durham Castle (Remnant, 41) is from the Bishop's Palace at Auckland.

50. M. Jones, 'The misericords', in *Beverley Minster: An Illustrated History* (Beverley 2000), 164–65, 171; see also, for his interpretation of the motif, idem, 'Folklore motifs in late medieval art I: proverbial follies and impossibilities', *Folklore*, 100 (1989), 208–09, and 'Notes on the last issue . . .', *The Profane Arts of the Middle Ages*, 7 (1998), 78–81. Jones argues ingeniously that the motif is derived from a depiction of one of the monstrous races, a naked pigmy arising from a hole next to a hydra; in the later depictions, the bands of earth have been transformed into the coils of a shell (see also, on this point, Grössinger, 'Chester Cathedral misericords', 104, pl. XXVIIA). In complete contrast to the image of the snail-warrior as apparently representing courage, there are many depictions from the 13th century onward of men attacking or surrendering

to snails, as an image of cowardice; for this well-known genre, see especially L. M. C. Randall, 'The snail in Gothic marginal warfare', *Speculum*, 37 (1962), 358–67; M. A. Dollfus, 'Les mollusques terrestres dans l'art et l'archéologie', *Bulletin de la Société nationale des antiquaires de France* (1978–79), 30–39.

51. Remnant, *Catalogue of Misericords*, 164; Jones, 'Notes on the last issue . . .', ill. on 79 (a rather similar example, at Windsor, is illustrated on 78).

52. Cave, *Roof Bosses*, 187.

53. For the 'abduction' interpretation, see, for example, the anonymous leaflet 'The Prior's Tower Museum, Carlisle Cathedral' (n.d.).

54. Another 'nonsense' in her appearance is, however, the result of modern repainting: the low square neckline typical of the early 16th century has been misunderstood by the restorer, who has painted her flesh the same red colour as the dress.

55. D. Park, 'Rediscovered 14th-century sculptures from the Guesten Hall', in *Archaeology at Worcester Cathedral: Report of the Eighth Annual Symposium*, ed. C. Guy (Worcester 1998), 18–21.

56. Grössinger, *World Upside-down*, 130, pl. 187.

57. For use of the term 'prince' with reference to the king, see, for example, the writings of the rebels and of Henry VIII himself at the time of the Pilgrimage of Grace in the 1530s: 'for princes should choose such virtuous men as would regard the commonwealth above their prince's love' (rebel tract); 'How presumptuous then are ye . . . to find fault with your prince' (Henry's response to Lincolnshire rebels). See R. W. Hoyle, *The Pilgrimage of Grace and the Politics of the 1530s* (Oxford 2001), 61, and also 62, 314.

58. F. W. Steer, 'The heraldic ceiling at the Bishop's Palace, Chichester', *Chichester Papers*, 10 (1958); E. Croft-Murray, *Decorative Painting*, 154, pl. 33.

59. E. L. Blackburne, *Sketches of the . . . Decorative Painting applied to English Architecture during the Middle Ages* (London 1847), 80 and pl.; D. Park, 'Survey of the medieval and later polychromy of Worcester Cathedral: a report for the Dean and Chapter' (unpublished report, 1997), no. 29, fig. 29.2.

60. W. H. St J. Hope, 'Castleacre Priory', *Norfolk Archaeology*, 12 (1895), 150–1, pl. iii.

61. ibid., 149.

62. J. Newman and N. Pevsner, *Dorset* B/E (Harmondsworth 1972), 210.

63. We are indebted to Philip Hughes and John Newman for discussion of these unpublished paintings, and particularly to Laurence Keen who first recognised their pre-Reformation date. Photographs of the paintings, taken *c.* 1976, are held at the National Monuments Record. For other aspects of Abbot Chard's work at Forde, see RCHM(E), *An Inventory of the Historical Monuments in Dorset, I, West* (London 1952), 240–46.

64. K. Miller, J. Robinson, B. English and I. Hall, *Beverley: An Archaeological and Architectural Study*, Royal Commission on Historical Monuments [England] Supplementary Series, 4 (London 1982), 49, fig. 10.

65. A. W. Oxford, *The Ruins of Fountains Abbey*, 5th edn (Ripon 1967), 19–25, figs 12–19.

66. C. Woodforde, 'Some medieval English glazing quarries painted with birds', *JBAA*, 3rd ser., 9 (1944), 1–11. The finest surviving examples in wall-painting are those of *c.* 1520–30 uncovered in the 1980s in a house in Silver Street, Ely, each with an appropriate motto: for example, a dove with 'Deale Justlye' and a peacock with 'Be not proud'; see Courtauld Institute, Conservation of Wall Painting Department, 'Secular wall paintings in Ely: recently discovered 14th- and 16th-century schemes and their architectural context', in *Medieval Wall Paintings: Silver Street, Ely*, ed. H. Davis (Cambridge 1990), 6–12.

67. C. Hussey, 'Haddon Hall, Derbyshire – iii', *Country Life*, 106 (1949), 1814–17; Croft-Murray, *Decorative Painting*, 16, 176, pl. 32; A. Emery, *Greater Medieval Houses of England and Wales 1300–1500, I, Northern England* (Cambridge 1996), 388, pl. 194.

68. A. E. Middleton, *An Account of Belsay Castle in the County of Northumberland*, 2nd edn with introduction by M. Apted and G. Dickinson (Stocksfield 1990), 27–30, 37–39, pl. opposite 28; C. Babington, T. Manning and S. Stewart, *Our Painted Past: Wall Paintings of English Heritage* (London 1999), 70.

69. Middleton, *Belsay Castle*, vi. Two drawings of the shields by Dugdale are in his 1666 Visitation of Durham and Northumberland, and an associated book of church notes; London, College of Arms MS C.41, f. 13 and verso; *Church notes, Yorkshire, Durham and Northumberland*, 210B. We are grateful to the Archivist of the College of Arms, Mr R. C. Yorke, for assistance with this material.

70. E. Chappell, 'New light on the "Little Men" of Naworth Castle in the Victoria and Albert Museum' (unpublished M.A. dissertation, Courtauld Institute of Art, University of London, 2002). See also Croft-Murray, *Decorative Painting*, 16, 158–59; G. Worsley, 'Naworth Castle, Cumberland — i', *Country Life*, 181 (1987), 74–79, figs 9–10, 14.

71. Chappell, 'New Light', 37.

72. For these observations, and for the references to the Leconfield and Wressle texts below, we are indebted to unpublished correspondence by Dr Priscilla Bawcutt and Professor Philip Edwards of the University of Liverpool in the Cathedral archive (CCA F15).

73. T. Tusser, *Five Hundreth Points of Good Husbandry, united to as many of good huswiferie* (London 1573); see J. Fleming, *Graffiti and the Writing Arts of Early Modern England* (London 2001), 29–31, 170–71, ills 6–7.

74. J. Bertram, 'The painted texts in the Long Gallery', in the forthcoming volume on Acton Court, edited by Kirsty Rodwell. We are most grateful to Mrs Rodwell for information about these paintings. See also N. Cooper, *Houses of the Gentry 1480–1680* (New Haven and London 1999), 319, pl. 334.

75. See Emery, *Greater Medieval Houses*, 516, for these paintings which have yet to be studied in the detail they deserve.

76. E. Flügel, 'Kleinere Mitteilungen aus Handschriften', *Anglia*, 14 (1892), 471–97.

77. I. Lancashire, ed., *Two Tudor Interludes: The Interlude of Youth; Hick Scorner* (Manchester 1980), 28–90. Not all these verses were too forbidding, however; of the many 'prouerbis in the rouf of my lorde percy closett at lekyngfelde'one can still empathise with

> As the cause requyrithe to stody is goode
> But allway to be in a stody dryethe up a mannes blode.

78. J. Savage, *History of the Castle and Parish of Wressle* (Howden 1799). This decoration has been attributed to the time of the fifth earl by D. Neave, 'Wressle Castle', *Archaeol. J.*, 141 (1984), 59, and Emery, *Greater Medieval Houses*, 419. Savage recorded the date 1525 in one of the windows. See also, however, C. V. Collier 'The heraldry', *Yorkshire Archaeological J.*, 22 (1912–13); in this discussion of other 18th-century evidence for the arms then surviving at Wressle, Collier interprets one shield in the 'Dining Room' as indicating that the heraldic display dated 'in part at least as late as the middle of the sixteenth century'.

Archibald Campbell Tait, Dean of Carlisle 1850 to 1856, and Ewan Christian, Architect

GRAEME KNOWLES

The appointment of Archibald Campbell Tait as dean of Carlisle in 1849 proved to be a milestone in the history of the fabric of the cathedral. On his arrival, he found a building much in decay and a ministry in the same state. With zeal, and backed by funding from the newly-founded Commissioners, almost single-handed, Tait pushed through a programme of restoration with the distinguished architect, Ewan Christian. This paper will sketch the character of Tait himself and his background, and it will examine briefly the main points of Christian's survey of the fabric. Lastly, it will underline the main areas of lasting change and alteration to the fabric which give us largely what we see today.

WHEN I was first ordained, I worked in the parish of St Peter-in-Thanet in Broadstairs. As I celebrated the Eucharist for the first time, I faced a small window in the chancel dedicated to Craufurd Tait, only son of the archbishop of Canterbury, Dr Tait. As the old palace in Canterbury had not yet been restored, the archbishops used Stone House, on the North Foreland, as a summer retreat within their diocese. It was here that Craufurd Tait died, acting as his father's chaplain at the time.

On arrival in Carlisle, I found myself living in a deanery extended to cope with Tait's large family. Within the cathedral itself the north window of the north transept stands as a memorial to five of his children who died between 6 March and 6 April 1856. It could be said that Archibald Tait and his traumatic family losses are rather dogging my own ministry. What, then, was this man like who came to Carlisle in 1850, following Dean Hinds who only managed one year in office before he was consecrated to the See of Norwich?

Archibald Campbell Tait was born in Edinburgh in 1811, the first of a succession of Scottish-born archbishops of Canterbury. He was brought up a Presbyterian, and was educated in Edinburgh, Glasgow and at Balliol, becoming a fellow in 1834, having taken a first class in the Final Classics School. As Edward Carpenter says, 'along with prodigious industry there went undoubted ambition'.[1] He followed the redoubtable Dr Arnold as headmaster of Rugby School, and again as Carpenter says, 'it is the highest compliment to say that his tenure of office was not an anticlimax'![2] He was only thirty years old on appointment.

Tait was born with a clubbed foot and overcame his disability with the aid of special tin boots prescribed by a Lancashire farrier. His life was haunted by bereavement and illness. He nearly died of scarlet fever at the age of seven. At Rugby, in 1848, a sudden illness all but killed him. It was rheumatic fever, affecting both his heart and lungs. The move to Carlisle was in fact dictated by his health.

Lord John Russell, the Prime Minister at the time, first offered the deanery to Arthur Stanley as a 'tribute of respect' to Stanley's father, the late bishop of Norwich. Stanley preferred to stay in Oxford, so the job was offered to Tait, who at once said 'yes'. Bernard Palmer, in writing of this move, says, 'Although he had seemingly made a good recovery from his illness, his physical powers were clearly no longer equal to the strains of a schoolmaster's immensely busy life: a deanery, by contrast, was considered a post of comparative ease'.[3] Carlisle was Tait's consolation prize! As Anthony Trollope wrote in *Barchester Towers*: '"I do not find myself fit for new duties" urged Mr. Harding. "New duties! what duties?" said the Archdeacon, with unintended sarcasm. "Oh, papa," said Mrs. Grantly, "Nothing can be easier than what a dean has to do".'[4] Tait's biographers, Randall Davidson and William Benham, comment, 'the position of Dean was regarded as one of dignified retirement rather than active usefulness'.[5]

Tait was installed in Carlisle on Saturday 5 January 1850. The Chapter Minutes Book tells us that Archdeacon Harcourt, as canon in residence, was present together with Canon Goodenough. As his biography notes:

Next day he entered in his diary, with much dismay, that though it was Sunday and the feast of the Epiphany, there were only nine or ten communicants. Some days were spent in a vigorous inspection, not only of the Cathedral precincts and all belonging to them, but of the condition generally of the various parishes in the town. He noted the want of order in one of the National Schools, the fact that there was no chaplain at the Infirmary, and many other details of Cathedral and parochial shortcomings; interchange of duty and the attendance of the bedesmen at divine service, and returned to Rugby, having given evidence that, in Lord Cockburn's phrase, he at least did not mean to 'doze on the decanal cushion'.[6]

It goes on to say that

At Carlisle he rapidly regained a large measure of his former strength, and though he was never again a robust man, and his heart was always irregular in its action, the work he succeeded in doing during the six Carlisle years was sufficient evidence of his physical energy. In the Cathedral itself there was much to be done; but his reforms did not greatly commend themselves to all his colleagues, and he had an uphill fight to wage before he carried them. There was special difficulty, for example, about the establishment of an afternoon sermon in the Cathedral on Sundays, although he took the entire responsibility of it upon himself. But he was not easily daunted, and he gained his points one by one.[7]

In the six years he was dean of Carlisle, Tait achieved two major reforms. First, he reorganised the entire Capitular revenues under the scheme which had just been approved by Parliament, 'to facilitate the management and improvement of Episcopal and capitular estates'.[8] Second, he carried through the restoration of the seriously dilapidated fabric of the cathedral itself, which the reorganisation of revenues made possible. This paper will address only the second of these tasks.

By 3 June 1850 the restoration of the fabric was on the agenda of Dean Tait's first chapter meeting. The necessity of taking steps towards the restoration of the cathedral was discussed and it was ordered that the dean and the canon in residence be empowered to confer with the bishop of the diocese on the possibility of uniting such restoration of the cathedral with a scheme for re-building and increasing the accommodation in St Mary's Church, located in the nave of the cathedral.[9] At the chapter meeting held in November 1851 the matter took a step forward when it was resolved 'that Mr Benjamin Ferrey of London, Architect, be consulted as to the restoration of the Cathedral, and if it should be thought proper of St Mary's Church, and that leave be given to any member of the Chapter who desires it to restore his stall under the sanction of such Architect'.[10]

A paper read to the chapter by the dean about the means of bringing before the public the question of the restoration of the cathedral and the re-building of the parish church of St Mary 'should be adopted by the Chapter, and the Dean and Canon in Residence be empowered to have the same printed and circulated. It was also resolved that the Dean and Canon in Residence be empowered to engage the services of Mr Ferrey for the purposes stated in the Resolution above, having first ascertained and approved of his terms'.

Following a thoroughly Anglican row between Mr Chalk, Secretary to the Ecclesiastical Commissioners, the Chapter, and Mr Ferrey, there emerged Ewan Christian, the Ecclesiastical Commissioners' choice, as the architect for the restoration.[11] A Manxman, Ewan Christian had been born in 1814, and was a pupil of Matthew Habershon. During his career he was much involved in ecclesiastical and domestic architecture, but also added buildings to the National Portrait Gallery. In his day he was highly regarded, becoming the President of Royal Institute of British Architects and receiving its Gold Medal in 1887. After his major programme at Carlisle no other cathedral work of consequence came his way, but his ecclesiastical portfolio was nevertheless impressive, including designing over forty new churches and restoring some 150 others as well as dealing with parsonages amongst many other commissions. He continued to work to the end of his long life and died in 1895.[12]

His manuscript 'Report of the Cathedral Church of St Mary, Carlisle, descriptive of its present condition and of the repairs and alterations necessary or desirable to be made therein' is dated August 1852.[13] The importance of this report is that it gives a detailed description of the condition in which Christian found the cathedral.

It should be appreciated that the present appearance of the cathedral church, both outside and inside, owes a great deal to Christian's restoration. He was responsible for the elevation of the south transept with his new porch and buttresses, for the restoration of the east front, for the north transept with his new window, and for the renewed west front. Christian, based in London, delegated much of the day-to-day oversight of the works to Charles Purdy, who was superintendent of the works of restoration and who in the process gained a detailed knowledge of the building.

From the report it is possible to follow Christian's thought processes as he assessed the condition of the cathedral and made his proposals. The building he inspected in 1852 was clearly in a parlous state — 'wholly defective', 'very unsatisfactory condition', 'completely decayed' are descriptive phrases which crop up in virtually every paragraph. The great east window is described as 'split and shaky — the glazing is so greatly dilapidated that in bad weather the rain pours in'.[14] Over and over again comes the statement that sections of the church 'require to be wholly taken down and restored'.

Christian also tackled the problem of St Mary's parish church located in the nave, the interior wall surfaces of the cathedral which were covered with a coloured wash, and the need for a proper main entrance to the cathedral. As we look at these practical issues, we hear Tait's voice in the background. Lady Wake, a close family friend, describes a visit in 1855 to Carlisle:

Besides the two services in the Cathedral, at one of which he preached, he found time for a most touching meeting in his night school-room with a number of old people and invalids who were not able for a Cathedral service. He sat among them like a young apostle, making choice of such portions of Scripture as brought comfort, and hope, and strength to their failing powers; pointing out to them the bright Beyond to which the Saviour was beckoning them, and praying with them, no printed formula of prayer, but the very voice of their hearts, taking to God all their infirmities and wants. Later in the day there was a similar gathering of young women, most of them mothers, to whom he spoke so earnestly that they evidently hung upon his words. Later still there was a children's class examined by him, and quite late in the evening, when, exceedingly fatigued, I thought the duties of the day entirely over, I found a most interesting gathering of young men in the Dean's study, to whom he gave instruction more like that given to the Sixth Form at Rugby, recognising in them the craving for knowledge felt by thoughtful and educated minds. His zeal for the gospel underlines all that he strives to achieve in the building itself.[15]

THE PARISH CHURCH

THE parish church of St Mary's was situated, until 1870, in the two bays of the nave. Christian describes this space as 'wholly inadequate to the wants of the parishioners. It is certain that the present arrangements are most inconvenient, unwholesome and devoid of a propriety'.[16] The ground floor seated 192, and the gallery (erected in 1813) a further 268, making a total 460! Christian's advice was 'to build a suitable church on another site and restore the Nave to the Cathedral for purposes to which it may be usefully applied'.[17] It was only in 1870 that this dream was accomplished with the erection of a new St Mary's to Christian's design opposite the east end of the cathedral. Photographs reveal that this was a rather drab, uninspiring building, squeezed awkwardly into a narrow space. It was closed in 1939 as surplus to requirements, and demolished in 1953.

THE GENERAL AND INTERNAL APPEARANCE

IN the tightrope that is the tension between restoration and destruction, it is in the stripping of the walls in the interior of the building that we encounter a sad loss in the cathedral. Christian writes under his General Remarks:

2nd The whole of the interior surfaces of the Cathedral are dirty and unbecoming. The Stone Work has been repeatedly washed over with Colour, until it has become quite clogged, and the rough surfaces thus formed upon it have acted as Collectors of Dust in motion. To colour the walls again would cleanse them for a time, but would only perpetuate and increase the evil before alluded to. Nothing therefore short of the restoration of the natural surface of the stone can be of permanent utility, and although the cost would necessarily be considerable, in no other way could money for this object be satisfactorily expended.[18]

This scraping took place and nearly all trace of the medieval wall-paintings was lost. The building was obviously filthy! Christian describes

the accumulations of dust which exist in various parts of the church, and are now, from draughts and other causes, a constant source of annoyance. In the triforium Galleries of the Choir, there are thick deposits of this kind in the spandrels of the vaulting and it has been suggested and the scheme is worth attention, that a floor of concrete might be formed over the Vaulting at a moderate cost.[19]

Despite the merits of the sandstone effect, it is interesting to ponder what was lost when all this colour wash and debris was removed.

THE NEW ENTRANCE DOOR

IT was clear that the cathedral was a difficult place to get into! Christian proposed that 'The present North Entrance to the Church, widened and improved, would give access to the Cathedral at a convenient point'.[20] He goes on

In connection with this improvement the two present inconvenient gloomy and miserable doorways might be blocked up, and a large Southern Entrance to the

Transept substituted the doors of which might always remain open during fine weather and thus supply the present grievous deficiency of pure warm air.[21]

Thus the new south transept entrance was born, but it suffered two defects. The arched entrance consisted of two doors separated by a pillar. First, it provided two narrow entrances where one wide entrance was required. Secondly, the design copied from Southwell Chapter-House was too intricate for the soft, local sandstone which tends, in consequence, to break away.

The high walls which separated the Choir form the Aisles, erected by Bishop Charles Lyttelton and his architect Thomas Pitt in 1764, were stripped out, together with most of the rest of the woodwork of this 18th-century restoration. The archway between the choir and the transepts, closed by Lyttelton and Pitt, was opened up, giving sightlines from choir to crossing.[22] The unsightly wooden spiked gates hung at the end of the side aisles were taken away, but only to be replaced by Dean Francis Close with cast iron gates.[23]

The restoration saw the reinstatement of the old choir ceiling, to a scheme by Owen Jones; a project favoured by Christian who thought that it might be judged too expensive. New glass was put into the lower part of the east window, in memory of Bishop Hugh Percy, and the medieval glass restored. The restoration included the provision of one of the finest Father Willis organs in the country, under the supervision of Henry Ford, the Master of the Music.[24]

Other factors in the project caused concern. Christian's controversial decision to replace two late-15th-century Perpendicular windows either side of the high altar when it was one bay further west, with those of Early English style, did not go unchallenged! The scraping of the walls meant the loss of mural paintings, only one of which was recorded as it was revealed and removed.

All this was not achieved without incident. Tait's diary speaks of the conflict within the chapter: 'This day in Chapter I was betrayed into unseemly anger. O Lord, forgive me! I will not let the sun go down upon my anger. O Lord, give me self-denial as a Christian and more regard for the feelings of others, through Jesus Christ.'[25] A few days later:

At times I feel greatly depressed here by the uncongenial spirits amongst whom I am thrown. But, O Lord, give me to understand that nothing great was ever done without effort, and amidst much opposition. Lord, give me wisdom, zeal, love and make me faithful in every work. This day we have been engaged in very important business as to the transfer of our estates to the Commissioners. Guide us, O Lord. May all the matter redound to Thy glory. We hope to rebuild our Cathedral, and thus infuse a love for the outward house of God.[26]

The cost of the Tait and Christian's restoration of the fabric of the cathedral was in the region of £15,000, but to this must be added the cost of the new organ, stained glass and the new ceiling, for which donations were sought.[27] In 1851 an Act of Parliament had been passed 'to facilitate the management and improvement of Episcopal and Capitular estates', and in 1852 Carlisle and York transferred their chapter estates *en bloc* to the Ecclesiastical Commissioners. The commissioners were to give a fixed annuity in return. The commissioners, as a result of the transfer, arranged for the £15,000 to be found for the restoration of the building from the chapter's estates at Hesket-in-the-Forest. Without Tait's foresight in pushing through the transfer to the commissioners, it is unlikely that the work would have been so easily funded. It is a measure of Tait's energy that Carlisle was one of the first two cathedrals to respond to the commissioners' initiative.

Ewan Christian went on from restoring the cathedral to build additions to the deanery and the house of the third canon, the new St Mary's Church and a new house for the fourth canon. However, it all ended on a sour note when in 1871 the Dean and Chapter turned to the more eminent G. E. Street for the interior furnishings of the cathedral, claiming that Christian, whose limitations had become evident, had only ever been the Ecclesiastical Commissioners' appointee, and had never been appointed by them.[28] Ironically, Street's altar and reredos, pulpit and lectern were all later stripped out, leaving only his bishop's throne which fits well with the early 15th-century choir-stalls.

Had it not been for Tait's 'prodigious energy', the scope and extent of the Carlisle restoration under Christian would not have been carried through. His diary entry for 5 May 1850, soon after his arrival in Carlisle reads:

Carlisle, Sunday 5th May 1850. This is our first Sunday in our new home. What great blessings have we received from God! How graciously has He dealt with me in providing a quiet useful retirement when the bustle and work of Rugby seemed too much for me! O Lord, enable me to use the retirement of this place for my own increase in spiritual-mindedness, by Thy Holy Spirit's help. Enable me to labour faithfully for others. Pardon my sin, and bless to my soul the Holy Communion which I have this day received. Through Jesus Christ. Amen.[29]

Tait's last word on his work of restoration of the cathedral can be taken from a lecture that he gave in Carlisle on 9 January 1855:

Most earnestly do I trust that our church, now rising to somewhat of its old splendour, may be getting ready to bear its share in a great work of Christian revival, which shall spread sound religion and enlightenment through every dark region of our land.[30]

In the event, Tait went on from the 'quiet useful retirement', which he had first envisaged, to be bishop of London and archbishop of Canterbury!

NOTES

1. E. Carpenter, *Cantuar, The Archbishops in their Office* (London 1971), 336.
2. Carpenter, 337.
3. B. Palmer, *A Class of their Own* (Lewes 1997), 44.
4. A. Trollope, *Barchester Towers* (London 1902), Chapter XLVI, 673.
5. R. Davidson and W. Benham, *Life of Archibald Campbell Tait* (London 1891), 148.
6. Davidson and Benham, 154.
7. Davidson and Benham, 155.
8. 14 & 15 Victoria Cap. 104.
9. Chapter Order Book, Dean and Chapter Archives, D & C 1/13, 280.
10. D & C 1/13, 301.
11. D & C 1/13, 330.
12. Christian died on 21 February 1895; his obituary appeared in the *Carlisle Journal*, 26 February.
13. E. Christian MSS Report 1852, Index of Visual and Technical Information, 79.0 in Carlisle Cathedral Archive, f. 35.
14. Christian, 6.
15. Davidson and Benson, 185.
16. Christian, 28.
17. Christian, 30.
18. Christian, 25.
19. Christian, 25f.
20. Christian, 30.
21. Christian, 31.
22. Christian, 33.

23. Christian, 33.
24. Christian, 33.
25. Davidson and Benham, 178.
26. Davidson and Benham, 178.
27. Printed letter of 1855, in Carlisle Cathedral Archives, B21.
28. Chapter Order Book 1855–74, D & C 1/14, 213.
29. Davidson and Benham, 155.
30. A. C. Tait, *An Historical Sketch of Carlisle Cathedral* (1855), 46.

The Architecture of Holm Cultram Abbey

STUART HARRISON

Various elements of evidence for the plan of Holm Cultram Abbey suggest that the long-held belief, that the presbytery was of aisleless design, may be erroneous and that the church had an aisled presbytery which was lost when the tower collapsed in 1600. Through the evidence of early illustrations and the remaining standing fabric it is possible to chart the development of the west front and recover the bay design of the nave arcades. Two sections of 13th-century trefoiled arcading survive as loose fragments and can be reconstructed to show their design. Elements of the nave arcades, such as the piers, can be related to contemporary work at Furness Abbey.

THE Cistercian Abbey church of Holm Cultram is one of only two English Cistercian churches to have remained in use since the Dissolution of the Monasteries.[1] It owes this distinction to the unusual arrangement, for a Cistercian church, of having been partly parochial. At the Dissolution of the Monasteries the parishioners petitioned Thomas Cromwell to retain the whole church for their use and this was granted. Unfortunately, due to lack of repairs, as well as the collapse of the crossing tower and a fire, the eastern parts of the building were damaged beyond economical repair and demolished.[2] The parishioners continued to worship in the gradually deteriorating nave until 1730 when a radical remodelling saw the original nine-bay nave reduced in size by the removal of the aisles, the three eastern bays, the clerestory and the blocking up of the arcades.

The abbey had been founded in 1150 by the Scottish royal house when Prince Henry, earl of Cumberland and son of King David, settled monks at the site from his father's foundation of Melrose Abbey in the Scottish borders.[3] The abbey appears to have prospered and the details of the surviving architecture suggest that the church was commenced within twenty years of the foundation.[4] Little is known of the monastic buildings, though it is thought that some of the buildings on the western edge of the site may embody parts of the monastic ranges.[5] Archaeological investigations in the late 19th and early 20th century identified part of the north nave aisle wall, north-east crossing pier, the adjoining upper choir entry doorway, the position of the east wall and parts of the south transept, slype and chapter-house. At the time the trenches were of necessity small in size because of the churchyard cemetery which covers the eastern parts of the church. Unfortunately, apart from a few published comments, drawings and photographs, there is no adequate surviving record of the excavations.[6] Later, unrecorded work exposed the south-west corner buttress of the west front and a section of the south nave aisle wall. Today the site of the main claustral nucleus is open fields, marked with some earthwork features. John Sumpton's drawing engraved by J. Cole, depicting the church from the north-east, also shows some ruined buildings on the western side of the site, and the Buck engraving of 1739 shows a building on the site of the present visitor centre with an embattled parapet. This building, though now largely modern in aspect, retains a chamfered base plinth and a first-floor fireplace with the monogram of Abbot Robert Chamber. The possible survival of a medieval building on this site may relate to the lodging granted to the last abbot at the Dissolution which included 'the sellaras chamber, and the chambre at the stayr hed adjoyning the same'.[7] The cellarer's chamber was most likely located on the western side of the monastic ranges.

One unusual aspect reported in the excavation of the slype and chapter-house area is that they were said to be at an angle to the south transept of the church.[8] This angle is perpetuated today by a large hawthorn hedge which extends southwards from the churchyard and may mark the western wall of the east range. If the reported misalignment is correct it suggests that either the church was built on a different alignment to existing monastic buildings and may have replaced an earlier church, or that they were extensively remodelled and their alignment changed. Geophysical survey by Philip Howard and the Department of Archaeological Sciences at the University of Bradford in 1976 revealed the outlines of some of the monastic buildings including the refectory, set at right angles to the cloister in the usual Cistercian manner. Unfortunately this survey did not include the area of the east range.[9]

THE PLAN OF THE PRESBYTERY

ALL previous commentators have suggested that the presbytery was of typical Cistercian aisleless plan with possibly three chapels in each transept. This interpretation is open to question for a number of reasons. The earliest depictions of the abbey church by John Sumpton engraved by J. Cole[10] shows the nave before it was reduced in size and also the outline of the lost transepts and presbytery (Figs 1–2). Sumpton clearly shows that the presbytery was much wider than would be expected if it was of simple aisleless form, suggesting that the building had arcades and aisles. He shows what appears to be part of a large buttress, which from its position would be at the east end of the north arcade. The topography of the churchyard also suggests that this was the case for the south-east quadrant extends out as a platform, beyond the line that would have been taken up by a aisleless presbytery.[11] A complaint by Mr Mandeville, the vicar in 1590 states, 'In the Chancell there were maye coneres where in people were always jangling and talking in tyme of devine sevice which abuse I thought to redrese for the honor of God'.[12] This might also suggest that the chancel was larger than a simple aisleless structure and that the offending persons were causing disquiet in the aisles. J. H. Martindale reported the excavation that revealed part of the eastern buttresses and because of their deep projection and the character of the masonry, suggested that the church had been extended in the Early English period.[13] Notably, the buttress he refers to coincides in position with that shown in the Sumpton drawing (Figs 1 and 2). Finally, loose architectural fragments from a blind arcade (see below), of 13th-century date, may have originated in a presbytery screen wall that enclosed the ritual presbytery from the aisles. Although the idea that the presbytery of Holm Cultram, in its final form, was a fully-aisled structure cannot be proved without further archaeological investigation, the factors listed above strongly indicate that this was the case. Martindale's opinion that the presbytery had been extended cannot be lightly dismissed, but in the absence of photographs and drawings of the excavation it is difficult to be sure. The fabric of the north-east crossing pier suggests that the church was built with an aisleless presbytery, but that this must have been subsequently remodelled.

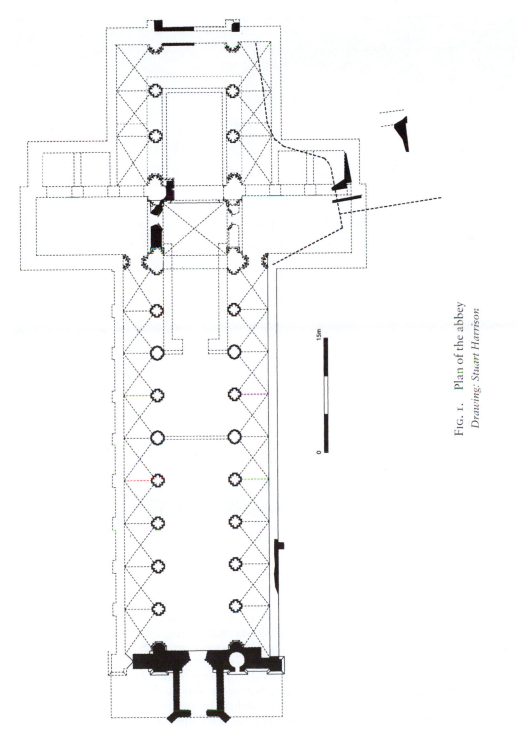

FIG. 1. Plan of the abbey
Drawing: Stuart Harrison

FIG. 2.   Early 18th-century engraving of the abbey from the north-east by J. Cole from an original
drawing by John Sumpton

Photograph: Stuart Harrison

THE SURVIVING CHURCH

THE church in its reduced form retains six bays of the nave arcade, shorn of the aisles
and clerestory, the lower half of the west front and a western porch of early-16th-
century date. The architectural detail is early Gothic with arcade piers incorporating
eight round shafts, standing on moulded bases with individual squared sub-bases.
There is a mixture of waterleaf and chalice capitals and pointed arches with simple
unmoulded offset and chamfered orders. The first pier from the east on each side is of
different design, with ten smaller shafts set around a stepped core, presumably to mark
the position of the rood screen. The spacing of the arcades becomes uneven towards
the west so that there is a substantial difference in width between the western bay on
the north and south. The fourth arch from the west in the south arcade has a moulded
soffit. This, and a change in the design of the capital abaci in the south arcade, might
indicate the progress of building, with the north arcade slightly in advance of the south.
The western doorway is a magnificent design with an inner order of continuous
mouldings and four orders of detached shafts supporting waterleaf capitals and
moulded arch orders which include bobbins on the outer order (Figs 3–5). It is covered
by the porch built by Abbot Robert Chamber in 1507. This porch was heightened
during the remodelling of the church and lost the upper part of a large niche positioned
above the entrance doorway. Fortunately, Sumpton shows the porch before it was
altered and the canopied head of the niche, flanked by pinnacles and topped with an
eagle, is clearly shown (Fig. 6). This eagle is now reset upon the western gable of the

242

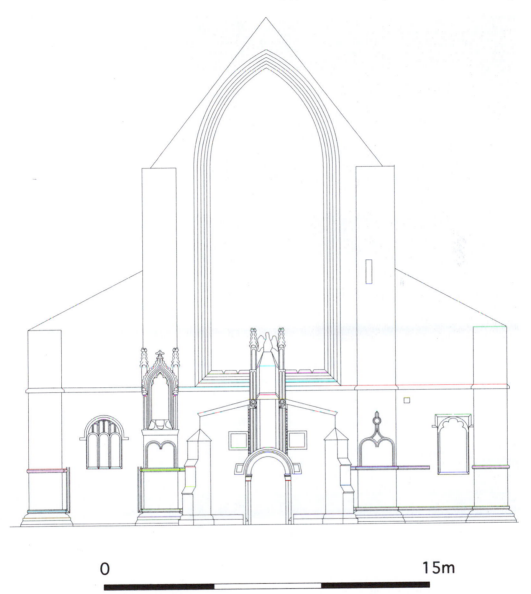

0   15m

FIG. 3.   Reconstruction of the west front following the alterations by Abbot Robert Chamber
based on the surviving fabric and the engraving by Cole

Drawing: Stuart Harrison

church. The sides of the niche are unusual in the use of archaic dog-tooth ornament,
combined with perpendicular panelling. Lying loose in the porch is a section of the lost
upper part, with dog-tooth on the angle and the cusped head of the blind panelling on
the front. Sumpton shows that the original 12th-century arrangement of windows had
been replaced by a huge traceried window, though by his time the tracery had been lost

243

FIG. 4.   The west doorway showing the moulding of the base plinth carried up the side to frame the doorway. This originally formed a hoodmould over the doorhead but was removed in order to accommodate the ceiling of the 1507 porch

Photograph: Stuart Harrison

and only the blocked up frame remained, with a smaller inset perpendicular window. The head of the window completely filled the steeply pitched gable and indicates that the internal ceiling must have been of pointed barrel or trussed rafter design. By Sumpton's time the nave roof had been reduced to an almost flat pitch which may have been one of the reasons the window tracery had been removed and the window reduced in size.[14] All traces of this great window were removed during the later remodelling of the church, but one large moulded stone lying in the porch may represent part of its jambs. Just when it was inserted into the west front is difficult to tell, but it is tempting to associate it with Abbot Chamber who, besides building the porch, also added a canopied niche on the surviving north-western nave buttress.[15] The ends of the aisles had perpendicular windows, probably also inserted by Chamber, that on the south side had a square head with a stepped hood-mould. Its north jamb now remains on the

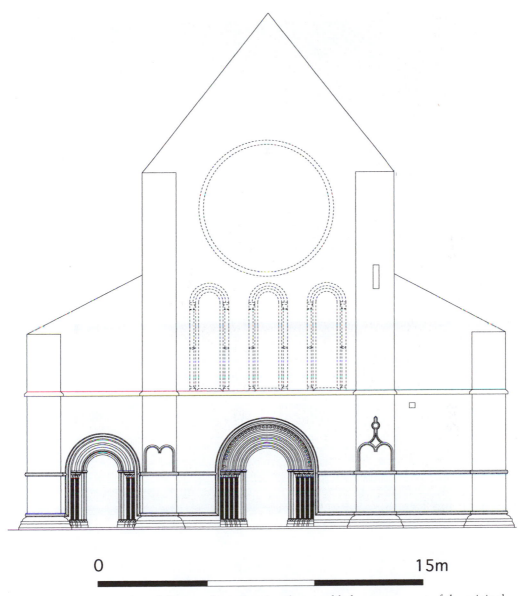

0   15m

FIG. 5.   Reconstruction of the west front showing the most likely arrangement of the original
windows and the north aisle doorway

Drawing: Stuart Harrison

south-west angle of the 18th-century buttress constructed when the aisle was demolished. From the surviving remains of the front and the pictorial evidence it is possible to draw a reconstruction of the west front before its alteration (Fig. 5).

FIG. 6.   Early 18th-century engraving of the abbey from the west
showing the building before it was reduced in size. By J. Cole from an
original drawing by John Sumpton

Photograph: Stuart Harrison

THE ORIGINAL DESIGN OF THE WEST FRONT

INTERNALLY, above the west doorway, there is a gallery which is reached by way of a newel stair behind the respond of the south arcade (Figs 1, 7). This staircase was originally entered from a doorway in the south aisle that has been blocked up and a new doorway from the west forced through the southern buttress of the west front. The stair turret reduces in diameter as it ascends and there are traces of a small blocked circular window in the west side. This can be identified on the outside as part of a panelled roundel on the face of the buttress. At each side of the gallery there remain parts of the moulded jambs of the original 12th-century windows (Fig. 8) and these suggest that the lower part of the west front had a group of three large round-headed windows. The space between them was rebuilt extensively when the church was reduced in size and ragged misalignments can be seen externally where new masonry was inserted. The arrangement of the lower part of the west front with a very thick west wall carrying an internal gallery and a lower tier of three windows, relates it to a specific class of Cistercian west front design. Such galleries are a particular feature of the Yorkshire group of Cistercian churches at Rievaulx, Fountains and Kirkstall. The galleries at Fountains and Kirkstall (and probably Rievaulx) were surmounted by a lower tier of windows with a rose window above. In each case the windows were surmounted by a relieving arch that carried the main gable. Although it is now impossible to prove that this was the case at Holm Cultram, it seems that a lower tier of three round-headed windows surmounted by a large rose window was the most likely original fenestration. One other detail links the west front into the mainstream of Cistercian church planning. The wall on the south side of the southern buttress retains a moulded 12th-century corbel and just above it the buttress is banded by a chamfered weather-mould, which clearly once continued across the west front. These two pieces of evidence strongly suggest that the whole of the lower part of the front was originally enclosed with a Galilee porch, a feature that appeared at numerous Cistercian sites.

One other important lost detail of the west front can also be reconstructed. The front has a bold base plinth of unusual design which is topped by a triple roll moulded string. This was carried up the sides and over the head of the west doorway as a hood-mould (Fig. 5), though only the vertical jamb section now remains at each side. The section over the doorway has been cut back flush with the surrounding wall face to accommodate the roof framing of Chamber's porch. A similar contemporary plinth moulding carried over a doorway as a hood-mould remains over the north transept doorway at Dundrennan Abbey in Galloway and many of the doorways at Kirkstall Abbey in West Yorkshire have this feature. The base plinth is carried around the surviving north-western buttress where it stops and the top string is then extended up vertically against the north side of the buttress (Fig. 9). This identical articulation to the west doorway surround suggests that there was once a north aisle doorway that had a similar hood-mould. There is no obvious sign of it in Sumpton's drawing of the west front, though he shows the surviving vertical jamb moulding and also a second one to the north, where a northern door jamb would have been. Instead of a doorway a perpendicular window is shown in this position (Fig. 2). This suggests that the doorway was removed as part of Chamber's renovations; when the original Galilee porch was destroyed and replaced by a smaller porch there would be no need for a north aisle doorway. Perhaps parts of the moulded south jamb remain immured in the later 18th-century buttress that now overlies its position. Both west front buttresses are articulated by moulded blind arches that stand on a string-course. On the north buttress these

FIG. 7.   Interior of the west front showing the gallery over the west doorway
Photograph: Stuart Harrison

FIG. 8.   The blocked internal south jamb of the
12th-century windows in the west front
Photograph: Stuart Harrison

FIG. 9.   The hood mould surround of the lost
north aisle doorway rising from the base plinth
to frame the south jamb of the doorway
Photograph: Stuart Harrison

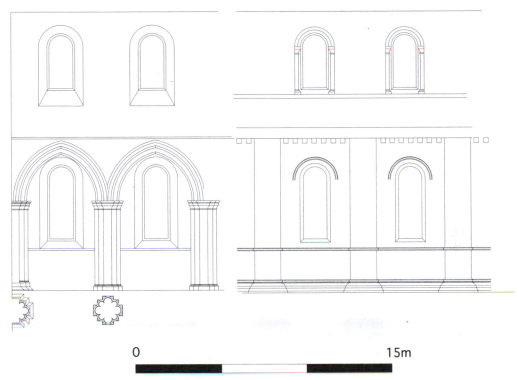

FIG. 10. The bay design of the nave with the clerestory reconstructed based on the engraving by
Cole and the surviving fabric

Drawing: Stuart Harrison

comprise two moulded round-headed arches but on the south buttresses there is an
additional ogee-shaped moulding above them that rises to a pointed finial above a small
roundel. The details of the articulation of the panelling where it rises from the string-
course indicates that these are original 12th-century features of the buttresses (Fig. 9).

THE DESIGN OF THE NAVE ARCADE

THE surviving parts of the nave arcades are difficult to appreciate because of their
reduced height and loss of the aisles. By 1703 Bishop Nicolson noted that,

The inside of the church was full of water, the rain falling in plentifully everywhere. The
parishioners, about fifteen or sixteen years before, took off the lead from the south aisle (the arches
of which are drooping down) to cover that on the north; the fabric is large, though only the body of
the church is standing, of nine arches on each aisle, and very high.[16]

From this description it seems safe to assume that the aisles were vaulted with ribbed
vaults.[17] Following the remodelling, it was said that seven yards in height had been
taken off the upper parts of the church.[18] Above the arches of the main arcade is a
string-course and a band of plain masonry. This retains no trace of triforium openings,
except over the third piers from the west where a blocked opening can be seen on each

249

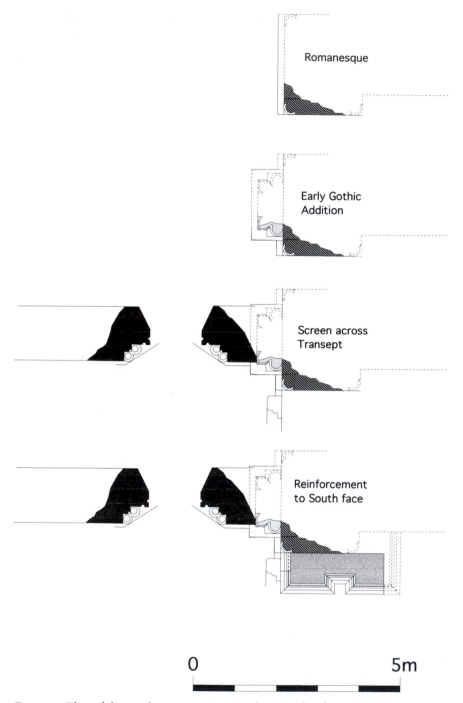

FIG. 11.   Plan of the north-east crossing pier showing the phases in its construction

Drawing: Stuart Harrison

FIG. 12.   The remains of the north-east crossing pier

Photograph: Stuart Harrison

FIG. 13.   Base with Romanesque profile and pellet decoration detached from the north-east crossing pier

Photograph: Stuart Harrison

side. What purpose these served, except to possibly allow some light into the aisle roofspace, is difficult to tell. It seems clear that there was no triforium and the clerestory shown in Sumpton's drawings shows that it had round-headed windows with external bases, jamb shafts and capitals (Fig. 10). Apparently, there were no clerestory buttresses. The aisles were divided by wide pilaster buttresses, except in the western bay where the window was also omitted, but this may have been a later alteration. The aisle windows were tall and round-headed. One obvious omission from the Sumpton drawings is the depiction of string-courses. He shows one below the north aisle windows but omits some that still exist on the west front. It is likely that more existed for extensive lengths of string-course are reused on the exterior of the remodelled 18th-century north and south walls and in the window jambs of the upper storey of the porch. The heads are also reused medieval arch hood-moulds that match the lengths of string-course in profile.[19]

THE CROSSING

EVIDENCE of the structural failure in the crossing that eventually caused the collapse of the central tower was confirmed in an excavation which discovered part of the north-east crossing pier. Built against its south face as reinforcement was what Martindale identified as a 17th-century moulded base for a pair of pilasters.[20] Fortunately, this excavation was partly consolidated, the trench sides revetted and the remains largely retained for display. They include part of a screen wall beneath the north crossing arch with the lower jambs and bases of a 13th-century doorway, presumably the upper choir entry (Fig. 11). Examination of these remains shows that some masonry has been lost since they were first exposed (Fig. 12).[21] The south-west corner of the north-east pier remains with a circular base for a shaft on the angle. This base is Romanesque in profile with a decorative band of small pellets and it stands on a chamfered plinth, though a large section has become detached (Fig. 13). North of this base there are remains of two others. Their profiles are early Gothic in style and they overlap the chamfered plinth of the Romanesque base, clearly showing that they are a later addition to the crossing pier. On Martindale's plan they are both shown as round shafts but careful examination shows that the western base is designed to support a large keeled shaft (Fig. 12). The south side of the Romanesque base is abutted by the deeply moulded plinth for the added pilasters. Measurement shows that these are deeper in projection than Martindale's plan indicates. Despite his suggestion that these pilasters are post-monastic in date, there seems to be no reason why they could not be part of a late medieval reinforcement of the crossing.[22] The interpretation of these features is fundamental in understanding the development of the church. The presence of the Romanesque base strongly suggests that the monks initially built a typical aisleless presbytery with three chapels in each transept arm. This church may have been designed without a crossing tower, and when construction commenced on the early Gothic nave, the crossing pier was reinforced on its western face by the addition of at least two extra shafts. This suggests that a tower was then raised over the crossing, although it is unlikely, at that time, to have risen to the nineteen fathoms mentioned by later commentators.[23] Later, structural problems possibly brought about by raising the tower to its final height led to the addition of the large pilasters on the south face to underbuild the eastern crossing arch (Fig. 13).

Sumpton shows that the western crossing arch had been underbuilt at a low level by a moulded, segmental pointed arch and the space above it walled in to support the original arch above, though no trace of that is shown in his drawing (Fig. 1). It may have been obliterated or removed in the later blocking off when the transepts and choir were abandoned and demolished.[24] Above the arch he shows a perpendicular window in the blocking that seems likely to have been dismantled and reset in the new east wall of the reduced church. In the wall above the window was a reset pair of shields.[25] The accuracy of Sumpton's drawing is substantiated by that made by the Buck brothers in 1739. The church by then had been remodelled and reduced to its present size, but they clearly show part of the abandoned three bays of the north arcade still standing together with the north-west and south-west crossing piers. Spanning between them is the same low-set arch shown by Sumpton. Notably, both illustrations show that it sprang from a lower level than the nave arcades. The Buck engraving is deficient in detail but it does show that the crossing pier shafts carried up above the level of this inserted arch. This low-set arch must surely be connected with the repairs carried out following the fall of the central tower on 1st of January 1600. The surviving records show that for two years the site was pillaged for stone, timber and lead, and that eventually the vicar built a new chancel from the materials of the old chancel and the transepts.[26] Presumably this was a completely new structure that was much lower than the surviving nave and the indications of an offset in the wall above the arch shown in Sumpton's drawing, may mark the level of its roof. This would explain the presence of the low-set arch which must have been provided as a new entrance to the chancel.[27] The new chancel was burnt down shortly after its completion in 1604[28] and repaired again. Repairs to the chancel were called for in 1671, but whether these were carried out is not known. It must have been demolished by 1703 when Bishop Nicolson made no mention of it and described the church as 'The fabric is large, tho' onely the Body of the Church is standing, of nine Arches on each Isle, and very high'.[29]

THE 13TH-CENTURY ARCADING

LYING in the porch are several sections of 13th-century trefoiled arcading. Examination of the pieces shows that they represent two different arcades although employing identical profiles. The smaller is a blind arcade with springers and keystones and may be associated with a single moulded capital. One of the springers is clearly from an

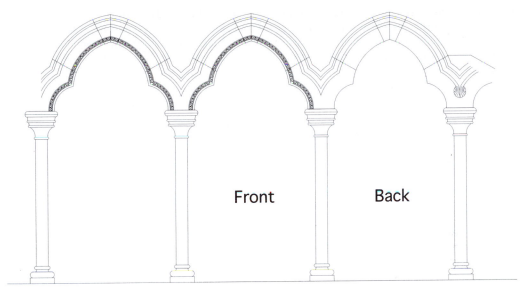

Front   Back

Open Arcade

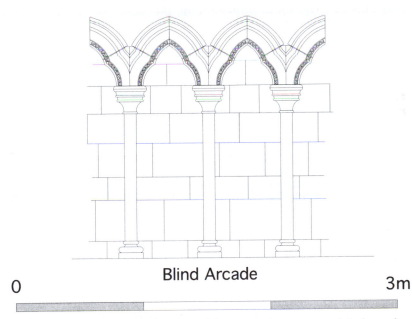

Blind Arcade

0   3m

FIG. 14.   Reconstruction drawing of the two 13th-century trefoiled arcades
Drawing: Stuart Harrison

internal corner position and shows that the arcade occupied at least two adjacent walls. When reconstructed this arcade shows a typical blind arcade such as was employed to enclose the ritual presbyteries in aisled Cistercian churches (Fig. 14). Substantial loose remains of such arcades survive at Fountains, Jervaulx and Rievaulx,[30] and have been reconstructed *in situ* at Byland. The second arcade has a wider span than the first and shows that it formed part of an open arcade which could be seen from both sides, although only one face is elaborately moulded (Fig. 14). It can be associated with a trefoiled hood-mould that has a foliate stop at the springing and which is designed to fit into a rebate in the rear spandrel of the arcade. The relatively unworn appearance and freshness of the pieces shows that they can never have been exposed to the weather, which suggests that they are the product of excavation somewhere on the site. It may be that they are some of the stones reported by Baxter as being found in the excavation of the crossing.[31] They may both have formed part of the same structure in which the bay spacing and arch size was varied between open and blind sections. Alternatively, it may be that the open arcade formed part of a transverse screen and the blind arcade a enclosing screen.

The architectural links of Holm Cultram with other buildings has never been fully explored and insufficient space permits only a brief exploration of this aspect of the abbey.[32] The details of the waterleaf capitals and the design of the main arcade piers are closely related to those at Furness Abbey. The piers with their eight round shafts and the treatment of their bases in particular are virtually identical, though the arches at Furness used developed early Gothic mouldings, rather than simple offsets and chamfers. Similar piers can also be seen at Ripon Minster in the presbytery and may also have appeared at York Minster. Bobbins like those on the west doorway at Holm Cultram also appeared in some profusion in the choir of York Minster. These similarities seem to point to a Yorkshire regional link, but whether the Cistercians were influencing the cathedral lodges or vice versa has been the subject of some discussion.[33]

Nominally Furness became a Cistercian house in 1147 following the merger of the Savigniac Order but, in effect, due to a dispute it was probably only fully Cistercian by 1150. There was an existing stone monastery which included a church that was progressively rebuilt and enlarged following the merger. This rebuilding started with the construction of a new western range and followed on with a reconstruction of the presbytery and transepts. It probably commenced in the early 1160s, and employed much early Gothic detailing. Some of the mouldings relate to those employed in the new choir of York Minster then being constructed by archbishop Roger Pont l'Eveque. The new nave followed on from the transepts and crossing but was built in an intentionally archaic style to match the eastern parts of the building, though it did employ lancet windows.[34] The use of round-headed windows throughout the nave at Holm Cultram and the details of the west doorway suggest that the church was finished before that at Furness. Although this might be explained by the fact that the Furness monks already possessed an existing church that was being replaced piecemeal. At Holm Cultram the surviving north-eastern crossing pier shows that the initial build on the presbytery was Romanesque in character probably without provision for a crossing tower. This was soon revised and the pier was reinforced in the new early Gothic style, suggesting that a formal crossing with a tower was then introduced.[35] Unfortunately, the presence of the graveyard overlying the eastern parts of the church makes it very unlikely that further excavation will determine the exact form of the presbytery and transepts.

ACKNOWLEDGEMENTS

I am indebted to various people who generously assisted in the research for this article including Canon David Weston, the Revd David Tembey, Minister of Holm Cultram, Donald Forster churchwarden of Holm Cultram, Phil Howard for providing a copy of his geophysical survey and in particular Denis Perriam who supplied much detail on the Cole and Sumpton engravings and drawings.

NOTES

1. Other Cistercian churches in present day use include Dore in Herefordshire, Margam in Wales and Culross in Scotland.

2. C. J. Ferguson, 'St Mary's Abbey, Holm Cultram', *Transactions Cumberland Westmorland Antiquarian Archaeological Society*, I (1874), 263–75.

3. VCH, *Cumberland*, II (1905), 162.

4. P. Fergusson, *Architecture of Solitude* (Princeton 1984), 128, suggests a date of 1160 as plausible for the start of building.

5. J. H. Martindale, 'The Abbey of St Mary, Holm Cultram; recent investigations and notes on the ancient roof', *Transactions Cumberland Westmorland Antiquarian Archaeological Society*, ns, XIII (1913), 244–51.

6. W. Baxter, 'Excavations at Holm Cultram Abbey, Cumberland', *JBAA*, XII (1906), 139–41, 284–86; 'Excavations at Holm Cultram Abbey', *JBAA*, XIII (1907); 'Proceedings of the Congress, Tuesday, July 14th', *JBAA*, XIV (1908), 198–99; T. H. Hodgson, 'Excavations at Holm Cultram', *Transactions Cumberland Westmorland Antiquarian Archaeological Society*, ns, VII (1907), 262–68.

7. VCH, 171.

8. Martindale, 245.

9. I have to thank Phil Howard for supplying me with a copy of his survey plan and for discussions relating to the layout of the monastic ranges. Unfortunately, this survey remains unpublished but moves are now in progress to try and reassess the original data using more refined techniques of processing. This will hopefully produce a clearer picture of the buried remains that can be interpreted more easily.

10. Three drawings of the abbey were probably made by John Sumpton, curate of Bowness on Solway, and are now bound in Oxford, Bodleian Library, St Edmund Hall Todd MSS, 7/3. I have to thank Denis Perriam for this information. The drawings were engraved by J. Cole and appeared as illustrations in John Stevens, *The History of the Ancient Abbeys, Additional Volumes to Dugdale's Monasticon Anglicanum*, II (1723), 54–56. Comparison of the drawings and engravings shows that they were faithfully rendered by Cole.

11. Martindale, 244–45. Martindale's description of the buttresses at the north-east angle suggests that he saw two buttresses, one projecting eastwards and one northwards. His plan, however, shows only the south-eastern side of the eastward projecting buttress. The Revd W. Baxter reported of these excavations that 'Adjoining the wall, at the north-eastern end, the foundation of the buttress was also clearly discernible'. W. Baxter (1907), 127.

12. Martindale, 249.

13. Martindale, 244.

14. Martindale, 247–51, suggests that the present roof timbers are of medieval date and were taken down and reused when the church was reduced in size. He also points out that this ignores the statement that the fire of 1604 'destroyed both the body of the chancel and the whole church except the south side of the Low Church which was saved by means of a stone vault'; F. Grainger and W. G. Collingwood, *The Register and Records of Holm Cultram*, Cumberland Westmorland Antiquarian Archaeological Society, Record Series, VII (1929), 179. It seems most likely that they represent the reused timbers of the post-1604 low-pitched roof of the nave.

15. Ferguson, 268.

16. Ferguson, 274.

17. The report of the fire of 1604 stated that 'that within three hours it consumed and burnt both ye body of ye chancel and ye whole church except ye south side of ye low church which was saved by means of a stone vault'; G. E. Gilbanks, *Some Records of a Cistercian Abbey* (London 1900), 139–40.

18. Ferguson, 263.

19. Gilbanks, 98, shows a drawing of the west front which indicates that the porch windows have been altered by the insertion of the subdivisions.

20. Martindale, 245.

21. A large tree root has grown beneath part of the pier and lifted the masonry 7 cm in places. This has broken off a large fragment of the Romanesque corner base which has been recovered and placed in the church porch.

22. Similar late medieval buttressing of crossing piers can be seen at Fountains Abbey, Bridlington Priory and Furness Abbey, Cumbria.

23. Grainger and Collingwood, 178.

24. A parallel for this would be at Bridlington priory where all trace of the western crossing arch was also obliterated by the inserted blocking wall.

25. At Raby Cote are two similar shields which may be the ones shown in the engraving.

26. F. Grainger and W. G. Collingwood, 178.

27. What form the new chancel took is difficult to establish. It presumably comprised the outer walls of the presbytery, together with the repaired, but reduced in height, arcades and possibly a reduced crossing. The transepts seem to have been abandoned and were probably walled off along the line of the nave and presbytery aisle walls.

28. ibid., 179.

29. ibid., 181–82.

30. P. Fergusson and S. Harrison, *Rievaulx Abbey, Community, Architecture, Memory* (New Haven 1999), 162.

31. W. Baxter (1906), 139–41. Baxter's description is vague and ambiguous, but it may be that he is describing the trefoiled springers.

32. P. Fergusson (1984), 62.

33. C. Wilson, 'The Cistercians as 'Missionaries of Gothic' in Northern England', in *Cistercian Art and Architecture in the British Isles*, ed. C. Norton and D. Park (Cambridge 1986), 86–116.

34. S. Harrison and J. Wood, *Furness Abbey* (London, English Heritage guidebook 1998), 9.

35. One large voussoir with an early Gothic profile, presently lying in the field south of the abbey church, may have originated in the crossing arches.

Rose Castle

TIM TATTON-BROWN

The See of Carlisle was created in 1133 by Henry I and for some time it is thought that the Bishop's residence lay within the precinct of the cathedral, which was also an Augustinian priory. From the 1230s it seems likely that the bishops occupied a house near Dalston known as La Rose, but no trace of this survives. The present buildings belong to the mid-14th century and have been much modified since. Rose Castle is an important building in Cumbria, but no detailed discussion of the surviving structures has been published since James Wilson's account in 1912.

FOR over 700 years Rose Castle has been the principal residence of the bishops of Carlisle. This fine house, in a beautiful setting, lies about 6.2 miles south-south-west of Carlisle beside the River Caldew. Over the last century or so quite a lot has been written about the history of Rose Castle,[1] but rather surprisingly no detailed study has yet been made of the fabric of the surviving buildings, even in the most recent accounts.[2] James Wilson's *History of Rose Castle*, published in 1912, is by far the most important work, and has a useful 'Appendix of illustrative documents'.[3] These include the grant of 1230, the licences to crenellate, Bishop Bell's building accounts, and the Parliamentary Survey of 1649. The one published paper that does deal with architectural history, a most interesting article, is Blake Tyson's account of the rebuilding of the chapel in 1673–75.[4] This paper will look briefly at the earlier architectural history of Rose Castle, and will suggest that the principal buildings were all put up in the 14th century to create a strongly fortified castle against the Scots. Before this, however, a brief account will be given of all the bishop of Carlisle's other residences in order to try and place Rose Castle in a wider context in the medieval period.

THE BISHOP AND HIS RESIDENCES

THE see of Carlisle was created in 1133, eleven years after the new Augustinian priory of St Mary in Carlisle had been founded by King Henry I.[5] The prior, Athelwold, became the first bishop and it is highly likely that at this time the prior's house became the first episcopal residence, and that this house was situated in the west range of the cloister. After Athelwold's death in 1157, no further bishops were elected until 1204, when Bernard became the second bishop. Unfortunately, his episcopate (1204–*c*. 1214) was during the later part of John's reign when the country was under an interdict for much of the time. His successor, Hugh, who had been abbot of Beaulieu, was bishop of Carlisle from 1219–23, and it is known that in June 1221 he was given twenty good oaks by Henry III from his forest at Inglewood 'to build himself a house in the city'.[6] Hugh of Beaulieu had been a key figure in the many negotiations between the Pope and King John between 1206 and 1215, and although he was a Cistercian abbot he was often accused of having an extravagant lifestyle when acting on the king's behalf.[7] As abbot he attended the famous Lateran Council in 1215, and when he died at the abbey of La Ferté, in Burgundy, on a return journey from Rome on 3 June 1223, the chronicler of Lanercost recorded that

Hugh, bishop of Carlisle, disgracefully dispersed the community of that same church and halved its possessions by a deceitful and iniquitous division, by the just judgement of God, as he was returning from the court of Rome, through over-eating, died wretchedly without the viaticum.[8]

This division of the conventual possessions of Carlisle began to give the bishopric a more adequate income (the process was not completed until 1249), and it is clear that from this time Bishop Hugh started to acquire residences for himself, not only in Carlisle, but also at the nearby *dominium* of Linstock (north of the River Eden and just two miles from Carlisle), and at Bewley, three miles north-west of Appleby (Bishop Hugh no doubt gave it this name, Beaulieu, himself).[9] It is also possible that it was Bishop Hugh who first had a residence in London, but it is equally likely that it was his successor, Mauclerc (bishop 1224–46) as an ex-courtier and royal treasurer, who acquired the house. This was situated on the south side of the Strand immediately to the west of what was later to be the great Savoy Palace, and from the early 13th century until 1539[10] it was much used by the bishop while at court or attending Parliament.[11] While travelling between Carlisle and London the bishop was also able to make use of his two other major properties at Melbourne in Derbyshire and, from 1230, Horncastle in Lincolnshire.[12]

Despite the comments of some earlier writers, it seems certain that the bishop had a major house in Carlisle itself from *c.* 1220 until the Civil War period. Once again James Wilson has gathered together many of the documentary references to this residence, but without drawing them together in a broader way.[13] When the new Dean and Chapter was established in 1541, they were given all the old Augustinian priory buildings, 'provided that they meddle not with the house called the bishop's lodging within the precincts of the late monastery'.[14] The most likely site for this lodging in 1541 was in the western corner of the precinct, immediately to the south of Prior Slee's western gateway to the precinct of 1528. This vaulted gateway had buildings attached to it, both on the north-east and south-west,[15] and it is possible that the range on the south-west was part of the bishop's lodging which, from the early 16th century, had a large tower attached to it.[16] All these buildings, except the gateway itself, seem to have been demolished in the Civil War or the Commonwealth period, and after this the bishop had no residence within the cathedral precinct, although his registry was built on this site in 1699. In the 13th century, however, there is documentary evidence to suggest that the bishop was building his Carlisle residence on a separate site north-west of the cathedral precincts. This is in the area between the cathedral and the castle and one should remember that the castle was often under the control of the bishop (on behalf of the king) at this time. On 5 April 1222 Walter Mauclerc, then sheriff of Cumberland, took possession of the castle and, when Bishop Hugh died the following year, he became bishop of Carlisle as well.[17] From 1227 he was also Treasurer of England, and it is possible that he started to build, or rebuild, his residence, with a great hall and chamber block somewhere in the area between the priory and the castle. During the siege of 1216, Alexander II of Scotland's army had attacked and mined under the southern curtain wall of the castle from within the city,[18] and this part of Carlisle must have been waste when the Scots army left at the end of 1217. It would, therefore, have made a good site for first Bishop Hugh to start his new residence in 1221, and then for Walter Mauclerc to have continued the work. As an important royal servant, Bishop Walter would have been well aware of the house building activities of other bishops close to their cathedrals in the early 13th century. At this time many bishops were erecting aisled great halls and great chambers commensurate with their own status,[19] and as Treasurer of England Walter Mauclerc would certainly have needed a fine residence in Carlisle as well as in London. Sadly, there appears to be no documentary evidence for this, although Bishop John Halton (1292–1324) is known to have been permitted to build a prison (for criminous clerks) on a site 360 ft long by 18 ft wide 'between the walls of the city and the priory on the west side'.[20] It is even possible that the bishop's great hall was used for the parliament in Carlisle in the spring of 1307, just before the death of Edward I.[21] In summary, large new residences for the bishop of Carlisle must have been constructed by the 1230s in both Carlisle itself and on the Strand in London. By the early 14th century and the beginning of the Scottish Wars both these houses must have been large building complexes[22] that were the principal residences of the bishop.

ROSE CASTLE

IN February 1230, the manor of Dalston, with the advowson of the church, was granted to Bishop Walter Mauclerc by Henry III,[23] and soon afterwards he must have started to build a new house for himself, near the River Caldew, 2.2 miles due south of Dalston church, which was quickly given the name 'La Rose'. Despite the suggestions of earlier writers, there is no historical or archaeological evidence for an earlier castle on the site,[24] and the present building does not even contain remains of a 13th-century house. Nevertheless, the documentary evidence does tell us that by September 1300, when Edward I, Queen Margaret and their court were at 'La Rose', the bishop of Carlisle had a large residence there, although there is no indication that it was a castle at this time. It is very likely, therefore, that Bishop Walter and his immediate successors built a large house here with the usual sequence of buildings — great hall, kitchen, bishop's chambers, chapel, and so on.[25] This house may have had a moat around it, but the main buildings were probably all free-standing structures, and it is these buildings that were occupied and then destroyed by first Edward the Bruce, King Robert's brother in 1314, and then by King Robert the Bruce himself in June 1322.[26] Only archaeological excavation can now determine their plan.

Most earlier writers suggest that the surviving buildings of Rose Castle were put up in various stages, with the oldest part being the so-called Strickland Tower on the north-east corner of the castle.[27] It was suggested that this was a pele tower built by Bishop Halton at the end of the 13th century that was 'later altered and restored by Bishop Strickland' *c.* 1400.[28] However, an examination of the fabric of the so-called Strickland Tower shows that it is all of one period,[29] and bonded to the north curtain wall of the castle. Small-scale excavations in 1994[30] also seemed to show that the Strickland Tower was joined to the east or hall range of the castle (the latter demolished in the late 17th century), with the outer curtain joining the tower beside the still-existing (but heavily rebuilt) southern spiral staircase (Fig. 1).

The external south-west faces of the Strickland Tower also still show the scars for the roof crease of the large first-floor chamber east of the chapel. The north curtain wall west of the Strickland Tower was considerably lowered by Bishop Law (1769–87),[31] but earlier views, particularly the Buck engraving of 1739, show the whole of the corbel table running from the Strickland Tower to Bell's Tower, the latter added to the curtain wall in 1488 (see below), and as far as the early 19th-century Percy Tower

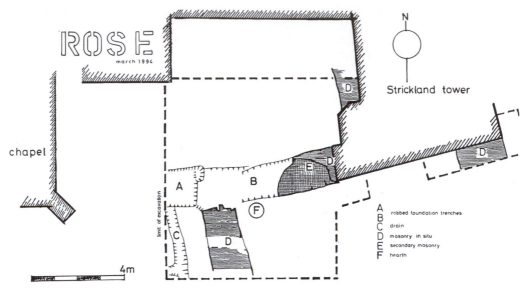

FIG. 1.   Plan of the 1994 excavation south-west of the Strickland Tower

(now the front door). All of this suggests that the Strickland Tower, and the north curtain wall, were built at the same date. The style of the architecture in the Strickland Tower, although fairly plain, and the form of the corbel table, perhaps suggest a date in the 14th century, and this work can probably be associated with the two licences to crenellate of 1336 and 1355.

Rose Castle is today only really an L-shaped building, but a most useful plan of *c.* 1671 in the Machell manuscript[32], shows that before about 1650 the present ranges were joined to others on the south and east and that the whole building was indeed a concentric castle built around a roughly square central courtyard (Figs 2 and 3). This plan is inscribed:

A Platforme of Rose Castle in Cumberland / wherein, what is coloured read was found in re-/paire by Bishop *Sterne* first Bishop of *Carlile* / after the returne of K. Charles the 2nd from / his exile; *whence* he was translated to the / Archiepiscopal See of Yorke: What is colour'd / black was repaired by Bishop Stearne: what / is gray were the old walls pulled downe / by him in order to his repaires: And wt / remains white, were the old walls stand / ing when Bishop Rainbow entered upon it.

Richard Sterne (bishop 1660–64) moved to York and was succeeded by Edward Rainbow (1664–84), and this map is a most useful record of Sterne's changes to Rose Castle in the years immediately following the Restoration.[33] In 1648 the castle had been captured and burnt, and during the Commonwealth period (1649–60) most of the castle was left in ruins after the stripping of most of the lead from the roofs. Only the west (gatehouse) range was occupied by its new owner, William Heveningham. The plan is also most useful in having marked on it, in a faint hand, the names of all the principal rooms in each of the ranges,[34] and these names are confirmed by the Parliamentary Survey of 1649.[35] This survey tells us of the 'void quadrangle' in the middle with

the house incompassing it, viz [b], the chapell on the north side, the great chamber and hall on the east side, the grannery, brewhouse and bakehouse on the south, and severall decayed chambers on the west, with one tower called Constable Tower on the north quarter, one tower on the east quarter called Strickland Tower, the kitching and two little turrets on the south and one tower called Pettinger Tower on the west, the whole castle being full four square.

It seems very likely, therefore, that this was a completely new castle erected for Bishop John Kirkby (1332–52) in the later 1330s, in the period following Edward III's defeat of the Scots at Halidon Hill in 1333 (Fig. 5). This castle would have been built in the typically English style of the 14th century that is best known from Bodiam Castle, although in some ways Bolton-in-Wensleydale Castle (of the 1370s) is perhaps a better example with its large, square corner towers and smaller intermediary turrets.[36] Bishop Kirkby's licence to crenellate was given on 9 April 1336, but in October the following year the castle was recorded in the Lanercost Chronicle as having been burnt by the Scots.[37] Then in 1338 Bishop Kirkby requested a lifetime grant of Carlisle Castle from the king 'because he had nowhere to live in his diocese'. His petition was not granted, but he did become constable in June 1339 'during pleasure'.[38] This, perhaps, suggests that Rose Castle was not completed until some time in the 1340s, although it was probably sacked again by the Scots in 1345 on their homeward march.

If we return to the *c.* 1671 plan of the castle, we can see that, as in the Parliamentary Survey, already quoted, the great hall was in the east range, with the bishop's great chamber to the north of it, and the great kitchen in the corner tower on the south-east. Behind the south curtain wall were the fairly menial service buildings (granary, brewhouse and bakehouse), which were no doubt rebuilt and enlarged in the later medieval period. In the north range, the chapel was certainly rebuilt by Bishop Richard Bell (1478–95), with a completely new tower added outside the curtain wall in 1488[39] while the west range must have contained the original gatehouse. This gatehouse is known as Kite's Tower, and it has been assumed that it was built by Bishop John Kite (1521–37), as there is documentary evidence relating to his building work at Rose Castle in 1522–24, and Kite's arms, impaling those of Armagh, where he had previously been archbishop, can be seen on the upper string-course of the gatehouse.[40] However, as James Wilson pointed out, the masonry of the lower part of the gatehouse is more ancient than the upper storey.[41] One can also see that in the lower three floors the pairs of windows with sub-rounded heads, typical of the early Tudor period, have been inserted into the masonry while in the top floor alone the windows are contemporary with the neighbouring ashlar masonry. This must mean that only the windows and the top storey were made in Bishop Kite's time, and that the gatehouse itself is an original 14th-century feature, lying on the other side of the central courtyard from the main entrance to the great hall. It also seems likely that Bishop Kite refurbished the west range of the castle at this time, and put in additional lodging chambers behind the curtain wall, which after about 1650, became the principal rooms in the reduced castle.

The original form of the north-west corner of the castle is difficult to work out today, as it has been rebuilt and given a new front entrance put in by Bishop Edward Rainbow (1664–84) and Bishop Thomas Smith (1684–1702).[42] This new entrance and façade is shown in Buck's engraving of 1739 surrounded by fine casement windows and with, above it, a small pediment (Fig. 4).

All of this was completely refaced by Rickman in 1829–30, and given a new corbelled out and crenellated parapet to make a new 'fake' tower, the Percy Tower. To the right (west) of this entrance is Smith's Tower which was also refaced on the north by Rickman. Much of the lower west face of this tower, which still contains a small blocked window, is of medieval masonry, and there can be little doubt that the south

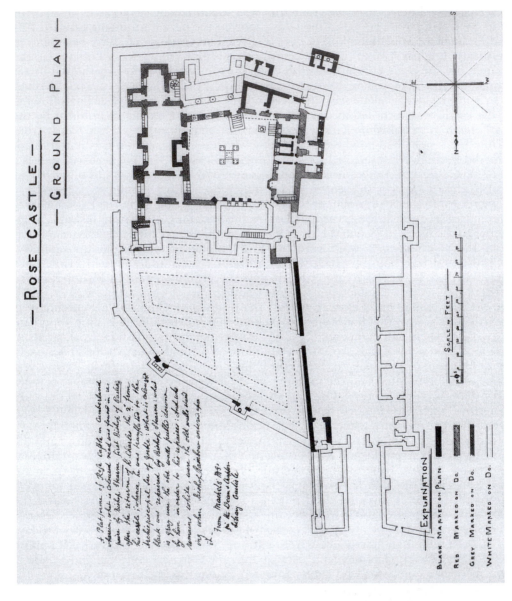

FIG. 2.   Plan of Rose Castle in *c.* 1671 in the Machell MS (re-drawn by Charles Ferguson, 1875)

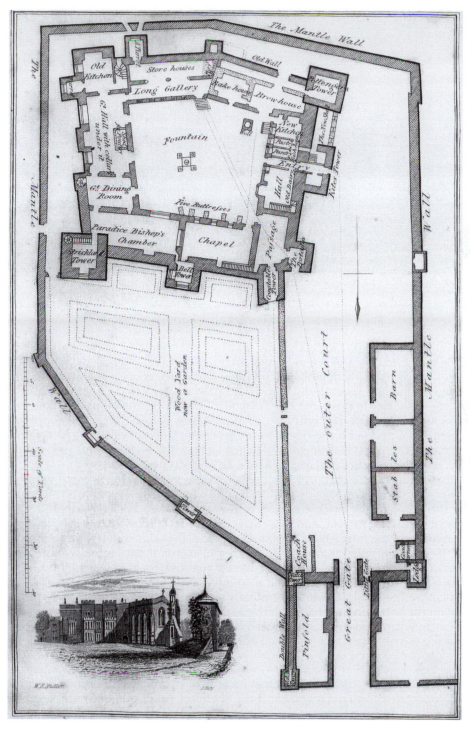

The Mantle Wall

Old Kitchen · Store houses · Old Wall · Pottengar's Tower
Long Gallery · Bake house · Brew house
Gt. Hall with cellar under it · New Kitchen · The Nursery
Fountain · Well · Pastry · Pantry · Kitts Tower
Gt. Dining Room · Entry · Hall out saving
Paradice Bishop's Chamber · Five Buttresses · Chapel · Passage · Kitts Tower
Stricklad Tower · Constable Tower · Bell Tower · The Dovehouse

The Mantle Wall

Wood Yard now a Garden

The outer Court

Barn · stables · The Mantle Wall

Pond

Coach House · Wall Tower · Great Gate · Kitts Gate

Double Wall · Pinfold

Scale of Time

W.B. Nutter   J. Roe

Fig. 3.   Jefferson's redrawn version (1838) of the *c.* 1671 plan

263

FIG. 4.   Buck's engraving of Rose Castle, 1739

and west walls of the tower were also the walls of the medieval tower called 'The Portcullis' on the *c.* 1671 plan. A second tower, to the east of this and called 'Constable's Tower', was already partially demolished by 1664, and its foundations may one day be found outside the modern front door. The *c.* 1671 plan suggests that there was another main entrance to the castle through 'The Portcullis' (the name Portcullis also suggests this), but this must be a secondary entrance, as its passageway into the central courtyard is cut through, on a diagonal, the north-west corner of the courtyard. In the original 14th-century castle, built at a time when defence against the Scots was of paramount importance, only the entrance gateway in Kite's Tower was perhaps in use.

Around the outside of the curtain wall and towers one might have expected to find a ditch or moat, but there is no sign of this. Instead the remains of an outer terrace wall can still be seen close to the castle on the east and south sides. To the north and west this outer wall had small turrets, and is further away from the castle. It connects with the main gateway on the north-west, and it seems clear that this outer wall, known as 'the mantle'[43] was an original feature of Rose Castle, even if it was actually built after the main castle. Its completion could have been marked by the second licence to crenellate in 1355,[44] but the mantle could also have been built in the 1330s. Around most of its course, particularly on the southern side,[45] the mantle wall has been cut down,[46] but on the north, in the vicinity of the outer gateway,[47] it still survives to its full height with a crenellated parapet. This crenellated parapet must have continued all the way around the top of the mantle wall, and additionally on the north and west sides it would have connected via a wall walk with small square or rectangular turrets. The best preserved of these is that which still survives, much hidden by vegetation, on the north-west corner. Part of another turret can be seen in the middle of the west mantle wall (nearly opposite Smith's Tower), and the shells of three others are still visible (their upper walls have long been cut down) on the north-east side of the mantle. This

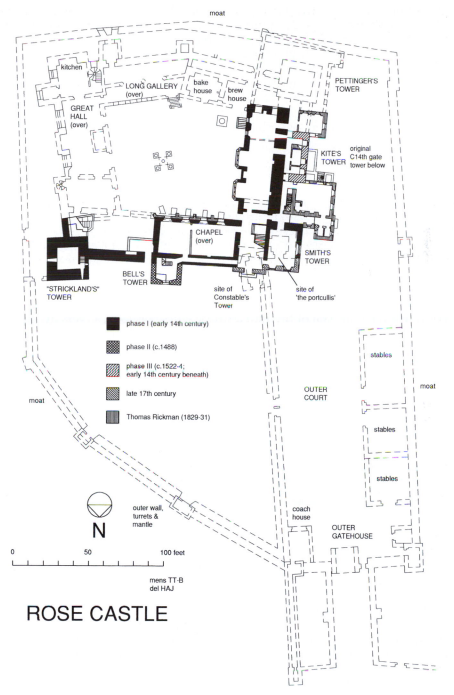

moat

kitchen

LONG GALLERY
(over)

bake
house

brew
house

PETTINGER'S
TOWER

GREAT
HALL
(over)

KITE'S
TOWER

original
C14th gate
tower below

CHAPEL
(over)

SMITH'S
TOWER

BELL'S
TOWER

"STRICKLAND'S"
TOWER

site of
Constable's
Tower

site of
'the portcullis'

phase I (early 14th century)

phase II (c.1488)

phase III (c.1522-4;
early 14th century beneath)

late 17th century

Thomas Rickman (1829-31)

stables

moat

OUTER
COURT

moat

stables

stables

outer wall,
turrets &
mantle

coach
house

OUTER
GATEHOUSE

N

0   50   100 feet

mens TT-B
del HAJ

ROSE CASTLE

FIG. 5.   Phased plan of Rose Castle

outer line of defence was particularly necessary on the more vulnerable north and west sides of the castle, and it was also built to allow for an outer court between the outer gate and the inner gate (Kite's Tower).[48] Beyond the mantle wall a large ditch would have been built all the way around the castle, and traces can still be seen as the ponds on the north–west side, and down the hill from the mantle wall on the east. On this side, a second outer wall, with buttresses against it, had also to be built because of the steepness of the hillside down to the flood plain of the River Caldew. The very wide outer moat on the east has been obscured by the landscaping carried out in the mid-19th century.[49] At this time an outer ha-ha wall was built to separate the castle grounds from a new park.

CONCLUSION

EXAMINATION of the fabric in conjunction with the maps and written sources allow a tentative phasing of the castle to be attempted (Fig. 5).

Rose Castle was probably a new castle built in the reign of Edward III for the warlike bishop of Carlisle, John Kirkby (1332–52), although it may not have been finished until the time of his successor, Gilbert Welton (1353–62). This was at a time when they were much involved with the king's Scottish Wars, and Cumberland was constantly being overrun by the Scots. It should therefore be compared with other new concentric castles of the mid-14th century, which had evolved from the great castle-building activities in Wales of Edward I at the end of the 13th century. These bishops, as very active wardens of the western march, were great secular lords, and Rose Castle was built for them as both a strong residence and as an important status symbol.

ACKNOWLEDGEMENTS

I am most grateful to Henry Summerson and David Weston for all their considerable help with this paper. Dr Summerson also most kindly sent me a copy of Bishop May's inventory of 1598, as well as many other most helpful references. My wife, Veronica, has, as usual, word processed this paper immaculately from my messy text. Figure 5 was kindly drawn for me by Howard Jones.

NOTES

1. C. J. Ferguson, *The Development of Domestic Architecture: Rose Castle and Dalston Hall* (Kendal 1875), 5–15; J. Wilson, *Rose Castle: the residential seat of the Bishop of Carlisle* (Carlisle 1912); C. M. L. Bouch, 'Rose Castle', *Transactions Cumberland Westmorland Antiquarian Archaeological Society*, ns, LVI (1956), 137–41; C. G. Bulman, 'Rose Castle', *Archaeol. J.*, 115 (1958), 246–47 are the principal accounts.

2. A. H. Emery, *Greater Medieval Houses of England and Wales*: i, *Northern* (Cambridge 1996), 244–46; D. R. Perriam and J. Robinson, *The Medieval Fortified Buildings of Cumbria*, Cumberland Westmorland Antiquarian Archaeological Society Extra Series, XXIX (Kendal 1998), 216–17.

3. Wilson, n. 1, 200–58.

4. B. Tyson, 'William Thackeray's rebuilding of Rose Castle chapel, Cumbria, 1673–75', *Transactions Ancient Monuments Society*, ns, XXVII (1983), 61–76. There is also a brief, but well illustrated account by J. M. Robinson in *Country Life*, 183, no. 47 (23 November 1989), 70–75.

5. H. Summerson, *Medieval Carlisle: the City and the Borders from the Late Eleventh to the Mid-Sixteenth Century*, Cumberland Westmorland Antiquarian Archaeological Society, Extra Series, XXV (Kendal 1993), 32; H. Summerson, 'Athelwold the bishop and Walter the priest: a new source for the early history of Carlisle priory', *Transactions Cumberland Westmorland Antiquarian Archaeological Society*, ns, XCV (1995), 85–91.

6. Summerson, *Medieval Carlisle*, 99; Wilson, n. 1, 22.

7. Dom. F. Hockey, *Beaulieu, King John's Abbey* (1976), 23–26.

8. *Chronicon de Lanercost, 1201–1356* (1839), 30, quoted in Hockey, n. 7, 26. This is, no doubt, a biased account, coming from another Augustinian priory.

9. For a fuller discussion of the bishop's manors, see Wilson, n. 2, 8–16. For plans of a 15th-century tower at Linstock, and the ruins of part of an early-14th-century chamber block at Bewley, see Perriam and Robinson, n. 2, 84, and 260–61. The bishopric's income is more fully discussed in H. Summerson, 'The King's Clericus: the life and career of Silvester de Everdon, Bishop of Carlisle', *Northern History*, 28 (1992), 70–91.

10. In 1539 the bishop was forced to give up this house to Lord Russell, and to receive in exchange the Bishop of Rochester's house on Lambeth Marsh, made vacant by the execution of Bishop John Fisher. This remained the property of the Bishop of Carlisle until 1827, when it was described as 'very ancient and much out of repair'. See *Survey of London*, 23, *St Mary Lambeth*, pt 1 (1951), 75.

11. For more details of Carlisle Inn on the Strand, which was also used by the prior of Carlisle in the 15th century, see Wilson, n. 1, 16–21.

12. For Melbourne and Horncastle, see Wilson, n. 1, 12–16.

13. Wilson, n. 1, 21–28.

14. Letters Patent Foreign and Domestic of Henry VIII, Add. I ii 1499, 25 May 1541.

15. David Weston, *Carlisle Cathedral History* (2000), 96.

16. Weston, n. 15, 106.

17. Henry Summerson in M. R. McCarthy, H. R. T. Summerson and R. G. Annis, *Carlisle Castle, a survey and documentary history* (1990), 127.

18. Summerson, n. 17, 126.

19. For example at Lincoln where the ruins of the fine aisled great hall built by Bishop Hugh of Wells (1209–35) is still visible. See P. Faulkner, *Archaeol. J.*, 131 (1974), 340–44.

20. Wilson, n. 1, 22. Henry Summerson tells me that by the 1280s Bishop Ralph was able to maintain a harper and singing men in his entourage, and had an income of about £600 per annum, so he may have completed the large residence.

21. Henry Summerson points out that there is still no evidence for a bishop's great hall in Carlisle (pers. comm.). He suggests that the Parliament was probably held in a new timber great hall in the castle, n. 17, 134.

22. Bishop John Halton also held Carlisle castle for Edward I from 1297–1304, see Summerson, n. 17, 133.

23. Wilson, n. 1, 200–02. In April 1230 a commission was set up to determine the bounds between the bishop's newly acquired woods at Dalston, and the king's forest of Inglewood to the south.

24. Bouch, n. 1, 132, who suggests that the earliest manor house here 'was of the mote and bailey type'.

25. The chapel is first mentioned in a licence to build it, dated at Rose, 23 February 1255. See Bulman, n. 1, 246.

26. Wilson, n. 1, 42.

27. See, for example, Bulman, n. 1, 246.

28. idem.

29. The Strickland tower was, however, redesigned and rebuilt by Anthony Salvin in 1852 for Bishop Hugh Percy, but various early views of it exist, including a plan and internal view in W. Hutchinson, *The History of the County of Cumberland*, II (1794), 435.

30. I am grateful to David Weston for a copy of this plan, which was drawn by Peter Strong.

31. Wilson, n. 1, 73.

32. Reproduced best by Wilson, opp. 96. This plan was also redrawn by Ferguson, n. 1. The original is Machell MSS, VI, 622 in the Dean and Chapter's archives.

33. The long and complicated dispute between Rainbow and Sterne is described in Wilson, n. 1, 91–95. See also Tyson, n. 4, and Bouch, n. 1, 136–39 where further documents of this period are transcribed.

34. These names are usefully transcribed onto another redrawn version of the plan in S. Jefferson, *The History and Antiquities of Carlisle* (1838), 376, also reproduced in Bouch, n. 1, opp. 140.

35. Wilson, n. 1, 232. Dr Summerson has also very kindly sent me a copy of a very full inventory role in Carlisle Record Office of Rose Castle, taken in 1598 just after the death of Bishop John May in 1598. This lists all the rooms and their contents.

36. For plans of both these castles see R. A. Brown, *English Castles* (2nd edn, 1976), 143–45. Dr Summerson points out that Bishop Kirkby's register tells us that Kirby spent about six weeks at Rose in the autumn 1333, returned briefly in July 1334, and then began to reside regularly at Rose from the end of 1334.

37. Wilson, n. 1, 44 and 209–10.

38. Summerson, n. 17, 140.

39. Wilson, n. 1, 214–19, where the account roll is fully transcribed.

40. Wilson, 76–78.

41. Wilson, 77.

42. The new front entrance was probably made by Bishop Rainbow, as the front door still has a splendid lock dated 1673, which was given to Rainbow by Lady Anne Clifford.

43. The 'mantle wall' and its turrets are described in the 1649 Parliamentary Survey, n. 35 above, and on the *c.* 1671 plan.

44. Wilson, n. 1, 210.

45. On the south-west side the cut-down mantle wall is now buried beneath the ground.

46. In Bishop Osbaldeston's Register, among a list of works carried out in 1762, is mentioned 'the old ruined mantle wall repaired and reduced to 4 foot high, and covered with new stone coping round the castle'.

47. The well-known carving of a rose within a quatrefoil, set in a square plaque still survives above the main gate arch. Though restored it is also perhaps 14th century in date.

48. At a later period stables and outhouses (and a coach house) were built in the outer court.

49. Though its position is well shown on the Ordnance Survey 6-inch map (2nd edn, 1901), Cumberland Sheet XXX S.W. The landscaping is said to have been carried out by Sir Joseph Paxton, Bulman, n. 1, 247. In the 1649 Parliamentary Survey 'an oarchard without the south and east quarter of the castle containing about 3 roods of ground' is mentioned; Wilson, n. 1, 232. This probably lay in the already filled up moats here.

Romanesque Architecture and Architectural Sculpture in the Diocese of Carlisle

MALCOLM THURLBY

This paper discusses the Romanesque churches of the diocese of Carlisle and the gatehouse and curtain wall of Egremont castle. The study commences with small, two-cell churches with square-ended chancels and considers aspects of the reuse of Roman stonework and the continuity of Anglo-Saxon building techniques after the Conquest. The problem of dating uncarved and carved tympana, and interpreting the latter, is examined, and the relationship of smaller churches to Carlisle Cathedral is explored in detail. The form and function of the west towers at Morland, Burton-by-Kendal, Dacre, St Lawrence at Appleby and St Michael at Workington, is investigated. The north nave arcade of Kirkby Lonsdale, with its incised decorated columns so often related to Durham Cathedral, is placed in the architectural context of St Mary's Abbey, York, to which monastery it belonged. The west portal of the former priory church of St Bees is discussed in relation to arches decorated with heads in Scotland, Ireland and, locally, at Great Salkeld. Other doorways and chancel arches, some carved with beakheads and other heads, are studied in connection with sculpture in Yorkshire. Late-12th-century north nave arcades at Great Ormside, Lowther and Crosby Garrett are briefly examined. Finally, the problems associated with the dating of the Norman fabric of Egremont castle are explored.

TWO-CELL CHURCHES AND THEIR DECORATION FROM THE LATE 11TH TO THE MID-12TH CENTURY

TWO-CELL plans comprising a square-ended chancel and an aisleless rectangular nave survive at Cross Canonby, Gilcrux, Isel, Kirkbride, Long Marton, and Upper Denton. Upper Denton is built of Roman stones and, according to Pevsner, the chancel arch is a reconstructed Roman arch, probably brought from Birdoswald.[1] There are two massive, side-alternate quoins at the south-east angle of the chancel and megalithic stones in the jambs of the chancel arch. These features continue a church-building tradition from the earliest pre-Conquest times in the north, as at Escomb (Co. Durham), but the relatively large scale of the chancel arch is in keeping with a post-Conquest date. In contrast to this, the tall narrow chancel arch at Crosby Garrett, which is now cut by its Gothic replacement, belongs to the pre-Conquest tradition, although whether or not it is pre- or post-Conquest in date is a moot point.[2]

At Cross Canonby the unbuttressed north wall of both the chancel and the nave is built of reused Roman stones. The plain, single-order chancel arch rests on plain jambs and damaged imposts. In contrast to many Anglo-Saxon examples, it does not use through-stones, and the thin mortar joints make a date before 1120 unlikely. At Kirkbride the unadorned, single-order chancel arch is matched by simple north and south doorways. To either side of the west face of the chancel arch there are altar recesses; the one on the left appears to be cut in awkwardly but on the right it seems to be original. Similarly placed niches are found elsewhere in small Romanesque churches in England, as at Barfreston (Kent), Castle Rising (Norfolk), Patcham (Sussex), Scawton (Yorks.), Wakerley (Northants.) and Worth Matravers (Dorset).[3] The plain tympanum of the south doorway at Cross Canonby comprises six pieces of ashlar in two rows on a plain, single-stone lintel, and is topped with plain voussoirs.[4] The manner of construction is related to the plain, recessed tympanum of the south doorway at Great Ormside.[5] The doorway has tall proportions and the massive size of lintel, versus the relatively small tympanum, suggests a date no later than the first quarter of the 12th century, as at Bredwardine (Herefs.).[6] A cruder example of a plain tympanum is in the south doorway at (Little) Clifton, where there is a roughly finished, plain stone with smaller stones and render between the top of the tympanum stone and the voussoirs. This surely indicates that the tympanum was rendered and painted as at Saint-Savin-sur-Gartempe, Vienne.[7] Fragments of plaster may still be seen on the tympanum of the doorway to the south vice at the west end of the nave of Blyth priory (Notts.) which was founded in 1088 and probably completed by the early years of the 12th century. Plain tympana continue into the 12th century in Cumbria, as at Carlisle Cathedral in the first storey of the west wall of the presbytery. This has an important bearing on dating in that Cross Canonby was given by Waltheof to Carlisle Cathedral and, given the similarity in construction between the tympana at the two places, Cross Canonby is unlikely to pre-date the start of the cathedral in 1122.[8]

The north doorway of St Michael's, Appleby-in-Westmorland, has a hogback tomb reused as the combined tympanum and lintel.[9] The manner of construction, with separate voussoirs above the tympanum between ten and two in terms of a clock face, was fairly common in the first half of the 12th century, not least in Herefordshire.[10] Ranulf de Meschines gave St Michael's to Wetheral Priory which he had founded as a daughter house of St Mary's Abbey, York, c. 1106–12, and the construction of the church may coincide with this gift.[11] Calverley gives a drawing of the tympanum in a better state of preservation and also illustrates it from inside the church.[12]

The north wall of the nave at Long Marton has side-alternate quoins at the north-east angle and rendered rubble masonry. The north doorway is cut through the earlier masonry and rendering. The church is unusual amongst two-cell churches in the region in having both a south and west doorway, both of which have carved tympana. The south doorway has plain jambs of large blocks of stone topped by a plain lintel above which plain voussoirs frame the carved tympanum.[13] In construction it is like the Great Ormside south doorway where the tympanum is plain, but the subject matter of the tympanum is unusual. To the lower right is a dragon or leviathan with back-turned head and knotted tail above which is a shield carved with a small cross. Behind it there appear two large wings and, pointing towards the upper left, a sword. Immediately to the left of this there is an open quatrefoil knot while to the left is a quadruped with giraffe-like neck from which spread huge wings and a tiny bird head with long curved beak. This creature seems to stand on what, for Calverley, 'resembles the conventional ship of art; and there seem to be waves of the sea beneath it'.[14] The iconography is not easily interpreted, but it may refer to Isaiah (xxvii, 1), 'In that day the Lord with his sore and great and strong sword shall punish leviathan the piercing serpent, even leviathan that crooked serpent, and he shall slay the dragon that is in the sea'.[15] The leviathan is paralleled on the ironwork of the south door at Staplehurst (Kent) and more closely on the lintel of the south doorway at Dinton (Bucks.), as well as the lintel of the west tympanum at Ault Hucknall (Derbs.).[16] At Dinton the leviathan faces a demi-figure of an angel holding a cross, while at Ault Hucknall it is met by a standing figure with shield and sword, presumably St George or St Michael. This signifies triumph against evil in much the same way as the wings, shield and sword at Long Marton. Band knots were supposed to have powers to fascinate or charm evil spirits and the quatrefoil form of Long Marton may be compared with ironwork on doors at Kirby Bedon and Leathley.[17] Geddes observes that on 'Swedish doors a knot is often found beside keyholes, an area vulnerable to evil influences. A fourfold knot is wrapped around a quatrefoil lock plate lying dramatically loose beneath the bound devil in the Harrowing of Hell mosaic at St Mark's, Venice. It emphasises the proximity between evil and protection'.[18] Allen equates the monster on the left with a serra, a sea monster which has huge wings. According to the *Bestiary*,

When the serra sees a ship in full sail on the sea, it raises its wings and tries to keep up with the ship for four or five miles; but it cannot keep up the pace and folds its wings. The waves carry the wary creature back into the depths. The serra is like the things of this world, while the ship is the image of the just man, who sails unharmed and without shipwreck through the storms and tempests of this world. The serra which could not keep up with the ship signifies those men who at the beginning set their hand to good works, but cannot continue them, and are overwhelmed by all kinds of vices, which drag them into the depths like the waves of the sea. 'He that endureth to the end shall be saved' [Matthew, x, 22].[19]

Stylistically there is related work in a panel above the north doorway at Bolton. In particular the tail of the serra relates to the tails of the horses on the Bolton panel (Fig. 1).[20]

The west doorway at Long Marton has a plain, single-order arch on plain jambs with a lintel carved with a pattern of connected equilateral triangles, and a tympanum with a lower section of two stones carved with saltire crosses above which are two figurated panels carved in low relief.[21] To the left is a scene traditionally associated with the legend of St Margaret — she was swallowed by Satan in the form of a dragon — and on the right a dragon with a knotted tail (the emblem of Margaret is a dragon).[22] The closest comparison for the left scene is on the north tympanum at Stow Longa (Hunts.), with the fins on the body of the 'dragon' and the raised arms of 'Margaret', but even here there are significant differences.[23] At Stow Longa 'Margaret' has breasts and long hair; at Long Marton the breasts are lacking, the hair is short and the face looks bearded. It would therefore seem better to interpret the Long Marton scene as Jonah and the Whale, which also helps account for the fish swimming below. This was a popular scene since early Christian times as an Old Testament type that prefigures Baptism and Resurrection.[24] The inclusion of the cross to the left of the whale indicates salvation through Christ and the church, and triumph over evil as on the south tympanum.

AFFILIATIONS WITH CARLISLE CATHEDRAL

THE north and south doorways at Bolton are typologically in advance of Long Marton. Both doorways have a plain, continuous inner order and an outer order with an angle roll and a narrow hollow (N door only) on the front of the arch. It is carried on capitals atop detached shafts of which only the right shaft of the south doorway survives. The juxtaposition of the angle roll-and-hollow moulding with a single-billet hood is matched on the second window of the north nave clerestory at Carlisle Cathedral. With the exception of the right capital of the south doorway, all the capitals are cushions

Fig. 1.   Bolton, All Saints, north doorway
© *Malcolm Thurlby*

with incised outlines on the faces, in the manner of a number of capitals at Carlisle Cathedral. The left capital of the south doorway has a double band of saltire crosses on the chamfer of the abaci and arrowheads at the lower angles. The latter are found on a clerestory capital at Carlisle Cathedral and other sites discussed below. The arrowheads between scallops may reflect a lost source at York as the motif appears regularly in Yorkshire churches, as on the chancel arch at Old Edlington, Seamer and Hauxwell (Yorks.), and the north doorway at Hilton.[25] On the south doorway the hood-mould is carved with a row of discs adorned with six spokes outer order while on the north doorway there is a single-billet hood-mould. An eight-spoked version of the discs appears on the soffit of the south doorway at Corbridge, Northumberland, a church given to Carlisle Cathedral by Henry I.[26] The former chancel arch of St Leonard at Warwick has been reset at the west end of the nave. It relates in detail to Carlisle.[27] The chapel of Warwick was given by Ranulph de Meschines to St Mary's Abbey, York.[28] The multi-scalloped capitals have single-incised chevron on the chamfer of the abaci as on the east capital of the south aisle arch at Carlisle Cathedral (Figs 2 and 3).

FIG. 2.   Warwick, St Leonard, tower arch, detail, north capitals
© *Malcolm Thurlby*

FIG. 3.   Carlisle Cathedral, S crossing arch, detail, east capital
© *Malcolm Thurlby*

The various arrowheads and foliated central form on the north soffit capital relate also to the cathedral. The outer north capital at Warwick has a swollen angle scallop as on the east respond of the north nave arcade at Carlisle. The soffit roll is flanked by broad hollows as in the arch from the south transept to the south presbytery aisle at Carlisle (Figs 2 and 4). The bases of the Warwick tower arch also have angle spurs in the manner of the east respond of the south nave arcade at Carlisle. The apsidal east end at Warwick is beautifully constructed in ashlar and has a very unusual set of tall, narrow niches (10 ft 8 in x 1 ft 5 in) on the exterior.[29] It has been suggested that these may reflect the original east end of Carlisle Cathedral.[30] Be that as it may, the uniformity in the size of the ashlar in the external wall arcade speaks of a highly accomplished mason akin to that in the incised columns at Durham Cathedral.[31]

The neo-Norman, cruciform church of St Bride at Bridekirk, which was constructed between 1868–70 by Cory and Ferguson, incorporates two portals and the chancel arch

FIG. 4.   Carlisle Cathedral, arch from south transept to south presbytery aisle, detail, north capitals

© Malcolm Thurlby

from the original Romanesque church.[32] The reset arch in the east wall of the north transept, and now filled with the organ, was probably the original chancel arch. It has plain cushion capitals and a soffit roll flanked by broad hollows like Warwick and Carlisle Cathedral. The outer order has an angle roll and hollow like Bolton north doorway and a hood-mould with medallions like Bolton south doorway, although at Bridekirk the medallions are spaced. The south portal at Bridekirk has chevrons in the arch and a double-billet hood with double-scallop capitals on *en delit* shafts and a tympanum with a shallow carving of Christ in Majesty. The carving appears to be unfinished and the whole must have been completed in paint. The left shaft is covered with saltire crosses.

St Michael at Isel has a two-cell plan with square-ended chancel with one original window remaining in both the north chancel and nave walls. The chancel arch employs motifs emanating from the cathedral; the soffit roll with broad angle hollows, and scalloped capitals with incised edge and spearheads between the undersides (Figs 3, 4 and 5). The broad, spear-like ornament on the bases is virtually identical to the north base of the north transept arch at Bridekirk. The south doorway has two orders with

FIG. 5.   Isel, St Michael, chancel arch   FIG. 6.   Isel, St Michael, south doorway
© Malcolm Thurlby   *© Malcolm Thurlby*

an angle roll moulding with a chevroned underside atop double-scalloped capitals with an incised edge and spears between the undersides of the scallops as at Carlisle Cathedral and Warwick (Fig. 6). The inner order has chevrons in the arch carried on chamfered imposts atop plain jambs. The chevron is not paralleled at Carlisle Cathedral but is close to the south doorway at Corbridge (Northumberland). Thus it is possible that both Corbridge and Isel reflect lost chevron at Carlisle. A more complex version of the Isel-Corbridge chevron is found in the arch to the vestry at St Kentigern at Aspatria, the former chancel arch of the Romanesque church with scalloped capitals with incisions and spears underneath. Like Corbridge, Aspatria belonged to Carlisle Cathedral.[33]

At Aikton the plain, two-order chancel arch is carried on various scalloped capitals atop a half shaft for the inner order and formerly on detached shafts for the outer order. There are troughed arrows between the undersides of the scallops as at Warwick and elsewhere.

At Kirkbampton the north doorway has a single pair of columns with scalloped capitals. The right capital has upright stumps between the scallop undersides as in certain clerestory capitals at Carlisle Cathedral. The tympanum is not well preserved; on the upper register there is a simply incised chevron in the manner of abaci at Carlisle Cathedral and Warwick. On the lower register the only feature now discernable is a figure on the right carrying a crook or crozier in his right hand. Antiquarian descriptions record 'a rudely sculptured bas-relief representing two animals, and what seems to have

Fig. 7.   Kirkbampton, St Peter, chancel arch,
north capital
© Malcolm Thurlby

Fig. 8.   Carlisle Cathedral, S transept, east
clerestory, detail of capital
© Malcolm Thurlby

been designed for an abbot'.[34] Calverley observes that the figure 'carries something which looks like David's sling; and possibly the subject was David with his crook and sling attacking the lion and the bear'.[35] The chancel arch at Kirkbampton is of two orders with a chamfered hood, channeled chevrons outside an angle roll on the outer order and a set of truncated inverted triangles outside an angle roll on the inner order. The angle roll with chevron on the face is paralleled in the Carlisle Cathedral clerestory, albeit not with exactly the same type of chevron. The capitals are scalloped with various geometric designs on the faces except for the outer left capital on which there are two scallops on the right, a drooping angle volute and a head with gaping mouth on the west face. The droopy volute is remarkably similar to a capital in the east clerestory of the south transept at Carlisle Cathedral, while the incised chevron on the abacus relates to the cathedral and Warwick (Figs 7 and 8).

Like a number of churches under discussion, as well as the lost Wetheral Priory, St Michael's, Bromfield, belonged to St Mary's Abbey, York.[36] The tympanum of the south doorway at Bromfield has a countersunk chequer board pattern like the face of the inner left capital at Kirkbampton (Fig. 7), a motif used in the region in the late 7th century on the Bewcastle cross.

TOWERS

THE west tower at Morland is entered through a narrow arch in the west wall of the nave. There is no west doorway to the tower but there is a mid-wall-shaft in each of the narrow, plain, paired belfry openings.[37] Pevsner calls the tower Anglo-Saxon or 'possibly even of after 1066' but the Royal Commission dates it immediately pre- or post-Conquest, and the Taylors to 1050–1100.[38] The church was given to St Mary's Abbey, York, by Ketell or Chetell, son of Eltreth, who was alive some years after 1120.[39] The date of the gift of a church is not a foolproof means of dating, but it is often associated with work on the fabric. It is therefore possible that the west tower and the fragments of chevron reused in the church may both date from around 1120. Pre-Conquest motifs can last well after the Conquest as indicated by the west tower at Thurlby (Lincs.), consecrated in 1112, and Dymock (Glos.), of the 1120s. There is a similarly narrow, unmoulded, single-order arch to the west tower at Caldbeck. As at Morland, this is the only entry to the tower, and the same is true at St Lawrence at Appleby, Burton in Kendale, Dacre (rebuilt 1810) and St Michael at Workington. All of these towers are likely to have served as baptisteries in the tradition of the westwork and St Ricquier at Centula.[40] The tower at Workington was rebuilt in 1780 and again after a fire of 1994, but the lower part remains from the Norman church.[41] In contrast to the plain arches to the towers mentioned above, the arch at Workington has a large soffit roll flanked by hollow chamfers. This is the form encountered in the arch from the south transept to the presbytery south aisle at Carlisle Cathedral and elsewhere in the region (Figs 2, 4 and 5). The stair turret at Workington projects into the north-east corner of the tower, a feature paralleled in the transepts and west towers at Durham Cathedral and Lindisfarne Priory.[42] Workington belonged to St Mary's Abbey, York, and it is possible that the projecting stair reflects a link with that church.[43] Workington also has a large double scalloped capital with deeply incised edge reset in the tower which may come from the Norman chancel arch.

The tower at Long Marton is an addition to the early Norman church and is unusual amongst Cumbrian Romanesque towers in having a west doorway (now blocked).[44] The heavily restored belfry openings have a plain enclosing arch with paired sub-arches on a mid-wall shaft with scalloped capitals. This articulation contrasts sharply with that of the belfry openings at Morland, and probably indicates a date in the third quarter of the 12th century.

Barton had a central axial tower of a type common in England.[45] In the tower there is a transverse barrel vault with a remarkably clear impression of the wattle centering, although whether or not this is 12th century is a moot point.[46] The Royal Commission suggested that a similarly planned church may have originally existed at Warcop, but I found no evidence for this.[47]

KIRKBY LONSDALE

THE three western bays of the north nave arcade at Kirkby Lonsdale are usually compared with the nave of Durham Cathedral (Fig. 9).[48] Formally there are many similarities, including the alternation of columns with a compound pier, the incised decoration of the columns with lozenges, the octagonal cushion capital of the eastern column, and the plinth moulding. Moreover, the multi-scalloped capitals of the compound pier may be compared with examples in the dado arcade capitals of the Durham choir aisles. Such a list clearly indicates a close affiliation between the two buildings but that it suggests a direct connection between them may be questioned.

Kirkby Lonsdale was given to St Mary's Abbey, York, by Ivo de Taillebois, between 1090 and 1097.[49] In the Yorkshire Museum there is a section of painted plaster from St Mary's Abbey, York, with the very same design as on the eastern columns in the Durham nave arcades (Fig. 10). The alternation of compound and columnar piers also relates to the nave of Selby abbey where the first column of the south nave arcade has the same incised pattern of double-outline lozenge as the west column of the Kirkby Lonsdale north nave arcade (Figs 9 and 11).[50] A multi-scalloped capital from St Mary's Abbey, York, has four scallops on each face as on the eastern capital of the Kirkby Lonsdale north nave arcade pier (Figs 9 and 12). This same St Mary's capital has incised edges to the scallops like many of the Carlisle Cathedral and associated capitals (Figs 3, 5, 6, 8 and 12). The interlaced designs on the scallop faces of the western column capital at Kirkby Lonsdale are closer to Selby nave arcade capital S1 than to the carved capitals

FIG. 9.   Kirkby Lonsdale, St Mary,
north nave arcade from north-east
© *Malcolm Thurlby*

FIG. 10.   Yorkshire Museum,
painted plaster from York, St
Mary's Abbey
© *Malcolm Thurlby*

FIG. 11. Selby Abbey, south nave arcade, column 1, capital from west-south-west

© Malcolm Thurlby

FIG. 12. Yorkshire Museum, scalloped capital from York, St Mary's Abbey

© Malcolm Thurlby

FIG. 13. Kirkby Lonsdale, St Mary, north nave arcade, detail, west column, capital from south-west

© Malcolm Thurlby

FIG. 14.   Gosforth, St Mary,
chancel arch, detail, north capital
© *Malcolm Thurlby*

on the processional doorways at Durham (Figs 11 and 13). Moreover, the arch mouldings in the Kirkby Lonsdale arcade change from bay to bay as at Selby whereas at Durham there is not this variety. Given these similarities it seems possible that Selby Abbey and Kirkby Lonsdale reflect a common source in St Mary's Abbey, York.

Allied to the sculptured capital of the western column of Kirkby Lonsdale are the capitals of the chancel arch at Gosforth, a church that also belonged to St Mary's Abbey, York.[51] Specifically, the two heads on the north capital at Gosforth with doughy facial modelling, large almond-shaped eyes, a moustache growing to the sides of the nose, and a glum expression, relate to the head at the south-west angle of the west column of the Kirkby Lonsdale north nave arcade (Figs 13 and 14). Moreover, the beaded strands that frame the Gosforth heads compare favourably with those on the middle scallop of the west face of the same Kirkby Lonsdale capital.

The west portal at Kirkby Lonsdale goes with the addition of the late-12th-century west tower to the nave. It has four orders and combines traditional and progressive elements. The inner order of the jamb with coursed shafts to either side of an angle fillet is a common motif in north English Romanesque including Durham and Selby. The inner order of chevron differs little from Durham Cathedral nave before 1128, yet the third order 3, with foliage in the triangles, speaks of development in the north first encountered in the work of Archbishop Roger of Pont l'Eveque at York Minster (1154–81).[52] Similarly, the fluted capitals bring to mind examples in Bishop Henry of Blois' hospital church of St Cross at Winchester, while figures following the line of the arch on the outer order of the doorway reflect French Gothic portals.

ST BEES

THE former Benedictine priory of St Bees was founded *c.* 1120 by William Meschin, the first Norman owner of Coupland, as a cell of St Mary's Abbey, York.[53] Bees, or Bega, was the daughter of an Irish king who reigned as a Christian king in the 7th century and the church possessed a bracelet of St Bega.[54] The priory was the monastic counterpart to William Meschin's castle at Egremont. The elaborate west doorway has four orders, the outer three of which are carved with chevrons occasionally topped with heads carved in deep relief (Fig. 15). The foliated cushion capitals are badly weathered but enough remains to relate the principles of design to the capital of the

FIG. 15.   St Bees, west doorway
© *Malcolm Thurlby*

first column of the Selby south nave arcade and the allied work at Kirkby Lonsdale (Figs 11, 13 and 15). The projecting heads on the St Bees doorway relate to the south doorway at Dalmeny (Lothian) and the west doorway of Dunfermline Abbey, founded in 1128.[55] The reset south doorway at Killaloe Cathedral provides a very close parallel for the central head at St Bees and the south doorway at Great Salkeld (Fig. 16).[56] There are also allied heads loose at St Finn Barre's Cathedral, Cork, and on the chancel arch of Cormac's Chapel at Cashel (Tipperary).[57]

Built into a wall in front of the west doorway of St Bees is a lintel carved with what is usually identified as St Michael killing the dragon.[58] The interlace that flanks the scene may be seen in connection with Ireland, as appropriate to the patron saint of the priory.[59] The representation of the saint carrying a sword rather than the more usual spear has been allied with the hero of the Norse saga, Sigurd, the dragon-slayer.[60] Representation as a soldier may also suggest identification as St George killing the dragon; Calverley suggests St George, or parenthetically, St Michael.[61] Similar soldiers fighting dragons are found on the lintel of the west doorway at Ault Hucknall (Derbs.), the tympanum of the south doorway at Pitsford (Northants.), the inner north capital of the chancel arch at Steetley chapel (Derbs.), and on a tomb at Conisborough (Yorks.).[62]

At Great Salkeld the south doorway hood-mould has spaced roundels. Plain versions of this motif on the inside of the west processional and west doorways of Durham Cathedral, and the south nave doorway at Riccall (Yorks.) (Fig. 16).[63] The unruly interlaced designs on the cushion capitals relate to the west doorway of St Bees (Figs 15

Kilnwick (all in Yorks.). Variants on this theme are also found on the north doorway at Burgh-by-Sands.

The south wall of the nave of St Michael at Burgh has Norman masonry and a doorway with one order of columns, lozenged abaci, an inner order with big 'beakheads' and outer order with chevrons (Fig. 18).[68] Three of the heads have paired symmetrical leaves issuing from the mouth as on the south portal of St Margaret's at York. The size of the one remaining Norman window in the south nave aisle at Burgh-by-Sands, larger than tiny early Norman windows and also with a chamfered surround, suggests a date in the third quarter of the 12th century.

St Michael's, Torpenhow, which belonged to Holyrood Abbey, preserves its Norman chancel arch and south doorway.[69] The chancel arch has two richly chevroned orders on carved capitals and coursed shafts (Fig. 19). The outer capitals are scalloped with an incised edge of the faces and daggers between the undersides of the scallops as at Carlisle Cathedral and elsewhere. The inner left capital has four standing stylised nude figures with interlocking arms and legs, while the inner right capital has six heads — human, animal and bird — in deep relief atop stalks. The abacus above the latter capital has countersunk chequerboard as on the Bromfield tympanum. The south doorway has two orders, the inner of chevron, the outer with three rolls of cable, and the hood-mould is ornamented with bobbin (Fig. 20). The latter motif is very useful for dating in that it is used by Archbishop Roger of Pont l'Eveque's at York Minster (1154–81), and at St Albans Abbey in the work undertaken by Abbot Robert de Gorham (1151–66).[70] Locally, the motif also appears on the west portal at Holm Cultram Abbey.

In the second half of the 12th century it was common to add one or two aisles to an earlier nave or build new churches with nave aisles.[71] At Great Ormside a two-bay arcade with round-headed arches and multi-scalloped capitals was added on the north side of the nave. Somewhat grander is the four-bay north nave arcade at Lowther with plain, round-headed, two-order arches on columns with square capitals. Capital 3 is multi-scalloped with arrows between the undersides in the Carlisle tradition, but the faces of the capitals have symmetrical stylised foliage patterns that suggest a date later in the 12th century. Other capitals are variants on the waterleaf family as associated with Archbishop Roger of Pont'l'Eveque of York. A cruder version of the Lowther capitals is found in the nave north arcade at Crosby Garrett.

EGREMONT CASTLE

EGREMONT Castle was founded by William Meschin, probably around the same time as he founded St Bees Priory. Of the 12th-century fabric there remains the gatehouse, which is constructed in good-quality ashlar, and the adjoining curtain wall in which there are stretches of herringbone masonry (Fig. 21).[72] The difference in masonry may suggest that the gatehouse is later than the curtain wall, whilst parallels for the form of the entrance in other castles, would seem to support a date in the second half of the 12th century for the gatehouse. Specifically, the segmental arch recessed beneath the round-headed enclosing arch is found in the main gate at Newcastle Bridgend (Glamorgan), in the main doorway inside the forebuilding at Orford (Suffolk) (1165–73), and in the outer forebuilding doorway at Newcastle-upon-Tyne (1168–78).[73] In the late 12th century segmental barrel vaults became popular over gate-passages, as in Henry II's inner bailey gatehouses at Dover. Be that as it may, the vault at Egremont is not a segmental barrel but a quadripartite rib vault. The juxtaposition is analogous

Fig. 19.   Torpenhow, St Michael, chancel arch
© *Malcolm Thurlby*

Fig. 20.   Torpenhow, St Michael, south
doorway
© *Malcolm Thurlby*

Fig. 21.   Egremont Castle, gatehouse and curtain wall
© Malcolm Thurlby

Fig. 22.   Egremont Castle, gatehouse, detail of vault
© Malcolm Thurlby

to the quadripartite rib vault and segmental rere-arch in the gatehouse at Castle Rising, which was probably built soon after 1138.[74] Moreover, in Normandy the segmental arch beneath a round-headed enclosing arch is used for the doorway at the Exchequer at Caen as early *c.* 1100–25.[75] In the ecclesiastical realm a round-headed arch enclosing a segmental arch was originally included in the gatehouse of Bury St Edmunds Abbey and, following that, in the south doorway at Wissington (Suffolk). Other examples include the north transept west portal at Dorchester Abbey (Oxon), in the south portal of Sherborne Abbey (Dorset), in the former pulpitum of Ely Cathedral, and the south doorway at High Ongar (Essex) and Kirkburn (Yorks.).[76] Of these, the Bury St Edmunds tower dates from the time of Abbot Anselm (1120–48) and there seems no reason to date High Ongar, Kirkburn or Wissington later than the middle of the 12th century. Indeed, the High Ongar doorway is remarkably similar to the south portal at Montgaroult (Orne) which Maylis Bayle dates shortly after 1100.[77] Returning to Egremont, the rubble plinth continues uninterrupted through the curtain wall and gatehouse, and the ashlar of the gatehouse appears to key into the curtain wall without any sign of having been inserted. Herringbone masonry is usually associated with an early post-Conquest date as in the curtain wall at Richmond castle (Yorks.) and Tamworth (Staffs.). Ashlar was used for the keep of Carlisle Castle possibly as early as 1122 and almost certainly by 1133.[78] In the absence of unequivocal evidence to the contrary, therefore, it seems pertinent to date the gatehouse and curtain wall with the foundation of the castle in the 1120s.

The Egremont gatehouse is remarkable for the remains of the quadripartite rib vault, which is unusual in the context of English Romanesque rib vaults in that its trajectory is domical (Fig. 22). The ribs formerly rested on double-scalloped capitals atop coursed shafts on attic bases with angle spurs. The use of a four-part rib vault in a 12th-century castle gatehouse is paralleled at Castle Rising (Norfolk) and Durham, to which should be added the gatehouse at St Augustine's, Bristol, with two bays of quadripartite rib vaults. More generally, there are barrel-vaulted gatehouses at Prudhoe and Norham castles and the Court Gate at Canterbury Cathedral precinct. In broad iconographical terms the vaulted gatehouse may be related to the vaulted church porches, as at Southwell Minster and Tewkesbury Abbey (barrel vaulted), and Malmesbury Abbey, Sherborne Abbey, Bishop's Cleeve (Glos.) and Bredon (Worcs.) (rib vaulted).

CONCLUSION

IN the light of its pre-eminent ecclesiastical position in the region, it is not surprising that Carlisle Cathedral influenced a significant amount of Romanesque architecture in the region. The loss of Wetheral Priory, however, raises the important question of its role in this development. As a daughter house of St Mary's Abbey, York, it may well have been an avenue through which the architectural influence of that great abbey church was disseminated in the area. In the absence of Wetheral, however, the evidence at Kirkby Lonsdale and elsewhere suggests that St Mary's Abbey, York, and, more generally, Romanesque in Yorkshire, was an important influence in the architecture and sculpture in the Diocese of Carlisle.

ACKNOWLEDGEMENTS

I am grateful to Canon David Weston for kindly facilitating access to the clerestory of Carlisle Cathedral. Stuart Harrison and Karen Lundgren accompanied me on the fieldwork for this

MALCOLM THURLBY

research. They provided good company, excellent map reading, and the observation of many features which otherwise I might have missed. Moreover, Karen very kindly checked numerous details in Yorkshire churches for me. Thanks are also due to Jane Geddes, John Goodall, Stephen Heywood and Richard Plant for advice on various aspects of this paper.

NOTES

1. Pevsner, *Cumberland and Westmorland* B/E, 121.
2. H. M. Taylor and Joan Taylor, *Anglo-Saxon Architecture*, 2 vols (Cambridge 1965), 184–85.
3. D. Kahn, 'The Romanesque Sculpture of the Church of St Mary at Halford, Warwickshire', *JBAA*, 133 (1980), 64–73 at 69 n. 19.
4. For a list of plain tympana in English Romanesque churches, see Duncan Blair Cameron Givans, 'English Romanesque Tympana: A Study of Architectural Sculpture in Church Portals *c*.1050–*c*.1200', 3 vols (unpublished Ph.D. dissertation, University of Warwick, 2001).
5. RCHME, *Westmorland*, pl. 147.
6. For Bredwardine, see M. Thurlby, *The Herefordshire School of Romanesque Sculpture* (Almeley [Herefs.] 1999; reprinted with additions, 2000), 128, fig. 201.
7. Raymond Oursel, *Haut-Poitou roman*, 2nd edn (La Pierre-qui-Vire 1984), pl. 20.
8. R. K. Rose, 'Cumbrian Society and the Anglo-Norman Church', in *Religion and National Identity: Studies in Church History*, ed. S. Mews, 18 (Oxford 1982), 119–35 at 129.
9. Richard Bailey and Rosemary Cramp, *Corpus of Anglo-Saxon Stone Sculpture, II, Cumberland, Westmorland and Lancashire North-of-the-Sands* (British Academy Oxford 1988), ill. 25.
10. Thurlby, *Herefordshire School*, 21, 105.
11. VCH, *Cumberland*, II, 184.
12. William Slater Calverley, *Notes on the early sculptured crosses, shrines and monuments in the present diocese of Carlisle*, Cumberland Westmorland Antiquarian Archaeological Society Extra Series, XI (Kendal 1899), 59, and ill. opp. 59.
13. RCHME, *Westmorland*, pl. 139.
14. Calverley, *Notes*, 229.
15. J. Romilly Allen, *Early Christian Symbolism* (London 1887), 369.
16. Jane Geddes, *Medieval Decorative Ironwork in England*, (London 1999), 43 and 69. For Dinton (Bucks.), see C. E. Keyser, *A List of Norman Tympana and Lintels, with figure or symbolic sculpture still or till recently existing in the churches of Great Britain* (London 1927), fig. 46; for Ault Hucknall, ibid., fig. 145.
17. Geddes, *Medieval Decorative Ironwork*, 43.
18. ibid.
19. Richard Barber, *Bestiary* (London 1992), 205; Allen, *Early Christian Symbolism*, 369.
20. Calverley, *Notes*, 58, records an inscription on the adjoining slab which has now weathered away.
21. RCHME *Westmorland*, pl. 139; C. E. Keyser, *Norman Tympana and Lintels*, fig. 144.
22. Calverley, *Notes*, 229; Keyser, *Norman Tympana and Lintels*, 34. Allen, *Early Christian Symbolism*, 369, identifies this as a male syren or merman.
23. Calverley, *Notes*, records St Margaret and the dragon is on the tympanum let into the west wall at Ault Hucknall (Derbys.); Calverley, 230, who also lists Stow Longa (Hunts.), and refers to J. Romilly Allen, *Early Christian Symbolism*, 316–17, 366 and 368; Keyser, 26, fig. 145).
24. Gertrud Schiller, *Iconography of Christian Art*, I (New York 1971), 130.
25. Thanks to John Goodall for Hauxwell.
26. VCH, *Cumberland*, II (1905), 8.
27. Pevsner, *Cumberland and Westmorland* B/E, 198.
28. William Whellan, *The History and Topography of the Counties of Cumberland and Westmorland* (Pontefract 1860), 188; VCH, *Cumberland*, II, 184.
29. ibid., ill. 15.
30. Pevsner, *Cumberland and Westmorland* B/E, 198.
31. J. Bony, 'The Stonework Planning of the First Durham Master', *Medieval Architecture in its Intellectual Context: Studies in Honour of Peter Kidson*, ed. Eric Fernie and Paul Crossley (London and Ronceverte, 1990), 19–34.
32. Pevsner, *Cumberland and Westmorland* B/E, 77–78. Bridekirk church was given by Waltheof, first lord or Allerdale to Guisborough Priory (Yorks.), Whellan, *Cumberland and Westmorland*, 285. The 12th-century font

288

is also reused in the present church — see George Zarnecki, *Later English Romanesque Sculpture 1140–1210* (London 1953), 59, pls 71–72.

33. Rose, 'Cumbrian Society', 129.

34. Whellan, *Cumberland and Westmorland*, 173.

35. Calverley, 214, ill. opp. 214.

36. VCH, *Cumberland*, II, 185.

37. Taylor and Taylor, *Anglo-Saxon Architecture*, 446–48; plan and plate of west tower, RCHME, *Westmorland*, 176, pl. 144.

38. Pevsner, *Cumberland and Westmorland B/E*, 17, 278; RCHME, *Westmorland*, lix; Taylor and Taylor, *Anglo-Saxon Architecture*, 446–48.

39. *The Register of the Priory of St Bees*, The Publications of the Surtees Society, 126, ed. James Wilson (1915), 233–34.

40. Carol Heitz, *Recherches sur les rapports entre architecture et liturgie a l'epoque carolingienne* (Paris 1963), 31, 79–80, 98; idem, *L'architecture religieuse carolingienne: les formes et leurs fonctions* (Paris 1980), 233.

41. Whellan, *Cumberland and Westmorland*, 473.

42. M. Thurlby, 'The Roles of the Patron and the Master Mason in the First Design of Durham Cathedral', in *Anglo-Norman Durham 1093–1193*, ed. D. Rollason, M. Harvey and M. Prestwich (Woodbridge 1994), 161–84, pl. 22.

43. VCH, *Cumberland*, II, 181.

44. RCHME, *Westmorland*, pl. 140.

45. Barton plan, RCHME, *Westmorland*, 36. For a list of central, axial towers in English Romanesque churches, see Karen Lundgren and Malcolm Thurlby, 'The Romanesque Church of St Nicholas, Studland (Dorset)', *Proceedings Dorset Natural History Archaeological Society*, 121 (1999), 1–16 at 14. Remove from this Pirton (Herts.), which is a cruciform church, and add Maiden Newton (Dorset); see M. Thurlby, 'Aspects of Romanesque Ecclesiastical Architecture in Dorset: Wimborne Minster, Sherborne Abbey, Forde Abbey chapter house, and St Mary's, Maiden Newton', *Proceedings Dorset Archaeological Natural History Society*, 122 (2000), 1–19.

46. M. Thurlby, 'The Use of Tufa Webbing and Wattle Centering in English Vaults down to 1340', in *Villard's Legacy: Studies in medieval technology, science and art in memory of Jean Gimpel*, ed. Marie-Therese Zenner (Farnborough 2001), in press.

47. RCHME, *Westmorland*, lix.

48. RCHME, *Westmorland*, lix; Pevsner, *Cumberland and Westmorland B/E*, 18–19, 261. Plan in RCHME, *Westmorland*, 134.

49. W. Dugdale, *Monasticon Anglicanum*, III (1830), 553.

50. Stuart Harrison and Malcolm Thurlby, 'Observations on the Transepts, Crossing and Nave Aisles of Selby Abbey', in *Yorkshire Monasticism, Archaeology, Art and Architecture*, ed. Lawrence R. Hoey, *BAA Trans.*, XVI (Leeds 1995), 50–61.

51. VCH, *Cumberland*, II, 181.

52. Malcolm Thurlby, 'Roger of Pont l'Eveque, Archbishop of York (1154–81), and French Sources for the beginnings of Gothic architecture in Northern Britain', in *England and the Continent in the Middle Ages: Studies in Memory of Andrew Martindale*, ed. John Mitchell (Stamford 2000), 35–47.

53. VCH, *Cumberland*, II, 11, 179.

54. VCH, *Cumberland*, II, 178, 181.

55. Neil Cameron, 'The Romanesque Sculpture of Dunfermline Abbey: Durham Cathedral versus the Vicinal', *Medieval Art and Architecture in the Diocese of St Andrews*, ed. J. Higgitt, *BAA Trans.*, XIV (Leeds 1994), 118–23.

56. Tessa Garton, 'A Romanesque Doorway at Killaloe', *JBAA*, 134 (1981), 31–57. Tessa Garton, 'Masks and Monsters: Some Recurring Themes in Irish Romanesque Sculpture', in *From Ireland Coming: Irish Art from the Early Christian to the Late Gothic period and its European Context*, ed. Colum Hourihane (Princeton 2001), 121–40.

57. John Bradley and Heather A. King, 'Romanesque Voussoirs at St Fin Barre's Cathedral, Cork', *J. Royal Society Antiquaries of Ireland*, 115 (1985), 146–51.

58. Keyser, *Norman Tympana and Lintels*, 47; *English Romanesque Art 1066–1200*, cat. 124.

59. ibid.

60. ibid.

61. Calverley, *Notes*, 259.

62. The standing figure of St George killing the dragon is discussed by Keyser, *Norman Tympana and Lintels*, lxxxii-lxxxiii.

63. R. W. Billings, *Architectural Illustrations and Description of the Cathedral Church of Durham* (London 1843), pls XXXVII–XL; for Riccall, see F. Henry and G. Zarnecki, 'Romanesque Arches Decorated with Human and Animal Heads', *JBAA*, 3rd series, X–XII (1957–58), 1–34, pl. XIII (4).

64. Henry and Zarnecki, 'Romanesque Arches', 31–32.

65. *English Romanesque Art 1066–1200*, cat. 129.

66. Henry and Zarnecki, 'Romanesque Arches', pl. VIII (I).

67. Riccall was held by the canons of York Minster (VCH, *Yorkshire*, III, 498).

68. Brough plan in RCHME, *Westmorland*, 49; S. doorway, ibid., pl. 12.

69. VCH, *Cumberland*, II, 15.

70. M. Thurlby, 'The Place of St Albans in Regional Sculpture and Architecture in the Second Half of the Twelfth Century', in *Alban and St Albans: Roman and Medieval Architecture, Art and Archaeology*, ed. Martin Henig and Phillip Lindley, BAA Trans., XXIV (Leeds 2001), 162–75.

71. Eric Fernie, *The Architecture of Norman England* (Oxford 2000), 227–32.

72. J. F. Curwen, 'Herring-bone Work, as seen at Egremont Castle', *Transactions Cumberland Westmorland Antiquarian Archaeological Society*, ns, XXVIII (1928), 142–48. Plan in D. R. Perriam and J. Robinson, *The Medieval Fortified Buildings of Cumbria, Cumberland Westmorland Antiquarian Archaeological Society*, Extra Series, XXIX (1998), 103.

73. John Goodall kindly supplied these examples and information on Dover castle.

74. R. Allen Brown, *Castle Rising* (London 1978), 24–26.

75. Edward Impey, 'La demeure seiggneuriale en Normandie entre 1125 et 1225 et la tradition Anglo-Normande', in *L'architecture normande au moyen age*, ed. Maylis Bayle, I (Caen 1997), 219–41, fig. 16.

76. Thanks to Stephen Heywood for the examples at Bury St Edmunds and Wissington. For Bury St Edmunds, see P. L. Drewett and I. W. Stuart, 'Excavations in the Norman Gate Tower, Bury St Edmunds Abbey', *Proceedings Suffolk Institute of Archaeology*, 33 (1975/6), 241–52, pl. XX; for High Ongar, see Pevsner, *Essex B/E*, ill. 6.

77. Maylis Bayle, *Les origines at les premiers developpements de la sculpture romane en Normandie: Art en Basse-Normandie*, 100 (Caen n.d.), 100, fig. 340.

78. On Carlisle keep, see Goodall's paper this volume. I am deeply indebted to John Goodall for generously sharing his views on Carlisle keep and related work.

Copies of these may be obtained from Maney Publishing, Hudson Road,
Leeds LS9 7DL, UK
www.maney.co.uk